The Wayward and the Seeking

Books Authored and Edited by Darwin T. Turner

Katharsis
Nathaniel Hawthorne's "The Scarlet Letter"
In A Minor Chord: Three Afro-American Writers and Their Search for Identity
Afro-American Writers (Bibliography)

Black American Literature: Essays
Black American Literature: Fiction
Black American Literature: Poetry
Black Drama in America: An Anthology
Black American Literature: Essays, Poetry, Fiction, and Drama

To my wife Jeanne

Photo by Marjorie Content Toomer

"They can pile up records and labels a mile high,
and in the end they will find, pinned under
that pile, not me but their own intelligence."

Jean Toomer

The
WAYWARD
and the
SEEKING

A Collection of Writings by
JEAN TOOMER

Edited with an Introduction by
DARWIN T. TURNER
University of Iowa

HOWARD UNIVERSITY PRESS
Washington, D.C.
1980

Library of Congress Cataloging in Publication Data

Toomer, Jean, 1894-1967.
  The wayward and the seeking

  I. Turner, Darwin T., 1931-   ed.   II. Title.
PS3539.0478W3   1980   818'.5'207   74-11026
ISBN 0-88258-014-0

Contents

Acknowledgements

I wish to express my indebtedness to the many people who contributed to this volume. Knowing my admiration of Jean Toomer's writing, the late Arna Bontemps encouraged me to examine the materials in the Toomer Collection at Fisk University and recommended me for an American Council of Learned Societies Grant-in-Aid, which supported my initial research. O. B. Hardison, Professor of English at the University of North Carolina, encouraged me to apply to the University of North Carolina-Duke University Fellowship Program, which enabled me to extend my research about Toomer. A grant from the Rockefeller Foundation enabled me to complete my collecting materials for publication.

Staff members of the Fisk University Library have been very helpful. Dr. Jessie C. Smith, Director of the Library, took a very kind personal interest in the work; Ann Shockley, Director of Special Collections, helped me collect materials; and librarians Beth Howes—and especially Clarencetta Jelkes— graciously labored overtime to assist with assembling and photocopying the manuscript.

I also wish to thank Éliane Clifit, Brenda Parker, Estella Sales, Patricia Schmid, Alsatia Shank, and others for helping to prepare copy. Mrs. Marjorie Content Toomer very generously shared memories and materials of her life and her husband's, including, of course, the original manuscripts that she permitted me to use. Words are too few to express my admiration for the charm and talent of this remarkable woman. And my wife Jeanne, at considerable sacrifice, created the freedom for my work.

The Wayward and the Seeking

Introduction

T. S. Eliot, Robert Frost, Ezra Pound, Amy Lowell and the Imagists, Edna St. Vincent Millay, Countee Cullen, Langston Hughes, Sinclair Lewis, Sherwood Anderson, and Gertrude Stein, F. Scott Fitzgerald, Ernest Hemingway, William Faulkner, Eugene O'Neill: even a partial list of American authors of the 1920s resembles a Hall of Fame of American literature. In 1923, twenty-eight-year-old Jean Toomer, born December 26, 1894, in Washington, D.C., was one of the brightest stars in this galaxy. Waldo Frank, a highly respected author and social critic of the 1920s, proclaimed that Toomer was creating new dimensions for American literature. Sherwood Anderson envied him: Not only did he seem to be the only artistic Negro author whom Anderson had read, but he could portray Negroes as Anderson desired to present them himself. And Lola Ridge, editor of the American edition of *Broom,* predicted that, in future years, he would be discussed and studied more than any other author of that generation.

Twenty-five years later, however, when I first read selections from *Cane* in *The Negro Caravan,* Toomer was not being discussed or studied. I was almost embarrassed to confess my admiration for Toomer's work because surely, I reminded myself, if the man is as brilliant as I believe him to be, some of my professors of American literature would require me to read his work; or at least they would mention his name occasionally.

Within another generation, the memory of Toomer had become so dim that when he died in 1967 in a nursing home near Philadelphia, some admirers of *Cane* were startled because they presumed that he had died many years earlier. Ironically, as Toomer was dying, *Cane* was being discovered by a new generation of readers who, fascinated by the lyric, suggestive, and sometimes enigmatic sketches, poems, and stories, wanted to know more about the author and to read more samples of his art. This volume of autobiographical selections, stories, poems, dramas, and aphorisms—its title taken from an unpublished collection of Toomer's poems—is a response to that wish.

I have summarized many of the materials in this collection in "Jean

1

Toomer: Exile'' (Turner, *In A Minor Chord,* Carbondale, Ill.: Southern Illinois University Press, 1971). But by summarizing I became an interpreter: Unavoidably, I filtered Jean Toomer through my own perceptions and biases.

I began this book with the intention of opening a line of direct communication between Toomer and the literary public interested in him. Rather than depending upon summaries and interpretations—in short, encountering an intrusive intermediary—readers would look at Toomer directly and interpret him as they desired.

I know now that my original assumption was naive. I cannot remove myself entirely from the position of intermediary between Toomer and his readers; by the mere act of deciding which materials to include within a slim volume, I have imposed upon readers my vision of Jean Toomer. Therefore, in fairness to readers of this book, I must explain what that vision is.

I have not attempted to encompass the totality of Jean Toomer within the covers of this book. Instead, I have focused on Toomer the imaginative writer by selecting autobiographical materials that reveal his psychological and intellectual development before *Cane* and by selecting imaginative literature that illustrates his style before and after *Cane*. (No selections from *Cane* have been included except "Karintha," which Toomer originally wrote as part of the drama, *Natalie Mann*, and "Conversion," which he presented as the concluding stanza of an untitled poem in "Withered Skin of Berries.") My selections have been governed by my belief that most readers, knowing Toomer as the author of *Cane*, will be primarily interested in learning about his life before 1923 and about his literature after that date. This collection is divided into five sections: Autobiographical Selections, Fiction, Drama, Poetry, and Aphorisms and Maxims. Each section is preceded by an Editor's Note, which includes an explanation of how the critical editorial decisions were made. For the moment, however, the broader considerations that went into the making of this book must be noted.

The task of compressing the life's work of any person into a few hundred pages becomes complicated immeasurably when the subject is an author who wrote prolifically. Like the proverbial child in a candy store, I suffered the frustration of choosing from a treasure-lode: four autobiographies and several drafts of others, a volume of stories, two collections of poems, three full-length dramas and two shorter ones, two collections of aphorisms, four novels and a novelette, two book-length philosophical statements, and numerous letters and essays.

The limited size of this book and my desire to present a variety of Toomer's writing governed the first decision—to exclude any book-length fiction or nonfiction. But a more significant question remained: Which of Toomer's talents, images, and attitudes should be emphasized in the selections? I have emphasized four aspects of Toomer: (1) his personality; (2) his attitude toward race; (3) his career as a writer of imaginative literature; and (4) his philosophical-psychological proposals for a reformation of American behavior.

Because little was known about Toomer when he was rediscovered during the 1960s, scholars who wrote about him created varied images of the man. Therefore, it is advantageous to examine Toomer's own record of his personality. Because he was rediscovered during a period when many Americans interested themselves in the concerns of Afro-Americans, it is important to know his attitudes about race. Because most of the recent attention to Toomer has focused on his talent as a writer of fiction and poetry, it is necessary to emphasize materials relevant to a knowledge and understanding of his career as an author of imaginative literature. Finally, because Toomer considered his work as a spiritual reformer more important than his work as a poet or fiction-maker, one must consider his ideas for reform. These aspects of Toomer's vision of the world, amplified through his own voice in this volume, are central to an understanding of his development before *Cane*. In this introduction, however, I feel compelled to call attention to some of the more significant episodes of Toomer's life and literary development after *Cane*.

Shortly before *Cane* was published (1923), Toomer had begun to move in a significantly new direction. With the guidance of Waldo Frank's wife, Margaret Naumburg, and with the assistance of Gorham Munson, an editor and literary critic, Toomer became a disciple of Georges Gurdjieff, founder of the Institute for Man's Harmonious Development, the purpose of which was "to understand clearly the precise significance ... of the life process on earth of all the outward forms of breathing creatures and, in particular, of the aim of human life" (G. Gurdjieff, *Herald of Coming Good*, [New York: Samuel Weiser, Inc., 1971], p. 13).

Although a brief introduction does not permit a detailed analysis of Gurdjieff's program, a summary may reveal concepts that influenced Toomer. Gurdjieff asserted that, because civilization has educated modern man to be out of harmony with himself, a new education is necessary. First, each Gurdjieff student was required to complete an introspective analysis and record of the principle functions of his or her organism: the specific traits of individuality; the degree of attention, memory, speech, temperament; and the form of physical and psychic reflexes—smell, taste, and reaction to colors. Second, each student followed individualized programs designed with particular attention to needs that resulted from such "pathological" symptoms as weakness of will, willfulness, laziness, unreasonable fears, fatigue, apathy, alcoholism, drug addiction, and irritability. The program itself would provide a "line of work" selected according to individual capacities and needs. Also, students were to choose courses from a curriculum that included the social and physical sciences, trades, handicrafts, the arts, and psychic and physical exercises.

As one may perceive by reading the autobiographical selections in this volume, Toomer, even before being influenced by Gurdjieff's system, examined diverse ideas as he sought to understand himself and his world. But Gurdjieff, Toomer believed, manifested ideas that Toomer could not. After studying with Gurdjieff at the Institute in Fontainebleau, France, Toomer became a disciple-teacher, first in New York, then in Chicago. Because he judged his mission as a spiritual reformer to be more important than his ambition to win praise as an imaginative author, Toomer temporarily abandoned literature. When he returned to it, he was no longer the impressionistic lyricist of the *Cane* years. He had become a teacher who considered imaginative literature profitable only as a vehicle for the education of readers.

In *Cane* Toomer had questioned the harmonies and values of his society. He had written about men who war with themselves; men who cannot save themselves or others; men who succumb to vanities—jealousy, materialism, possessiveness, fear of ridicule; men who substitute fantasy for action. And he had written about women who clash with a society that, refusing to comprehend them, seeks to redefine them according to the perverted concepts of male chauvinism. The stories, sketches, and poems in *Cane* were impressionistic, sensuous, and elusive. In them he questioned and suggested more often than he taught; he adumbrated messages. The components of *Cane* resembled an artist's sketches rather than a reformer's sermons.

After *Cane,* however, Toomer used a heavy, sometimes satiric or even farcical style to caricature or allegorize men out of harmony with themselves. Although he occasionally published didactic messages in magazines of the 1920s, book publishers refused to accept his novels, his collection of poems, his collection of stories, his autobiographies, or his collection of aphorisms. He published privately one collection of aphorisms, *Essentials,* in 1931. Still, partially encouraged by the enthusiastic admiration of disciples in his Gurdjieff group, the dogmatic Toomer refused to believe that publishers might question the artistic merit or the thematic interest of his work. Instead, he persuaded himself that publishers opposed him for racial reasons. Because they identified him as Negro, he thought, they expected him to write as a Negro: They expected another work like *Cane*.

The year 1931 was an important one for Toomer. Inspired by the model of Gurdjieff's institute in Fontainebleau, Toomer and several followers from Chicago spent the summer on an estate in Portage, Wisconsin, where they attempted "to achieve harmonious development." Among the group were Chauncey Dupee, a business executive, and Margery Latimer, a talented, emotionally insecure writer, who traced her ancestry to the well-known colonial poet Anne Bradstreet. The experiment ended in scandal. Suing for divorce, Dupee's wife alleged that the Portage group had been a "free-love" cult. Group leader Toomer, who had married Margery Latimer, was castigated for miscegenation and for "radical instruction."

Toomer was astonished by the virulent attacks—perhaps because he rarely comprehended the schizoid nature of a nation that could wallow in sensational journalistic reports about "love nests" while it pretended that extramartial sexual intercourse did not exist in the United States. Or perhaps, Toomer was baffled, understandably, by the antics of a nation that glorified Afro-American exoticism and simultaneously raged at the thought of physical contact between black and white.

With equal innocence or naiveté, Toomer wrote a book, "Portage Potential," to explain the experiment. But Gorham Munson, also a Gurdjieffan, suggested that Toomer not publish it: Most Americans of the 1930s, Munson insisted, were not ready to accept Gurdjieff's ideas. Toomer then defended himself with his final novel, "Caromb," whose title combines "somber" and "Carmel" (California), where he was living with Margery when the journalistic attacks began.

In 1932 Margery Latimer died in childbirth; and in 1934 Toomer married the brilliant and affluent Marjorie Content.

For the student of American literature, little needs to be said about the final three decades of Toomer's life. Continuously seeking answers for a harmonious life, Toomer turned to the Society of Friends, Jungian psychology, psychoanalysis, and Eastern mysticism. Still wishing to educate the world, he lectured and occasionally published short pieces—especially in the *Friends' Intelligencer*. But he still could not persuade publishers to accept his books of philosophy. He died on March 30, 1967.

Any intelligent person quickly learns the impossibility of encompassing a creative spirit, an author, an artist, and a spiritual leader within a few hundred pages. A work of such length might be needed merely to illustrate Toomer's views about women and their relationship to men, to cite only one of the intricate human relationships that perplexed and enticed him.

Nevertheless, I hope that even this restricted presentation, bared in his autobiographical conceits and insights, his fictional failures and successes, his literary disasters and triumphs, will help readers of the present distinguish the man from the myth. For, even after the shortcomings are noted, the man Jean Toomer must be recognized as a singular creative artist and teacher and a fascinating human being.

Section I

AUTOBIOGRAPHICAL SELECTIONS

Editor's Note

Although biographical facts may be irrelevant to the study of some writers, they are important to a comprehension of Jean Toomer. He valued autobiography as an end in itself: It constituted a Gurdjieffan exercise in introspection that led a person to understand himself or herself; it served as a podium from which he might explain his attitudes and actions; and it offered a format for instruction in psychological-spiritual reform.

In addition, Toomer frequently wrote autobiographically in his imaginative literature. Sometimes he merely inserted a somewhat romanticized version of himself as a major or minor character—the narrator in "Fern" (*Cane*), Lewis in "Kabnis" (*Cane*), or Prince Klondike in "The Gallonwerps." Sometimes he included details about his life and his relationships with people, as in his presentation of Paul in "Bona and Paul" (*Cane*) or Nathan Merilh in *Natalie Mann*. In other instances, he even created an entire work to explain a particular episode in his life: *York Beach* recounts a trip to Maine with Paul Rosenfield, and "Caromb" describes the journalistic attacks on his first marriage and his responses to them.

Toomer's autobiographical writing, I believe, is most effective when he does not disguise it as fiction. Readers who examine Toomer's autobiographies wish to learn more about Toomer's character and experiences; consequently, they do not regard this information as a digression from some more important topic. In addition, Toomer's posturing seems less offensive in autobiography, for perceptive readers anticipate some romanticizing. They know that few individuals will—or can—bare themselves realistically to the public. In his autobiographies, Toomer appears as a delightful personality—candid, self-assured, persuasive, witty, poetic, and informative.

Unlike most writers of autobiography, Toomer did not restrict himself to a single approach. Most people who quest for immortality through autobiography consider it sufficient to record their thoughts and their achievements. If they write a second autobiography, they merely wish to describe additional achievements or to identify a significant change in thought. Toomer, however, wrote several autobiographies in order to focus on different aspects of his development.

The first, "Earth-Being," written about 1928 or 1929, but probably revised early in 1930, is perhaps the most detailed account of his formative years, his relationships with family and friends, and his personality.* As usual in reading autobiography, one must remember that the records of youth are being presented from the perspective of an older person. Consequently, some of the arrogance of spirit may be less characteristic of Toomer the youthful subject than of Toomer the mature author, whose self-esteem had been heightened both by his own success and by the tutelage of Gurdjieff, whose method—according to Marjorie Content Toomer—inspired extreme self-assurance in all of his students. Nevertheless, "Earth-Being" has values not duplicated in his other autobiographies. Because he wrote it earliest, it may provide the most accurate reflection of his youthful years. Even when one makes allowances for Toomer's coloring of his youth, one perceives evidence of early attitudes important to Toomer's adult life: his desire to be a leader, his tendency to isolate himself when he failed to win, his ambivalent attitudes about his grandfather, and his admiration for Uncle Bismarck's literary habits. Furthermore, because Toomer prepared the manuscript for submission to a publisher, "Earth-Being" is a more accurate illustration of Toomer's style than are the notes and unpublished drafts that constitute many of his later autobiographies. For all of these reasons, I have used "Earth-Being" as the basis of the story of Toomer's life from birth to the age of fourteen.

Wherever they seemed relevant to expand Toomer's statements about these early years, I have borrowed passages from three other autobiographical works. In the 1940s Toomer wrote an expanded, more romanticized autobiography entitled "Incredible Journey." Because this book presents the most detailed descriptions of his family, I have drawn upon it occasionally—especially for descriptions of his mother and father. Another editor might have favored this manuscript above "Earth-Being," for, in some respects, it is a more exciting document. Nevertheless, I have chosen the candor of the earlier book.

Two unfinished manuscripts, written during the 1930s, offer important additional insights. About 1931 or 1932, Toomer drafted notes entitled,

---

* There is evidence that Toomer intended to publish an autobiography, "Earth-Being," as early as 1928 or 1929. In the manuscript of "Earth-Being" used for this book, however, Toomer identifies his age as thirty-five.

"Outline of an Autobiography." It is not clear whether he intended this to be an exercise in introspection or whether, as is more probable, he intended to return to the notes later to develop them into a complete autobiography. Stylistically, this work is the weakest. In places, Toomer merely jotted down enigmatic notes about ideas to be developed later. In other places, he drafted full accounts of incidents that seemed significant to him. Despite these discordances of style, "Outline" seems to be the most perceptive presentation of Toomer's intellectual development. Therefore, I have borrowed passages from it to illuminate segments of his early life, and I have used it as the basis of the story of Toomer's life from 1909 to 1922, the years of wandering that formed the persona who wrote *Cane*.

About 1934 Toomer, frustrated by the conviction that the public did not understand his attitude about race, drafted "On Being an American (The Brief Statement of a Human Position)," in which he proposed to explain his attitudes by describing how the circumstances of his life had shaped them. Although he summarized these attitudes later in a more concise essay entitled "A Fiction and Some Facts," I consider this earlier unfinished manuscript more important, and have selected materials from it to supplement "Earth-Being" and "Outline of an Autobiography." I have also used "On Being an American" as the basis for the story of the genesis of *Cane* and of the circumstances immediately following *Cane*.

The abrupt ending of the autobiographical selections has resulted from my decision to use "On Being an American" for the conclusion of the story. Toomer ended the essay with the statement that he could not complete "On Being an American" because (1) he could not explain his attitude about race without explaining his attitudes about love, family, and life, and (2) emphasis on the racial question had caused him to "introduce the big events of [his] life only as a means of putting the small events in their place." He probably decided later to complete the book as "Incredible Journey."

Since I have discussed Toomer's attitudes toward race elsewhere*, I do not want to repeat myself. Nevertheless, I must recall a few facts relevant to "On Being an American." While corresponding with editors in 1922, Toomer had included "Negro" as one of the strains in his ancestry. In correspondence with Sherwood Anderson during the year prior to the publication of *Cane*, he never opposed Anderson's obvious assumption that he was "Negro." In fact, Anderson began the correspondence because Toomer had been identified to

---

* See Turner, *In A Minor Chord* (Carbondale, Ill.: Southern Illinois University Press, 1971), and Turner's introduction to *Cane* (New York: Liveright, 1974).

him as "Negro." Furthermore, Walter Pinchback, an uncle who influenced Toomer, insisted that Toomer's paternal grandmother had been a slave.

By 1934, when he wrote "On Being an American," Toomer's attitudes about his identity had changed. Recalling the attacks on his first marriage, he may have worried about similar diatribes against his new marriage with a Caucasian. He continued to rationalize his failure to publish books as resulting from the restrictions publishers placed upon the work of "Negro" authors. In addition, by 1934 his grandparents were dead, and his father, if still living, could not be located. Consequently, no one was likely to step forth to contradict his assertions concerning the ancestry of the Pinchbacks and the Toomers.

In one respect, of course, Toomer's denial that he was "a Negro" can be validated technically. Certainly, enough "Caucasian" blood flowed in his veins and his appearance was sufficiently Caucasian that in many European countries he would have been identified with the "white" group. In his homeland, however, the general practice was to identify as "Negro" anyone who could be linked to any African ancestor. Moreover, Toomer probably truly believed that Americans should be considered a new race. Walt Whitman had certainly expressed similar ideas one-half century earlier.

The least controversial summary of Toomer's changing position is that at one period during his life—from 1920 to 1922, while he was living primarily in Washington, D.C., advising such Afro-American friends as Mae Wright and Henry Kennedy, and teaching in an all-black school in Sparta, Georgia— Toomer identified very strongly with black Americans. Later, after Margaret Naumburg Frank and Gurdjieff had become fundamental to his psyche, he articulated the position described in "On Being an American." Although he continued to clarify this position in "A Fiction and Some Facts" and several long essays about racial prejudice, he did not significantly alter it during the remaining years of his life.

The major autobiographies that I have not used are "From Exile Into Being" (1940), revised as "The Second River" (1941)—explanations of his spiritual development. Although these two books also reveal important aspects of Toomer, my decision to concentrate on his literary life required me to select only those autobiographical materials most significant to his image as a creative writer. "From Exile Into Being" and "The Second River" have greater importance as records of the experiences guiding his career as a spiritual reformer and should be the substance of a future book about Toomer.

Originally, I proposed merely to quote verbatim sections from "Earth-Being," "Incredible Journey," "Outline of an Autobiography," and "On

Being an American." Unfortunately, however, Toomer's repetitions from one manuscript to another seemed tedious and confusing. Therefore, the editors at Howard University Press and I attempted to create a reasonably coherent, single story from these four documents, which were developed, as I have stated, from four different perspectives.

The task has been extremely difficult, for while telling a coherent story, I wished to preserve Toomer's form as far as possible. Let me illustrate some of the complexity. The original manuscript of "Earth-Being" is constructed as a series of "Books" (chapters). Recounting a particular time-span in Toomer's life, each "Book," which has a title, consists of a series of essays on different topics or events, such as "Saratoga," "School," "Mother," and "Sex." Each of these subdivisions is numbered and titled, just as a chapter in a book might be. Toomer's organization for each "Book" then, was not a single coherent chronological essay but a collection of essays sustaining cohesion only by their relevance to the years that he was recalling. Because of the space limitations of this volume,* I have deleted some subdivisions that do not focus directly on Toomer or his family. (Examples of such deletions are Toomer's recollection of his grandmother's stories of Mike, a red-haired handyman, or Toomer's memory of the annual excursion to Saratoga, New York for the racing season.) The decisions were mine, but I hope that they have been wise. Because I have deleted some subdivisions and included others, consequently disrupting Toomer's organization, I have deleted all numbers and titles of subdivisions.

I have imposed an organization upon this material for ease of reading. Since my overall objective has been to provide a coherent account of Toomer's life, I have divided the story, where it breaks naturally, to indicate broad stages of development. The title I have given each of the resulting parts is only a reference to the period being recalled. It should be remembered, however, that the frequently abrupt jumps from one topic to another within each part represent Toomer's designations of "Books" and their subdivisions in the original manuscript.

As I have stated, I have shifted from "Earth-Being" as a base to "Outline" and later to "On Being an American." I have noted the places where this occurs. Even when one manuscript is being used as a base, I have borrowed illuminating materials from other manuscripts, and I have even transposed materials from that autobiography which is the base. Italics have been used to indicate both intrusions of material from other manuscripts and transposi-

---

* The impossibility of including all of "Earth-Being" in a book of this limited size is indicated by the fact that Toomer's account of his family and his life from 1894 to 1906 is 227 double-spaced typed pages.

tions. At the end of each such extract, I have given the name of the autobiography from which it has been borrowed or transposed.

In footnotes, I have attempted to provide additional information to explain certain points that Toomer does not develop fully, and I have provided
information that contradicts some of Toomer's statements about himself.

As far as possible, I have preserved Toomer's writing style. However,
because I have needed to use ellipses (three periods with spaces between
them) to indicate my deletions of sentences and paragraphs from the
text, I have been forced to modify Toomer's use of two to four spaced
periods, which indicate his pauses in thought. I have used two periods
with spaces between them, both within a sentence and at the end of a
sentence, to reflect Toomer's pauses. (In the sections following these
autobiographical materials, any deletions that I have indicated are shown
by ellipses within brackets. All other punctuation of two to four periods
will reflect Toomer's suggested pauses.) Occasionally, I have revised sentences that are not clear. Otherwise, I have only corrected obvious typographical or spelling errors, and changed punctuation that would be mis-
leading.

Reflections of an
Earth-Being

"Reflections of an Earth-Being" and "The Early Days" have been taken from "Earth-Being" except where indicated.

I have a curious compulsion to write only about what I understand. I desire to write of what I know most. I have more knowledge of myself than of any other person or thing. Hence I will write about myself. I will take my own life as material because my understanding of it exceeds my understanding of any other material, because it suits my purpose. So I aim, certainly, to give a record of my experiences.

But I see myself as one of countless millions of human beings. I also see some fraction of these others. I aim, then, to give a picture and critique of all life as I see it. This is to be my critique of mankind. From this point of view, my own life is but a necessary starting point. If I knew as much of some other as I know of myself, if I saw in his life equivalent significances, if his material would equally suit my purposes, I could take this other as my central figure.

As it is, I try to treat myself as if I were a second person. ... I am trying to record the essential experiences of one of the beings born and existing on earth. That this being is myself is important mainly only because, as I have said, I understand him better than any other. At least I believe I do. I must write about what I at least believe I understand best.

[Preface to "Earth-Being"]

In the memory of Earth there is recorded the birth of a man-child when America was in winter the day after Christmas '94. In my own memory there is record of the same birth. Some cells within my then small body were indelibly impressed with the sensations experienced when, passing through a burning body, I was projected into this, the next larger world. Some cells heard my birth-cry. Something within me remembers the first entrance of air into my lungs.

From one point of view it is difficult for me to dramatize the career of a tiny cosmic speck, even if that speck is myself. For all events in this universe from the birth of atoms to the death of stars are local events important only if the observer has a local view or if he has a true view of the whole. In this latter case the local episode is seen to have significance because one realizes that it is a necessary unit of the sum total. I have outgrown the local. I have not yet crystallized the universal. My consciousness swings in a wide arc between the two.

On the other hand, I am nothing if not a dramatist; and, together with everyone, I make drama of even the minute features and behavior of myself and others. Only the other day, for example, I vividly visualized the entrance of my infant self into the world. I saw a diminutive, red wrinkled mite emerging from its mother's body. That mite was myself. I was that, just as truly as I am this today. It was a strange sight. It gave me queer sensations and effects.

It gave me, among other things, a personal experience of a very ancient hatred of the womb. Certain ancients called the womb "the slimy." With them it was a symbol of the truth that ordinary men are bound on the wheel of life, committed to an endless recurrence of births. But they did not, as so many of us moderns do, hate life. This is the difference. They hated the wheel of life, man's enslavement to rebirths; and they aimed to use this hatred as an energy for liberation. They did not hate life itself. They did not hate birth. On the contrary, they had an amazing affirming sense of life's possibilities; and, in particular, their literature is explicit as to the need and value of reproduction. Some of us in the modern world, having acquired a mechanistic view of life bereft of possibilities, hate life itself. Both before and after conception we strangle it. The symbol of this view and feeling—well, we have two of them, neither of which is philosophic or religious. One is chemical—the contraceptive. The other is mechanical—the machine gun.

But to return to my experience of the other day.

Coupled with my understanding of the hatred of rebirth, I had a strange sense—pictured as magic darkness—of the source behind the womb from which I came. My consciousness seemed to pass beyond the border, touch the invisible, and then make swift transit back into the visible universe. As if looking from that side, I had a kind of synoptic flash of this waking world as seen when I first entered it.

There was the room in which I was born. It was a gas-lit room, heated by latrobe, with rose patterns on the wallpaper—a typical front bedroom of a typical red-brick house built in Washington in the 1890's. And this is interesting—that I, who am fashioned on no antecedent, but who will be a prototype for those to come, should have sprung to life in a standard house.

My mother lay on a large bed with brass posts. Her mother and two friends were near. A nurse was moving swiftly. The doctor plied his business.

There were no signs or portents other than a sufficiently reassuring tragi-comic birth-cry.

From warmth to coldness, from darkness to light—I had emerged from a unitary world into the life of contrasts and of opposites.

And thus the more or less nine-month process of Nature was fulfilled. I squirmed in my first independence and submitted to the laws which govern the growth and development of human beings on this earth.

In the days following I was, it seems, a normal child; that is, I did none of those amazing things attributed to legendary infants who are born to great destinies. I did not astound my elders by at once speaking an unlearned tongue with unlearned wisdom. Indeed, it was a year or so before I acquired the rudiments of baby-talk. I did not immediately stand up and exhibit phenomenal powers of locomotion and influence. Not till I was three could I rule my nurse. Not till I was seven could I rule my mother and grandmother. Not till I was twenty-seven did I finally conquer my grandfather.

And in truth the elders who saw me were not looking for extraordinary signs. They were very much concerned with the simple matter of resemblance. Did I take after my mother or my father? Was I a Pinchback or a Toomer? . . .

. . . Some people said I looked just like my mother; that I gave signs of having the same proud spirit and the feeling that I was of the salt of the earth. They even found resemblances to my grandfather, her father, saying that I had the Pinchback temper and a Pinchback nose. Others thought I was the image of my father, with his wide-spaced eyes, fine forehead, and well-set chin. To them I was unmistakably a Toomer. If I could have spoken for myself, I would have told them that I resembled myself. . . .

. . . Both of my parents were, to the ordinary American eye of that day, unusual looking. Both were tall, fine featured and fine boned. They had quality, and that intangible yet distinct thing referred to as class. Their carriage and manner were those of aristocrats. My mother's complexion was Italian-olive, my father's, that of an Englishman who has spent time in the tropics. Yet in no way was their appearance foreign. It was straight American—and this was the unusual thing; for what could be more unusual than an American face in a country whose people then and still do largely view themselves as if they were not American but

Irish or English or German or Jewish or Negro or Polish or Swedish or French, and so on? In truth, it is only the exceptional American who views himself and others, who feels himself and others, to be just this, namely, American. . . .

As I grew up, as I began to develop and differentiate spiritually, as I became psychologically individualized, my expression and even my features underwent a corresponding change. Now, at the present time, they are such that—to judge from the responses I get—I have the appearance of a sort of universal man. According to their own subjective experiences, various people have taken me for American, English, Spanish, French, Italian, Russian, Hindu, Japanese, Romanian, Indian, and Dutch.*

---

* Interestingly, Toomer does not include "Negro." Although he may have meant that he identified only as "American," most readers would presume that he is denying that he is of African descent. When he states that such a misunderstanding about his race would not have developed if Waldo Frank had not identified him as "Negro," Toomer is mistaken. In a letter to Claude McKay, associate editor of *The Liberator,* Toomer in 1922 wrote:

> Racially, I seem to have (who knows for sure) seven blood mixtures: French, Dutch, Welsh, Negro, German, Jewish, and Indian. Because of these, my position in America has been a curious one. I have lived equally amid the two race groups. Now white, now colored. From my own point of view I am naturally and inevitably an American. I have strived for a spiritual fusion analogous to the fact of racial intermingling. Without denying a single element in me, with no desire to subdue one to the other, I have tried to let them live in harmony. Within the last two or three years, however, my growing need for artistic expression has pulled me deeper and deeper into the Negro group. And as my powers of receptivity increased, I found myself loving it in a way that I could never love the other. It has stimulated and fertilized whatever creative talent I may contain within me. A visit to Georgia last fall was the starting point of almost everything of worth that I have done. I heard folk-songs come from the lips of Negro peasants. I saw the rich dusk beauty that I had heard many false accents about, and of which till then, I was somewhat skeptical. And a deep part of my nature, a part that I had repressed, sprang suddenly to life and responded to them. Now, I cannot conceive of myself as aloof and separated. (*Cane,* Perennial Classic edition, New York: Harper & Row, 1969, pp. viii-ix.)

Furthermore, Toomer is quite wrong when he insists that he did not know or care whether other authors considered him Negro. In the fall of 1922 he received a letter from Sherwood Anderson, who presumed that Toomer was Negro. For several months afterward, even after the publication of *Cane,* Anderson continued to refer to Toomer as a "negro artist," and Toomer made no effort to correct Anderson. (See Darwin T. Turner, "An Intersection of Paths: Correspondence between Jean Toomer and Sherwood Anderson," *CLA Journal* 17 [June 1974], pp. 455–467.)

All of this has served to nonidentify me from any special group and to contribute to the experiences which give rise to my realization that I am a human being existing on this earth.

While we are on the matter of resemblance I would like to make a note as to the question of inherited psychological features. Did I or did I not, along with the materials of physical structures, inherit from my parents certain psychological traits, tendencies, attitudes? Personally, I doubt that I did. I am skeptical of the theory that our psychology is inherited as our biology is. Much of one's psyche is, I think, the result of environmental conditioning, the result of the interplay between the environment and the person. As for the rest, I incline to the view that we are born definite essential types. Each type has its own peculiar characteristics, its own way of unfolding. Each individual of a given type has his or her own variation or type-characteristics and type-ways of experiencing. I do not think this type is determined by our parents. What does or may determine it is another matter.

Man has the potentiality of forming three distinct, and, in a sense, independent bodies: a physical body, an emotional body, and a mental body. Of these three, the physical body is the only one which is actualized. We obviously get the original stuff of this body from our parents.

I can, however, mark one major resemblance, inherited or not. Both mother and father were heart people. I mean that emotions, feelings, were the ruling forces of their lives. Of these, love was dominant. So with me. All of my life I have had one main quest; and in so far as I have been moved by inner impulse, my turns, returns, leaps and crossings have followed love. And as with them, so my sufferings and joys have sprung from love's defeats and fulfillments.

But this is not altogether accurate. One part only, though a strong part, has been a lover. Another part has been an understander. Still another part has been concerned with incorporating my ideas and ideals in living. I am both an idealist and a realist. As an idealist I have visioned various perfections. As a realist I have tried to give these visions tangible here-and-now on earth embodiment. Nor has it been enough that I understand; I must see my understandings produce results in human experience. Productivity is my first value. I must make and mould and build life. As an artist I must shape human relationships. To me, life itself is the greatest material. I would far rather form a man than form a book. My whole being is devoted to making my small area of existence a work of art.

I am building a world.

To build a world is, from a personal point of view, to make and shape a portion of the external world so that it progressively corresponds to one's own developing needs and functions. From an impersonal point of view, it is to make and shape a portion of the world which includes oneself so that it progressively corresponds to the developing needs and functions of all who compose and participate in this world.

True building is at once personal and impersonal.

Life, and any living organism such as human society, is a field of force, a situation of tensions of forces. In society these tensions must exist. The trouble is, the tensions which now exist arise in the main from artificial oppositions, from unnatural prejudices, preferences, and mutual antagonisms, such as national differences; false patriotism, class and caste lines. They eventuate in destructive crises, such as wars. The tensions should arise from natural oppositions—force against inertia, value against the valueless, the essential against the non-essential, the new against the old, reason against the irrational and stupid, will against body, feeling against the feelingless, one type of man against another type, the individual against the mass. They should eventuate in constructive crises, namely, in periods of especially active creation during which the culture of man is greatly advanced.

There are, I know, so-called creative men who have despair and hopelessness written on their inner hearts. They merely enact the role of a creator of a better world because of the economic or social pressure brought to bear on them. In fine, like business men or any others who have stuff to sell, and who must sell it in order to live, these so-called creators simply hawk their wares and try to induce the public to buy them. Their fine phrases, their high values, their insistence on the worth and good of their own, are merely means of inducing a demand for the only things they can supply. Poor souls, they do suffer—because, who wants them? And occasionally there comes from them a spark of great beauty. But they too, like the entire world, struggle in the Relentless Stream for food, pride, and air. . . .

As for writing—I am not a romanticist. I am not a classicist or a realist, in the usual sense of these terms. I am an essentialist. Or, to put it in other words, I am a spiritualizer, a poetic realist. This means two things. I try to lift facts, things, happenings to the planes of rhythm, feeling, and significance. I try to clothe and give body to potentialities.

I am both pessimistic and optimistic, a realist and an idealist. I am an egotist; I can be genuinely humble. I am promiscuous; I am single. I have regard for nothing; I am devoted and sincerely deeply care. To care for—this is one of my main feelings. I am crude and cultured, weak and strong, slow and quick, without morality but with conscience—and all of these in extreme degrees.

I am complex and involved; I am quite simple. I am secretive and revealing, round-about and direct. I am concentrated; diffused; formed and unformed. I have essential organization. I am chaotic. I can work intensely. I am lazy and heavy with inertia. I can rise from the depths of inertia to the height of force. When idle I too am sex and a stomach. I am younger than a child and a thousand years old.

I am a chicken; I am a hawk. A sheep, a wolf. A reliable person and a pirate.

I am a home-man and a wanderer, a patriarch and a lone nomad.

A devil and a saint. . . .

Just now I understand something.

That my life is made up of *two* flowings. One, the flowing within myself. Two, the flowing of factors and forces in what I have hitherto regarded as the external world. Up till now, I have thought that my life was solely the flowing of things within my organism; but now I see, or believe I see, that the flowing of so-called outside things is not only necessary to the maintenance of my life, but that it is an integral part of it. For, just as I would die if the internal flow ceased, so would I die if the external flow ceased. I can control neither, and both are one.

I make my way as a man who has sight just enough to see that he is blind.

There are some people so isolate or in other ways outside the run of common affairs that we seldom associate them with parents, relatives, families, or with the forms of life which are usual to the majority of us. Their presence is such that it suggests an uncommon genesis. They appear as if they had stepped upon this planet already grown and differentiated, to pursue a course of life remote and strange, as if they had wandered here from some other solar system to dwell amongst us temporarily and startle us. So strong is this impression of uniqueness that we feel shock when we see or are told that they too did in fact have parents, that they do in truth share with us many of our own experiences.

It is with a similar feeling of surprise and strangeness that I now begin to link myself up. It has been a long time since I have felt the enveloping warmth and security of blood-relationships; not so very long in point of time, but quite—in terms of intensity of alone-experiences. I have seen myself without family for so many years—my mother and father passed from my life and from this life years ago,* and even before then I was much within a personal world, having already begun to walk the earth

---

*Toomer's mother died in 1909.

alone. I have a queer sense, as if I were writing fiction, relating myself
to those who did, after all, produce me.

But now I see that if I am to tell their story—and I must, briefly, in
order to give the human background of my early life—I will have to go
back one step further and sketch in my mother's family, particularly
her father, P. [Pinckney] B. S. Pinchback of Louisiana, who was the
dominant overshadowing figure of us all.

*My grandfather on my mother's side, P. B. S. Pinchback, was born in
Macon, Georgia. I must mention and emphasize that all of this concerning my family was told to me; I do not* know *it to be fact. Do you?
Who* knows *about his family, which swiftly branches out to include more
than a million ancestors if we follow the tree back through a few hundred
years? Most of it is hearsay. Besides, even as regards what is known, the
known facts are but a very small portion of the total number of facts.
Thus, most that we speak and write is fictional.*

*Pinchback's father was what is called a white man. He was of Scotch-
Welsh-German stock. Pinchback's mother possibly had some dark blood.
I have seen a photograph of her but from it I could not say precisely what
dark blood. It might have been Negro or Indian or Spanish or Moorish
or some other. The photograph shows a woman of olive complexion with
straight black hair and high cheek bones, with a general cast of features
that would not be particularly noticed one way or the other unless you
were looking for something. In general, the family appears to have been
similar to many others who existed in the South of those days, with this
exception—that one of the boys was to grow up and make a name for
himself as a political figure of national prominence.*

[''On Being an American'']

. . . He was still young when his father, following the movement westward, went to and bought a plantation in Mississippi. There, dissatisfaction
with home conditions made Pinckney run away. This was the first act
of independence of a more than usually independent career. He never
knew what became of his brothers. He got a job on a Mississippi steam-
boat and plied up and down the great brown river. In time, he reached
New Orleans and decided to make it the city of his fortunes. He had
ambition and energy; and perhaps even then he pictured himself as a
dominant person, as a coming leader of men.

Just what he did in New Orleans during those early years I do not
known, but one may guess that his life was difficult and precarious. I

remember him once making a laughing reference to that period. He said he had so little money that he had to live on cakes and apples. He added, "I ate cakes to fill my stomach, and apples to empty it." In any event he secured enough to build up a sturdy active body with drive behind it. And, whatever the difficulties, they seem to have had the effect of stimulating him to overcome them. His ambition increased. He was a fighter. His fighting spirit increased. And it was during this time that he must have formed his desire and design of entering public life. When the Civil War came he saw a first opportunity. He mustered a company for the Federal army and was made captain of it. Just before this he had married Nina Hethorn.* Their first child was born while he was in active service.

I have photographs of Pinchback and his wife which probably were taken at about this time. The one of him shows a strong headstrong self-confident face with intense dark eyes and a black beard. It has a certain flare, suggesting physical courage and a sort of picturesque recklessness. Though the forehead is high and broad, one knows that it belongs to a man of action rather than to an artist or a thinker.

Her picture is in striking contrast. It shows a soft gentle face, sensitive and delicate, touched with a strain of timidity or meekness. It portrays a woman, essentially a wife and mother, the maker of a home, who will see the world only as it comes within her house or as it passes before her window at which she sits embroidering. And this in truth was my grandmother. Yet it was not all of her. For, as sometimes happens with apparently retiring and timid souls, somewhere in her there was a surprising courage and fortitude. She went with her husband to a war-camp and there nursed her first child. She stood without flinching at Pinchback's side all through his stormy and dangerous political career. She saw the rise of the family and, out-living her husband and all but one of her children,** she endured its rather tragic fall. She was the one person in my home who sustained her faith in me after I turned black sheep,† who supported me through thick and thin. . . .

Then, the war ended and the black men freed and enfranchised, came Pinchback's opportunity in the political arena. He claimed he had Negro

---

* In "On Being an American," Toomer identified her as a "white woman, of English-French stock."
** Nina Emily Hethorn Pinchback died in 1928.
† A reference to his wandering from school and job to job from 1914–1920.

*blood, linked himself with the cause of the Negro, and rose to power.
How much he was an opportunist, how much he was in sincere sympathy
with the freedmen, is a matter which need not concern us here. In my
autobiography I will attempt to give as complete a record of Pinchback as
I can. In the present book ["On Being an American"] I am limiting myself to the one theme of his racial strains, his racial position.*

*It would be interesting if we knew what Pinchback himself believed
about his racial heredity. Did he believe he had some Negro blood? Did
he not? I do not know. What I do know is this—his belief or disbelief
would have had no necessary relation to the facts—and this holds true
as regards his Scotch-Welsh-German and other bloods also.*

*I would judge that the admixture of dark blood or bloods, whatever
they were, occurred in his mother's line two or more generations before
her. It is probable, then, that his mother herself did not know. Whatever
she believed had reached her by hearsay. Certainly what reached him
was hearsay.*

*I, who write this, am in much the same position as my grandfather was.
You who read this are in much the same position as I am. It seems to me
that if we all with one accord frankly avowed that our records of the past
are but partial and uncertain, that our behavior of the present is what
really counts, we would greatly simplify and advance the cause of genuine
human relationships. "I am I." Let us begin with this primal affirmation,
let us live it, let us be it throughout the course of our lives. This, I firmly
believe, is the key to the kind of existence that every human being, because he is a human being, essentially desires.*

["On Being an American"]

I say he [Pinchback] was an adventurer. I think he was. I doubt that he
saw himself bearing a mission to secure and maintain the rights of the
freedmen. To a certain extent, yes. I remember hearing of how on two
occasions he risked his life in an effort to enact legislation favorable to the
Negro. One was during the time when he was president of the state senate.
Pinchback had been told that when a certain bill came up, his opponents
would be armed and would try to stop him by force. Pinchback armed
his supporters and had them stationed about the house. At his signal
they were to fire. But they did not have to. With excitement running
high, but with no violence, the day came and passed.

The other was the then famous railroad race with Warmouth. Warmouth
was governor. Pinchback was lieutenant-governor. Both of them were in
New York at a banquet. Pinchback had an act he wished to put over;

and he could do this if he could return to Louisiana before and without Warmouth, for then he would be acting-governor. When the banquet was at its height, Pinchback slipped out and boarded a train for New Orleans. At some little town down south this side of Louisiana he was called from the train to receive a telegraph message in the station. Once he was in the room the door was shut and bolted—and there he was kept prisoner until Warmouth's special arrived. Warmouth, missing him, and suspecting his design, had telegraphed ahead to have him detained. Having arrived on the spot he had Pinchback released and told him that he was glad they had caught him just there. Otherwise, Pinchback would not have been among the living. Warmouth had sent orders that he was not to enter Louisiana alive.

But even these episodes, risky though they were, and done to a certain extent for the Negro, show the tactics, not of an idealist and liberator, but of a bold dramatic venturer. More than anything else Pinchback saw himself as a winner of a dangerous game. He liked to play the game. He liked to win. This—the reconstruction situation in Louisiana—was the chance his personal ambition had been waiting for. He was not a reformer. He was not primarily a fighter for a general human cause. He was, or was soon to become, a politician—but far more picturesque, courageous, and able than the majority of the men who bear that name.

His rise was rapid. He became Collector of the Port of New Orleans. He became state senator. He edited a newspaper and wrote for it. He became known as a sure-fire stump speaker and political orator. A state commission sent him on an official trip to Paris. He attended national conventions of the Republican party. He became governor of Louisiana— the key-man of Louisiana politics. He was sent to the Senate at Washington, but his seat was contested, and, after a long and hard battle, he lost it.*

Meanwhile, though not primarily a businesss man, he had accumulated money and had come to be regarded as a wealthy man. The Louisiana Lottery, in which he owned shares, and his friendship with the owner of it, Howard, doubtless had considerable to do with this.

Also, he had formed a passion for horse-racing. He loved the horses, and at one time himself owned several. This was his undoing. For, as his political career declined, he followed the races more and more and not only lost money on them but failed to take advantage of numerous business opportunities. (In our family also there is the story of how he turned down

---

*Actually, he was refused twice.

a chance to buy property in the Loop district of Chicago.) Whenever the
political situation allowed of it, he would travel about to the various
tracks; and, during the summers, he would take his family with him,
usually to Saratoga Springs which then was a brilliant place.

Pinchback believed in having large families. By now, he had a fair-sized
one, three boys and a girl, Nina, who was to be my mother. He probably
saw himself as a patriarch. In any case, he was the dominant and sometimes tyrannical head of his household. At the same time he was a loving
and devoted husband and father; and, like many another playing-the-
game man, he made a sharp division between the world of affairs and
his home. Politics, lotteries, horse-racing—these he tried to keep outside.
Within his house he wished only the finest and best influences. To the
limit of his powers he had it so. His ideals and aims for his children, derived from reading—he was quite a reader and had accumulated a good
library from his numerous contacts and travellings—were similar to those
of most ruling-class Americans of his time.

When the time came, he sent his eldest son off to school up north.
This boy, named Pinckney, after his father, graduated from college, I
believe it was the University of Pennsylvania. He became a pharmacist,
opened a store near the university, married a Quakeress, and continued
living in Philadelphia till his death.

The next boy, Bismarck, was sent to Yale to become a physician.

Walter went to Andover. Pinchback had decided that this son should
become a lawyer, and, perhaps, follow in his political footsteps.

Nina was sent to a finishing school near Northhampton. He evidently
wished that she, his only daughter, gentle like her mother yet spirited
and of proud temper like himself, should have the graces of society and
the desirable contacts such a school offered.

In doing all this, my grandfather had the very best intentions, without
doubt. He was, as I have said, devoted to his children. But, in the first
place, though part of his nature was affectionate and sincerely good-
wishing, another part was egotistical, domineering, and headstrong. With
too little wisdom he cut his children's patterns, particularly the boys',
and then tried to force them to fit in—with unfortunate results . . . . And,
secondly, as time went on, though he remained as willful as ever, he
gradually lost his grip on life and lost his money, so that he could not
stand back of his children and help them carry through the plans into
which he had thrust them.

Pinchback was a good-liver and he believed that his family should live
well. He gave them the best things to be had. When travelling, he would

stop at only the best hotels. I remember hearing tales of their stays at the old Hoffman House, New York, where he liked to give what I believe were then called banquets, not large banquets but what we nowadays would call dinner parties—a number of people to dinner, and then the theatre or opera. He liked plays and music. He liked to be surrounded by friends and admirers and had the reputation of being the best of hosts.

But, like many other men of his temperament and wealth, he held the purse-strings. He himself would spend lavishly, and it never hurt. But he would not give money to his wife and children for them to spend. A new suit or dress? Yes. A trip to Saratoga? Yes. Ball gowns, trunks and furnishings, everything of the most expensive. But let them try for a few dollars for their own pockets and they had the devil's own time getting it. He wanted to see money when spent yield a social return for the group of which he was the obvious head. . . .

His career had been stormy and brilliant owing to unusual conditions which in the very nature of things could not last long. Shortly after his governorship things began to change. Old-line southerners gradually regained their power. Control slipped from the hands of the Republicans, and the Democrats again got in the saddle. The days of the carpet-baggers were over. And Pinchback's local regime was ended, though he still remained an influential figure in the national Republican party.

He decided to leave New Orleans for good, and establish himself in Washington, D.C. This was about 1890.

In this latter city he bought property on Bacon Street in a desirable and growing residential district . . . .

The Early Days

*F*irst it was called Bacon Street. Later the name was changed to Harvard. It began, as I remember it, at 14th Street and ran westward to end at a farm, an old place not yet out through the city thoroughfares, a relic of days before the Civil War. It was over and behind this farm that the sun used to set. Beyond it was 16th Street; and from here it was but a short distance to the Zoo and Rock Creek Park. Rock Creek Park was a favorite place for horse-back riding. Once I ran across a man there. I didn't know who he was. He told me he was Theodore Roosevelt and picked me up and gave me a ride too. Going south on 16th Street you passed two or three impressive-looking embassies, you sloped down Meridian Hill and finally ended at the White House.

This was in the Nineties, when the northwest section of Washington, the hill beyond the boundary line, was rapidly being built up.

City people, fairly well-to-do people who had come from other parts of America, from Europe, and from other sections of Washington, had only recently been drawn there; and their houses, solid three-story affairs of red and yellow brick and brown stone, were still sufficiently few to leave open lots and fields all around.

These families were middle and upper class. They had a tone of fineness and refinement, and each seemed to have a marked feeling for life, some special interest, talent, or ability. There was very little of what I have since come to know as bourgeois smugness and complacency. . . .

The entire setting and atmosphere of our neighborhood, delightful blendings of city and country, the urban and the rural, civilization and Nature, provided not only a happy playground but conditions especially well adapted to stimulate the all-around growth of children. There is no doubt that these early surroundings were indelibly impressed upon me as desirable; that they gave me a sense and standard of where and how human beings ought to live.

Bacon Street, as I first knew it, was little more than a short dirt road made regular by curbstones. When it rained, puddles were formed, and carriage wheels cut furrows in the rich mud. If our mothers permitted us,

28

we children with bare feet would run joyously from homes and play in
the puddles and dig our hands in the mud and feel strange elation at the
touch and smell of earth.

Trees grew in the fields and in the yards of rambling frame houses:
tulip trees, firs, cedars, oaks, walnuts; fruit trees, cherry and sickle pear,
peach and mulberry. When spring came, and blossom time, these trees
released into the waiting world a quiet riot of color and fragrance. The
children of Bacon Street knew beauty.

[''Earth-Being'']

[On Bacon Street Pinchback built] a red brick and brown stone house
which, as he phrased it, would be his home for the rest of his days. We
called it the Bacon Street house. It was one of the first brick houses in
a neighborhood of open fields and old frame structures set back in yards
and peering out from lilac bushes, shrubbery, and the leaves of trees. It
was less impressive than the New Orleans dwelling, due perhaps to the
fact that, having lost considerable money in the closing of the famous
lottery, and on the races, my grandfather felt he ought to be more economical.

In a way it was typical of the brick affairs built in Washington, New
York, and Boston in the 1890's. It was of the kind I call a modified
fortress. Built solidly and four-square—though narrow for its height—it
seemed to stand there ready to defend its inhabitants from all comers.
Also, it had a sort of aggressive tower-like effect. In this it was typical of
Pinchback. . . .

So he came to live there. His days were spent downtown where he kept
his hand in the political game. Sometimes he would be away evenings
also, at stags or banquets. Most often, however, he returned for dinner
with the family which was had at five o'clock, preserving the southern
custom of early dining. Now and again he would have receptions at the
house. There would be a swirl of people and the house would blaze with
lights. He still loved to be the host and entertain, to be the central figure
of an admiring crowd. They called him Governor and made much over
him. They gave him to feel that there never had been and never again
would be one like him.

Advancing age, though reducing his vigor, had given him additional
weight and dignity. His hair and beard were turning silver white. His
forehead seemed higher and more prominent—and also more prominent,
the Pinchback nose. His eyes still looked out boldly. There was less fiery
challenge and aggression in them. There was more of an expression of

self-confidence and satisfaction which came from knowing that he had put his stamp upon the world. He had never had a sick day in his life, and, save for the gout, contracted from too many banquets, so he thought, he was as hale and hearty as anyone could wish to be. He always dressed well, usually in the habit of a diplomat with cut-away coat. He was an impressive figure advancing, it seemed, to the state of a grand old man.

This was my grandfather as I knew him. I saw him as a dashing commanding figure, the centre of an unknown but exciting world. He created an atmosphere which thrilled me; and there is no doubt that his image, and the picture and sense of his life, were deeply impressed upon me, later to function as an unconscious ideal for myself, for how I wished to look and be;* and also to serve as standards by means of which I measured men and life.

There was enough resemblance between him and Andrew Carnegie for him to be mistaken for Carnegie. Several times on crowded street cars I heard men address him as Mr. Carnegie and offer him their seat. Why Mr. Carnegie should be riding on Washington street cars never seemed to puzzle these men. Nor did it puzzle grandfather. He was pleased by the mistake. He considered Carnegie one of America's greatest men and would have liked very much to have had his wealth. The other way around—if Carnegie admired bold dramatic power, he might well have been pleased to have been mistaken for Pinchback.

Life, then, in terms of ordinary tests and standards, had treated Pinchback fairly well.

But the lives of his children were troubled. Pinckney, with his pharmacy in Philadelphia, was the only one tolerably established. Bismarck, having graduated in medicine, had been subjected to his father's ideas as to how a man is made, the main notion being that a young fellow should be put through the mill and made to endure and overcome hardships, the harder the better. Pinchback held to this conviction with all the force and stubbornness of his nature. In Bismarck's case, he would not in the slightest help him get started, but sent him off on his own. Nor would he permit practice in Washington where his son would at least have had conditions similar to those he had known all his life, and friends and companions of his own kind and class. No, he packed Bismarck off to a mud-hole along the Mississippi. The son did not have the stuff of the father. Life was so intolerable there that, before a year was out, Bis had to leave the

---

*In other autobiographical statements, however, Toomer rejects his grandfather and cites his father as an ideal.

place. Having no funds he pushed off on a raft and drifted down the river, finally reaching New Orleans. There, some of his father's old friends helped him a bit. Pinchback learned of what had happened and sent him money to come home.

Perhaps he then tried to practice in Washington. I don't know. But if so, his attempt was not successful and he soon gave it up. He took and passed the civil service examinations. His good standing in these—for Bis, though lacking in some respects, was quite a student—got him a job in a governmental department. He was sent out West to do something on an Indian reservation. He disliked the place and the work. Pinchback used his influence to have him transferred to Washington. At length this was accomplished. He came back and began living with the family in the Bacon Street house. In the eyes of the world he had not panned out so well; and in the eyes of his father he was, one may guess, a disappointment.

Walter also had returned to the Washington house. But he was younger than Bis. The mark he would make, or fail to make, was not so evident and decided. Pinchback still had hopes of him. He too, I believe, had a job with the government and was studying law at night.

And Nina [Toomer's mother] was there. . . .

In person, she was fine-boned, highstrung, proud of bearing, gracious, and had a decided impish streak. By now she had outgrown the plumpness that marked her adolescence and was developing into a well-proportioned rather tall woman. Neither beautiful nor pretty, there was something about her that made people sit up and take notice. Her motions were quick and lithe and she was very much her gay sparkling self at a ball. She had an olive complexion and lovely dark eyes that could be haughty, were sometimes pensive, but most often were twinkling with fun. In later life a hurt expression, an injured, baffled, somewhat hardened and defensive look took the place of the laughing loveliness.

Poise she had, distinction, independence of character, independence of mind too, and despite the fact that her life had been so strictly supervised.

["Incredible Journey"]

. . . She wrote occasional poetry, played the piano, sang, danced marvelously, and had the graces her father had wished that she have. She captivated everyone and was, naturally, the apple of his eye. And she had reached the age of marriage.

Like many another loving but dominant parent, Pinchback watched

over her with an eagle eye, holding a firm tight rein. He decided whom
she might see, how, and when. Everything she did had to meet his ap-
proval. His disapproval was final. I don't know how many young men had
come and tried to win her, meeting rejection either from him or her or
from both, when Nathan Toomer at length came on the scene. . . .

*Toomer, at the age of 52, was an upstanding figure, above medium
height, broad shouldered, well-nourished, weighing around two hundred
pounds. A flare for living invested his substantial physique with a roman-
tic glamour. There was dignity in the man, a certain richness and largeness, and charm. He had, in fact, quite a presence. And he had a way
with people.*

*His clothes, worn carelessly, were carefully selected, in good taste, and
of the finest materials. He liked silks. His bearing was a mixture of slouch
and poise. His manner was by turns off-hand and lordly, suggesting
that he was accustomed to giving commands and having his own way.
He lived well when things went well. At such times he was a pretty fine
person to be with. He got petty and cross when things went wrong. When
the tide turned against him he suffered and caused suffering. He seems
to have lacked sustained zest to overcome difficulties, nor did he seem to
have any real ability to extract profit from adversity.*

*I never heard of him having any kind of physical illness. I am of the
opinion that he took his own good health for granted and was one of
those healthy people who scorn sickness in others as a moral defect. If
you were ill, his contempt for your moral reprehensibility prevented him
from sympathizing with your physical distress. Yet when he was sick in
mind, which he was fairly often, he saw no sign of moral turpitude in
this, and he wanted plenty of sympathy.*

*I saw this father of mine but once with my remembering mind. I used
to have a picture of him, an enlargement of a photograph. I draw on these
two sources for my portrait of him.*

*The picture showed his complexion fair. As I recall him in life his
color was more swarthy. He had a fine head on his broad shoulders, well-
modeled features, soft greying hair. His face was unlined and rather
youthful looking, clean shaven except for a trim grey mustache which bore
no resemblance to the "handlebars" that were fashionable in those days.
His lips and chin were not particularly strong, not noticeably weak. His
eyes, generously spaced apart, were level-looking, quick with feeling. The
one time I saw him he had a brooding expression, a rather extraordinary
expression. It came from deep within him and seemed to reach towards*

*something far away. As I reflect on that expression now, a feeling comes
to me that among his many puzzling features he may have had a streak
of genius in him—a streak that, never finding its proper occupation,
disturbed his inner life and sometimes came to the surface in a mood
of creative brooding.*

*I search my memory of his picture. I search my memory of his face
as I saw it in life. I search in vain for visual signs of the deceits and weaknesses that undoubtedly were there.*

*Arrived in Washington, he set about his affairs. No one seems to have
known exactly what these affairs were. He kept them pretty much to
himself, thus becoming a sort of man of mystery, while at the same time
creating the impression that he did have definite business in the city,
and ample means with which to conduct it. People looked up. They felt
his strange power and attractiveness. People were convinced. A planter, a
wealthy man from Georgia, a handsome stirring man at that—so he was
accepted.*

["Incredible Journey"]

*His father, a plantation owner, had left him some money, and Toomer
lived as a gentleman of leisure with a taste for luxury and elegance. He
was of English-Dutch-Spanish stock. I gather that he lived in the south as
a white man. Did he have Negro blood? It is possible.*

["On Being an American"]

He quickly fell in love with Nina and proposed to her. Pinchback
objected—but this time, the force of life over-ruled him. Despite his
objection they were married. I have been told and have reason to believe
it was a love marriage. This was the one clear affirmation of her life.

Toomer bought her a house and they started making a home.

For a short while all went well. But then it developed that he had run
short of funds and would have to go south to procure more. He went
south. He wrote back that he was doing his best but would have to stay
longer than he had expected. His letters came less and less frequently,
and finally there was a longer period during which she had no word from
him.* She, meanwhile, was having a hard time trying to make ends meet.

---

* The story which seems to emerge from other members of the family is that
Nathan Toomer married Nina for money. When he learned that P. B. S. Pinch-
back would not loosen the purse strings, he deserted. At times, however, Jean
Toomer blamed Pinchback for breaking up the marriage and forcing Nathan
Toomer to leave.

With a child on its way she struggled on alone, too proud to ask help of her father and deeply not wishing to, because this would mean a break of faith in her affirmation. Her mother, though having practically no money of her own, and her brothers, were the good angels of this period.

The whole thing seems to have been one of those unpredictable abrupt happenings which occur with no apparent relation to the desires or characters of either person, but which fling the people apart with such finality that one is inclined to view the happening in terms of predetermined life-patterns.

To all appearances, Toomer had disappeared from the face of the earth.

And so, at length, despairing of help from him, she was forced to forfeit all she had struggled for and appeal to her father. Just what happened then I do not know. This too was a closed chapter in our household. Indeed, as I grew up, I soon sensed that even the name of my father was not to be mentioned. But, from bits dropped here and there I have pieced things together. . . .

Only once had I seen my father. Mother and I were visiting somewhere, or, rather, she was visiting and I was playing on the street in front of the house. I do not remember just how it came about. I do not know how I knew him. But, soon, I was running up the way a bit towards a large man who was holding out his arms to me. He took me in them, raised me and kissed me, and I liked him very much. He said things to me which I didn't understand, but I knew he was my father and that he was showing how much he loved me and what a fine little man I had grown to be. He raised me high in the air, and then he saw mother come out. He lowered me, pressed a bright silver half-dollar in my hand, kissed me again, and told me to run back to her. He went off.

I do not remember how mother explained it, or if she tried to explain at all. In any case, I seem to have been satisfied with things as they were. I never saw my father again, and seem not to have missed him. Perhaps grandfather had taken his place.

Toomer's name, as I have said, was seldom or never mentioned in the Pinchback house. I do remember, however, someone, mother or grandmother, once or twice telling me on special occasions, one of them during a summer when we were in Saratoga, that I must not wander far away from the house or from them because my father might be around and might steal me. Their words, if they were meant to frighten me, did not. I didn't want to leave them, but, recalling the one time I had seen him, I thought it would be nice to be with him.

Mother had resumed her maiden name and was known as Nina Pinch-back. I was known as Eugene Pinchback.

My first name was Nathan—after my father. Later it was changed to Eugene. Still later I gave myself the name Jean. To Dutch, and to all the children of the neighborhood, I was Pinchy—short for Pinchback. To them I was a Pinchback. They knew nothing of Toomer.

In my own home there were still other names. Mother called me Booty. Uncle Bis called me Kid. Uncle Walter—Snootz. And grandfather—the little whippersnapper. I was, then, well-supplied.

[''Earth-Being'']

I was altogether a member of this family; and, as I have mentioned, my grandfather seemed in a sense to have become my father. I liked him very much, and he liked me. Whatever grudge he may have held against Toomer was not carried over. I was his little man, his little whipper-snapper.

But, dominating person that he was, he seems to have followed towards me a policy of hands off. In this sense—that though he frequently showed his affection for me, he never took an active hand in my upbringing. Something must have restrained him. Perhaps he was realizing that his methods had not proved so well in the case of his own children. Perhaps—and more than likely—my mother had stood up to him and had demanded that he not interfere. But if so, then just the fact that she was able to win her point indicated that he was having doubts of some kind as to him-self. No purely outside pressure could have budged him; and besides, as I shall soon show, he was still exercising a sort of tyranny over her.

For myself—I was fascinated by him. His goings and comings were the big events in the house. I liked to see him get ready to go downtown. He took special care of his beard, trimming it with a pair of sharp scissors which he would never let me touch. Most often he polished his own boots and kept them as spick and span as patent-leather. He had a number of fine suits and, according to the occasion and weather, he'd wear a dif-ferent one each day of the week. His speech was jovial and hearty, with many vivid words and turns of phrase peculiar to him. No one could speak to me and make me laugh and get me excited the way he could. He made me feel I was having a part in everything he did. Now and again I felt very much a man when he'd place me in a high chair and use his sharp scissors to cut my hair. Sometimes he would take me downtown with him and I might even have lunch with "the men," who made much to-do over me, giving me a feeling that I was the scion of a great family. One day he walked me a long distance to see Little Red Riding Hood in a store window.

Sometimes of evenings he would ask me to come with him in his bed for a short while and we would lie there in the dark and I'd tell him about many times: myself and Dutch and what went on in the neighborhood; stamps, or whatever bump I happened to have at the time; my school lessons, history, geography, and arithmetic. At such times he seemed not a grownup forceful man but a young fellow, even a boy of my own age.

I used to recite for him. There was one special piece he always asked for. I did this one best. It seemed, as it were, to match my temperament and give me maximum opportunity for self-expression. My face was very serious when I did it; but also, my eyes had a roguish twinkle. I carried it off with a boyish flourish and not a little style. When finished, a round of laughter and praise and handclaps greeted me. I liked to do it. Other people usually were present. I say I recited it for grandfather because he particularly encouraged me. Perhaps he took it as a sign that I had the makings of an orator and would grow up to follow in his footsteps.

When I got older I'd sometimes wait up for him of nights. Coming in from downtown he'd be hungry. There'd be a light supper for him on the table. He'd talk to me and I'd watch him eat. Perhaps he would give me something, especially if it were cold turkey, which I liked very much. He'd eat and eat with evident relish; my mouth would be just a bit watering. I never got much. We had a standing joke. He'd explain to me with a twinkle in his eyes that it wasn't good for a young whippersnapper like myself to have heavy food just before going to bed. I'd agree with him. I had worked that idea out for myself in connection with nightmares. Indeed, he'd continue, it wasn't altogether good for himself. But—and this was the place where we'd always laugh—he simply ate things to keep them from wasting. So, on these nights, I'd watch him keep delicious turkey, almonds, cheese, salad, bread, cold biscuits .. from wasting. But in any case it was a happy time for me. We were almost comrades at a supper party.

With mother, the thing was as different as it could be. He treated her as if she were still a young girl in her teens. Her marriage, her year and more of experience with my father, the difficult maturing conditions, herself being the mother of a rapidly growing son—these did not change his attitude towards her in the least. She was still his only daughter and he kept an eagle eye on her. She had callers. But it was he who said who could and who could not come. Also, he set the time of their departure. Ten o'clock sharp was leaving-time. And I well remember what happened if they didn't leave then.

They'd be in the downstairs parlor. Grandfather and grandmother would be in their rooms on the second floor. If ten o'clock came and passed and there were no signs that mother's visitor was about to depart, first you'd hear grandfather stirring around. Perhaps he'd cough several times and let them hear him walking back and forth. If this did not produce the desired effect, soon you'd be jolted by the slamming of blinds. Nothing yet? An alarm clock would go off. If still the gentleman didn't move, grandfather would come to the head of the stairs and call down in a voice formidable enough to eject anyone, "Nina! It is after ten o'clock!"

And this performance was enacted night after night, whenever anyone not forewarned or forgetting the warning in the flush of courting mother, overstayed the time-limit. One can imagine how it made a grown woman feel; and, with this as a sample of her father's treatment, one can understand how at length she could endure it no longer, but married again simply to escape this ridiculous tyranny.

Grandmother, though sympathizing with mother, was not able to do anything. Grandfather was too strong and too stubborn for her.

To me this slamming the blinds, alarm clock business was highly amusing. It made me giggle and I looked forward to hearing it come off. Then too, the gentleman caller had such a sheepish beaten look as he said goodnight and scuttled out the door. I liked this. I was jealous of the men who came to see mother. I wanted to keep her to myself. I didn't want them to come. After they were there I wanted them to go soon. Indeed I sometimes sat myself in the parlor and they couldn't get rid of me. Once I got so sleepy I didn't know what I was doing and started undressing. The alarm clock couldn't go off soon enough. In fine, both grandfather and myself were leagued against her callers—but it really worked out that we were also leagued against her. Unconsciously I too was a factor in her troubles. I displayed an animal possessiveness and a total disregard for others which really called for a sound thrashing. I should have been whipped and sent about my own business. . . .

Mother was having a very difficult time. Her life, and all life, must have appeared to her strange and baffling, tragic and unjust. As a young woman, like most women of her kind and training, she had placed large hope in love and marriage, in the having and making of her own home. Freedom, a chance to have and live a personal life, the intimate satisfaction of working out life-problems with the man she loved—all her wishes and ideals were centered on and promised fulfillment by just these two. Love had come to her and she had affirmed it, opposing the one person in the world she had never before dared oppose. And love had failed her. Her marriage and home had broken about her head and within her heart. She had been beaten back into the very house she had left so independently and with such faith.

Her very presence in her father's house was a constant reminder that a strange fate had caused the best impulses of her nature to suffer disappointment and defeat. Her faith in them, her confidence in herself, were severely shaken; and, since they were so basic a part of her life, her doubt of them led to doubt of all life. Having had such experiences in the past she could not look forward with conviction to a happy future. Toomer had failed her. What could she expect from other men? Besides, there was me, her responsibilities to me and my demands, to complicate matters.

Meanwhile, from day to day, she was living in conditions which must have frequently given her the feeling that she was caught and trapped. If she had never ventured away into a life of her own, her sense of Pinchback's domination would have been less acute. Nor was her condition made easier by the fact that she loved her father, that he loved her. She feared his power. She resented his tyranny. But, despite his headstrong and sometimes petty ways, he was the kind of man to evoke deep affection. It would have been simpler to have withstood him had she hated him, or if she could have felt that his supervision was a mean sort of interference. She knew it was not. She knew that though he was lacking in understanding of what was wise to do, he was completely good-willed towards her. What could she do? There is no form of relationship harder to escape or alter than that in which our affections are enlisted in favor of the one whose superior force controls us.

I do not know what attitudes and beliefs she held, general views of life which may have helped her to meet the situation. She had probably started out with some kind of idealism, some strength of belief in the Christian picture of the world; for, though there was very little formal religion in our house, and though grandfather kept his own views of important life-matters pretty much to himself, my grandmother was a devout believer in God, Christ, and the Christian doctrines, and she had doubtless instilled them into mother. But we know what happens to youthful idealism and to immature faiths when they are subjected to a reality which has a tragic outcome. Perhaps some of her idealism had survived; and, probably, like everyone, she had worked out a philosophy of life; but, as later events showed, it was not sufficient to have formed in her an attitude enabling her to profit and learn and construct herself from her experiences. Beauty of a kind she had, and vivacity, pride, small talents, independence of spirit; but, though brave and enduring in certain ways, she was very sensitive and vulnerable through her heart. She was not formed with large capacity for overcoming the difficulties and disappointments of life. Nor could she long endure acute heart-suffering.

From me, at the time, she successfully concealed her troubles. Because I nearly always saw her so, I believed her as happy as myself. She would laugh and play and romp with me. When Dutch came into the house she was the same with him. Now and again, I knew, she had sick headaches and would have to stay in bed. And once she had an operation.

For several days she had been lying in the big bed in grandmother's room, and the doctor had been coming regularly. I did not like to see her like that. I did not want to enter the room. Whenever I did, I felt restless and aimless. I couldn't say or do anything. I just had to stand there and see that she was sick. Her face made me sad.

One day, grandmother and the whole house seemed nervous. Two doctors came and arranged a long table in the middle of the room. I was told they were going to do something to mother, and then she'd feel better and get well. I wanted to see. I saw them lift her from bed and place her on the table. She groaned a little. I squirmed and wanted to yell that they should leave her alone. The doctor was very gentle and kind and spoke to her as though she were a little girl. They fussed about her. I began smelling a peculiar odor. And then, suddenly, I heard her voice. It was hers, and yet it wasn't. It sounded small and weak and far off. "Not yet. Not yet." Later I understood that she was telling them not to operate until the anesthetic had had its effect. She was letting them know she was not yet under it. Again her voice, "Not yet." But it was weaker and even farther off. It gave me a sinking feeling and terribly frightened me. The doctor discovered me concealed near the door and put me out. I went away and thought very seriously about everything.

The operation, a minor one, was successful; and she was soon up and about again, as vivacious as ever.

But it was not long after this that I made an observation: there was beginning to be a difference in the way she looked when about the house during the day, and when she primped for her callers or got ready for a ball. In the day-time she seemed, as I would not phrase it, preoccupied and just a little worn. She was fading. Only at night when stimulated by a gay event did her cheeks bloom and her eyes sparkle with their wonted snap or soft brilliancy. . . .

. . . I had an attitude towards myself that I was superior to wrong-doing and above criticism or reproach. I resented anyone thinking I was wrong or guilty. I wanted them never again to think this way of me. To gain this end, I'd let them hurt me. The minute they did so, then *they* were very wrong and guilty. And then I, strong in the knowledge of my right and righteousness, would confront them, fresh from this mistake. It was a quick turn-over, a kind of moral or emotional jiu-jitsu. I seldom failed to induce in them a feeling of wrong-doing, shame or regret or remorse— sufficient to make them feel inferior to me at the moment, to make them in the future at least think twice before accusing me. And, as I say, for this moral triumph I would undergo considerable physical or emotional discomfort. I would endure someone's bad opinion of me, a belief, say, that I had played Dutch false, for a week in order finally to establish my blamelessness in such a way that the bad opinion could not easily be held again. . . .

Melvin, or Dutch, as we soon nicknamed him, and I were about the same age, I a month or so older. But they tell me that I used to lean over the side of my carriage, and, in the role of a much older person, greet him, "Nice baby." . . .

As we grew up I retained my "nice baby" older-than-thou attitude— sometimes to his irritation, sometimes to his comfort. For if, on the one hand, I bossed him and showed him what to do and how to do it, on the other I fought for him. I would take up for him when larger fellows wanted to hurt him. More than once I got into scraps which made me wish to goodness there was someone to take up for me.

I had soft brown hair and eyes that were roguish to pensive. Dutch was freckled-faced and mischievous. I too had freckles but they weren't so noticeable because my skin was darker. My head was rather large and roundish with full healthy cheeks. My nose was inclined to be short and stubby. Now, it is so noticeably pointed and long that a person, asso- ciating it with my incisive critical temper and disliking it, once made a caricature showing me as an old thin man with nose much elongated, hooked, and touching my chin—a sort of grotesque Danté gone to seed and turned misanthrope. But then, as I say, it was just a little stubbed; and, for others, I suppose, more likeable and far more comfortable.

I used to laugh often and usually my face wore a smile. It was a roguish smile. But there was this difference between it and Dutch's. There was no doubt as to what his meant. It meant straight mischief. One could not quite tell about mine.

I wore a stout little reefer, leather leggings, and a winter cap. With this outfit on I often assumed the pose of a little Napoleon. For summer, I had rather tight short pants and a white blouse with large collar. The only picture I have of Dutch shows both of us, in just this kind of dress, with our respective smiles, seated cross-legged under a peach tree which grew in the Bergmanns'—his parents'—backyard. . . .

The Bergmanns had come from Germany. They had brought with them a feeling for the old world; and I dare say that it was during the time I played with Dutch and was often in his home that I overheard the conversation of his parents and absorbed some portion of their feeling for the German world. In no other way can I account for the strange nostalgia, the spell of beauty, the dim haunting memories which come over me whenever the Rhine is mentioned or when I read or see something which contains the essential German. Years later, Goethe's Wilhelm Meister *was to touch this same vein.*

["Earth-Being"]

It is generally understood that the things of this world go to the clever, and to those who have a strong desire to possess them. Here then, at the age of boyhood, I was giving evidence of having just the two qualities which above all others make for material success and earthly princedoms. Here were signs that I might grow up to be, not a second Christy Matthewson, not a musician, not a photographer, but a baron of finance, commerce, or industry.

Then something happened which swiftly transferred my interests from the world of things to the world of ideas and imagination. Uncle Bis and I suddenly discovered each other. He had been there all along, and his sensitivity and affection had drawn me to him. I had been there all along, and he had loved me. He had probably been aware that despite the difference of our ages and my restless activity our temperaments were similar. He had certainly noticed that the minute he spoke to me of interesting things I became attentive, pensive, and even grave—save when some particularly fine thing made my eyes flash or glow and caused a flush of eagerness, curiosity, thrill, or enthusiasm to irradiate my face. All the years of my young life we had been there together. He had been my uncle and I his kid. But now the time was ripe for a special relationship. All at once the veils of familiarity dropped from our eyes and each in his own way beheld the wonder of the other.

He had a habit—but it was more than habit; it was a passion—of coming home from work, having dinner with the family, and immediately retiring to his room. There he would get in bed with a book, cigarettes, and a saucer of sliced peaches prepared with sugar in a special way, and read far into the night. Sometimes he would write, trying his hand at fiction. . . .

This position—my uncle in bed surrounded by the materials of a literary man—was impressed upon me as one of the desirable positions in life. It is no wonder that later on I responded positively to pictures of Robert Louis Stevenson and other writers spending most of their lives in bed. Nor is it surprising that in time I inclined to a career which would let me live this way if I wanted to. At that early date, I certainly did want to live like Bis. I knew nothing of his day; but his life at night was completely desirable.

Not every evening but many he would ask me to come and see him, saying he would show me things and talk about whatever interested me. When I went in he would drop his book, look up with his large thoughtful eyes, and welcome me with a quiet undemonstrative but very deep affection, "Hello, kid." "Hello, Uncle Bis." I always found him in a mood of what I would now call lovable reflection. He gave the impression of having experienced much of life. Defeats, ignorance, bitterness, disillusion—these doubtless had left their marks on him, but from it all he seemed to have distilled a certain sweetness and wisdom. I never saw him angry or in any way distempered. His most characteristic expression was a kindly understanding smile, slightly drooping with humorous resignation. He had the quiet withdrawn air of a man who, having tested his wishes and ambitions and having found that his force would not win him more than a minor role in life, accepts his limitations and devotes himself to books. By nature he was far more the artist and thinker than a man of action; and, as far as possible, he evoked the thinker in me.

I would sit on the bed beside him and look and listen with rapt attention, or ask questions in a grave tone of voice. These meetings were very serious—lightened by my laughter and enthusiasm and by his luminous kindliness.

Among the things he showed me and talked about, one stands out with particular vividity. It was a book of physical geography. In it was a picture illustrating the sun shining above raining clouds. In the lower corner a segment of what was meant to be a sphere represented the earth.

Midway up was a heavy cloud with rain pouring from it. Below the cloud earthward all was dark. But above the cloud the sun shone, and in this bright world a balloon sailed with men in its basket. This was the first time I had ever seen such a thing, ever heard such ideas, and my eyes were wide with amazement. And as Bis continued explaining it to me I experienced something but little short of revelation.

I was seeing the earth and hearing ideas about the earth's nature and size—for the first time; that it was spherical-shaped like a pear or apple; that it existed, rotated and revolved, and, despite its great weight, almost floated like a toy balloon in space; that, though very large, thousands of times larger than Washington, it was very small when compared with the sun and with the great stars of the universe. The stars, then, those tiny twinkling lights in the night sky, were enormous bodies. They appeared small only because of their great distance from the earth. I was seeing the clouds in perspective, I was seeing the sun and hearing ideas about the sun, for the first time. It was all wonderful. And, young though I was, I was growing a sense and forming an attitude towards my and our position on earth in the universe. I had a new way of seeing things.

If, like other children, I was an unconscious natural poet of Nature, finding beauty and delight in trees, flowers, rain, snow, sky and clouds, moon, stars, so also was I a natural poet of man's artifices. Copper sheets were as marvelous to me as the petals of flowers; the smell of electricity was as thrilling as the smell of earth after a spring shower.

["Earth-Being"]

From that day to this, the attitude and vision then formed have never left me. True, they have often been eclipsed, forgotten for a time; but, consciously or unconsciously they have continued growing, deepening and widening and filling out down to the present period. They are integral to my mature way of viewing life—man, earth-beings. In fine, my picture and idea of the universe were born that night. This was the beginning of my world view. And for this alone I will be forever grateful to my uncle for having taken such interest in me.

Seeing that I was so eager to learn more about the earth and sun and stars, for many evenings thereafter he went into detailed descriptions and explanations of these things. I could hardly wait for night to come. Dutch was almost forgotten, and the activities of Bacon Street seemed comparatively unimportant.

Bismarck had wide interests, and as time went on he led me along other interesting paths. I learned of history and particularly of Napoleon, whom he saw as a superman of force, courage, love, ambition, and ability to conquer and rule. Bis had been named after Bismarck of Germany whom my grandfather considered one of the world's great men. He himself preferred Napoleon and probably wished he had been given this name. It is a bit odd that the Little Corporal should have captured his imagination, for he seemed to have so little of the soldier in him. But perhaps just this was the cause of the attraction. Perhaps he sensed in himself a tragic lack of the Napoleonic traits and was drawn to complete himself by reading, by gathering from this literature materials for a fanciful self-creation. In any case, his admiration for Napoleon engendered a similar feeling in me.

In the parlor of our house there was a steel engraving of Napoleon bidding adieu to Josephine. I was much taken by the eagle lines of Napoleon's profile. I would stand before the picture and gaze at it; and, as I did so, my imagination, filled with what Bis had told me of the man and of his career, would enact and dramatize a life-like scene. I would see Napoleon himself in life stride into the ornate high-ceilinged French room to take leave of queenly sad Josephine and depart for battle.

I suppose I began seeing myself as a Napoleon; but I did not have to do much acting. As I have already shown, in relation to the children of the neighborhood I was by nature a little Napoleon.

Bismarck also used to read me myths and fables, folk tales, romances and adventures. Often he would phrase the tale in his own words and himself tell it. He liked to do this. He had a decided bent for story telling, and, as I have said, now and again wrote short stories.

For myself—I eagerly absorbed them. My imagination took flight and I was thrilled to follow it into those worlds of wonder.

There are, I know, intelligent people who are so conditioned by the dominant temper of our time which is matter of fact, factual, and rationalistic, that they would prevent children hearing fairy tales and myths in order, as they say, to safe-guard children from the illusions and delusions caused by this, in their eyes, fantastic nonsense. Certainly there is reason for this point of view. But it seems to me that those who hold it often are themselves the victims of two main errors. They fail to distinguish between true myths and meaningless inventions. They fail to recognize that the harm is caused, not by hearing fables, but by confusing fables with facts. This confusion can be avoided, just as we can learn to avoid confusing ideals with actuality. Those who attempt to solve the problem by eliminating one of its factors, in this case, by eliminating legends, are robbing children of the material needed for the growth and expansion of their imaginations. A factual person may not consider this a great loss; and he may be unwilling to credit it, but it is true nonetheless that facts without fables no less than fables without facts make for incomplete lopsided human beings.

With Bismarck I was fortunate enough to have a balanced diet.

And it was to him that I brought my serious questions about life. I felt I could ask him anything. I always received answers which satisfied me for the time and stimulated my mind to further inquiry and pondering.

Some things I asked mother. Some things I asked my grandfather or grandmother or Uncle Walter or, on occasion, one of my playmates. We children used to exchange and compare what our various parents had told us. There was fun in this, but also much bewilderment caused by the different conflicting reports. We felt there was something wrong somewhere. Who? What? We usually settled it by each one loudly and proudly proclaiming his own parents right, all other parents wrong. One effect of this, in my own case, was to diminish my confidence in the elders, and to increase my doubt of them.

Bis was the exception. I held him in the highest regard. I was devoted to him as to one beyond doubt wise and knowing, one capable of holding my complete faith and trust. He was, in truth, my real teacher. In comparison with him and with what I learned from him, my formal teachers and schooling were as nothing.

To me, the conventional side of elementary learning—reading, spelling, penmanship, arithmetic, history—was irksome, tedious, and unrewarding; and, having plenty of energy and some independence of spirit, I did not fail to register my feelings: I was the class-room cut-up and the teacher's problem.

In the beginning, it is true, I had had difficulty learning to read. For some reason or other, try as hard as I would I couldn't get on the inside of the thing: the letters and characters obstinately withheld their sense from me, and the lines of words behind which meaning lurked were like closed doors which stubbornly refused me entrance. I gazed with hopeless amazement at the older children, the teacher, the grownup members of my family who read so easily and seemed to think nothing of it. I wondered by what miracle they, when they were my age and had been confronted by just this baffling task, had been transported past the barriers into the magic land. One thing, however, had encouraged me. Even before this I had had a similar difficulty with learning to tell time. Then, suddenly,

quick as a flash, something had happened, and lo and behold I knew
what the face and figures and hands meant. So it might be with reading.
A second thing had helped me. The teacher had threatened severe punishment for all the dullards or lazy fellows who persisted in remaining stupid
after a certain day. This had served to concentrate as never before all
my force on the task; and I did indeed succeed in taking the prize literally
by force. Before judgment day arrived I had rent the veil. This had been
a mighty achievement; and as long as the thrill of it lasted, I had been
impressed not only with myself but with school.

In time, however, reading had become just an ordinary thing which I
was compelled to continue. I found but little to attract me in the various
school readers. Some of the stories I liked, but they were not half as wonderful as those told me by Bismarck, and moreover, whatever pleasure or
interest they may have had for me was spoiled when they were put through
the mill of classroom recitations. I preferred history and arithmetic.

The system of instruction under which my teachers labored, like all the
schooling of that period, worked on the assumption that a child is naturally
recalcitrant and hostile to learning; and that, therefore, the adult world,
knowing what was best, had to constrain and enforce his education by
cramming stuff into him and by punishing him if he failed or rebelled
against swallowing his allotted portion.

Each evening with Bismarck I was unconsciously demonstrating just the
contrary. Thousands of children of my own age all over the country were
doubtless doing likewise. But the school system. blindly assuming its role
to be that of a literate policeman, took no notice of the real nature and
disposition of any of us. And even now, in the enlightened 1930's, the
school system still does not know that the child's brain, like the child's
muscles, is eager to exercise itself if only it is given the right materials
in a corresponding way. Because the so-called adult brain, already long
since spoiled by the miseducation it was subjected to, and long since
having forgotten the eager way in which it used to function, will not work
unless flogged, the possessors of these spoiled brains assume that children
are as inert and wayward as themselves and must similarly be flogged
into action. This flogging they called education—or discipline, or some
important name. And they never suspect that it is just this education
which hurt their own minds and which will harm if not spoil the minds
of coming generations.

Under the given conditions, my teachers, good souls, were as well-
meaning and competent as the next; but they did not and could not do

other than follow the established method. I resented and resisted it. I had an almost constant feeling that I was being maltreated.

At the same time, I had a lot of fun in school. Some of this fun was natural to the gay spirit of childhood. Some sprang from an instinctive resistance to authority. No small amount of it was tinged with a malice due to my resentment against mishandling. And certainly the conflict produced in me by my relation to my mother and her callers found vent in this way. Poor teachers! I threw crayon and erasers about the room. I emptied ink-wells and rolled them up the aisle against the teacher's desk. I teased the girls. I sent notes. I stomped my feet and made strange noises. During recesses I'd race in and out raising all possible racket. I felt somewhat privileged and immune owing to grandfather's position and influence. ...

... There was much fun and interest in my early schooling, despite the yoke of education. Indeed the yoke was but the smaller part. For in this world also, as in human affairs in general, the conventions, though coercive, were not enough to strangle; and life, that irrepressible electric flowing, overflowed and burst out and away from the set moulds. It bubbled and laughed and did a multitude of fine and mean things even while the disciplinarians exerted watchful strain to hamper it.

I sometimes think that the only form of fun we human beings experience is that which we have when we do things despite the taboos and prohibitions. In a sense, it is a perverse pleasure, under cover and indirect. We can't be frank and straight-forward about it. It can never be given our unqualified acceptance. Often it causes us to feel a false shame and guilt. In my opinion, a large amount of the feeling of guilt which burdens us is induced by just this idiocy which makes us try to snatch our fun when no one is looking.

In another sense, it is the pleasure an unusually intelligent and capable sheep might have if he devised and executed a plan for outwitting the shepherd—and the shambles.

Still another way of viewing it—it is the thrill of independent power exercised by a man of the human aristocracy who knows that the taboos were made by his ancestors, men of his psychological class, not for him but for the herd.

Surely we have no fun being conventional; but convention serves a purpose because it gives us opportunity to be unconventional. We put up with rules because we have fun breaking them. We subscribe to laws for the thrill of being outlaws. We accept morals for the delight of immorality. What a tame thing life would be if society and everyone approved of all one's actions. What dull people! If, on the contrary, society disapproves, if we nevertheless do it, life is dramatic and adventurous. It calls from us our utmost cleverness and skill.

There are, perhaps, two kinds of people: one, those who believe that the conventions should be conformed to; and, two, those who believe that the conventions should be broken. The difference is mainly a matter of belief, of attitude; for in practice all classes and all people more or less break away from the conventional order. Only the second kind of people act independently with little or no feeling of guilt, and hence have more fun. The first kind of people seldom have fun, and then merely vicariously, when they see a Charlie Chaplin or some other kick the established order in the pants and blithely go his way.

In school there were those who did and those who did not have fun. I, as I have said, had fun. But this had nothing directly to do with what is called learning. I was taught comparatively little.

I truly learned with and from Bismarck. He had, I am sure, an unusual natural aptitude for teaching; and it just happened that, with me, conditions were favorable for its exercise. Our evenings together were periods of genuine education. He met me as being to being, one of them older and wiser and more experienced than the other. What he told me was related to my individual needs, interests, and capacity. And he did achieve a living balance, a right proportion, between what was called forth and what was put in. My increasing understanding, my voluntary increasing interest and application, were proofs of this. My mind was born and nurtured during those times with him. . . .

. . . In the early days there was, as I have shown, graded school on the one side and Bismarck on the other. During a later period there were high school, my independent readings, and studies and discussions with a close friend. In my college years—classes and self-directed inquiries.* And, in mid-life, the world of accepted formal knowledge in contrast with my personal experience, with my literary work, and with the Gurdjieff method and body of ideas.†

---

*For Jean Toomer, there were often as many self-directed activities as there were formal classes.
†Toomer's formal relationship with Georges Gurdjieff endured almost a decade after 1923. (See Introduction.)

During my formative period I was in the midst of constuctive human activity, of building, from which I derived the germ of my sense of the joy and value of just this kind of productivity. This is why, later on, I myself thought of becoming a contractor or an architect. This was the starting point of my interest in houses, churches, and cathedrals. My desire to have things constantly happening dates back to these experiences. And—my use of the symbol of building to express my general creative aim in life.

[''Earth-Being'']

I had not, and I doubt that any of the children on our street had, been intelligently informed by their parents about sex. Many years were to pass before new views of life and new ideas of education revolutionized the relation of parents to children in this respect. Not that the new views are now held by everyone, or that they have enabled us to solve the problem; but at least it is recognized that there is a problem, and that the effort cleanly to face it is better than an attempt to avoid it. Then, sex was still regarded as an issue of the devil to be kept out of sight, with the curious hope that it would not lift its head. Our parents themselves, misused— and misusing-themselves—beings, had been left to stumble upon it. They in turn closed their eyes and indulged the ridiculous hope that we, the new generation, were constructed differently and would not fall into the snares and tangles which they all life had suffered through. Knowing from experience that sex will out, yet not knowing what constructively to do with it, they, like their parents, tried to wish it out of existence; or, should this pseudo Christian-Science fail, they, again like their parents, were furtively prepared to meet its manifestations with prohibitions and punishments. Thus were the adults equipped to deal with the most powerful of man's forces, the key-force of life, the one prime energy which sets the tone and temper of our entire existence. Inevitably we children stumbled upon it. Indeed it seemed to arise all at once like an epidemic striking everyone.

One day in a tree an older boy showed me what he could do with his organ to make a milky fluid come from it. I told Dutch. The next day in an old barn we witnessed the same boy in the same demonstration. He explained things to us about boys and girls. Girls were made different, but they too liked it. Maybe one of them would give us a piece if we asked them. He told us about grownup men and women and why they slept together at night. Revelations were coming thick and fast. They thrilled me. Some things I resisted. Some sickened me. But there was no

holding back. A force of attraction greater than me, stronger than anything I had ever felt, was pulling and sweeping me through an unlocked
door into an amazing almost unbelievable world. All life was suddenly
utterly changed.

Not long after, Mr. Bergmann caught Dutch and me playing with a
dog. He made Dutch go in the house and sent me off, my ears ringing
and all of me stinging from a tongue-lashing.

A girl got a note from a boy one day at school. She brought the note
home and showed it to her mother. Thereafter she was not allowed to
play with boys. If she were with a group of girls and some boy came up
she'd immediately go in the house. Of course, we all knew why; and
thus her actions, just the things which were intended to prevent sex,
increased our consciousness of it. We boys giggled when she turned her
back and went away. We looked at each other knowingly.

More and more we saw and felt that girls were girls and boys were boys.
A division was coming between us and we ceased being an unconscious
group of playmates.

My only cousin came to visit us. I proposed that we show each other
things. My family saw that something was up and she didn't stay long.

Mother suspected me. She wanted to know what I knew. Now and again
she gave me a probing but always furtive look. She dared not ask me.
I concealed everything. I knew I had her guessing. I felt superior to her—
mother, the loving but blind adult who could see no more than the surface aspects of a fraction of the things at work in her child.

Through ignorance and fear she had already forfeited the opportunity
of being the first to inform me, to inform me cleanly and correctly, and
thus at the outset to place in me constructive views of this most important
matter. Now she was failing the chance to intercept the forming of a
practice* which, as the years unfolded, gave rise to the most desperate
struggles of my life. My superiority to her was gained at a price I would
not willingly pay for anything on earth. And she, dear suffering soul, had
gone through it all herself, as had her parents and their parents on back
through the ages of human history—save in those times and at those
places where young growing beings came under the care and direction of
men who possessed objective knowledge of man's structures and functions;

---

* Possibly repressions of sexual desire, but more probably masturbation. A prolonged illness in youth frightened him into believing, at times, masturbation to
have been the cause of it.

or when, though not directly under such wise guidance, they were within the still surviving customs first originated by such men.

We boys learned a song:

> If you like me, and I like you,
> And you like me the same,
> Just pull up your dress
> And I'll do the rest,
> Under the bamboo tree.

We'd sing it sometimes changing the last line to mulberry or tulip or cherry tree—whichever we happened to be near at the time. We thought we were very clever and wise and devilish.

The climax of the business occurred late one summer while I was away and our house was vacant. Some older boy took a girl under our back porch. She told her mother. The news spread. When I returned I soon found that most of the girls of the neighborhood were no longer allowed to play with boys. Some could play during the day but not at night. This prohibition was strictly enforced and strictly obeyed only for a month or so. In time it was gradually relaxed, but not forgotten. The knowledge of so-called good and evil had visited us. Bacon Street had definitely become a street of the two sexes.

Sex had indeed willed out. Met with prohibitions and punishments it became furtive and truly a thing of abnormal human nature which is the only devil in the world; and more than one of us was started on that practice which more than any other bleeds away the body and soul of growing beings on earth. ...

... Dorothy Hanvey was my first love. Just suddenly I was rapturously completely in love with her—and she with me. We became inseparable. Everything I did I wanted her to do, or at least to be there with me. No longer was I content to climb trees alone, or with Dutch, or some of the other boys. Dorothy had to be there. And if it were a fruit tree, a mulberry or cherry, I'd toss down to her the largest and ripest berries. We'd find vines of honeysuckle and smell them and bite the stems, tasting the aromatic juice. I'd catch butterflies for her. I'd give her buttercups and four-leaf clovers. We see-sawed. We'd play I-spy, and Dorothy and I would run off and it would take a long time to find us. The boys teased me. Her mother called her Mrs. Nathan.

I cut our initials in fences. I brought her trophies: June bugs, lady bugs, bumble bees, a bird's nest, strange insects, fine stones. On holidays I had gifts for her. Presents for Christmas, bunnies and eggs for Easter—

and we'd roll the eggs down the terrace until the shells were broken and then we'd eat them. And fire-crackers for the Fourth of July. On the Fourth I liked to show off. Once or twice I fought for her, or for myself. It was the same thing.

In spring and summer the houses of our block had screen doors which banged as people passed in or out. Of all the sounds of all the doors in the neighborhood I knew the special sound of Dorothy's. I was alert for it. It meant, or might mean, that she was coming out to play. I wanted to miss no chance of seeing and being with her. Whatever part of the house I might be in, upstairs, downstairs, in the dining-room, I could hear the bang of her door. Whatever I might be doing I would hear it. A great joy and eagerness would seize me. I'd instantly drop everything and rush through the house. If I could not go out at once I'd speed to the front window and wave to her, saying by word, gesture anyway, that I'd soon be out. My family came to accept it that whenever I heard that screen door all else was forgotten.

We were still young enough to have our mothers bathe us. We were bathed at the same time of the afternoon; and in some way the custom was formed that right after bath our mothers would stand us in the front second-story windows and let us wave across the street to each other. Both of us, I certainly, looked forward to this event each day. I was over-joyed by it. The other children knew. They teased us a little, but in a good way. They were as innocent as ourselves, and accepted it as being in the natural order of things.

But it came to an abrupt end. An older boy, a newcomer in the neigh-borhood, learned of it and said things that reached our mothers. They suddenly stopped it, explaining to us that we were getting too old for such things. But we knew the real reason. That new boy had said things. I had never liked him to begin with. Now I hated him.

Until this happening, our attachment had been free and as natural as breathing. After it, we became somewhat uneasy and seemed to feel unfriendly eyes on us. And so it may well be that just this circumstance caused the beginning of the end of our young love. In any case, after continuing a short while longer, it gradually diminished; and then, just as suddenly as it had started it stopped. Dorothy and I, as children of a larger group, continued seeing each other frequently and playing together. But the days of wonder were over. Neither of us was the marvel to each other that we had been.

That I had such an experience while still so young indicates a number of things, signs of my type and temperament. Among these, it showed that even then my emotional nature was strong and active; and—looking ahead—it suggested that personal affections would play a large part in my future life. And so they have. Dorothy was the first. With her I began my love-career. Then it was Bernice Carson, and then another and another and another down to the present time.

Of course, like all boys I had periods of withdrawal into a strictly boy's world from which we and I looked out and down a bit contemptuously on all that had to do with girls. But with me these phases were neither prolonged nor acute. The greater part of the time I was so obviously fond of the girls that had I not been able to give good account of myself as a fighter and runner and tree-climber I would doubtless have lost caste.

But I was a good fighter. In fact I was the leader of our, as it were, gang. I could lick any boy my size in the neighborhood. Sometimes I took on larger fellows. Scraps would only occasionally occur among the original children of our group. We got along surprisingly well. But sometimes when new boys came in, fighting had to be done. A family named Dowd moved in. There were three boys, one younger than myself, one my own age, one older. A larger boy, Horace Clark, put us up to fighting, and it was a comic thing. The Dowd boys would call me a name. I'd fight and beat the little fellow and send him in the house bawling. I'd fight and beat the second boy. And then the largest—one after the other. Almost every single day for a month this thing kept up. There was no sense to it. Perhaps we had been mad at each other at first, but now we weren't really ... . But, having started it we seemed not able to stop. Finally, we just got tired. We made up; and the Dowd boys became my good friends.

But to return to Dorothy. One other thing she did was to stamp me with, to indelibly impress upon me, her image. It was the image of a fair girl. My mother was dark. Already her picture, also fixed permanently, lay within me. And so the two, dark and fair, existed side by side, to govern my taste throughout life.

And in truth, often enough I have found myself now strongly drawn towards the one, again towards the other. And sometimes I have been in situations involving a choice between them, situations which, in a sense, were repetitions of my childhood circumstance.

Still again—for this matter of attraction is, in reality, far more complex than our formulae suggest—I have liked girls and women who were neither dark nor fair but in-between—such a one, for example, as Bernice Carson.

Blonde and brunette—two physical types, two kinds of women with whom a man can be in love. But in life nothing is only physical. There is also the symbolical. White and black. West and East. North and South. Light and Darkness. Day and Night. In general, the great contrasts. The pairs of opposites. And I, together with all other I's, am the reconciler.

The seasons came to our small piece of the surface of the earth, each with its own unique gifts—turning leaves and russet sunsets; white frosty days and snow and ice; thawings, blossoms, fragrance and blue skies; the full ripe days of heat and drowsy droning opulence—each to evoke from children corresponding moods and rounds of activity. The adult world was not much affected by seasonal changes. If adults thought of it at all, they probably prized their withdrawal from the influences of Nature and their commitment to the business of men which demanded that the same kind of thing be repeated day after day throughout the year. But the world of children was sufficiently close to natural forces to respond to the rich variety of the earth's logically changing moods. While adults, cut off in a strange sphere of their own fashioning, inertly or with strain repeated themselves month after month, each self each month the same, the children, still harmoniously within the universe, and behaving accordingly, grew into the new days of the new seasons, and in a year they had a complete cycle of experiences.

For me, then as now, the year ended with summer and began with autumn.

The long heavy days of heat passed. Days were cooler. Snap and chill came into the air; and the sun rose later and set earlier. Bees and insects stopped buzzing. No crickets made racket. No birds chirped or warbled. But something in the air, perhaps the air itself, hummed and sang with hushed expectancy. By now, all the families had returned from their vacations, and the neighborhood, strangely vacant without them, again had all its children. The earth quickened, and I with it. Fall was here, with gloriously colored leaves, with falling leaves and great heaps of them to jump into or burn in blazing bonfires—and Hallowe'en, Thanksgiving, and Christmas were in the offing.

I had grown into a sturdy little fellow, with a strong active body bursting with energy. My senses were more alive than ever. My feelings were mobile and impressionable. My mind worked like a flash. All of me was alert. My life was the life of outdoors. I was in the house only when I had to be, and took no notice of the grownup members of my family, save when I wanted something which only they could give, or when, for some reason or other, they compelled me to.

I awoke early and was eager to get up and out. Before breakfast I'd run from the house while the dew or early morning frost was still on the ground. I'd gulp something to eat and run out again, headed up the street for Dutch's house. I'd whistle for him, the special whistle of the boys of our block. If he didn't make an appearance right away I'd call, "Dutch, come on out." From somewhere inside I'd hear him yell, "I'm coming, Pinchy." And so he would. And then the day would really begin.

We'd join other children or they'd join us. Perhaps the Dutton boys, "D.D." and "H.D.," Carlie Joss, Herbert and Tuney Snyder. Maybe several of the girls, Dorothy Hanvey, Bernice Carson, Alice Hoover.

I was still the leader of this group. I still could run faster, climb trees better, skate, play marbles, better than any of them. Carlie Joss was heavier and stronger than I. But he was slower, and seemed not to have my wish or ambition or whatever it was to be ringleader. In a fist fight he could have beaten me. He never did, and never challenged my position—save once. For over a month I had wanted to sock him. I was standing next to him. All of a sudden I hauled off and cracked him one—and then ran like the devil. I was a hundred yards away before he knew what had happened. He got furious and started chasing me. He chased me all over the place, and I didn't dare come home till I knew he had gone in for dinner. For several days he had me running. Then his anger passed over. He was very good natured. He forgot about it. Carlie was the only boy of my age I ever ran from.

And, yes, once I walked away. It came about like this. Over on 16th Street were several old shacks which looked as though they had been standing there ever since the time when that part of Washington belonged to Maryland. They housed a number of tough ill-kempt boys who formed a gang. These fellows seldom foraged our neighborhood, but once or twice during our rambles we had run into and fought with them, our group winning. They had it in for us, and especially for me.

One day as I was sauntering down Bacon Street towards my house I heard a noise behind me. I looked around and saw the tough gang whooping in my direction. None of my bunch were about. I stood my ground and faced them. Now we've got you, they cried. I said nothing, just looked straight at them. Come on fight, they taunted me. I didn't budge. He's scared to fight. Soak him! Kick the piss out of him, they yelled. The leader said to the very smallest boy in the gang, slap his face. The little rascal slapped my face with a whack. I winced, but otherwise did not budge. I had very little bravado in me. I was a strategist. I was too wise to fight when my forces were so obviously outnumbered. Unconsciously, I was bringing to bear on them a different kind of strength.

Slap him again, said the big fellow. The little rascal whacked me again. I flared with anger but held myself in check. I glared at them contemptuously, saying by my look, you know very well not one of you would dare to fight me by himself. With that, I wheeled around and walked away. They stood gazing at me, not knowing what to make of it. I walked with dignity to my house and in the door—and that was the last of our trouble with that bunch. They never visited our street again.

As for myself—I was in a double state for several days. My feelings smarted. They smarted more than my cheek had. But, I was satisfied with the way I had handled the gang. I felt proud of myself. I knew I had had the better of it. I had won a moral victory. This was my first experience of such a thing. I became conscious of a new power.

We adventured in the lots and fields, continued investigating houses which were being built, played follow-the-leader, and cut our initials and signs in the bark of trees and on fence-boards. My sign was the arrow. I cut arrows on all possible places. I was proud of my skill and craftsmanship. I was fascinated with and proud of the sign itself. It was my first symbol. If anyone spit on the sign you had cut, this meant fight. One day Dutch spit on mine and I spit on his and we fought like cats and dogs. The next day, both of us were perched precariously on a real estate for-sale board. Without warning he suddenly spit straight in my eye. He jumped from the board yelling and laughing and beat it for home. Perhaps his Tanta still remembers what I did to him when I caught him.

We roller-skated. One sidewalk of our street was of cement and smooth. Along this we'd roll and race and fall. There was a big dog named Booze. He was a bulldog belonging to one of the families. He was our favorite. He'd let us hold his tail while he pulled us along. Also, he was a great scrapper. He and another bulldog fought whenever they saw each other. We'd yell and cheer for Booze. He always won, but several times he almost got chewed up.

We had our cave-making. For this we had to go what then seemed far down 16th Street where a high face of red earth arose to the summit of Meridian Hill. We dug into this face and hollowed out a cave which was wider and deeper than the entrance-hole showed. We'd stay away a good portion of the morning and afternoon. Our parents would not know what had become of us. They got worried and frightened. Somehow they found out, and forbade our going down there any more. Perhaps it was dangerous. The earth may have caved in. I don't know.

Then came the building of houses in trees. To the side of our house there was a marvelous big tulip tree. I had climbed all over it and knew every limb. Once I had fallen, a drop of about twenty feet. A passerby thought I was hurt. But I wasn't. My bones were still pliant. I was stunned a little, but that was all. Well, high up this tree some of the older fellows helped us build a house. It was quite an affair, cosy, and covered with tar-paper to keep out the rain. We practically lived up there. It was our club. We smoked Indian cigars, corn-silk, dry leaves, real cigarettes if we could get them. The problem was to take the breath out of your mouth so that your family wouldn't know. After a time, grandmother got worried. It was our lot and she felt that if any thing happened she would be blamed. So, with much wailing from us, she had Old Willis tear it down.

Old Willis was quite a character. He had been a slave, and now was very wrinkled, grey-haired, and old, how old neither he nor anyone exactly knew. But he was still active. According to the season he tended our furnace, watered and mowed the lawn, did odd jobs about the place. When grandmother was having trouble with cooks, he helped out in the kitchen. I particularly remember him washing dishes. Something about the way he did it, perhaps it was his own quiet quaintly happy mood, made me want to do it too. He wouldn't let me. But later on, years later, I did wash them; and, like him, I found that it was a good time for singing. Old as he was, he was spry enough to climb the tree and, as I have said, tear down our house. Old Willis, with a kindly wise smile on his wrinkled face, pushing an ancient grey wood-cart with a lawn-mower, a rake, and a bag of grass sticking out, was one of the familiar figures of the neighborhood. People hired him for these odd jobs. I was very fond of him.

By this time we had graduated to bicycles. Learning to ride a bicycle had been quite a stunt. Once done, we could range over the entire north-west section of Washington, the Zoo and Rock Creek Park.

Quite early I had a tennis racket in my hands; and to this day I remember the smell of gut as I experienced it then. I was a streaky, a flash player. When in form I could play better than most of them. My service was good. I knew both forehand and backhand strokes. When not in form some dub would give me a hard tussle.

In season we had baseball. I was the pitcher of our team. The Berliner boy had taught me how to throw curves. I imitated a long rangy fellow named Langley who pitched for Gunther Church in the church league. Most of us possessed season tickets to the games of this league, and after a game we'd return to our lot full of enthusiasm and have a contest ourselves.

Baseball gloves, by the way, were not merely things with which to play ball; to me they were experiences with leather, the various kinds, their textures, the treatment they needed, the rubbing in of neatsfoot oil. I liked leather very much. I still do. The leather of shoes, wallets, bags, briefcases. A store window with a leather display will almost always stop me. And I can tell quite a bit about people according to their tastes in this material.

Of all the days of early autumn, we looked forward most to Hallowe'en. It was preeminently a boy's day, or, rather, a boy's evening. Then we could indulge in a more than usual number of pranks and feel that we had a semi-official festive sanction. Pumpkins, jack-o-lanterns, putty, and bean blowers, tick-tacks .. We scared children younger than ourselves and chased them indoors. We were scared and chased by the older fellows.

This chasing business is a queer thing, not confined solely to boys or to the race of men. Dogs like to chase each other as well as chase cats. Horses like to put their ears close to their heads, look devilish, and chase cows. What is this strange passion?

Once, a young gentleman who came from some other part of town picked just this of all nights to call on his young lady, an older girl who lived on our street. He had a handsome automobile which he left standing in front. This car had a wonderful musical chime. Several times in the past we had monkeyed with it. This night we decided to blow it and chime it for all it was worth. Which we did. Just when we had the whole street echoing, who should dash from the house but our young gentleman, hot after us. He was quite a big fellow. Our boldness vanished and we ran as fast as our legs could carry us.

I had a feeling he had singled me out and was determined to catch me. I didn't look back but I knew he was coming. The others were scattering. I wanted to reach a certain lot and dive through a fence and out on the alley. Each of us had his own special and private way of escaping trouble. This was mine. Midway this lot I sensed him gaining on me. "Look out, Pinchy! Look out!" the others yelled. Just then he pounced on me. I shook myself free. He caught me again. "Why don't you pick on somebody your own size?" I asked him. "I'm going to pick on you and teach you a lesson." He was shaking me. "How do you know I blew your old horn?" "Well, didn't you?" The bunch, off at a safe distance, cried, "Fight him, Pinchy! Fight him!" But I wasn't in a fighting mood. He was too big. I was trying to trick him and escape a sound licking. ''What if I did? I didn't break anything, did I?'' This thing has been going on long enough. I want it to stop, do you understand me?'' ''Let me go.'' ''Will you stop it?'' ''Let me go.'' ''Well, I will this time, but if I ever catch you again—'' I got free and walked away in a sulk. I knew he was standing there watching. At what I thought to be a safe distance I wheeled around—''Go to hell, you big stiff!''—and started running. I got caught in the fence and he dashed up and gave my rear-end one of the stiffest whacks it has ever had . .

We harassed the staid adults, peppering windows with beans and putty, slamming doors, ringing bells. If we had it in for the people of any particular house, this was the time to take it out on them. We'd steal their mats, lift their gates off the hinges, sometimes burn them—and, to one party, we made a present of a large carefully wrapped package of juicy horse-turds. Our only fear was of bicycle cops. They could come swiftly and silently and be on us before we knew it.

But . . what a difference between the policemen of those days in that neighborhood and the burly crude fellows to be met with in most large cities today. Comparatively, those cops were refined, unassuming, and not one of them but what had a lively sense of humor, and a sense of what is to be expected of boys—and, for that matter, of men. Having caught us at our worst mischief they would do no more than try to frighten us into better ways, saying we ought to know better, or that they would tell our parents, or lock us up if they caught us at it again. Of course, they never did.

Once, however, I was really in fear of the lock-up. We had been playing fire on that same lot to the side of our house. I would start a fire in some high bushes and brush. When it had reached a fair blaze I'd run to the sidewalk and put in the alarm. The gang would come clanging along and put it out. Each time I'd let the blaze get a little higher, a bit more difficult to control, before calling the fire-fighting squad. Finally, it actually did get beyond our control. It blazed and swept through the bushes and caught the wood fence of the house next door. It spread down the fence and threatened to run over the next yard. In this yard was an old frame structure which, once afire, would have gone up in sparks with a great roar. We were frightened to death, almost paralyzed. Laborers working on the Copeland house across the way saw the danger and rushed over with pails of water, often stumbling. Passing men began beating the flames. The hubbub was considerable. Just then a bicycle cop wheeled up. We spied him; and our fear of him broke our paralysis. One fear overcame another, and we scrambled for cover. I ran in the house, upstairs to the top floor and crawled under a bed.

Soon I heard our doorbell ring. I knew it was the cop, and I believed he was coming for me. I wanted to fly away through the air. But also, I was curious. I stole to the banister and listened. Grandmother, though perhaps suspecting me, or Dutch, told him she did not know who had started the fire. He thanked her and went out. I waited a long while before creeping downstairs. Before I did so, I went to my window from which I could see the window of one of the culprits who lived in the Savoy apartment. He also had reached home and was standing there. I wig-wagged him that the danger was over. Down I went and outside where a few people were still gathered. I mingled with them and as innocently as anyone looked regretfully at the charred fence. But that was the end of playing fire. I had acquired a sense and understanding of how swiftly and powerfully flame worked. I was taken back. Indeed, I stood in awe of it.

For a number of days thereafter my thoughts were preoccupied with the question of fire. What was it, this hot, consuming, swiftly spreading, brilliant, flaming thing? I would gingerly light a match and look at it. It was fire; but now that my eyes were really open to it, now that I had seen what it could do to solid things, to say that it was fire was not to explain anything. I would touch it to a patch of dry grass and watch it catch. Its crackling sweep would frighten me and I'd quickly stomp it out. I asked my mother. It was simply fire, she said. Uncle Bismarck, who seemed to know more about things than anyone in the house, told me about combustion. But this by no means satisfied me as to the mysterious nature of fire itself. A flame might come from sulphur, or from hay piled in a barn, or from striking flint against flint. All right. But fire was not sulphur, or hay, or flint. It was itself. What was it? Then too, there was this question: when I had put fire out, where had it gone?

Needless to say, these queries were not answered. Just about this time, however, I had a chance to witness what a real fire would do. It was at night. I had gone to bed and was sleeping. Mother awakened me. I sat up, and, looking through the window, I saw the whole sky apparently ablaze. I leapt from bed. It was the Hanvey stable. Flames and smoke were pouring from the windows and spurting upward.

People were running and shouting and I could see them and the ground and the nearby buildings almost as plainly as if it were day. I felt as though something had stabbed me and I would choke. I knew the stable very well, and the stableman, and the fine horses. This would be the last of them. And I was fascinated. Engines came clanging to the spot. I put on my clothes and rushed out. I joined the crowd of excited people who had formed at a safe distance from the place. Even there you could feel the heat. Streams of water began pouring at the flames. The firemen were at work.

People talked. Were the horses out? Would they be able to get them out? Horses were hard to manage in a fire. They went blind or got panicky or something and you couldn't do a thing with them. They seemed to go straight for the flames. You had to cover their eyes. It would be a pity and terrible if they were burned. Such fine horses. I seemed to smell burning horse meat.

How did it catch? Who started it? I piped up, "Maybe it was spontaneous combustion." They laughed and asked what could a young fellow like me know about spontaneous combustion. Well, I knew, all right. I bet I'd thought about it more than they had.

After a while the flames diminished and everyone said the firemen had done a good job. It was night again, but against the sky you could see the brick walls, and the windows still smoking.

Next day I saw them drag out one charred stiff horse, and then another, and leave them in the alley until something came and carried them off.

I grew up in a comparatively free and open world, subject to but few of the rigid conventions and fixed ideas which contract the human psyche and commit people to narrow lives ruled by narrow preferences and prejudices. Neither by my family nor by Bacon Street was I deliberately conditioned to hold family, class, political, racial, regional, or religious preconceptions and antagonisms. This of course does not mean that I escaped being stamped positively and negatively by my environment with habits of various kinds, with likes and dislikes, with affirmations and denyings. No, I acquired them then. I have acquired more since. I still have a sufficient number. It simply means that no one went out of his way professionally to rivet me with those sweeping absurd beliefs which sink so deep into us as children that after we have grown up we assume them to have been inborn and swear by them eternally.

I was fortunate enough not to be victimized by the forms of insanity which induce people to believe that they love or hate entire classes, races, nations, religions. I like or dislike specific persons. Or, to be exact, I like or dislike specific traits or properties or ideas or values in the various individuals with whom I have had personal experience. I have yet to see a man whom I altogether denied and hated. I have yet to see a man whom I altogether accepted and loved. I doubt that anyone would believe that he completely loved or hated a person, to say nothing of such an enormous thing as a nation or a religion, unless he had been subject to a conditioning which paralyzed his critical faculties and hypnotized him to hold such a conviction. I was not thus hypnotized. *

How came such a thing? How did I partially escape?

. . . In the first place, the conditions in my household favored my being let alone. I have already told of how grandfather, the dominant one, checked himself and was checked by mother so that he took no active part in my upbringing. Mother herself—her type was not that of the fussy or domineering parent, nor was she the kind of mother who seems bent on devouring her child. Besides, she was very much occupied with her own problems, which were becoming more acute all the time. Thus she had neither the energy nor the inclination to keep me in constant surveillance and bondage. A fair portion of the care for me was given over to grandmother. But gentle and retiring grandmother never in this life would try to stamp her views on me or on anyone. Nor would Bismarck, for he was too tolerant and broadminded. It was native to them to live and let live. And Walter, though believing, as I have said, that I was being spoiled— well, after all, I was not his child and it was not his business. And so, in fine, I had the freedom of an orphan while at the same time living in an atmosphere of affection and sincere goodwill.

In the second place, I myself seemed to induce in the grownups an attitude which made them keep their hands off me; keep, as it were, a respectful distance. Just how and why was this?

I remember one episode which gave both mother and grandmother a queer feeling. There was one rule she strictly enforced. I had to report home at dusk, not later than the time when the street lamps were lit. This time I was very late. I had been playing some distance from our street. Mother was waiting for me in the front hall. She was so angry that grandmother thought she also should be present to intercede for me. The minute I entered I was yanked off my feet and given a thrashing. I did not cry. Something had happened in me and I was beyond tears and beyond anger. Mother was somewhat appeased. Grandmother was sorrow-

---

* In "On Being an American," Toomer states that his grandmother "was not fond of black men" but that neither he nor she took the prejudice seriously. Other members of the family, he asserts, had no prejudices. Race and color were rarely mentioned.

ful. I got to my feet, faced them without a quiver, and heard the strangest words come from me. "She can do no more than kill me." I spoke to grandmother, but it was meant for mother. I stood there. Both were taken back. Grandmother said I should not say such a thing. Mother said nothing, but regarded me with the strangest expression on her face. I went upstairs; and, still without feeling resentment or anger, I would have nothing to do with them for the next few days. I never forgot this episode, nor did they. That was the last spanking I ever had.

It would seem that my sense of becoming conduct had been violated. I deserved punishment for being late; but I knew I did not deserve being yanked off my feet and whipped with an anger which was out of all proportion to my fault. Children, I am convinced, have this sense. They have it more than adults, and in a purer form. If this pure form of it could be retained and developed as we grow up there would exist in man a function which of itself would act as an internal lever of behavior and tend to make the human world what it should be. We would be certain to have decent human relationships. Usually, however, something happens to it: it either ceases manifesting or becomes so twisted that it is hardly recognizable.

With the generality of adults the sense of becoming conduct is external, a thing acquired from the outside social world which tends to make the given person merely conform to what is considered becoming behavior in his or her environment. Under its influence we care only about appearing to behave well; we care nothing about really behaving well. With children it is an internal native thing. Many times I have seen children manifest it. Once I saw a child who had climbed a snow-bank after a ball yanked down by her nurse or mother. She freed herself from the grown person's grip and said, with dignity and a complete quiet assurance, "You ought not treat me like that." The adult looked confused and taken back. Perhaps she felt somewhat as my mother had.

. . . I still have the attitude that people, the world, life, can do no more than kill me. It has not changed. Of all the attitudes I am aware of and can trace, this one has undergone the least deviation, the least development. I remember just how I felt when I said it then. I have the same feeling of ultimate finality when I say it now. I have said it very seldom. There is no pose about it. I mean just what I say. It is a simple direct statement of what to me is truth. . . .

. . . I had in me a regular little demon that arose, showing hot temper, even rage, or an unyielding stubbornness, when I was told in a certain commanding manner to do something. Commands of certain kinds made me display a rage, behavior equal to that caused by pinning down my arms or in any way hampering my body-movements. I flared up and hated the person who told me. I would not do it. I would willfully do something else, or break something, or, if my nose were forced in it, I'd overdo it.

The way to handle me was to show me the thing, say you thought I should do it, and state with conviction that you believed I would. Then go away—leaving me entirely on my own, and with the feeling that you recognized my ability both to see that the thing should be done and to do it without anyone commanding or watching over me. If you did so leave me, you could be sure I would do my utmost not to fail your high estimate of me. But let me feel that you thought I was incapable, or that I needed a policeman, and I'd try my best to make you wish you had ten of them to help control me. . . .

As regards important matters, I was, as I have said, left singularly alone. My experiences with religion will illustrate this point.

I was told there was a God, but I was not told I must love or fear Him. I have never known these emotions. Heaven was described to me as a wonderful beautiful place; but no one made me long to go there. I was not induced to believe that residence in the land of harps and milk and honey was the reward I might look forward to if I were a good boy on earth. The Devil existed in our house only in grandfather's racy vocabulary. He was a roguish energetic fellow whom you could evoke to help you express your anger or high spirits. And, if I did not melt at the thought of Heaven, neither did I shudder at the picture of Hell. I had indeed seen pictures of Hell, reproductions of Doré's famous illustrations of Danté. They did frighten and awe me, but in my imaginative experiences they were on a par with illustrations of the *Arabian Nights* and other wonder-books. I once asked mother if they were drawings of an actual place. She shook her head and said no. I asked her if there was a Hell. She paused and for a moment looked doubtful, undecided. Then again she shook her head and said, "No, Booty, I do not believe there is, unless .." She left the sentence unfinished. Her completed thought probably was, "unless it exists here on earth." But I did not divine this, and I felt relieved to know that the place of pitch-forks and liquid fire was a thing of fancy which I need not fear having really to go to.

As for sin—sin was something I had never heard about and did not know even by name. Even when, years later, I went to college and one of my professors asked me if I believed in the doctrine of original sin, I looked at him without the slightest notion of what he was talking about.

On the corner of 15th and V Streets, N.W., Washington, there is a

Catholic church of white stone. I always see it as a cross of white and green, for the stone is crystal white and the lawn around is vivid green. In this church I was christened. I remember this event, or part of it. I recall the marble bowl and the stained glass window with sunlight coming through; and I seem to recall kicking up a big fuss when the water was put on me. But perhaps this latter is no more than a memory of what someone else told me. In any case, I was christened Catholic; and this was the first and almost the last of my formal religious experiences.

Grandmother was Catholic. But, as can be seen, neither she nor any member of my family was what is called a good Christian. They seldom went to church and had no religious prejudices. They did not compel me to attend Sunday school. And so, during my own formative period, I was, as I have said, free of the usual so-called religious influences. Not then, not ever, have I felt bias for or against any faith, sect, or creed. Nothing could be more remote from or abhorrent to my nature than that I take part in those perversions which are not ashamed to bear the names of religious persecutions and religious wars. But I have hated and I do hate the vices and vanities, the thirsts for power, the crafty acquisitiveness, that hide under religious cloaks. I do hate the oily piety, the sweet sugar frosting, the hypocrisy, the infidelity. And I do hate the organized religious machine. The majority of my contacts with conventional religion have caused mechanical pain or suffering.

Next to my christening, my first memory of anything having to do with churches goes back to the time when the big Congregational church was being built and I adventured about in the half-finished structure. Thus I associate a church with building.

Then, second, the following. Dutch and I were walking down Columbia Road one summer evening and there in a large yard we saw a lawn party in full progress. Fascinating Chinese lanterns swung from the trees, and happy children white and starched were romping and eating as much ice cream as they could get. Standing outside the fence we could see them; we could hear the click of spoons and the sounds of merry-making. It was a church lawn party. We wanted to go in—not, in truth, for religion's sake, but for the fun of it. We were told we would have to stay out because we did not belong to that church. I will never forget the sensation, the mingled sense of injustice, shame, anger, and regret caused by that refusal; and I was old enough to know that we were being kept out by a church. It was the way in which we had been told that rankled us. There was, of course, justification for the refusal itself. They had to limit the numbers, else, every child in the vicinity would have come in, and that would have been the end of the party. But the manner of the rebuff, the tone of voice, the hard flat righteousness of it . . I have heard that same voice time and time again issuing from church-lips, spitting the acid of an ugly belief on all outsiders.

In an informal way, however, I did receive religious ideas and views, and the rudiments of the Christian doctrine as revealed by the sayings of Christ. And it was grandmother who taught me to pray. Never a night came but what, before getting in bed, I knelt and prayed,

> Now I lay me down to sleep,
> I pray the Lord my soul to keep,
> If I should die before I wake,
> I pray the Lord my soul to take.

With me this became a very real observance. It evoked my feeling and my wish. Soon I came to enact it of my own volition; and had I skipped an evening I would have felt robbed of a very precious thing. Later on I learned the Lord's Prayer. So strongly did I feel the need of saying it that I continued praying through the years of boyhood, adolescence, and young manhood, having recourse, if necessary, to subterfuge should an overt practice of it be likely to subject me to the ridicule of my friends or room-mates.

Indeed there formed in me, despite or because of the lack of formal training, a deep, powerful, interior religious sense. Until my twenty-second year my main attitudes to life arose from religious views. So firmly and completely did my universe have God, so related was I to this religious world, that when the then to me irrefutable logic of atheism compelled me to accept it, not only did my ideational world collapse, but my very form of life, my life itself, was broken. I told a friend of that period that I had the sensations of a condemned man when the platform sinks and he is jerked by his neck to dangle in mid-air.

I was ten years old and the summer of 1905 lay before me, that summer which in my memory appears as a dark night streaked with fears and nightmares. It was as if the sun had gone into eclipse; or as if I, suddenly struck by a curse, had to stand hunch-shouldered with my face averted from it. No contrast could be sharper than that between this summertime and previous vacations. They had been gay bright seasons eagerly looked forward to because they set me free from school and took me to places like Saratoga which I loved. Doubtless, before I heard of the plan, I also anticipated this one, expecting it to be like all the others. Little did I know. The external conditions were to be quite different; and I myself was swiftly moving without knowing it towards the serious illness which was to change my entire way of life.

As vacation approached I sensed something unusual going on in the house. It was a time of sparks and thunderclouds. Mother was preoccupied and tense. Several times she had tilts with grandfather. He commanded and stormed at her. He flung her off, and she had all she could do to hold her ground. But she did hold it, as long as the set-to lasted. I opened my eyes in fear and amazement at the strength of her determination. Never before had I seen anyone successfully oppose grandfather when he was angry. But after each tilt she was more tense and remote than ever. Grandmother, usually so calm, was nervous and worried. Even so, she was nearer to me than mother. She gave me a more than customary amount of attention, and I instinctively went to her for things I wanted. I was very sensitive to the entire situation without being able to understand what it was about. I knew very well a crisis of some sort had arrived, but I could only feel it in the dark.

The school year ended and then I got the shock of my young life. Mother broke the news to me. She told me the summer plan. She was going off by herself. She would go to Atlantic City [and] Brooklyn, and I would remain in Washington. At first I thought she must be joking with me. Such a thing seemed impossible. She had never left me. I had never spent a summer in Washington. Soon, however, I saw she was in dead earnest. I realized that it was to be just as she said. I was terribly upset. I resisted her. I even argued with her and tried to stand up to her as she had stood up to grandfather. I couldn't see why she couldn't take me.

She did not try to explain. Now I understand that home conditions for her had indeed reached a climax, that they had at last driven her to seek a means of escape. I would have been a hindrance and a burden. Having reached the verge of desperation, she did in truth need a free period all to herself. She had fought the matter out within herself, settled it with grandfather, and was settling it with me. I too, whatever the mutual pain, would have to accept her decision.

To make things worse, grandfather and grandmother also were going away, and also without me. If I couldn't go with mother, then at least I wanted to go with them. But no, I was to remain in Washington. Bismarck, recently married, was off somewhere with his wife. But Walter would remain. He, however, was at work during the day. The Bacon Street house would be closed in the daytime. I'd stay with some people and have my meals there. Of evenings Walter would come for me and we'd go to Bacon Street for the night. It was all very complicated—to me, a disturbing whirl and puzzle I could not make head or tails of.

Each evening Walter would come for me. We'd take a street-car to Bacon Street. This was a brief respite and joy. I liked the ride up the hill into my old familiar neighborhood. But .. my street .. it was so silent and deserted that I hardly recognized it. It almost made me cry.

And there stood the house, shut and gloomy. It was like a blind thing looming out of the night. It seemed given over to a sinister spirit, the abode of ghosts and bats.

There had been rumors of burglars in the neighborhood. One house had been broken in and robbed. Walter had worked out a scheme. He left his big army revolver in the vestibule, with the storm-door closed. If a burglar entered, he would surely see the gun and take it. So then, the presence or absence of the pistol was to be our sign. If it were gone, we would not go in the house. If it were there—well, the chances were that nobody had been prowling about.

As we neared the house, ghost-like enough without this, Walter would laugh and say to me, "Well, Snootz, we'll see what we'll find this time." I'd also laugh and put on a brave face. In part, I was in truth both brave and thrilled. The thing had the proportions of unusual risk and adventure. All my boyhood I had wanted real danger. Now I had it. At the same time, my little body, hypersensitive because of my generally wrought up condition, would contract and tremble with fear.

We'd go up the steps, open the big storm-door, and peer in. The revolver would be there, and I'd feel great relief. Walter would pick it up and tell me everything was all right this time. But now would come another ordeal. He took no chances. Revolver in hand he'd enter the dark hall without switching on the lights. And then, still in darkness, and with me behind him clutching his coat, he'd make a cursory search of the house. I'd feel just as I did when I was having a bad dream.

And night after night all during the summer this thing went on. ...

There was, as one can see, a strange compulsion about the whole experience. The forces of life, and of each one of our separate lives, had increased their tensions and tempos to the point of compelling crucial situations and critical actions.

Mother had had to leave us all, and go off. Her action had the force and thrust of cumulative experience which has crystallized and formed an inevitable direction. For her there had been no alternative. The strength of her compulsion can be sensed by remembering that she not only broke away from the iron grip of her father but that she left me, a thing, as I have said, that she had never done before and which must have caused no little pain and tearing. For though it is true that for several years we had been gradually coming apart, she being increasingly preoccupied and concerned with her problems, I more and more transferring my affections and needs to grandmother, we were still bound together by very sensitive life-threads and by deep subconscious-holdings.

Her action had had to shock and upset me, throwing me into a conflict acute enough to gather and bind in struggle the entire train of my experiences with her, sweeping me on to a station of almost fatal illness which, in turn, was to be the cause of my life radically changing. Life held other things in store for me than that I was to remain yet a while a child of Nature and of Bacon Street and grow up to be a good but undifferentiated citizen of Washington. It had plotted for me a far-wandering complex course of suffering-experiences along which one might conceive a soul.

Walter had had to take me with him into that nightmare-house. This experience acted to intensify my state. My state intensified it. Thus was the law of reciprocal effects which produce crises fulfilled. Why couldn't I have remained of nights in the place I stayed by day? Simply, I could not. Why couldn't Walter have lived with me in a third place? Simply, he could not. I had to be played upon and worked up to the pitch demanded for that phase of my life. I could not be spared the tension produced by just that house.

The Unyielding Stream had tightened its grip and was sweeping us, grandfather and grandmother as well as mother and myself, sweeping us faster along the maze-like paths of our mutual and separate existences.

At last fall came. Mother and the family returned. As if nothing had happened we were again in the familiar Bacon Street house and the world seemed bright. I entered school. I was in the fourth grade. After school hours I threw myself into the activities of our neighborhood as never before. It was very good to have Dutch and the Dutton boys, Carlie, and the Snyders again. I made up for lost time. I wiped the taste of summer from my mouth.

Dorothy Hanvey was not there. It seems to me now that something had happened. Her father had died. She had been taken to Switzerland to school. I was sorry, but it didn't greatly matter. It had been long since I was in love with her. I was, and had been for sometime, crazy about

Bernice Carson. I couldn't tell what her feelings were. I didn't know whether she liked me or not. Now and again she seemed to, and yet she was often distant and chilly and acted as though she was stuck on herself. But in any case I was crazy about her and she too was there to play with.

I was, however, more sensitive and touchy than usual. Things easily hurt me or made me angry. A slight, a rebuff, one or another of the crudities and cruelties which children practice—the gives and takes I would ordinarily have thrown off without much thought—these hit like barbs and rankled and caused more pain than anyone could have made me admit.

And, inside home, though I and everyone had at first appeared much the same, things were different. The difference became evident as soon as the household settled down for the winter. Our habitual relationships were strangely altered. Everyone seemed to be fencing for a new position. No one quite knew how to meet the other, or what to expect. Often enough, what you did expect did not happen, and what you did not expect did happen. I began learning to expect the unexpected.

Mother showed the most marked change. She assumed an independent, superior, almost haughty, air towards grandfather which plainly told him that his storms would not intimidate her and that his commands would not be obeyed. She seemed to be carrying a secret knowledge which gave her strength and made little smiles play around her lips. Perhaps it was this same secret thing that allowed her to notice me more and give me more affection. But I too was changed. An ice had gotten in me. A hard chill-shield covered my heart. During the summer it had begun forming within me as an outgrowth of the bitter medicine, the astringent shattering reality I had had to swallow. It protected me from her uncertainties and was a buffer against future shocks. I was reserved and doubtful. The more she came towards me the more I withdrew.

But I missed Uncle Bis. We all did. A luminous kindly understanding had departed from the house. An affectionate sure presence was no longer there. Doubtless the grownups felt his absence more keenly than I did. He had been the peacemaker, the conciliating force, mediating between mother and grandfather. Mother had gone to him with her troubles. And even grandfather, recognizing his wisdom, his impartiality, his ability to deal with human matters, had occasionally sought his advice. In his absence each one was thrown sharply against the other; the jagged edges of the household were much in evidence; the warring factors had nothing to reconcile them.

Every home should have an Uncle Bis—especially if it contains an active dominant man like grandfather, a passive woman like grandmother, a resistant force like mother. The world of successful affairs can afford to release the men of loving understanding; these men can afford to fail in the eyes of the successful world, in order that they may hold families together.

Well, we had had our Uncle Bis. But, as so often happens, it was only after he had left us that we began to realize his full value.

One day mother asked me how I would like to have a father. I made a face and tried to forget it. As I would now say, I gulped it quickly into my subconsciousness and put up my front.

She did not mention the matter again. Perhaps experience had taught her that it was useless to try to conciliate me or anyone beforehand, that it was best first to act and then let us adjust to the accomplished fact.

Then, suddenly, I was taken down with a bad cold. The cold hung on. I couldn't seem to throw it off. I had a fever. I had to stop school and stay in the house. Mother gave me mustard foot-baths; and, lying in bed, I again had, so to speak, my milk and warm blankets. It was a decidedly pleasant sensation. A vapor-lamp burned in my room all night. I liked the little globe of light, the shadows in the room, the odor. It was very warm and cozy. I could hear the wind howling outside. In the grey morning the windowpanes were frosted.

And I liked the attention mother was giving me. The chill shield which covered my heart somewhat melted. Grandmother, even grandfather, attended me. Again I had them related to me with a subjects-to-king attitude.

Mother was worried. I had never at any time been very sick. I had had whooping cough and a few children's diseases, all of them comparatively mild and soon gotten rid of. Once the doctor has been called late at night. He had come and swabbed my throat with a pungent nasty-tasting something. Other than this, and occasional brief colds, I had been quite stout and healthy. This cold hung on. I enjoyed it. I didn't have to go to school and Dutch came in to see me most every afternoon.

However, before Thanksgiving I was well enough to go out. I found I was far behind in my lessons. I never had been. I didn't like it. Children and teacher were talking about things I did not know. She said I would have to study hard and make up. I didn't want to. I didn't want to go to school. I had tasted laziness and freedom. As often as I dared I made believe I was again sick and stayed home. But, when afternoons came and I saw Dutch and the others on the street I suddenly felt better. I was sure I was well enough to go out. I did go out. I whipped myself up and played passionately. I wanted to be with them so much that when my dinner time came I wouldn't leave them.

We dined at five o'clock. All the other families ate later, six or half past. I'd stay out and miss the meal. All along I had done this now and again. Now I did it regularly. I couldn't bear to think of my eating while they were still at play. To be with them that last hour was worth all the meals in the world. But when they went in, I suddenly felt hungry. I wouldn't let on to my parents. To them I pretended I had no appetite. This was my excuse for staying out. Really, as I say, my stomach would pinch. I'd take ten cents and go around the corner and buy candy.

For nearly a month this thing kept up. Mother would occasionally compel me to eat something substantial; but, in the main, my evening meal consisted of sweets. I thought I was very foxy. Indeed I did fox them, sometimes lying that I was going to have or had had dinner at the Bergmanns' or the Duttons'. And I did stay out.

But I paid for it severely. Shortly before Christmas I was suddenly taken sick with a violent stomach. I vomited—it seemed I would never stop. Everything turned over in me and out of me. I was deathly sick. I was put to bed. I kept vomiting, or having the wretched sensation that I wanted to. Mother got frightened and called the doctor. He prescribed medicine and said I'd be all right in a day or so. Mother was relieved. She jokingly said she knew I would get well for Christmas dinner. I thought so too.

Next day when they gave me light food it immediately came back. Neither that day nor the following nor the following would my stomach hold anything. Again the doctor was called and he gave me new medicine. He was grave this time. At the end of ten days I was very weak. Mother changed doctors. I still could not hold a single thing. My condition was very serious.

The second doctor had no more success than the first. He gave me up. The family thought they were going to lose me. Mother, grandmother, grandfather, Uncle Bis, Uncle Walter, and Dutch, came in to see me. I was so weak I could not move. I could hardly see them or know or care if they were there. Pinchy, Booty, Snootz, Kid, was going to die. With silent helplessness they watched me sink.

How she found him I do not know. His name was Kolapinski. He was a German doctor who lived in another part of town. When hope for me had been given up, he came and slowly slowly pulled me out. He prescribed two medicines, both so nasty that I would almost rather have died than take them. I had to be coaxed and coaxed. He said I must be fed on plain boiled rice and milk, a little at a time, and nothing else. He came regularly. He had a bushy beard, a large face, and small reddish twinkling eyes. He spoke quietly at first. Then he treated me with a sort of gruff humor, full of vitality. I think his presence had as much to do with my recovery as his medicine. He put something of himself into me. I liked him very much. I did not know he had saved my life.

If he still lives, or wherever in the great universe his essence may be, may he now receive the being-gratitude I was unable to express then.

. . . It was a sad day for me when I thought I was strong enough to get up. I was by myself. My feet touched the carpet. It was a queer sensation but I felt all right, just a little shaky. I stood up. I took a few steps across the room. I seemed to be walking all right. Without warning my legs gave way and I came to the floor with a thud. I felt sick and dizzy. I burst out crying. For the first time during my illness I cried and cried. Not once till then had I felt sorry for myself. Now I did. Now I realized how weak I was. The legs that had climbed trees, skated, played baseball and football, and out-run every boy in the neighborhood, were so wobbly they wouldn't even hold me. The strong Pinchy was weaker than a sick kitten. I crawled back to bed and didn't let anyone know what had happened. . . .

My illness had been the climax of the long train of my experiences with mother, experiences which started in that very first year when I was bathed in the pain and struggle and suffering caused by father's going away and the divorce and her return to the Bacon Street house, which continued and increased as I grew up and loved her and resisted her loving anyone else. The wonder is, I suppose, that the psychic strain had not made me sick more often, that it had not come to a head before. This was perhaps because I was sturdy and healthy in other ways. As the doctors would say, my exceptional constitution had enabled me to accommodate to and withstand the tension—until the crisis in mother's life produced a crisis in mine.

From one point of view, I daresay it had been a protest against what I sensed she was about to do. It had been a means of escape from a situation very distasteful to me. In my own mind there is no doubt that it had been emotionally caused and emotionally pointed. The physical circumstance—the apparent cause—that I had skipped meals and filled my stomach with sweets, was but a factor in a basically psychological situation.

My illness had been a means of securing through sickness what I unconsciously feared I would not be able to secure in any other way; namely, the complete concerned attention of my mother. Many times in life I have seen the human psyche behave in just this manner. It will resort both to sudden and chronic illness in order to gratify a wish which is threatened with defeat. It knows very well that a sick body not only commands the attention of but virtually enslaves whoever has affection for it. Indeed I once experienced just this in so acute a degree that I seriously questioned if it were not the invalids who rule the world.

Well, I had obtained what I wanted. I had made mother concern herself with me to the at least seeming exclusion of all else. More, I had compelled the whole family to group about and attend me with the subjects-to-king attitude which I, like every other young child, had once had, but which I had forfeited as I grew older. But .. I had lost Bacon Street. That I did not want. That I had not foreseen. Even the clever subconscious intelligence which may have maneuvered the illness had not envisaged this outcome—nor had it foreseen that its intrigue would take me almost to death and render my body thereafter miserably weak. Both mother and my street were very dear to me. The one, I had gained—temporarily. The other I had irrevocably lost. The law of compensation, or of alternatives—some law was giving me severe instruction.

By the way, it is interesting to note that the summer before, that which I have called the Dark Summer, I saw Bacon Street deserted in physical fact. Dutch and none of the others were about. But they would come back. Now, eight months later, I experienced it empty in spiritual fact. Dutch and all the others were there—but not for me. They were in a distance which no physical means could measure or lessen. They would, or I would, never come back.

From another point of view—and this one is more basic and inclusive than those above mentioned—my illness was a station, a turning point, a radical deflection of the course of my developing essence. The effects on my body, the effects on my psyche—these produced results in keeping with the exercises and struggles demanded for my growth and understanding in this life.

To arise from a severe illness calls for a new affirmation and a new effort from the human essence.

I had been strong. Now I was weak. I was compelled to exert effort to get strong again. Life had taken away what it had given, and I was forced over years to obtain it by exertion. In fine, I was made to become energized in a new way, and struggle with myself. The Stream no longer completely carried me.

I had been by nature a leader. Now I was deposed. I was compelled to make effort myself to become a self-made leader.

I was extremely sensitive and open to shocks, both positive and negative, as never before.

I had learned that familiar desirable conditions do not necessarily last forever, that no thing was necessarily permanent; but that, on the contrary, flux and change ran through life, converting this year's stability into next year's instability, this year's certainty into next year's uncertainty, this year's joy into next year's sadness.

I had experienced the collapse and loss of a world.

I had acquired self-pity. I had learned to be philosophic.

I had been active mainly externally. Now I could not be so. I gradually became active mainly interiorly and built up an inner world of my own in which intangible things were more real than tangibles.

I had been a member of a group, a participant in a common existence. Now I was different. I no longer belonged. I was thrown on my own and alone. Before, my family had practiced hands off. Perhaps they sensed my present emergency, but I did not tell them of it and they did not come forward to help me. Now, Bacon Street also had withdrawn. I was in all ways compelled to differentiate and learn to stand independently. In short, the entire experience and its consequences were the shock and the circumstance which started my individualization.

Those who see a human being merely as an organism stumbling through the accidents of experience, motivated solely by physical hungers, pain, fear, escape, pleasure, and ego mechanisms, soon to fall into the grave and be covered up by still living stumbling organisms—well, certainly they see what is apparent; but they see only these fractions of a being, and they have no sight and consequently no understanding of the essence of man, the essence of life, the processes and purposes of existence on earth. They themselves not having been born above the body, they can only see within themselves and round about them what a body can see. Their position is sincere and natural and understandable. It is the only intelligent and honest one they can take. It is when they assume that their limitations measure the whole of life that they cause mischief both to themselves and to those others who listen to them and would also like to believe that their two eyes have seen the universe.

I sat on my post. This post was the brown-stone post of our front steps, the steps leading to the porch. Occasionally before, I had climbed up and perched on it. It was a sort of observatory from which I could see up and down the street, across the field, everywhere. Alec Coleman had snapped a picture of me there because he thought it a characteristic pose. Now I made a regular habit of it. It was not altogether comfortable. It was, in fact, hard and chill and its top was rounded. But there I sat like a candidate-saint.

Most children, I think, take life philosophically; and, when they are in reflective moods, their attitude is so much the real thing that many so-called adult professional philosophers could not do better than try to emulate them. With me, this mood had become almost a permanent state. The sharp feelings of hurt, of loss, regret, and sadness had gradually left me. Bacon Street did not want me, or at least it was indifferent to me. Well, I had accustomed myself to not wanting it. I too was indifferent, that is, as far as active participation went. I was still rather weak. Well, so I was. The fellows and girls followed Horace Clark. So they did. I had weaned myself from them. I had even come to like the spectator's role, watching them play and do things, I making comments to myself, or my mind going wandering far off along some path of its own.

True, now and again I experienced quick heart-burns and pangs of suffering; but even through these my mind gazed out pensively upon the world and seemed to say impersonally with a sense of reality, ''Yes, life is just this.''

And, of course, I did not stay on my post all the time; for I still had a strong social sense, the larger part of which had not been embittered. Indeed, this joy of companionship, this wish to be with people, was active in me then and has ever been. It has weathered the antagonistic feelings manifested against me; it has lived through my phases of voluntary and enforced solitude; and my very individualization has strengthened it. Not then, not ever, have I been out and out anti-social. And so, as I say, ever so often I would quit my post and mingle with the group. But it wasn't any too comfortable. Despite my philosophy I was hypersensitive when in their midst. I was touchy, and tended to be on the defensive. A part of me was constantly secretly expecting that at any time some one might hurt me. I had a bit of a chip on my shoulder. In fine, I myself unconsciously caused just the kind of friction I did not want. Horace sometimes baited me. I had to swallow it. Once he sent me back to my post in a huff.

And once I got quite ruffled. Our bunch had gotten in a fight with a group on another street. They had returned to the house on the field to collect other fellows and hold a pow-wow. I went over. They completely discounted my fighting power. They said I'd better stay out of it; but, if I wanted something to do I could, as it were, keep the fort and protect the women and children. Off they went. After a while they brought back one of our boys with a gash in his forehead. They had been throwing sharp blue stones. He'd been hit and almost knocked out. I ran and got a basin and we bathed and bandaged him. He was a warrior. I was a camp-flunky. Napoleon Pinchy was reduced to this. . . .

I sat on my post. Once, when describing this pose to friends I said, "The candidate-saint was already on his pillar. He has been on it ever since." This is an exaggeration; but it is hard fact that I did then sit there. I saw the fellows come home from school. I watched them do things. I thought my own thoughts. Some of them were dark enough. Friends of the family had said from the very beginning that I was born an old soul. Now I looked it. I did indeed look disillusioned.

And I waited. It was as if I were waiting for something. It was as if I had a pre-sense that something unusual, a solving-something, was going to happen. I seemed to know that I was not going to spend all my life on Bacon Street sitting on the sidelines. I couldn't quite see myself ever being one of the group again. I couldn't quite feel that I was going to repeat the fourth grade in that school. I didn't think much about it. I just sat there and waited.

The day came when mother told me she was going to leave me for a short time. The news did not shock me. This, it seemed, was one of the things I had been waiting for. It was as if I were hearing what I had expected all the while. I was prepared for it—at least, I felt so. I would not resist her. She could go. I had already seen her reel off, with Dutch and Bernice, into an alien land. I had already suffered the loss and accepted it. All right, go. Grandmother would take care of me.

Mother went. It was an easy departure, with none of the tearing of the previous summer. She might simply have been going downtown for shopping. She did not say what for; but I sort of knew, and I steeled myself against it.

Now there were only four of us in the house; and Walter was away most every evening with a beautiful lady he had fallen in love with. . . .

Just grandmother, grandfather, and I would sit at the large table. It seemed almost empty. Grandfather was not happy. He'd have his toddy beforehand. He'd come down and storm at the absent Walter for not having told us he would be away that evening. His storm would fill the room for a short while; but when it subsided I'd feel everything more quiet and sad and vacant than ever. He'd talk to grandmother—

"mamma," as he called her. His words might be forceful, angry, banter-
ing; but she would understand him. She'd know that a pain in his heart
was reaching out to her for support and sympathy. In her calm clear way
she would answer this unspoken request. Her eyes would seem to tell
him, "Don't worry. Don't work yourself up. You'll see, everything will
turn out for the best."

Sometimes he would josh me, Foxy Grandpop. But I too would know
that his high spirits were trumped up. Now and again he'd fall into a
brooding, half wrathful, half sorrowful stare. I felt a bit like that myself;
but I couldn't, of course, altogether understand why he, the dashing,
commanding figure of my early years, should feel that way. I did not
realize that he was foreseeing the loss of a world, the breakup of his
family, the leaving of the house he had built to be his home for the rest
of his days.

After dinner [Pinchback] usually went downtown; and grandmother
and I would be left in the big house alone. Even had I wanted to go on
the street, I wouldn't have. I felt I ought to stay with her. Just suddenly I
came to feel that she needed me, that she needed me as much as I needed
her. It was an altogether new emotion. Someone who needed me! All
my life I had only thought and felt of what I wanted. Now I was beginning to know this other thing.

If the night were warm, we'd take mats and sit on the front steps a
while. Maybe Dutch would come up. The Hanvey house was dark. Dorothy .. with golden curls, my sweet first love .. where was she? In the
high snow-mountains of Switzerland, or by a deep blue lake, far off
there, playing with Swiss boys and girls, growing up to be a lovely princess?
Would I ever see her again? She was not like Bernice Carson. Perhaps
when we grew up and were man and woman we'd meet somewhere and
greet each other with our old names and remember the days on Bacon
Street when we tasted honeysuckle and I brought her four-leaf clovers
and I ran out whenever I heard her screen-door bang. This was the season
of screen-doors. But no one opened or closed hers. Lights glowed from
the Duttons' house, and from the Berliner laboratory. Far up in the soft
night-sky stars twinkled. Twinkle, Twinkle, little star, how I wonder what
you are .. And there were the Great and Little Dippers, the Bear ..
stars, tiny bright specks, great bodies greater than the earth, which Bismarck had told me about. Now and again Uncle Bis himself would visit
us and sit for a while. It seemed almost like old times. And how sweet
and fresh everything was, and soft and beautiful. There were the trees
along the street, trees I had watched grow from the time when they had

to have boxes around them. And the old lamp-posts, with insects buzzing around, and a soft yellow light shining from them through the new
leaves of nearby branches. And the old red bricks of the sidewalk, with
tufts of grass sprouting in the crevices. My feet had walked those bricks
many years and helped to wear them smooth. Our mothers, Dutch's and
mine, had pushed their baby carriages over them. I loved it. I loved Bacon
Street. I felt I would give anything on earth to sit there always and have
it friendly and soft and beautiful about me.

The time would come to go indoors. Grandmother and I would go to
her room, the big front room with the alcove where I as a baby had cried
for milk and warm blankets, where I had crawled the floor for pins to sell,
where mother had had the operation, where I had seen the women-folk
get ready for a ball.

Grandmother would get her embroidery-work and seat herself in a
rocking-chair near the mahogany bureau near the light. And as she worked
she would hum. Rocking quietly to and fro, using her fingers with an
easy skill and swiftness which fascinated me, she'd hum two or three
tunes over and over. She seemed very peaceful, and happy in a way that
was strange to me. She seemed untouched by the disturbed household.
The current of troubled events which had even me in its grip seemed to
divide as it approached her and flow to either side with the sensitive
knowing that it must not molest this slender delicate being of sweet faith.

At times, she appeared so frail that I wondered how she managed; and
yet, at the same time, she gave me the strange feeling that she was stronger
than us all, stronger even than grandfather.

Sometimes she would talk to me, tell me of New Orleans, the stormy
days . . . . And of Mardi Gras. As she described this festival, the wondrous
floats, the dazzling colors, the riot of masquerading people in the streets,
I would listen with rapt amazement, having a queer sense that she was
telling not of actual events in far off New Orleans but of some of the
wonderland figures of my dreams. . . .

Once during this time there was a very fine happening. Mrs. Terrell
came to visit us and brought her young daughter Phyllis. Mrs. Terrell
was an old friend of the family, but she lived in another part of town
and we, or I at least, seldom saw her. Nor did I see Phyllis. This time,
however, I met her so vividly that her image, just as she appeared that
day, was impressed on me to remain throughout life. She had the most
beautiful soft brown curls. Her eyes were brown and golden with dancing
light. She was the most vivacious sparkling girl I had ever seen. We played
together and had a great time. But, though I liked her very much, though

I fell in love with her on the spot, I had not the slightest suspicion that the years were to separate us, make us forget each other, and then bring us together again to fulfill the promise of that first forever vivid contact.

Then things moved rapidly.

Grandmother broke the news. Word had come from mother that she was married. His name was Coombs. I gave a start, but tried not to show anything. In truth, I felt less than might have been expected. During the past months I had been tempered, and my shield was working. Grandmother made no comment, save to say that she guessed I would go to Brooklyn or New Rochelle and live with mother and my new father. She looked at me rather sadly. I seemed to be her child. I said I didn't want to leave her. The thought of this pained me far more than the thought of my new father. I had not considered this possibility. I said I didn't want to leave grandfather. She answered, almost as if musing to herself, that perhaps we'd all go. Perhaps the Bacon Street house would be closed and we'd all move to New York.

I felt a heavy thud. I felt something click. This .. this was the whole thing I had been waiting for. The marriage of mother, the closing of the house, the end of Bacon Street.

I felt glad. I felt sorry beyond words. I was glad to have something definite at last happen. I was glad at the prospect of actually leaving the place, the group of children, to which I no longer belonged. I seemed to know that in a new place I could start fresh—as it were, begin my life over again. I was glad not to have to repeat the fourth grade in that school. I was sorry to think of finally going from the street I still loved, leaving Dutch to whom I was still deeply attached despite the change, leaving the dear old house, and Uncle Bis and Uncle Walter.

And I was a bit shaky, a bit apprehensive about New York. It was big and cold and unfriendly and I hadn't liked it very much. What would this new father of mine be like?

I was in conflict.

Mother returned. Again she was a changed mother. She was vivacious. Her eyes had snap. She carried herself buoyantly. She was less haughty and more sweet. She laughed and played with me. I had forgotten she could look and be this way. She said I'd like my new father. I looked doubtful. She said she'd buy me a pony, a nice Shetland pony, when we got to New Rochelle. This made me happy. I began seeing myself with him. We would like each other. I'd tend him and feed him and brush his hair. I'd get on his back and ride and race everywhere. I began looking forward to New Rochelle, forgetting that there would be a new father on the scene.

I wondered why he hadn't come to Washington with her.

The family held a conclave to which I was not invited. Bis came up. He was the same Uncle Bis, but on this occasion he too seemed happier. Everyone seemed more happy and hopeful, mother, Uncle Bis, Uncle Walter, even grandmother—everyone save grandfather. He was stern, and I knew he had thunderclouds in him.

They stayed in the room a long time.

When they came out I knew something had been decided. And so it had. Mother was to pack her things and my things and go on to New York ahead of us. Walter was to live in another part of town. The Bacon Street house would be closed and sold. . . .

It was a happy and hopeful time for . . . [Pinchback's] children. All of them were middle-aged or past, and now, for the first time, they were going to swing completely free of the life-long domination of their father, and pursue courses of their own. It was a sorrowful ironic time for him. Many of his hopes were down. First he had lost his political career. Now he was losing his home and family. The stream of his fate, having carried him from the stormy days of New Orleans, having permitted him to come to rest with seeming permanence in Washington, was again moving him on but now against his wish out of the harbor of Washington into the open seas of New York—and he was far past being a young man.

I have wondered what was the deciding factor. Did he wish to be near mother? Had grandmother persuaded him, because she wished to be near me? Did he feel that the phase in Washington had really come to an end for him also, and that he would do well to try his fortunes with politics in New York? Or was it that the Bacon Street home, like the cigar, had failed to draw, and he was casting it from him, never, as it were, to smoke again? It would have been like him. He was that way. He could command and hold; but, if his holding proved futile, he would let go with decisive finality. Thus he had done with New Orleans. Thus, doubtless, he was going to do with Washington.

Grandmother accepted the situation in her quiet way. Underneath, even though she sympathized with her children's wishes to be free, she must have had feeling no less acute than grandfather's as to the breakup of the home. From her own body it had sprung and she had spun it with the tenuous bright threads of her essentially woman's soul. Now the winds were to rend it and carry the separate strands to places beyond her gathering. But while he, with a dramatic temperament which was inclined to fight the stream, showed everything, she, flowing with the varying eddies and currents, revealed no more than tremors which only a person as sensitive as herself could read. . . .

I did not want to say goodby to the fellows and girls of the block. I had avoided them as much as possible. I wanted simply to go off. But I had to see Dutch. I couldn't leave without seeing and saying goodby to dear old Dutch. I went to his house.

It was as ever. It had the same atmosphere, the same mellow feeling I had known for years. Nothing had happened to it. No changes had occurred here. There had been no disrupting drama of family events. Dutch himself—yes, in physical growth he had kept step with me, and he too had passed through the various phases typical of the first ten years of boyhood, but he had experienced nothing similar to the reversals and tragedies of my life. The Bergmann household was quiet, intact, stable, and gave the impression that it would continue being so. It seemed almost uneventful. I could not help but see and feel it in vivid contrast to my own storm-visited dismantled house.

I was very conscious that I was going away, that I would no longer have a place in it. I knew very well that this mellow atmosphere which for years had extended its warmth to me, including me along with Dutch, was not now mine to share. I felt almost already a stranger, a complete outsider. A chill stiff feeling had me in its grip.

Dutch had known of my going. We talked about things but felt uncomfortable. Our respective roguish smiles tried to play on our faces without much success. We said we'd write each other, and maybe some day I'd come back. So long, Dutch. So long, Pinchy. We shook hands. I asked him to tell the others so long for me. I said goodby to Mrs. Bergmann. She, as always, was warm and motherly. I left their house, and I could hardly see the street in front of me.

That night after dinner I went out, saying I would be back soon. I wandered down the street. My legs were taking me somewhere. I let them. I crossed over to 16th Street and walked south. Soon I was standing on the brow of Meridian Hill, with twinkling evening Washington below me. I leaned against a tree which grew near the edge, and stood, looking. Washington lay in a cup surrounded by hills. I knew the Potomac River, brown and lazy, was down there, and over and away the hills of Virginia. It was a night of the South, soft and subtly perfumed. The lights of the city twinkled in answer to the stars. Nothing answered me. Perhaps I asked no question. But my heart swelled at this last view of the place which had been mine to love.

We arose early. The storage-men were coming at eight o'clock. Our train left at ten. We had breakfast, grandmother preparing it because the cook had been dismissed. We ate in the kitchen. The morning was bright and lovely. Sunshine came in the windows. It was still cool, but you knew it was going to be hot, as grandfather called it, a scorcher. Old Willis came in and we said goodby. Grandfather gave him extra pay. I wondered what would become of him. The storage-men arrived and took everything away. We closed and locked the windows and pulled down the shades. We were ready. I got my mandolin and a little suitcase. We went out. Grandfather closed and locked the big storm-door. The house looked just as it had last summer. We walked away.

The Pinchbacks were leaving. They were leaving the place of their home for fifteen years. No one seemed to notice. No one seemed to care. No one called out, "Don't go. We are friends. The world is a large place and we should not lose one another." Two silver-haired people and a boy were walking away with their backs to the old farm beyond which the sun set.

We stood on the corner and waited for a car. The car came and we took it. As my street swept past a large lump arose in my throat.

An hour later we were passing through the Baltimore tunnel. Before me—New York, alien, unknown, unfriendly, looming.

Behind me, the gate of the garden of Bacon Street had closed.

[I have omitted Toomer's brief summary of the years 1906 to 1909, when he lived with his mother and a step-father in Brooklyn and New Rochelle, New York, because these years seem less significant in his development than others. Despite new friendships, intensive reading—especially in novels and tales of knighthood, interest in boating and swimming, and early attempts at creative writing, Toomer recalled these years unhappily in "Outline of an Autobiography." He never accepted his stepfather, whom Toomer considered inferior to his mother and incapable of providing for the family financially. When his mother died, June 9, 1909, after an apparently successful appendectomy, Toomer was taken in by his grandparents, who had returned to Washington after a brief residence in Brooklyn. Recognizing the terseness of his account of his mother's death, Toomer appended a note to his manuscript: "It was characteristic of me to appear callous as to a thing which meant unbearably much to me. Thus, I seemed almost hardboiled about my mother's heartbreak and death."]

The Maturing Years

"The Maturing Years," "The Years of Wandering," and "The *Cane* Years" have been taken From "Outline of an Autobiography" except where indicated.

W e returned to Washington. I was again in my city, but in a different part of it, with different people. I hardly ever saw Dutch or any of the Bacon Street children. We lived with Bismarck and his wife on Florida Avenue; and I became acquainted with families who were friends of my grandparents. With the children of these families. With this world—an aristocracy—such as never existed before and perhaps never will exist again in America—midway between the white and Negro worlds. For the first time I live in a colored world. . . . *

It was not difficult to do so. I accepted this as readily as I had accepted living in Brooklyn and New Rochelle.

What I have just said may seem to the average person of either group a surprising statement. And it is—if you do not know the facts. So I will give them briefly.

In the first place it should be said in general that the two groups are not as different as they have been made to seem. Yes, there is considerable difference between the best of the white and the worst of the black, just as there is between the best of the black and the worst of the white— and it is these comparisons that prejudice is prone to make. But compare the best with the best and the difference decreases almost to the vanishing point. I am speaking of people, of human beings. I am comparing them as human beings. I am thinking, not in terms of range of opportunity or social position or achievement in some special field, but in terms of character, of fineness of body and of person—in short, in terms of quality. By any qualitative valuation the best of the people whom I met in that

---

*In "On Being an American" Toomer indicates that his neighborhood friends were white and attended a school in the neighborhood. In contrast, he was sent "quite out of [his] district . . . to a colored school," where for the first time he played with black children. His attending a colored school, however, did not affect his relationship with his white playmates.

colored group in Washington were not simply on a par with, but had obvious affinities with, the best people of any group I have met anywhere.

Whatever Negro blood they had was an asset. I do not mean that it was more of an asset than any of their other bloods, but I do mean to affirm (in opposition to the contrary superstition) that it contributed its share to the making of these splendid people. If I believed with certain of my countrymen that in all cases of admixture the Negro blood is the dominant blood, and if I therefore believed that these people were what they were mainly because of their dark blood, then I'd say let us have more of it in all the groups of America.

In the Washington of those days—and those days have gone now—there was a flowering of a natural but transient aristocracy, thrown up by the, for them, creative conditions of the post-war period. These people, whose racial strains were mixed and for the most part unknown, happened to find themselves in the colored group. They had a personal refinement, a certain inward culture and beauty, a warmth of feeling such as I have seldom encountered elsewhere or again. A few held or had held political posts of prominence. Some were in government positions. Others were in the professions. One was a municipal court judge. Several were in the real estate business. All were comfortably fixed financially, and they had a social life that satisfied them. They were not pushing to get anywhere or be anything other than what they were. Without bitterness, but with a sweetness and warmth that I will never forget, they were conscious that they were and had something in themselves. The children of these families became my friends.

With one or two exceptions, those of my new friends who became my best friends were, in a racial sense, no different from the boys and girls I had known in white groups. They behaved as American youths of that age and class behave. Their quality of person was considerably higher than the majority of boys and girls I had played with in the New York region. For this very reason I felt, if anything, more at home with them. They were my kind, as much as the children of my early Washington years had been.

These new friends of mine were not conscious of being either colored or white. They had no active prejudices against black people or white people. Knowing that I had been of, and had come from, a white world, they were not curious about this world and certainly they did not feel that it was either superior or inferior. Segregation, if known to them, meant nothing. They had never run up against the color line. In fine, they were as youths of fifteen anywhere.

What I have just written may sound incredible to those whose heads ring with the rattle of race talk, and who believe that all people of America from the moment they are born until the moment of their deaths are consumed with the race phobia. Even to more balanced minds the statement may sound strange. Young people in a colored group—and not feeling it? I can only give my honest word that it was so.

To explain it somewhat I may point out (1) that this was in 1910; the movement to make the Negro self-conscious and give him racial solidarity had not yet gotten under way effectively, (2) that propaganda is always a limited influence and never reaches but a fraction of people, (3) that only those who make an issue of race are conscious of this issue, (4) that no people label themselves and fix their consciousness on this label unless the thing has become ingrained in them by hearsay and education or unless external circumstances compel them to do so.

These youths whom I am now writing about had simply not been imprinted. They lived within their world, not on the antagonistic periphery of it where clashes are most likely to occur. (Even with a race riot going on, the deep centers of both groups can be quite calm.) These youths had their rounds of activity, parties, and interests—and were self-sufficient. In their world they were not called colored by each other. They seldom or never came in contact with members of the white group in any way that would make them racially self-conscious.

["On Being an American"]

Just before school began I went on an excursion down the Potomac River to Riverview. It was a gay, bright, sweet life, and here I met all the girls and boys with whom I was to live, to like and love and hate, for the next five years. Charlie Craft, Nettie Langston, Phyllis and Mary Terrell, Victoria Tunnel. I was fascinated by the pretty impishness of Vic Tunnel.

The difference between this life and that of New Rochelle. More emotion, more rhythm, more color, more gaiety. I begin to have my emotions fed directly from life.

I enter school, the eighth grade. Good school work, particularly in history and algebra. I take a leading role in the *Merchant of Venice*, and I find I like to declaim the sonorous lines of Shakespeare.

Vic Tunnel is in first year high school. She won't look at me because I'm only in the eighth grade and wear short pants. I fall in love with Ethel Evans, a girl in my grade. A boy teases me about her and we have a terrific scrap.

I give a party at Christmas, mainly because I want Vic there. I get kidded because I have a Christmas tree.

Out-door activities. Football, roller skating. I am not as rough as some other boys. Because I come from New York they expect me to be a terror.

How it worked out in the house of my uncle. Grandfather, though less able and showing his age more, still goes downtown and keeps his hands in politics. But, obviously, he has lost a fair portion of his money. Grandmother growing more feeble, and sometimes having protracted sick spells.

I like Bismarck very much.

Interior life. Dreams of Vic. Reading. First experiences with Dickens, and with novels and literature which described actual life-conditions.

The first year goes very well and I graduate with honors from the eighth grade. I look forward with great expectancy to the exciting life of high school.

Summer vacation. First to Harper's Ferry, a very beautiful spot. Then to Arundel on the Chesapeake. I saw the great warships come in and stand off Annapolis.

First year high school

I enter this strangely thrilling world. I meet the boy who is to be my closest friend for the next ten years, Henry "Son" Kennedy, a radical and rebel, a character out of Dostoevsky.

Vic begins to notice me.

The cadet company and drilling.

Studies—my special aptitude for algebra and physical geography.

Social life—parties and dances. Calling on girls.

The first year ends successfully.

Summer vacation. We go to Brooklyn. I begin to think about what I want to do in life. The matter of future schooling and a career. I talk this over with grandfather.

Just about this time he, owing to the speeches he had made during Taft's campaign for President, is given, or expects to be given a political appointment. He does get a position in the Department of Internal Revenue in New York, with an office in the Customs House. This enables him to hold out the hope that I may be able to go to prep school. One of my uncles had gone to Andover. I wanted to go either there or Exeter. And then to Harvard, and then perhaps to the Harvard Law School.

But somehow this never came about.

However, grandfather's job took him to New York. Grandmother and I remained in Washington but left my uncle's house and moved into a small apartment.

Second year high school.

Vic and I begin "going with each other."

The birth of my interest in physics, in the physics laboratory. I renew my passion for electricity and become devoted to everything having to do with it. I stay after school and work in the laboratory. Wireless. I have a set. The unfortunate experience that finished my love of the laboratory.

The sudden break and change of my entire state around the end of the first half of this year. The beginning of acute emotional and sex problems. My studies fall off. This is the beginning of my stress and strain period.

I become a rebel. My English teacher asked me if I didn't like poetry. My answer an emphatic No.

Son [Henry] Kennedy and I grow closer together and begin strongly influencing each other. One of our teachers calls us "The Twin Ruffians."

Our disregard of the value of school increases. But, off to ourselves, we hold many discussions, mainly critical examinations of life, its manners, customs, and values. On our own initiative we read books, particularly Shakespeare, and go off into the parks or woods to discuss them and to declaim our favorite passages.

My teachers begin considering me an indifferent student but a difficult and devilish young man.

I begin to grow deeply restless, and have phases of acute depression.

The year ends. Summer vacation. The lyric interludes at Harper's Ferry and Arundel.

Third year high school.

The above described conditions increase. Schooling becomes more and more irksome; I, less and less good at it. I decide to take extra work so as to finish high school in three and a half years.

Grandmother and I have moved again, and are now living in a big gloomy barn of a house with Uncle Walter, who had also married. She becomes more feeble, and, since grandfather is still away, and since neither my uncle or his wife give her much attention, she becomes my responsibility. I look after her, and often, instead of going out at nights to play, or to see Vic, or to the movies, I have to stay indoors and keep her company.

I want to work, to get a job after school hours and on Saturday to make money of my own. During the first year I had had this same impulse, and it had led me to selling the *Saturday Evening Post*. I had saved some money. With this I buy a motorcycle. Against my grandmother's wishes, I get a job with a cleaning and dyeing firm, as delivery boy. I learn how to press and clean clothes. Later on, I get a job in a drug store. The fun and experiences of this work.

Vic and I are close together all this year. Kennedy and I are called the inseparables.

Sometime during this year I had an avalanche of sex indulgences.* I felt and look wretched. Everyone noticed it. But neither teachers nor friends nor parents could help me meet my problems. My teachers, feeling something was wrong, alternately tried to punish or shame me into better work, and, on the other hand, they would extend to me a baffled but genuine sympathy.

At intervals my grandmother sensed there was something tragic in my life. I would sometimes surprise her eyes regarding me as though she feared for me and yet hoped it would all turn out well. I believe she prayed for me. She could do nothing else. Like most young people of that age and with those problems, I had to face and struggle with myself and the world, alone.

I saw myself falling to pieces. Some strength of my nature arose to fight, and I took myself in hand. I began searching to find a way of building myself up. I hit on a physical means; and this was the beginning of my self-imposed discipline.

I went in for physical training. I regularly took exercises at home. I took several correspondence courses in muscle-building and health promotion. Dumb-bells, wrestling. Finally, I began heavy-weight lifting. By force of nerves and indefatigable persistence I grew muscularly strong to the point where I could lift a hundred and twenty pounds with one arm.

I tried dieting and nature cure. I ran across the *Physical Culture* magazine and was thus introduced to Bernarr McFadden.† I bought his

---

*Masturbation.
†Nationally known for his programs for developing physical fitness.

encyclopedia, and, in addition to following his prescriptions, I began talking and arguing his ideas with everyone.

And then came another spell of sex which reduced me so low I feared I was going into decline. In a desperate condition I began breathing exercises, lived more carefully than ever, and, by sheer force of will pulled myself out. I entered high school athletics.

This entire series of experiences went on in almost complete isolation, only grandmother and Kennedy knowing I was doing the exercises, but neither of them knowing the critical nature of my state. No one knew the fight I was making. But, in time, everyone saw the results. They came to regard me as an exceptionally strong and healthy young man. Color came back in my cheeks, and I was again active in the affairs of young people.

Kennedy graduates from high school.

Summer vacation.

Fourth year high school.

Kennedy is gone off to college and I am a bit lonely.

I become increasingly disgusted with most of the life round about me. What are these people doing with their lives? Surely I do not want to be like them. I am not like them. I see and feel more in life than they will if they live to be a thousand years old. I feel seasoned, and mature. I have, as it were, gone down to the depths, and have come out.

Meanwhile, my grandfather, owing to advancing age, has had to resign from his job in New York. He has returned to Washington, and he and grandmother and I take an apartment on U Street, the place that was to be my home for the next number of years.

The obvious beginning of Pinchback's break-up, and the decline into almost poverty of our family.

I graduate from high school in three and a half years. I get an injury in athletics and have to remain in the house for over a month. When I come out, I find myself with a half year of free time, the time between March and the beginning of college next fall. I haven't yet decided to which college I'll go, but I know it will be some place other than the usual colleges where most everyone has gone.

My Uncle Bismarck introduces me to his world, a world of parties and dancing and gay times with men and women older than myself. Some of the women are beautiful, and for the first time older women, that is, older than Vic, begin to attract me. I am a good dancer. They make much of me, saying I am handsome and a sweet lover. Vic fades.

I get a job in a theatre. My first contacts with the inside of show-life. My first tastes of actors and actresses, and, in a sense, artists. I feel grown up and very mature.

But, much as I love it, I also strongly revolt against all this life. I have ambition, dreams, visions of achievement. I decide that Washington is no place for me. I decide to go to the University of Wisconsin, study agriculture—of all things—and, when I have finished college, to strike out for a life of my own.

And it was then, for the first time, that I formed and formulated my views as to my racial composition and position. Going to Wisconsin, I would again be entering a white world; and, though I personally had experienced no prejudice or exclusion either from the whites or the colored people, I had seen enough to know that America veiwed life as if it were divided into white and black. Having lived with colored people for the past five years, at Wisconsin the question might come up. What was I? . . .

Race is a biological phenomenon. It has to do with the organic heredity, with the physical composition of people. . . . On the basis of certain observed things about a person, an anthropologist can draw inferences as to what racial strains are in his make-up. Few anthropologists would attempt to define all the racial strains, but certainly some of them could be determined, while others could be guessed at. At the same time, it is not possible to analyze the racial composition of a person as we can analyze the chemical composition of a stone. In any case, and to repeat, race has to do with the organic actuality which exists in its complex identity as a thing distinct from our opinions of it. I may say of a given person that he is white or black, an oriental or an occidental; but what I say has no necessary relation to the nature and composition of the person himself. On the one hand we have actual racial composition; on the other hand we have my opinions about it together with whatever labels I may happen to use. A stone is a stone, whatever I may call it. It is, however, comparatively difficult to determine the nature of a stone; so most of us are content to have a name for it. It is even more difficult to determine the nature of a man; so most of us are even more content to have a label for him.

Now these labels, together with ideas, opinions, beliefs, emotions and their associated behavior constitute the sociological psychological factor of racial matters.

To a thoughtful person it is evident that a belief is something quite different from the thing itself; but as most of us are unthoughtful we easily follow into the assumption that the thing is as we believe it to be. Thus for example, we may believe, and therefore assume it to be fact, that all of the main races are pure races. In point of fact all of the main races are mixed races—and so mixed that no one can unravel them in all of their blended complexity. No one knows for sure, but guesses have been made as to the strains which make up the present day peoples of Germany, of France, of England—and the layman would be surprised at the results of such guesses. They lead back to Asia—into Africa.

In our own country it is comparatively simple to show the distinction between the racial and the sociological factors. There is a large group of people called "colored." Under this blanket label are to be found people with racial strains from every country on earth. Some of them are as white as anyone can be. The term "colored" obviously does not define their organic actuality. The term "colored" is a sociological psychological word which refers not to a racial but to a social group.

There is a larger grouping of people called white. As a matter of organic fact there are within the white group also racial strains from every race on earth. This racial or blood admixture is the organic actuality underlying the so-called white group.

What I have said above is known to almost everyone who has experienced the people of this country. Yet most of us play a game and agree not to see what we cannot help but see and know.

No one will ever know how many white people have been recorded in the books as colored. No one will ever know how many people with Negro blood have been recorded in the books as white. Nor need we know. I am simply mentioning this fact as an example of what I mean when I say that a person's race is one thing, that what he is labelled and how he is classified is another. . . . By hearsay there were in my heredity the following strains: Scotch, Welsh, German, English, French, Dutch, Spanish, with some dark blood. For the point of this book let us assume the dark blood was Negro—or let's be generous and assume that it was both Negro and Indian. I personally can readily assume this because I cannot feel with certain of my countrymen that all of the others are all right but that Negro is not. Blood is blood. My experience has been that on the one hand, all of it is pretty bad, and that, on the other, none of it is any too good, that all of it has potentialities far beyond anything that any race has yet actualized. I am I. My body is my body, with an already given and definite racial composition. As bodies go it is not so bad; I have been able to make some constructive use of it; whatever virtues it has are the result of all the bloods in it, whatever defects it has are similarly the result of all. So to return—

Suppose in my heredity there were all the racial strains I have mentioned. Of what race am I? To this question there is and can be but one true answer—I am of the human race. . . .

I was an American, neither white nor black, rejecting these divisions, accepting all people as people. Having intimately known splendid and worthless of both groups, I could say and know, "Human beings are human beings." I liked or disliked them, associated with or kept away from them, valued or scorned them, not on racial or color grounds, but on an individual person-to-person basis. If others had race prejudice, that was their affair as long as it did not manifest itself against me.

In my body were many bloods, some dark blood, all blended in the fire of six or more generations. I was, then, either a new type of man or the very oldest. In any case I was inescapably myself. My body was inescapably my body. . . . It was up to me to make the best that I could of it. If I achieved greatness of human stature, then just to the degree that I did I would justify all the blood in me. If I proved worthless, then I would betray all. In my own mind I could not see the dark blood as something quite different and apart. But if people wanted to say this dark blood was Negro blood and if they then wanted to call me a Negro—this was up to them. Fourteen years of my life I had lived in the white group, four years I had lived in the colored group. In my experience there had been no main difference between the two. But if people wanted to isolate and fasten on those four years and to say that therefore I was colored, this too was up to them. As for myself, I would live my life as far as possible on the basis of what was true for me.

Never having found them so in my personal experience, I did not believe that all or even most Americans were crazy, distorted, and split on this subject of color and race. I was sure that even if I discovered that some were, I would find a sufficient number who were not. And I was confident also that in the future as in the past I would have good friends and a good life.

I determined what I would do. To my real friends of both groups, I would, at the right time, voluntarily define my position. As for people at large, naturally I would go my way and say nothing unless the question was raised. If raised, I would meet it squarely, going into as much detail as seemed desirable for the occasion. Or again, if it was not the person's business I would either tell him nothing or the first nonsense that came into my head.

All the while these thoughts were working out in my mind, my feelings little by little became outraged; my aristocracy might be invaded; I might be called to question by louts, white, black, or any other color. But as I settled the thing for myself and my mind grew quiet, my feelings quieted also.

All of the foregoing, as I say, took place in me in advance of my having to use it; so when the time came to go to college I was prepared. I went to college, had no use for it [the statement of his racial position], and the question was never raised.

["On Being an American"]

And so, in June of this year, 1914, I left for summer school at Madison, Wisconsin. This was my first decided break-away from home, my first adventure into a new world completely on my own. . . .

I went to the University of Wisconsin. I went there to study scientific agriculture: the agarian movement moved me twenty years ago. Strange as it seems in the light of what I now know, at that time I had sincere dreams of a large farm in the middle west.* The middle west beckoned me then, and it has ever since. My various underlying motives for going to Wisconsin are interesting—this was my first real step out into life by myself—but this is not the place to detail them. Enough to say that I did go there to undertake a course of study for which, in all ways except the desire, I was unprepared—and the desire itself petered out before a year was finished.

This adjustment, for the first week or two, was the most difficult one I had had to make. Part of the difficulty was directly due to my anticipation of what could happen if I was called upon to put my racial position to the test. The rest was due to other matters, personal and scholastic, which we need not go into here. However, before two weeks were out I was in the current of my new life, taking this white world as a matter of course, forgetting that I had been in a colored group. I began being active in freshman affairs, was fairly popular, was proposed for the class president, made friends, went places, and studied when I had to.

I passed the courses; but as it became increasingly clear to me that agriculture was not what I was fated to do, I was thrown back upon myself and became involved in the sufficiently distressing problem of what I

---

* Toomer's "middle west" is defined from the perspective of an Easterner. His only prolonged residence in the "middle west" was in Chicago. Later in the 1930s, when he and Marjorie Content Toomer, his second wife, decided to move from New York City, they considered Massachusetts but settled in Bucks County, Pennsylvania. The land was farmland, and the estate was sufficiently large for Toomer to realize his dreams. Nevertheless, according to his wife, he never attempted to practice farming.

really wanted to do, of what I really could do best. Whatever my grades, to myself I felt that I was failing, wasting time and money. This was the first time I had ever felt myself failing, and it was a profoundly unpleasant state. Hitherto, I had thought pretty well of myself. I did not feel that I had any special talent: indeed, strange as it may seem, it had never occurred to me that people did have special talents—though from my reading, if from nothing else, I must have known they had. No, I felt myself to be a thoroughbred with a pretty active intelligence, with some strength of character, with some man-ness. But all of this did not help me solve the specific problem of what I was going to do.

Through the interest of a professor of the English department who urged me to write,* who urged me to read magazines such as the Nation, *the* New Republic *and the* Manchester Guardian, *I might, had I been ready to profit by it, have come in contact with the world of modern American literature then, in 1914. But other things were in store for me—a detour of groping and suffering and chaos during which I almost smashed myself on the nation's hard roads. In 1914 I was interested less in literature than in having a good time, talking, athletics, drinking beer and raising hell in the tradition of American college life.*

This same English professor, by the way, thought I might be a Hindu. He asked me if I were. He was disappointed, because he felt that if I had been I could have drawn upon some interesting material for my themes and stories. No, I was not a Hindu, nor was I much interested in drawing upon any material for any stories—not then.

Two interesting experiences, as regards race, came my way. I went out for football. Someone thought I was an Indian and the word went around. One day a fellow said to me, "You're going to make good. You've got them all scared." I was amazed and amused too that the idea of an Indian carried so much weight on a football field. Certainly I did not. Those beefy giants punished my body each day; it was only by will that I kept myself there. It was not long before my body cried so loudly that my will had to bend and call "time out" for good.

In our house there was a fellow who opened my eyes. In him I sensed something inimical to me. In me he sensed something inimical to him. I did not like his weasel face from the first. It was not long before I disliked him. He turned out to be prejudiced against everyone who was not white, bourgeois, and Christian. From him I learned that there was a

---

* Toomer identifies him only as Mr. Manchester.

prejudice against Jews, a prejudice against people who did menial work,
a prejudice against backward peoples who were heathen and benighted.
Nor was he charitable toward Swedes, Poles, "Dagoes," small town people,
fellows who went around with girls, and many other not-so-bad people
of this earth. As a nest of prejudices he was quite a sight—and this sight
was instructive to me. Besides, I had the pleasure of hating him a little
more than he hated me.

Wisconsin was a good place; but, in my condition, not the place for
me. I left it and returned home—to find myself on my hands.

["On Being an American"]

More and more I saw that I was not fitted for a farmer, scientific or
otherwise. I decided to change that course and switch to another. I did
so, but had a run-in with my advisor, which left a bad taste in my mouth.
I looked forward to Christmas in Washington as a prisoner looks forward
to his freedom.

Even then, imperfect though it was, I had a way of proceeding; and
this way sometimes rubbed against the stationary mass-people of my environment, causing in me friction for individualization but in them only
invitation.

Christmas came and I went home. Grandfather had a big dinner for
me, with champagne and everything. There, in Washington, I really saw
for the first a girl I had known for a long time—Phyllis Terrell. I fell madly
in love with her. She also was home on vacation from her school in Vermont.
We leave Washington together, I going as far as New York with her.

I return to Madison to finish the semester, but my heart is not in it.

The reasons for my leaving Madison were complex, but outstanding
among them was the compulsion I had to be nearer Phyllis. I could not
bear the thought of four long dull cold years at Wisconsin. It is a wonder
I did not plan and scheme to marry her at once. I passed my mid-year
exams and quit Madison for good.

I returned to Washington. Phyllis was away at school, but at least I was
there and would see her at Easter.

My return to Washington gave my grandparents quite a shock. I had
much talking and explaining to do. They were disappointed, but, in the
main, they seemed to accept my action. Other people, however, began
saying that I had failed at Wisconsin. Some of them had been wanting
to take a crack at the high and mighty Eugene Toomer or Eugene Pinchback, as many of them still called me. Here was their first real obvious
opportunity. This was the beginning of the attitude that I was a failure.

Also, here began the notion that I was a strange queer fellow, different from everybody else. They had had some evidence of this during high school; but now, and in the following years, they had more and more evidence. For myself, here was the beginning of my individualization. For now, more than ever, I had to fight and struggle for my own way—not without periods of great self-doubt.

I felt the need to justify my position. I became articulate. On the one hand, I began building up a world of my own based on fancies and rationalizations. On the other, I began a deeper and sincere and penetrating questioning of myself and of life. I remained convinced that I was right in feeling that I wanted to cut loose completely from Washington—in going to Madison. I remained convinced that I was right in leaving college. But I was shaken to see that these actions had led me into a sort of blind alley. I began looking for my next step.

Phyllis, as I have said, was away at boarding school. I read Shakespeare and used some of his words and phrases in letters to her.

Kennedy was at Illinois. I had no one to talk with.

Phyllis came at Easter. I loved her very much.

The rest of that half year I spent much to myself, and with my grandparents, helping to keep the apartment running.

To a certain extent I resumed going around with the friends of my Uncle Bismarck, but that life had somehow lost the joy and sweetness of my first contacts with it. And too, I could not really make love to any of the women. I was in love with Phyllis, and it has always been with me that the love of one person tends automatically and organically to exclude love for others. In fine, though I may love many, one after another, I am usually faithful to the one at the time.

That summer I was with Phyllis in Washington and at Arundel. It was one of the most lyric and joyous periods of my life.

And now we come to the beginning of the period of three or four years during which I literally batted about America, and within myself, increasing my knowledge of American places and forms of life, greatly increasing my personal experience and understanding, by being subject to an almost constant acute suffering, the suffering of an unformed extremely sensitive person who has a feeling of his own power and worth, yet who accumulates failure after failure. During this period, even my own family, with the exception of my grandmother—bless her heart—lost faith in me. She and Kennedy were my sole support during this phase. Phyllis, though she remained in love with me for a number of years longer, was not the kind of person who could understand. Her affection, and mine for her, created a place for my love emotions. But even these emotions soon came to be but a small part of my increasingly complex and troubled life. I was swiftly learning that life in general, and my life in particular, was a thing far more complicated and involved than even the sufficiently complex nature of love. Kennedy was the only one with whom I could talk. Often he was away. Or I was away, and I had only myself to communicate with.

The Years of Wandering

In the fall of 1915 I struck out—God knows why, seeing I had forsaken agriculture at Wisconsin—for Amherst and the Massachusetts College of Agriculture. Mass. Aggies, it was called. Amherst itself was lovely beyond description, and I felt I always wanted to live there. And I liked the fellows. I was taken to live at a fraternity. I started training for the football team. I was made temporary captain. The Dean let me begin classes. But there were difficulties. For some reason or other there was delay in getting my marks and standing from Wisconsin. Someone in authority there would not write the letter that the Mass. Aggies required. It began to appear to the Dean that I had flunked-out at Madison. There was much redtape, and the writing back and forth of letters—and, finally, I got so sick of it all that I resolved to leave this place also and face the people of Washington, if necessary. The proper credentials did at last come. But nothing could hold me at the Aggies any longer. I took train for New York.

I fooled around New York till my money gave out—and then returned to Washington. Grandfather, his second hope dashed, was sorely disappointed. He and my uncles shook their heads at me. People talked. I held my own but I had to become more independent and articulate than ever. . . .

Suddenly the idea struck me: why not capitalize on my athletic abilities and interests? I decided I would. I wrote for catalogs to various places and hit on the American College of Physical Training in Chicago.

In the winter of 1916, that is, soon after New Year's, I set off for Chicago, to enter the winter term.

This, then, was my second contact with Chicago, a more prolonged one. I liked it. I liked the work and the people. I did good work both in the physical and the academic aspects of the schooling. I developed as a gymnast. I flowered as basketball player. I became almost an expert in anatomy. A very good course, including dissection, was given there. The instructor, a doctor, began talking to me about entering medical school. He was also an instructor at the Jenner Medical College. He said I'd have no trouble getting in. He would vouch for my ability as a student. I gave the idea some consideration.

Meanwhile, I was having quite a marvelous time. I had become good friends with Harry Karstens. Sometimes I'd spend week-ends at his home in Wheaton. He and I were the only "acceptable" men in the college. Most of the other fellows knew little or nothing about the graces of life. The place was full of girls. We had our pick. Every Saturday and many times during the week we'd go dancing in cabarets. This was my first experience with the vivifying effects of ginger ale highballs. Harry was the best of company, and so were the girls. *

That summer I went to stay with him and his family at Wheaton.

We were ambitious. We had pictures of ourselves as being cut out for something much higher and grander than mere gym instructors. We were agreed that the American College was but a stepping stone to better things. Harry decided to continue and graduate. But I thought, though I'd carry on for a while mainly because I liked the life, I'd also do some work at the University of Chicago.

So, the next fall, I enrolled for some classes down at the Midway, † and continued at the American College.

But now, some surprising things began happening to me. First of all, I was introduced to socialism. One of the fellows at the College, a wrestler who had been all over, had a scar on his face from a fight in Mexico, and was somewhat of a rascal—this fellow was a socialist, not a bad arguer. I fought hard for my Republican ruling-class capitalistic ideas; but, though I outpointed him in debate, he really won. His views began soaking into me, undermining and eating away everything I had thought as to how society is, as to how it ought to be. In fact, this was the first time I'd ever seriously thought about society at all. All of my thinking had been individualistic, highly so. As for my political and social views—they merely existed in me as my grandfather, school, and reading had deposited them. Now I began thinking. There was a persuasive logic and sense of justice in what that socialist said. I did not think much of him as a person. His mind was none too good. In talk I beat him every time. But, as I say, his ideas got to me. Suddenly, to the surprise of everyone, I no longer argued against him. On the side I had gone to the library and gotten some books on the subject. Indeed I began reading up on society and sociology in general. And then, one day, I was convinced. I announced

---

*See "Bona and Paul" in *Cane* for a literary description of this life.
†The geographical location of the University of Chicago.

myself as a believer in the ideas of socialism. I became their chief ex-
pounder in the school.

I had been, I suppose, unconsciously seeking—as man must ever seek—
an intelligible scheme of things, a sort of whole into which everything
fit, or seemed to fit, a body of ideas which held a consistent view of life
and which enabled one to see and understand as one does when he sees a
map. Socialism was the first thing of this kind I had encountered. I responded
accordingly. It was not so much the facts or ideas, taken singly, that
aroused me, though certainly I was challenged and stimulated by them.
More, it was the *body,* the *scheme,* the order and inclusion. These evoked
and promised to satisfy all in me that had been groping for form amid
the disorder and chaos of my personal experiences.

I was turning serious and no longer went out on many parties. Both
Harry and the girls, not liking my new ideas any too well, out and out
objected to my, from their point of view, too great an indulgence in
reading and study. But one girl, a girl named Eleanor Davis,* a fine-
looking girl with more maturity than most of them, and with a decided
way of her own, began taking notice of me. We went out once or twice
together, and, to my great surprise and delight, I found that I could
really talk to her. She was the first girl of my own age who could meet
me in terms of understanding and interest in the ways of life. She stimulated me. Our attachment grew.

Meanwhile, my formal studies were being neglected. Those at American
College did not demand much of me. I did them easily. But the biology
course at the University was pretty stiff. I was failing in it. I didn't care.
Compared with ideas about society, the routine of the biological laboratory
seemed empty and valueless. I decided to quit.

This decision was hastened by the following circumstance. I had con-
tacted still another body of new ideas. I began going to lectures on naturalism
and atheism, which were held regularly in big halls downtown in Chicago's
Loop. Among the speakers was Clarence Darrow. Darrow . . . on Darwin
and Haeckel, and, before I knew it, the logic of his reasoning had completely undermined my picture of the world. Till then, I had believed in
God, in the religious universe. Suddenly into my world came the ideas and
facts of the naturalists and evolutionists. I read their books. I did a lot
of thinking. With the result that my old world suddenly and completely
collapsed. I found myself in a world without a God. I felt the founda-
tions of the earth had been pulled from under me. I felt like a con-

---

* Possibly the basis for Bona in "Bona and Paul" (*Cane*).

demned man swinging with a rope about his neck. For several days I was so stunned and broken that I could hardly do more than lie on my bed in a darkened room and feel I was dying. Also, I felt as if I had been somehow betrayed. I didn't want to see anyone. I didn't want to see the light. In truth, I did not want to live.

Only a short while ago my political structures had been toppled. Now my religious ones were down also. In comparison with this experience, what did the courses at the University, or for that matter, anything, mean to me? It was during this phase of this Chicago period that, to protect my too deeply impressionable nature from receiving too strong and too many shocks, to shield my sensitivities and prevent the world from trodding on them, I deliberately set about the forming of a buffer, of a protective mechanism, resolving to meet the world with, and to let it touch me only through, my mind.

Eleanor ran into this.

(The very fact that I did not already have a buffer indicates that during my formative period, during my growth up to this time, I had somehow partially escaped the influences which fit masks over people; that I had gone through the social milieu somewhat like a person dodging rain drops and not getting wet—though the dodging had been quite unconscious on my part. And of course I did get wet a little—but comparatively little.)

No one knew what was happening to me. I dropped the University. I cut classes at the College. I wasn't to be seen for several days.

Then, gradually, I began pulling myself together. Indeed, I swung into a period of intellectual activity such [as] I had never before even thought possible. I read and read. Not only books on socialism and evolution, but also novels. I became acquainted with Victor Hugo, and with Jean Valjean, whose story, although it nearly broke my heart, fired my imagination. Eleanor Davis and I were more and more together.

All of this activity culminated in my suddenly wanting to write and lecture. At the College I got permission to use one of the rooms as a lecture hall; and there, one evening each week, I gave lectures to whoever wanted to come. I usually had a fair crowd. I'd talk, it seems, on everything under the sun. Victor Hugo. Evolution. Society. The nebular hypothesis of the origin of the universe. Finally, to attract more people, I decided to talk on nothing less than The Intelligence of Women. I got my material from Herbert Spencer—who was one of my Gods—and from several others. But this was the end of of my lecturing. I offended the women. The Dean of Women got mad at me. The attendance dwindled and before long I stopped. But what an intoxicating spree it had been!

I continued reading and thinking and talking with Eleanor.

Eleanor had a guardian in Chicago, a wealthy man, who, I was sure, wanted her for himself. He tried to break up our relationship. Eleanor resisted him and kept going with me. She was sure I had the makings of a great man. She believed in me. She was the first girl or woman to really inspire my efforts. Because of her I regained all of the sense-of-myself which the failures with universities had caused me to lose. I felt new powers and abilities springing up.

But we did not really love each other. We decided that.

In the spring of this year I suddenly felt that my experiences in Chicago had come to what I would now call a psychological end. I could have stayed on and continued. But I began feeling with deep conviction that the thing for me to do was to leave. Just why, for what ..? Again the motives and reasons were complicated.

In any case, I did leave. Returning again to Washington, I made believe that I had graduated from the American College. It was no use trying to explain or describe the nature and wealth of my experience there. It would have been futile to have tried to tell the truth, which was that I had derived from my stay in Chicago a thousand times more value than any graduation from any college could possibly have given to me. I was in living and vital contact with the ideas and thoughts of my century. Chicago had indeed witnessed and brought about the birth of my mind. And, of equal importance, I was again full of strength—physical and moral and mental—again with zest for life, with greater self-confidence.

My grandparents must have seen and sensed the change. They were pleased, and grandfather began looking as though he were thinking to himself, ''That boy will make something of himself yet.''

In myself I was convinced of it; but I still had some rough roads to travel. Could I have foreseen the difficulties and struggles and sufferings that were ahead of me I don't know what I would have done.

That spring in Washington I got hold of Lester F. Ward's *Dynamic Sociology*. It fired me. Never in my life had I read such a book. I felt I must return to college where I could get an ordered study in this subject. I saw that the subject was so vast that I could not hope to get anywhere by chance reading. Further, my taste for study was so great that I wanted to graduate, get my degree, and then a Master's, and then a Ph.D., get a job in a school or university, and devote my leisure hours to the life of a scholar.

I went to New York for summer school, enrolling in the New York University for sociology and another subject, in the College of the City of

New York for history;* and never have I worked and so well. Sociology at N.Y.U., however, was a disappointment. The course was nothing. I transferred my energies to the history course at City College. In this I did so well that when the final examination came, I was on my thirty-eighth page and still going strong when the professor came over to me and said, "Toomer, give me that paper. You have your 'A'." It was very seldom that Professor Schuyler gave an "A." He introduced me to the Dean and said, "Dean, Mr. Toomer is an excellent student." On the strength of that I got an appointment as assistant to the librarian, the next year. And here I first came in contact with the works of Bernard Shaw. But there are several things about the summer still to be told.

Socially, I had a fine time that summer. I used to eat at the Psi U house and came to know and like the fellows. They liked me. We'd go on "tasting parties" to various saloons. Once I got so full that when I entered my hot room I almost passed out. Also, we'd sit on the porch late of nights— Saturday and Sunday—and tell stories. These "story parties" often lasted till near day-break. I played tennis, and danced. To the fellows I was a marvel. They could not understand how I could be so excellent in my studies, carry on courses at two places, and still have time and energy for all the other things. In truth, I was a dynamo that summer. My strength and zest seemed to be inexhaustible.

I got one shock. A letter came from Eleanor. We had been writing each other. This letter came just as I was about to leave my room at N.Y.U. for my final exams at City College. I read it in the subway. In it she said she wanted to tell me how her guardian had tried to keep her away from me—the device he had at length used, all others failing. He had told her he was sure that I had Negro blood. He had taken her to restaurants where there were colored waiters and had tried to make her see that some of the lighter ones looked just like me. Her reply had been, "What if he has? I like him because he is what he is, whatever that may be." The guardian's tactics had not prevailed against her, or against me.

So that was what Eleanor had been going through—and I had known nothing of it. I admired her all the more. But I felt swift hatred for that guardian. The little puppy, unable to oppose me, man to man, and win her from me, had resorted to this. All sorts of emotions flared up in me. But the train reached my station. I got off and hurried to write the thirty-eight-page exam.

---

*Elsewhere Toomer states that a professor from C.C.N.Y. taught the course on the campus of N.Y.U. during that summer.

To my knowledge, only three times in my life has the matter of race been used against me as a deliberate weapon. This was one of them. The First.

The next day I answered Eleanor and told her the facts of my racial composition, as I knew them, and also of my individual position. She wrote back saying she was glad to know. Her feeling and opinion of me were the same as ever.

The following fall I continued at City College, getting a job in the library to help out. My funds were getting low. So this made a pretty full day and night. Classes till three in the afternoon. Then work in the library till five or six. A hurried dinner—and study at home till far into the night.

I was rooming with Uncle Walter. His wife had died and he had thought to try his fortunes in New York. He had got a job at Macy's. Studies went well for a time—but I was far more mature than most of the men in my classes. It became tedious sitting there having to listen to them bungle through. And too, I began feeling the need to really go into one subject thoroughly. I was taking psychology with an exceptionally good professor. It interested me more and more. Soon I concentrated my entire energies on it, convinced that herein, rather than in social theories, lay the key, and the one fundamental approach, to life.

I didn't have much time for other matters. But one afternoon I went on the basketball floor. The coach saw me playing and immediately wanted me for the team. A fraternity got interested in me, asked me over, and at length pledged me.

And then—the World War reached a crisis in my psyche.

In 1914 when I was at summer school in Madison, Europe had declared war. I only heard the faintest rumbles. It seemed unrelated to my life. In 1917, when I was in Chicago, America had entered. This brought matters nearer home. I remember saying to a fellow, "Well, if I have to fight and get killed .. I feel I've had a pretty full life." But what to do? I let things drift until they passed the conscription act. This did involve me. Let myself be conscripted, or enter an officer's training camp? I was in conflict. My human values, my aims in life, were opposed to war. But something in me rather liked the idea of soldiering. Grandfather had been in the Civil War. Walter had been in the Spanish American. Both in high school and at Wisconsin I had drilled—and liked it. For the time, however, my opposition to war won. Returning to Washington, I had had sharp run-ins with grandfather and both my uncles. All of them were, first, patriotic, and second, realistic. They wanted me to feel I should fight for my country. Also, they pointed out that it would be far better to become an officer than to be drafted as a private. My views and position angered them. But I held my ground. I'd go my own way until I was drafted. I hoped the war would end, or something would happen, before that time.

But now, towards the end of the fall term at City College, the war fever, having increased everywhere, suddenly got into me and began giving me a bad time. My soldiering inclinations arose and started a strong contest with my aims and values. Besides, the day for me to be called for examination was swiftly approaching. What would happen? If I were drafted and sent over, well, what was the use of these studies I was doing at college? Everything would be wiped out. Harry Overstreet gave a talk in the large hall to the men. It was not by any means a typical war-speech, but it did give me a sense of the gravity of the whole thing—and, a sense of the terrible but intriguing adventure of it. I was all stirred up. I remember going in and talking with Overstreet afterwards. The upshot was, that, not long afterwards, I could endure college no longer. I had registered in Washington. I'd go there and see what my fate was.

In Washington I was examined and rejected, put in fourth class because of bad eyes and a hernia gotten in a basketball game. This was a great weight off my chest. But—what was I to do now? Return to college? Impossible. I had to do something more active.

On one pretext or another I went to Chicago, and lived with Harry Karstens in his fraternity house. He had graduated from the American College and was now a student at the University of Chicago. I had ideas of doing a number of things. One of them was to do farm work. I knew a fellow, originally from Rockford, whose father had a large farm there. Perhaps I'd see if they would take me on. Nothing came of this. My funds were low. I became a salesman of Ford cars. It was deadly cold in Chicago, snow piled high about the streets. I had to be on the job at eight a.m. I didn't even get a nibble. More experienced fellows told me I wouldn't be able to get a thing unless I myself had a car. My job was to go, as it were, from house to house, trying to interest people in Fords—in sub-zero weather! I quit the job. I swore I'd never spend another winter in the north temperate zone. Me for Mexico or South America, or somewhere where it was warm. I even tried to inveigle several firms into sending me down there with their goods. I pretended I was an experienced salesman with a particular knowledge of things South American. Nothing came of it.

Meanwhile—and at last—I was writing. On the train to Chicago, in sheer desperation as to what I was going to do, I had tried my hand at a short story—and it was terrible. At the fraternity house I used every spare moment to write at least something. All of it was pretty poor stuff. What on earth was I going to do? The world outside seemed to be frozen like ice. It offered not a single place for me. I couldn't stay on at the frat house forever and a day. I couldn't see how I could possibly return to Washington. Just when things had about reached a climax, I received from Milwaukee an offer to take a substitute job as a physical director in one of the schools. One of my old friends of the American College days was up there. But he was leaving to join the army. Would I come up? The thing would only last two or three weeks—until they found another suitable regular man. I jumped at the offer.

I was in Milwaukee about a month. The job was of no importance save that it gave me bread and butter. But something big happened to me there. I really discovered the works of Bernard Shaw. They came strongly into my life and gave it a radical turn.

Up to this time, having failed so often, having experienced so acute a discrepancy between what I felt I was and what I could manifest, I had gradually and then more and more resorted to bluffing. In time, this bluffing had become an automatic and unconscious property in me. I practiced it without being aware that I did so. Shaw's independence and candor showed me to myself. He as a person struck deep into me, convincing me that it was valuable to be as he was. I felt I could be and should be independent and candid. I experienced a sudden turnover—a spiritual bath, a complete cleansing. I became candid. And the minute I did so, I felt myself, for the first time in years, standing squarely and frankly on my own feet. I was what I was. The world could take me or leave me.

So intense and so wonderful were my experiences that I stayed on in Milwaukee some time after the job was finished. My funds ran so low that I had to live on bread and milk and raisins, occasionally having eggs, potatoes, and coffee. I had no money with which to leave. I wrote grandfather. He sent me just barely enough for my train fare to Washington, saying that that was the last money he'd send me. He was completely disappointed in me. I had failed him and I had failed myself.

I again returned to Washington, but the old man made it so unpleasant for me that I had to pull out. In the spring of that year I wrote ahead to New York to the firm of Acker Merrall and Condit Company. While at City College I had worked at one of their stores on Saturdays. They said they had a job for me. I got enough money from grandfather for train fare and a week's living, promising to pay him back, and went to New York.

Something led me to take a room on 13th Street just off Sixth Avenue. During the day—and what long days they were!—I worked in a store on Broadway and 110th street. I was on the job at eight a.m. and didn't finish till six p.m., sometimes later, and always eleven or later on Saturdays. I did good work and came to be noticed by one of the general managers.

Of evenings I was on 13th Street. And in the house I met a girl named Eleanor Minné, and she, or one of her friends, introduced me to the Rand School—and this was the beginning of my contact with radical, and, later, with literary, New York. Whenever I had time and energy I went to lectures there, thus hearing for the first time Scott Nearing and Alfred Kreymborg. I was still a socialist in my political and economic and sociological views—but now it was a compound of the ideas of Lester F. Ward and Bernard Shaw. They all knew me as a Shaw enthusiast. And so I was. Also, I was beginning to feel my oats as a potential poet and writer. But the work with Acker Merrall took all the stuff out of me. I could do no writing then.

That summer Acker Merrall sent me to Ossining to be district manager of the Ossining-Mt. Kisco region. I took one of their Ford cars with me; and in no time at all I had so organized the work that I could do it all in from three to four days a week. This left me a fair amount of free time. And I was earning enough to live on. I had no need to lean on my grandparents. I read much and wrote a little. I kept a notebook and often jotted down my thoughts and ponderings. These were in some abundance, and this form of writing seemed most natural to me. Of course I had no notion of getting them published. They were purely for myself, and for the satisfaction of giving form to my experiences. I was developing an aesthetic sense in literature. Indeed I became so interested in aesthetics in general that I took several large volumes on this subject from the local library.

I met a girl of the town. Her home was just up from the street from where I was living. Many evenings I visited her. She was very fond of music and could play the piano fairly well. As I listened to her, there gradually began awakening my own old love of music, first started by the singing and playing of my mother. Melodies of my own began coming into my head. Induced they began coming in such wealth that I began seriously wondering if, after all, I was not fashioned to be a musician, a composer. Just at the time, at least, music seemed much nearer to my heart, much more a natural and spontaneous form of expansion than literature. I decided to give it a serious trial.

So, when I returned in the fall to New York, one of the first things

I did was to rent a piano. So far, so good. But I needed lessons, and these cost money. So I looked around for a way of increasing my income. Happening to see an ad, "Physical Educator and Gym Director Wanted," I applied for the job. It turned out to be at the University Settlement on the East Side. I was quickly taken on. And this was the beginning of my settlement house experiences. I moved down there, piano and all, and became a resident. I still kept the job with Acker Merrall, working with them during the day, at the settlement each night. And I found a teacher, a very good one. I had to have the best. A Mrs. Tapper, wife of the well-known teacher of that name, Thomas Tapper, I think it was.

So, what a program I had! Breakfast, early. Piano exercises. Study of harmony and composition. Readings in literature—particularly Shaw and Ibsen. My own attempts at writing. Lunch. Then to Acker Merrall. I had maneuvered to work with them half-time. Three afternoons I had piano lessons. Then back to the Settlement, dinner, and gym classes till eleven at night. This pace was kept up for six months.

I met a number of interesting people. Elmer Rice, who was there teaching a dramatic group. And, among others, Moses L. Ehrlich, a very fine person, a young dentist just starting out with an office on the East Side. Ehrlich and I became very good friends. He introduced me to Santayana, Goethe, and to music—concerts at Carnegie Hall. I was rapidly entering my chosen sphere of the New York world.

Then, suddenly, I broke under the strain. Over-work caused what seemed to be a serious breakdown. For a day or two I was in a semi-coma. They were frightened by my state. One or two thought I was losing my mind. But I wasn't. I was there all the time, looking out at them. Only, I couldn't do much with my body. Seemed disconnected with it. I pulled myself together. I went on a fast, and for several days I wouldn't eat anything. I got very weak, but began feeling better. Then I went on a diet of milk and orange juice. As I began to pick up, they increased their advice that I should see a doctor. Finally, I did go to one, a specialist on nerves. He said I had exhausted one or another of my glands, and wanted to inject something into me. I wouldn't let him. I continued being my own physician. I got better and better. Before long I was well enough to travel. I went up to Ellenville, New York, a place I know of in the mountains. It was dead winter, but I wanted to be there.

The Settlement people gave me a warm send-off—and a check for two months in advance, though I had told them I would not return to my job. They were very good friends.

In Ellenville I continued my dieting till I was completely all right.

Then I was suddenly seized by a passion for writing. I wrote day and night. I wanted others to see what I had written. I sent for a small mimeographer and made copies. Each week I'd send out to friends and acquaintances in New York, Washington, Chicago, wherever I had them, my long letters which usually dealt with world-matters as I saw them. I got some interesting responses, and among them, replies from grandfather. He often disagreed with me, but I could detect in the wording his surprise and even his admiration that I had such ideas and was able to express them so well. When I still again returned to Washington, as I did when I felt I had had enough of Ellenville, he was more tolerant of me.

In the early summer of that year who should blow into Washington but Walt Palmer, another one of my friends of the American College days. He was quite a fellow, of marvelous physical build, bent on seeing and experiencing everything in the world. And he had a mind. He was pretty clever in philosophic arguments. Well, Walt proposed that since neither of us had any money, and since sitting still was a thing we could not do, we'd start off, bum our way to New York, and then, ride blind baggage from New York to his home in the western part of the state. There, we would at least have room and food, and we'd be free to do what we pleased. So, with grandfather again shaking his head, and with grandmother almost worried sick as to what might befall me, off I went with Walt. Luckily, we were picked up by a man driving a big Pierce Arrow. And this man deposited us on the corner of 7th Ave and 42nd Street, New York, at eight o'clock of that same day.

We knocked about New York a few days; hiked north; crossed the Hudson at Poughkeepsie; walked over the mountains, sleeping outdoors at night; reached Ellenville; reached Port Jarvis; and rode blind baggage all night. It was a terrible experience. Never again. Finally we reached Salamanca. All summer we stayed there, tramping about, swimming, and I, reading Shelley.

Early fall we were again in New York. He got a job. And I returned to Washington. For the old man, this was almost the last straw. Was I never going to do anything? All of his high hopes of me had long ago been dashed, but I might at least get a steady job and settle down to be a respectable if inconspicuous citizen. Even I, in truth, was getting a bit dizzy with all my returns and departures from Washington. I more than half agreed with the old gentleman. But something inside me was driving me on, and I felt it would eventually lead me where I wanted to go, though I didn't know where, though my course seemed as crazy and as aimless as they make them. Besides, I had thoroughly exploded the myth that an able-bodied intelligent young man could start at the bottom of American business or industry and work his way up. I had seen too much of business conditions in New York to be taken in by this fiction. If you didn't have pull, or if you didn't get a fortunate break, you just stayed down there where the majority of the workmen of the world were, and always would be. In short, I saw no future for myself in business. Once I told grandfather these ideas, and they shocked him. I spoke with such biting realism that even he, who in his day had played the game and knew pretty much what it was, was taken back. Never again did he open this subject with me.

But now I was having to fight him. It was at the stage of continual opposition. If I wanted to stay home, I could only do so by opposing him and, as it were, forcing him to let me occupy my room. In the apartment there was still a room with my things in it. It was still called my room. This was because of my grandmother's wish. But, as I say, it was mine only after I fought for it.

This was in the fall of 1919. I was twenty-five years old.

Towards Christmas, things got so bad that I left home with ten dollars in my pocket. It was the 20th or 21st of December, and cold as the mischief. I walked to Baltimore, and stayed there in a cheap room overnight. I walked to Wilmington. Near there a train of army trucks passed me. I got a ride on one of them to Rahway, N.J. I had eaten nothing. When I got off I was so stiff, so nearly frozen—well, I fell off. I could hardly walk. At the station I could only just barely open my jaws and make the agent understand I wanted a ticket to New York. I slept somewhere, I don't remember. Next day I got a little room on 9th Street near Fifth Avenue. The next day I got a job in the shipyards of New Jersey. I had to get up at five o'clock.

The work was hard, harder than I ever thought work could be. The steel of the half-finished ships was terribly cold. Just to touch it was enough to freeze you. (And I had once vowed I'd never spend another winter in the north!) All day long I had to cramp myself under heavy plates, in small compartments, and work the holes so that bolts could be slid in from the top. I was called a fitter. I got $22.00 a week. After ten days of it, I quit. And that, by the way, finished socialism for me. The men who worked in those yards—and they were real realistic workmen—had two main interests: playing craps and sleeping with women. Not God himself could have done anything with those men. Socialism ..? Well, it was for people like Shaw and Sidney Webb .... . It was the way they saw social life. But as for working a great betterment in the lives of the proletariat—this was a pipe dream possible only to those who had never really experienced the proletariat.

I got a comparatively gentlemanly job with Acker Merrall.

I renewed my friendship with Ehrlich. I moved over and lived on the East Side. Of evenings I went to concerts—and again my love of music returned stronger than ever. But also I was reading. I had discovered Walt Whitman.

Just about this time grandfather sold my house in order to get back what he had loaned me on it. He said he needed the money. I think he did. His financial affairs were going from bad to worse. Of all the property he had at one time owned—the Bacon Street house and lots, several houses in other parts of town—the whole thing had dwindled till now he had only one house; and he was living mainly on the rent from it. So, with my consent, he sold my house. There was about six hundred dollars left over. This he sent to me. I decided to live on it. I decided that I was at one of the turning points of my life, and that I needed all my time, and that the money would be well spent. I quit Acker Merrall. I devoted myself to music and to literature.

But soon I saw I couldn't carry on them both. In order to become proficient in either, I had to make a choice. Which would it be? I was in serious quandary.

Just then I happened to read Goethe's *Wilhelm Meister*. It must have come just at the right time, for its effect was tremendous. It seemed to gather together all the scattered parts of myself. I was lifted into and shown my real world. It was the world of the aristocrat—but not the social aristocrat; the aristocrat of culture, of spirit and character, of ideas, of true nobility. And for the first time in years and years I breathed the air of my own land. My God! how far I had wandered from it! Through the cities of America, through colleges, through socialism and naturalism and atheism, through the breakup of family and my home, through arid philosophies, Herbert Spencer and all the rest, and now at last I saw it again. It was like seeing it again, like seeing something you had known long ago but had forgotten. In fact, of course, I was seeing it for the first time. So this was the effect of Goethe on me. I resolved to devote myself to making of myself such a person as I caught glimpses of in the pages of *Wilhelm Meister*. For my specialized work, I would write. I would put music aside forever as a possible career. And indeed I did just this.

I continued in New York, reading and writing. I returned to Whitman because he was of America, and I felt he had something to give me in terms of the American world. I spent days in the library reading not only all he had written, but all that had been written about him: biographies, monographs, etc. The rest of my time I practiced writing. Things continued this way for several months. My money was getting low.

Just then I happened into the Rand School one evening. I saw a lecture that interested me. It was on Romain Rolland and Jean Christophe, by Helena DeKay. The name Helena DeKay didn't mean anything to me. And, in truth, I had heard little or nothing of Rolland. But something urged me to attend that lecture. I did. I got quite a bit from it. I looked rather hard at Helena DeKay. It was a series. The next evening I was again there. I went up and talked with Miss DeKay. She interested me very much, and Rolland, and Jean Christophe,—and I seemed to interest her. I asked her if she'd mind if I walked home with her. She would like it, she said.

Well, the upshot of all this was that one evening she invited me to go to a party given by Lola Ridge. She said I'd see and meet all the literary figures there. I was overjoyed. I did go and I did see and meet them. This was my first literary party.

Edwin Arlington Robinson, Witter Bynner, Scofield Thayer were there. There was talk about the *Dial*, a new magazine of the seven arts. And much literary buzz-buzz, a good bit of which was so much Greek to me. I had a queer mixture of feelings. I felt I was a hopeless novice in the presence of expert men and women. I felt I didn't quite belong. Yet, I had a strong feeling that I did. I seemed to feel that here was the first gathering of people I had ever seen in my life—people who were of my kind. It was simply a matter of my learning how to speak their language. Some of them noticed me. Some, after a brief nod at the introduction, immediately forgot me. But both Helena and Lola Ridge sort of kept me under their arms and prevented my feeling I was out of things. They were very good.

For myself—though my eyes were open wide taking it all in, they also were looking out. I had a habit of taking the measure of people, particularly of men. I was like the rabbit who stood on his hind legs and stretched to see who was the tallest. I had a pretty good opinion of myself. This habit was especially stimulated now that I was in the company of the chosen few. There was not a person in the room whom I felt to be a better man or as strong a man as myself. As for writing—well, we'd see about that. That would depend upon how much talent I turned out to have, and upon what I could make of it. In terms of life, of experience and understanding of life, of overcoming difficulties, of struggles, and so on, I felt I had as much or more than anyone I saw. My one criticism of the party was that there was far too much buzz about publishers, magazines, reviews, personalities; not enough talk of life and experience.

One man stood out. He wore a light suit and sat on the edge of a table. He had a fine animated face and a pair of lively active eyes. I felt there could be something between him and himself. I didn't know his name, but I marked him.

A week or so later I chanced to be walking through Central Park. A man passed me. In a flash I seemed to recognize him. But I wasn't sure, so I passed on. Then suddenly, drawn by some force, I stopped and turned around. At the same moment he stopped and glanced back at me. Now I knew it was the person I had marked at Lola Ridge's. We introduced ourselves. He was Waldo Frank. I vaguely remembered having heard of him through my friend Ehrlich. Ehrlich had said Frank had written a remarkable book called *Our America*. I had not read it. This was all I knew of Waldo Frank.

We went over and sat down on the grass and had a long talk. I felt immediately he would be a good friend of mine. I told him about my music. He offered to give me an introduction to Ernest Bloch, should I want it. I told him I had put music out of my life [and] was going to do nothing but write. He said he'd like to do whatever he could [to help]. I thanked him but said there was nothing he could do just then. I had decided to return to Washington and put in a long apprenticeship. However, he gave me his address and said that I should write him or call on him whenever I felt I needed him. I knew without doubt that I could count on him. We said goodby.

I had, in truth, decided to return to Washington. My money had given out. It was useless to think that I could at the same time work for my living and give the necessary time and energy to literature. I had made up my mind that I would go home, force my grandfather not only to accept me but to give me an allowance of five dollars a week, and stay there, come what might, until I had proven myself as a writer. In fine, I was going to Washington and remain there until my literary work lifted me out.

And that is just what I did. Grandfather put up a fight but I beat him. His age and enfeebled condition were no match for the strength and singleness of my determination. At last I was wholly convinced that I had found my true direction in life, and no one was going to stop me. On the contrary, everyone, including grandfather, was going to help me. But first and last I was going to help myself. In truth, I was so ready and so eager to help myself, whatever the pain and sacrifice, that, in comparison, I felt I was demanding hardly anything of him. So it was done.

And thus, in the summer of 1920, after five years of buffeting and knocking all-over America—the period between the ending of high school and this date—I came to comparative anchorage in the apartment with my grandparents.

They had greatly aged. I had matured considerably. And, I was filled with a purpose that was to keep me working for the next three years. But what terrible years they were!

The Cane *Years*

I was in the house with two old people whom, despite the continual struggle with grandfather—he never gave up completely; he was a game fighting cock to the end—I loved. And they were dying. No, they weren't dying. Grandfather gradually declined—a tragic sight—and, one day he broke. After that, he was a doddering old man, not dying, not living, yet hanging on. He might hang on for years and years. But I had to take over whatever of his affairs needed attention. And I ran the house, even cooking meals and sweeping and cleaning. In a way, it was a good thing for them that I had returned. Neither Walter nor Bismarck was much in evidence. Bis came over rather regularly a couple of evenings a week. But he had his work to do, and could not have been of any help during the day. Walter dropped in now and again, but he showed a certain coolness, a certain resentment against his father. He had cause enough to. His life had not turned out well. He was grandfather's favorite son. His almost brusque manner pained the old gentleman more than anything else.

Grandmother, however, was showing forth one of the miracles of life. Each day her body was growing more feeble. You could almost see it thinning away. For weeks at a stretch she would have to be in bed. And, though grandfather worried and feared about his near-poverty, it was she who really felt conditions most acutely. Yet she bore up. Not a whimper from her. She was glad to have me there. As far as I could I shared my life with her, and she began living in my life. She would say every now and again that she only lived for me. But this was the miracle—as her body failed her, her spirit began taking on a more and more vivid life. Her mind became sharper—and also her tongue. She showed a vein of humor and satire that was the delight and amazement of all who came in.

Most of grandfather's political friends had either died or deserted him. Very seldom did any of the men come in—and when they did, the picture of his decline was so painful to them that they left as soon as they could. But grandmother had several old and staunch women friends. They too were getting feeble, and they couldn't get around so well. But grandmother hardly went out at all. They had to come; and come they did. It was a tonic to them to hear her. Sometimes she would forget how weak her body was, and she'd begin planning to do this and that. And her criticisms of people, of life and manners, were penetrating to the degree of the uncomfortable. Yet, she usually gave everything a humorous turn which would take the sting out.

My days were divided between attention to the house and my grandparents, and my own work. At all possible times I was either writing or reading. I read all of Waldo Frank, most of Dostoevsky, much of Tolstoy, Flaubert, Baudelaire, Sinclair Lewis, Dreiser, most all of the American poets, Coleridge, Blake, Pater, in fine, a good portion of the modern writers of all western countries. In addition—Freud, and the psychoanalysts, and a miscellany of scientific and philosophical works. And I began reading the magazines: the *Dial, Poetry,* the *Liberator,* the *Nation, New Republic,* etc.

In my writing I was working, at various times, on all the main forms. Essays, articles, poems, short stories, reviews, and a long piece somewhere between a novel and a play. Before I had even so much as glimpsed the possibility of writing *Cane,* I had written a trunk full of manuscripts. The phrase "trunk full" is often used loosely. I mean it literally and exactly. But what difficulties I had! I had in me so much experience so twisted up that not a thing would come out until by sheer force I had dragged it forth. Only now and again did I experience spontaneous writing. Most of it was will and sweat. And nothing satisfied me. Not a thing had I done which I thought merited publication—or even sending to a magazine. I wrote and wrote and put each thing aside, regarding it as simply one of the exercises of my apprenticeship. Often I would be depressed and almost despair over the written thing. But, on the other hand, I became more and more convinced that I had the real stuff in me. And slowly but surely I began getting the "feeling" of my medium, a sense of form, of words, of sentences, rhythms, cadences, and rhythmic patterns. And then, after several years work, suddenly, it was as if a door opened and I knew without doubt that I was *inside. I knew literature*! And what was my joy!

But many things happened before that time came!

People round about wondered what I was doing. They said things. I was sufficiently individualized to hold and go my own way without stopping even to confound them. Once or twice I let fly. I got the reputation of being a very queer fellow. Those, even those who once upon a time had said what a fine dancer and what a sweet lover I was, gave me a sufficiently wide berth.

Vic had long since married someone and gone away. I never saw her after. Not till this day.

Phyllis was there but married. And, in any case, she no longer meant much to me. But somewhere in my heart I reserved—and still do—an affectionate place for her. But it was as though she and all the other people existed in another world. They could not enter mine. I did not want to enter theirs.

Kennedy alone was with me. I stretched him quite a bit, but he always came back for more. I wanted him to try writing. He had a life that, as I have suggested, read like Dostoevsky.* But I could not get him to. He was working now and again, and thinking a lot. But I was afraid that sex and drink would get him. He was burning all over, intense emotions, active brain, sexing and drinking and shooting pool—burning the candle at all three ends. He said I was the only person in life he trusted or gave a damn about. By now, his physical features were quite defined, set in the mould and with the expressions he would have for the rest of his life. A long slim body with long tapering fingers. He had the sensitivity of an artist, the lips of a sensualist, the eyes of a fanatic. He was tied up in a family complex—mother and sisters and brother whom he hated. He would not leave home and take a room by himself. He kept picking and flaring at them. He liked to walk the streets at night. I have never known anyone to feel the beauty of tree-shaded evening streets as he did. He liked to go to the zoo and watch the polar bears. He liked to talk with me. He'd read some of the things I'd written. "That's the stuff!" he'd exclaim. But he himself would not try to write a page. I worked very hard on him. Kennedy was the first one to enforce upon me the realization of how difficult it is to change human beings.

Two or three other people of my own age came in to see me.

As for my past life—the life of Chicago and New York, I seemed to have left it completely behind. I seldom wrote to or heard from my former friends in those cities.

Bismarck got very sick. I took over the running of his house also, and each day I went over and massaged him. He was over a month recovering. This took it out of me.

I met a sculptress, and she did a bust of me. But, of more importance to myself, two things happened. One, I suddenly found myself with a faculty for seeing into people. People had always interested me, and,

---

*Toomer attempted a novel based on Kennedy; but, as far as can be determined, he did not complete it.

through my experiences with so many and such different kinds, I had
acquired some understanding of them, some ability to read them. But
this was like the sudden functioning of an entirely new function. I would
see and understand that hidden and complex thing called motivation.
As if a veil had been taken from my eyes I began seeing into the lives of
grandmother, grandfather, my uncles, Kennedy, Phyllis, this sculptress,
in short, everyone, as never before. And, I felt a marked increase of
power to do things with and for people. Being able to see what and why
they were as they were, I was enabled to see what they needed.

I met a girl several years younger than myself.* She was pretty and
talented in music, but very bitter against life. I saw what she was, and,
by questioning and reasoning—this was psychological reasoning—I learned
how she had come to be that way. In her case I was more successful than
with Kennedy. I actually squared her with life and enabled her to make
a fresh start.

Meanwhile, conditions in the house were demanding more and draining
more from me. But I was still keeping up all right.

I came in contact with an entirely new body of ideas. Buddhist philosophy, the Eastern teachings, occultism, theosophy. Much of the writing
itself seemed to me to be poorly done; and I was certain that the majority
of the authors of these books had only third or fourth-rate minds, or
less. But I extracted the ideas from their settings, and they seemed to
me among the most extraordinary I had ever heard. It is natural to me
to put my whole heart into anything that really interests me—as long as I
am interested. For the time being, only that thing exists in the world.
These ideas challenged and stimulated me. Despite my literary purpose,
I was compelled to know something more about them. So, for a time, I
turned my back on literature and plunged into this kind of reading.
I read far and wide, for more than eight months. Then, I became dis-
satisfied with just reading. I wanted to do some of the things they suggested. I wanted to see some of the things with my own eyes. I myself
wanted a personal all-around experience of the world these books seemed
to open. I tried several of the exercises; but then, abruptly stopped them.
I concluded they were not for me. In general, I concluded that all of that
was not for me. I was in this physical, tangible, earthly world, and I knew
little enough of it. It was the part of wisdom to learn more and to be able
to do more in this, before I began exploring and adventuring into other
worlds. So I came back to earth and to literature. But I had profited in

---

*Probably Mae Wright, an Afro-American.

many ways by my excursion. The Eastern World, the ancient scriptures had been brought to my notice. Also, our own Christian Bible. I had read it as if it were a new book. Just simply as a work of literature I was convinced that we had nothing to equal it. Not even Shakespeare—my old God—wrote language of such grand perfection. And my religious nature, given a cruel blow by Clarence Darrow and naturalism and atheism, but not, as I found, destroyed by them—my religious nature which had been sleeping was vigorously aroused.

One other thing happened. From this reading, but not so much from it as from the ponderings and gatherings-up of impressions and experiences which it stimulated, there swung to the fore my picture and ideal of Man, of a complete and whole individual who was able to function physically, emotionally, and intellectually. This ideal was much fuller, with more substance and detail than that formed by my reading of Goethe, but it was in the same line and order of desirable and valuable human life.

But both my religious feelings and this ideal were gradually lost to my consciousness as I again got immersed in the difficulties and problems of learning the craft and art of writing. Literature, and particularly the craftsman's aspect of it, again became my entire world, and I lived in it as never before.

And now again I was reading only literary works. This was the period when I was so strongly influenced, first, by the Americans who were dealing with local materials in a poetic way. Robert Frost's New England poems strongly appealed to me. Sherwood Anderson's *Winesburg, Ohio* opened my eyes to entirely new possibilities. I thought it was one of the finest books I'd ever read. And, second, the poems and program of the Imagists. Their insistence on fresh vision and on the perfect clean economical line was just what I had been looking for. I began feeling that I had in my hands the tools for my own creation.

Once during this period I read many books on the matter of race and the race problem in America. Rarely had I encountered the nonsense contained in most of these books. It was evident to me, who had seen both the white and the colored worlds, and both from the inside, that the authors of these writings had little or no experience of the matters they were dealing with. Their pages showed very little more than strings of words expressive of personal prejudices and preferences. I felt that I should write on this matter. I did write several fragments of essays. And I did a lot of thinking. Among other things, I again worked over my own position, and formulated it with more fullness and exactitude. I wrote a poem called, "The First American," the idea of which was, that here in America we are in process of forming a new race, that I was one of the first conscious members of this race. . . .

I had lived among white people. I had lived among colored people. I had lived among Jews. I had met and known people of the various nationalistic groups. I had come in contact with my fellow countrymen from the bottom to the top of the American scene.

I had seen the divisions, the separatisms and antagonisms. I had observed that, if the issue came up, very few of these United States citizens were aware of being Americans. On the contrary, they were aware of, and put value upon, their hearsay descents, their groupistic affiliations.

True, they were conscious of being anything but Americans. Yet, underlying what they were aware of, underlying all of the divisions, I had observed what seemed to me to be authentic—namely, that a new type of man was arising in this country—not European, not African, not Asiatic—but American. And in this American I saw the divisions mended, the differences reconciled—saw that (1) we would in truth be a united people existing in the United States, saw that (2) we would in truth be once again members of a united human race.

Now all of this, needless to say, did not get into the poem. Years were to pass before that could happen, before the germ of "The First American" could grow and ripen and be embodied in "The Blue Meridian." But into "The First American" I did put something of my actuality, something of my vision of America—though it needed explaining.

Soon after I had written it I read it to a friend of that time, a colored fellow of more than ordinary mental grasp. I considered him a sort of prodigy. I read the poem, and he looked blank. I explained it, and he looked puzzled. So I plunged in and gave him my position and my experiences at some length. At the end he said three words, "You're white."

"What are you?" I asked.

"Colored."

I threw up my hands. "After all I've said you still don't get the point. I am not talking about whites or blacks, I am talking about Americans. I am an American. You are an American. Everyone is an American. Don't you see what I mean?"

He shook his head then, he shook it ever afterwards. My reality was but words to him, words quite unrelated to what was real for him.

Never before had I realized the extent to which a consciousness of being colored had become fixed in members of that group. But there it was, fixed unshakably in a man of unusual intelligence. Never before had I known what a thorough job had been done in the matter of racial conditioning. But there it was, having gone down from his head and emotions to become lodged in the behavior patterns of his body. And a similar kind of fixing and conditioning had doubtless occurred also in members of the white group at large. . . .

Who was I to attempt to unfix all this? As I was neither a propagandist nor a reformer I concluded that it was not my business and I had best let it alone. Which is just what I did. The whole thing had started as an individual position; so then, in the future, I'd restrict it to myself and to those who, because of their relations with me, were individually concerned.

["On Being an American"]

All of the above had taken place between the summer of 1920 and the spring of 1922.

It was during this spring that I began feeling dangerously drained of energy. I had used so much in my own work. So much had been used on my grandparents and uncles. I seldom went out. I seldom could go out. Sometimes for weeks my grandmother would be laid up in bed, and by now my grandfather was almost helpless. The apartment seemed to suck my very life. And this is no figure of speech. Everyone has had the experience of being with some person, of leaving this person and feeling bled. He is bled. This person has taken stuff out of him. Just so, only for a protracted period, had my grandfather taken energy from me. He was still taking it; and I began to see the situation as a struggle for life between him and myself. It was a question of who would die first.

There was nothing the matter with me organically, though I had contracted a severe case of almost chronic nervous indigestion. Mainly, it was a matter of energy. I felt utterly exhausted. Each morning I was up before nine. I'd try to work, and just simply couldn't. The little force I had gathered during sleep was soon spent, and I'd be in a wretched state. But neither could I rest. To do nothing was even worse than trying to squeeze something out of myself. I drank what whiskey I could get. But when its effects wore off, I was more drained than ever. I didn't know what on earth I was going to do. I had no money even for a short vacation. And even if I had had, I couldn't have left my grandparents alone. A nurse was out of the question.

But, when the heat of summer came on, I got desperate. I felt I would die or murder someone if I stayed in that house another day. Somehow I managed to get enough money for a week's trip to Harper's Ferry. And, luckily, I was able to make arrangements with an old woman to be in the apartment for that time. Grandmother, sensing my state, was glad I was going to have a slight breathing spell. Grandfather, understanding very little other than his own infirmities, was petulant. But I left.

I returned with a small store of force which was soon spent; and I found myself in the same condition as before. The situation was slowly but steadily growing worse. Never in my life before ... [had I felt] so utterly caught and trapped. It was as if life were a huge snake that had coiled about me—and now it had me at almost my last breath.

Just at this time a man, the head of an industrial and agricultural school for Negroes in Georgia, came to town. He was going to Boston in search of funds and wanted someone to act as principal during his absence. He was sent to me.

My situation was so desperate that any means of getting out of it appeared as a God-send. I accepted his offer. Besides, I had always wanted to see the heart of the South. Here was my chance.

I had grandfather sent to a hospital. I hired a woman to come and stay with grandmother. And off I went.

I arrived in Sparta and took up my duties. I still felt terribly drained, but the shock of the South kept me going.

The school was several miles from the village. All the teachers lived there. I had a little shack off to one side.

The setting was crude in a way, but strangely rich and beautiful. I began feeling its effects despite my state, or, perhaps, just because of it. There was a valley, the valley of "Cane," with smoke-wreaths during the day and mist at night. A family of back-country Negroes had only recently moved into a shack not too far away. They sang. And this was the first time I'd ever heard the folk-songs and spirituals. They were very rich and sad and joyous and beautiful. But I learned that the Negroes of the town objected to them. They called them "shouting." They had victrolas and player-pianos. So, I realized with deep regret, that the spirituals, meeting ridicule, would be certain to die out. With Negroes also the trend was towards the small town and then towards the city—and industry and commerce and machines. The folk-spirit was walking in to die on the modern desert. That spirit was so beautiful. Its death was so tragic. Just this seemed to sum life for me. And this was the feeling I put into *Cane. Cane* was a swan-song. It was a song of an end. And why no one has seen and felt that, why people have expected me to write a second and a third and a fourth book like *Cane,* is one of the queer misunderstandings of my life.

I left Georgia in late November of that year, after having been there three months. On the train coming north I began to write the things that later on appeared in that book.

Once again in Washington I had my grandfather brought back from the hospital. His condition there was too pitiable for me to bear. He touched my heart so strongly that I resolved to care for him till the very end. And this I did.

He sank very rapidly. All during December I nursed him; and, at the same time, I wrote the materials of *Cane*. In these last days he seemed to know just what I meant to him. I knew and realized all he had done for me. Our almost life-long struggle and contest was finished, and all my love and gratitude for the once so forceful and dominant but now so broken and tragic man came to the fore. He died the day after I had finished the first draft of "Kabnis," the long semi-dramatic closing-piece of *Cane*.

Walter and I took his body to New Orleans and interred it in the family vault, beside the remains of my mother.

Grandmother bore up remarkably well; and she and I continued living in the apartment. . . .

[The remainder of the autobiographical selections have been taken from "On Being an American" except where indicated.]

I resumed writing.

Some of the pieces were impure and formless. But some, I knew, were really written. These authentic ones I began sending out. The *Double Dealer* of New Orleans was the first to accept. Then the *Liberator* and, later, *Broom*. In these literary magazines I made my mark. Beyond them was Waldo Frank and the possibility of a book.

Now I felt warranted in sending something to Waldo Frank. I sent a batch of the best—and waited his response as if my whole life were at stake.

His words to me fed me as nothing else had done and confirmed my belief.

He too talked about a book. Now I wanted a book published as I wanted nothing else. I wanted it because it would be a substantial testament of my achievement, and also because I felt that it would lead me from the cramped conditions of Washington which I had outgrown, into the world of writers and literature. I saw it as my passport to this world.

But I had not enough for a book. I had at most a hundred typed pages. These were about Georgia. It seemed that I had said all I had to say about it. So what, then? I'd fill out. The middle section of *Cane* was thus manufactured.

I sent the manuscript to Frank. He took it to Horace Liveright. Liveright accepted it, but wanted a foreword written by Frank.

Frank himself had a book to write, based on Negro life.* It was arranged that he come to Washington and then both of us would go South.

Frank came. He stayed at the apartment with us. I took this opportunity to convey to him my position in America. I read to him "The First American." I explained my actuality and my ideas to the point where I felt sure he understood them. I did this because I wanted that we understand each other on this point too, and also because he was going to write the foreword to my book and I wanted this introduction of myself to the literary world to be accurate and right.

We went South. We came back. Frank returned to New York. In several of his letters he referred to what he called my "vision," and seemed to feel that it "protected" me. Perhaps it did. But because of the way he used this word "protected," I was mainly concerned with whether or not he understood that it was not a vision, but an actuality. Once or twice I suspected that he, like my colored friend, felt it was words, fine words to be sure, but unrelated to reality. But I argued myself out of the suspicion by reminding myself that Waldo Frank was the author of *Our America*.

One day in the mail his preface to my book came. I read it and had as many mixed feelings as I have ever had. On the one hand, it was a tribute and a send-off as only Waldo Frank could have written it, and my gratitude for his having gotten the book accepted rose to the surface and increased my gratitude for the present piece of work in so far as it affirmed me as a literary artist of great promise. On the other hand, in so far as the racial thing went, it was evasive, or, in any case, indefinite. According to the reader he would have thought I was white or black, or again he may have thought nothing of it. But in any case he certainly would not *know* what I was.

Well, I asked myself, why should the reader know? Why should any such thing be incorporated in a foreword to *this* book? Why should Waldo Frank or any other be my spokesman in this matter? All of this was true enough, and I was more or less reconciled to letting the preface

---

* *Holiday* (1923). It is important to observe that Toomer states that he had completed *Cane* before Frank completed *Holiday*.

stand as it was, inasmuch as it was so splendid that I could not take issue with it on this, after all, minor point, inasmuch as my need to have the book published was so great, but my suspicions as to Waldo Frank's lack of understanding of, or failure to accept, my actuality became active again.

As I found out later from several sources, my doubts were warranted. I have been told that Frank, after seeing me and my family, after hearing my statement, not of words or visions but of facts, returned to New York and told people of the writer who was emerging into the world of American literature. In any event, it was thus through Frank's agency that an erroneous picture of me was put in the minds of certain people in New York before my book came out. Thus was started a misunderstanding in the very world, namely the literary art world, in which I expected to be really understood. I knew none of this at the time. . . . *

I saw that it was important for me to be in New York. Grandmother also saw this. Walter had again married. He and his wife had taken a house. Grandmother went to live with them and I took a train for New York [in early summer, 1923]. And thus ended the three-year period of death and birth in Washington.

*In New York, I stepped into the literary world. Frank, Gorham Munson, Kenneth Burke, Hart Crane, Matthew Josephson, Malcolm Cowley, Paul Rosenfeld, Van Wyck Brooks, Robert Littell—*Broom, *the* Dial, *the* New Republic *and many more. I lived on Gay Street and entered into the swing of it. It was an extraordinary summer.*

I wrote reviews, especially for Broom. *I worked on the outline of a large complex novel that was to essentialize my experiences with America. I entered the aesthetic-machine-beauty program as sponsored by Munson in* Secession *and Josephson in* Broom. *I met and talked with Alfred Stieglitz and saw his photographs. I was invited here and there.*

I went up to visit Frank at Darien, Connecticut. And here I met Margaret Naumburg and felt the whole world revolve . .

. . . My birth, and it was truly a birth, came from my experiences with Margaret Naumburg. I do not wish to put these in outline. It is enough here to say that the very deepest centre of my being awoke to consciousness giving me a sense of myself, an awareness of the world and of values, which transcended even my dreams of high experience. All that I had been, all that I had ever done, were as if left behind me in another world.

---

*In this part of his autobiography, Toomer asserts that he should not have been identified as "Negro."

All the past would have seemed valueless had I not known that it was just this past which had prepared me for these experiences.

["Outline of an Autobiography"]

. . . It was very exciting life and work, giving me a taste and an experience of the literary life such as I had never known before and have never experienced since. There was an excitement in the air. Writing was a living thing. We had programs and aims, and we were all caught up in a ferment. These were the last days of *Secession* and *Broom*. But the *Dial* and the *Little Review* were still going, and what was not yet an actuality we had as a glowing potentiality in our minds.

Sometimes I wondered what if anything Frank had said to these other fellows about my race. But it didn't matter much, one way or the other. What they thought of my race was of no more consequence than what I thought of theirs. The life was the thing—and we were having that life.

The first jolt I got was when I received a letter from Horace Liveright asking, in effect, that I feature myself as a Negro for some publicity he was getting out in connection with *Cain* [*sic*].* Now I had seen, talked, lunched with Liveright. Once he had said to me that he had run into prejudice in college, and he asked if I had. I said, "No." That was that. Otherwise, the question of race had not come up even in a vague way. Looking back on it, I can blame myself for not having opened the subject with him. However this may be, I received the request I have just mentioned.

I answered to the effect that, as I was not a Negro, I could not feature myself as one. His reply to this did nothing else than pull my cork. He said he didn't see why I should deny my race. This made me mad, and I was all for going to his office and telling him what was what in no uncertain terms, even at the risk of losing him as my publisher. Friends dissuaded me, and I let the matter drop, but not without having explained to them the facts of my racial actuality.

Cain [*sic*] came out. The reviews were splendid. It didn't sell well, but it made its literary mark—that was all I asked.

Meanwhile, since I was a human being as well as a writer, since I was living in this modern world of multiple experience as well as in the world of words and books, some extra-literary things had happened to me. Of these happenings, the only line that I will follow briefly is that which led me into the Gurdjieff work.

---

*I cannot explain the reason for this interesting spelling error in the typed manuscript. The reference obviously is to *Cane*.

The Gurdjieff Experience

I t will be remembered that, on leaving the University of Wisconsin and returning home, I started on my way to chaos. Through the years that followed I got bumped and broken, mentally and emotionally. Only my body held out. Spiritually I was plunged into the fundamental problems of this era; and the plunge, though invaluable as a means to the expansion of my consciousness and my conscious individualization, dislocated my parts.

This dislocation, together with the accompanying need to integrate myself, persisted in my inner life even while exteriorly I achieved some measure of order, balance, and direction. (I was a bit of chaos dressed in formal attire.) Or, to be accurate, I should say that the dislocation persisted off and on, sometimes being resolved in the intensity of a period of functioning but then coming into evidence again when such a period passed.

During the winter of 1923, owing to a complex of causes, my writing stopped; and my disharmony became distressingly prominent. So it became clear that my literary occupations had not worked deep to make of me an integrated man. Had it done so for others?

Now I looked questioningly, not at the book, but at the writer of it. This was an heretical focus. Only their liking for me kept my colleagues from pronouncing excommunication. What I saw, or believed I saw, was at once disquieting and challenging. I saw that these people, writers and artists, men and women, were much like myself with respect to the chaos of their personal lives—but that, unlike myself, they were unwilling, or in any case uneager, to search for a whole way of living that would make them whole. True, some of them talked about it. Some of them talked about "the end of a direction" and "a new slope of consciousness." Few of them felt the urgent need to *do* anything about it. They suffered, therefore; and their art too. Great art, I was convinced, could issue only from great human beings. Small men could not produce really big books. Twisted, thwarted, confused men could only express their confusion.

The resistance of my fellows further aroused me. I talked to them and thus talked to myself. I studied them and thus learned about myself. I urged them, and thus urged myself.

Old sayings came to my mind as if they were my sayings. "Physician, heal thyself." "Know thyself." "The first duty of an artist in a sick world is to become well." And the like.

I became the champion of something nonliterary, nonartistic and—I must confess—at that time unknown to myself. I must also confess that I became a sort of Socratic pest. I realize it now, looking back. They were still writing, even if I was not. They were still going on in their way, bumpily and circular though it was, even if I had come to the dead end of a direction and realized that the course of my life had led through mazes into a blind alley. I should have let them alone.

True, a pest to most of my colleagues—but a discoverer to myself. I was working something out.

In the course of this work I came to certain realizations that prepared for the revolution of my life.

The modern world was uprooted, the modern world was breaking down, *but we couldn't go back.* There was nothing to go back to. Besides, in our hasty leaps into the future we had burned our bridges. The soil, the earth was still there, even under city pavements and congested sky scrapers.

But such peasantry as America had had—and I sang one of its swan songs in *Cain* [*sic*]—was swiftly disappearing, swiftly being industrialized and urbanized by machines, motor cars, phonographs, movies .. "Back to nature," even if desirable, was no longer possible, because industry had taken nature unto itself. Even if he wanted to, a city person could not become a soil person by changing his locale and living on a farm or in the woods.

So then, whether we wished to or not, we *had to go on.* We had to go on and accept the task of creating a *human world* that was at least as conducive to man's well-being and growth as the world of nature was conducive to the growth of plant and animal life. The creation of a human world, this was our task. Those who sought to cure themselves by a return to more primitive conditions were either romantics or escapists. We had to project real values and then realize them in full-bodied life. And this included everyone in America, and everyone in western civilization who had arisen—or who had been pushed—above the grass line. So I sought for the means of going on. I would work to be able to contribute my share to the building of a functioning civilization in these modern times. I too, because I must be, would be a builder of the world. This was my general outlook, my general stand.

The problems of life were not respecters of colors or of racial groups. The basic problems of modern life had caught up white and colored alike, Northerners and Southerners, Americans and Europeans. These problems were the modern boat. Everyone was in this boat. Each one had to pull his oar, else we sink. The task of solving them was at every man's door, in his house, in his body and soul.

Specific problems like race problems, nationality problems, and others which were outgrowths of the general condition, could move towards a fruitful resolution only on the condition that the general basic issues were thus moved. Any attempt to solve a specific issue on the assumption that it was isolated and could be cured by itself, was foredoomed to failure. On this ground I rejected such attempts, without of course denying that they sometimes had good and necessary immediate effects in the matter of improving practical day to day living conditions.

The basic issues were, in my view, (1) economic, and (2) psychological and spiritual.

Our economic system had run away with itself and was doing damage not only to the proletarians and the petty bourgeoisie, but to the capitalists as well. All classes and all groups were involved in the mutilation.

Our psyches were split and chaotic. Our spirits were shrunken. Our souls were empty. To compensate for this emptiness, to avenge our tortured slow deaths, we had grown fangs and sacks of poison; and we used these fangs—race fangs, sex fangs, class fangs, national and religious fangs, all manner of personal fangs—with typical man-insanity against each other.

The unhappy person, unless great, is poisonous. The happy person, even if small, is sweet. It is not reasonable to expect that a man who is being destroyed will help others to live.

So, what?

(1) A constructive change of the economic system. I, however, had no special talent in this field. From experience, temperament, and interest, it was not my field, except insofar as I, together with everyone else, was involved in it; hence, my contribution at best would be minor. Hence, I would leave this field to others, and concern myself with the issues which, more and more, I had come to realize I could handle best—namely, the psychological spiritual issues.

Because of my personal experience, my ups and downs, my I-am-I states, and my I-am-nothing states, I was fairly well convinced that in man there was a curious duality—an "I," a something that was not I; an inner being, an outer personality. I was further convinced that the inner being was the real thing, that the outer personality was the false thing; that the "I" was the source of life, that the personality was the sack of poison. The question was—how to bring man together into an integrated complete whole. My answer was—by increasing the "I" while at the same time eliminating the personality. But I had no method, no means of doing this.

Also because of my personal experiences, my disorganization of parts, I was convinced that the parts of man—his mind, emotions, and body— were radically out of harmony with each other. But how to bring them into harmony? I did not have a means of doing this.

I discussed these matters with almost everyone I came in contact with. To me they were the really vital matters, and my heart and mind were concentrated on them.

Nobody could help me. Many people did not even get the point. Each one himself a specialist, and therefore lopsided, was content to pursue his speciality; achieve, if he could, some distinction in it; and let the rest— namely, his *whole* life—go hang.

It was just at this time that first A. R. Orage and then Gurdjieff himself came to America. A pamphlet of the Gurdjieff Institute came into my hands. In it I found expressed, more completely and with more authority than with anything possible from me, just the conditions of man which I myself had realized. More-over, a method, a means of *doing something about it* was promised. It was no wonder that I went heart and soul into the Gurdjieff work.

Here was a work that gave man direction and helped him move on the way out of the chaos of modern civilization. Here was a work that indicated what must be done in order to achieve a balanced development. Here was work whose scope was greater and more complete than anything I had dreamed of. Here, in fine, was truth.

That summer I went to the institute at Fontainebleau, prepared to stay there or in some similar place for the rest of my life or in any case until I had fulfilled my human needs as far as possible under those extraordinary conditions. After a time, because of a motor accident to himself, Gurdjieff closed the institute. I remained there a month or so longer and then returned to America and became a member of the groups then being conducted by Orage. These groups and the life that grew out of them became my life. I was worlds removed from the literary set. I knew little or nothing of what was happening in it. That I had once written a book called *Cain* [*sic*] seemed remote. What had happened to it I neither knew nor cared. Much less I knew of what was happening in the Negro world.

Gradually, however, I began making other contacts, I began awakening with interest to the wide activities of that time. Then I discovered, among other things, that a ferment was in the Negro world also, a literary ferment, and that it was producing a new literature. I was sufficiently moved to write an article. After this I viewed the movement as a splendid thing but as something that had no special meaning for me. *

Time passed.

The next I knew I received a visit from Alain Locke. Locke said he was getting together a book of Negro material and wanted something I had written, preferably a new story or a story from *Cain* [*sic*]. I replied that I had written no new stories of that kind and did not want *Cain* [*sic*] dismembered. He pressed. I thought of the article. I offered it to him. It turned out that he did not want it. My expressed attitude was—this article or nothing. I concluded that the matter was finished. Before Locke left he talked to me about Winold Reis, the artist. He said Reis was doing interesting things and had expressed a desire to do a portrait of me. He urged me to sit for Reis, never mentioning that he himself would use the portrait in his book.

Out of curiosity or vanity or something, I did sit for Reis; and, so far as I knew, that was that.

But when Locke's book, *The New Negro,* came out, there was the Reis portrait, and there was a story from *Cane,* and there in an introduction, were words about me which have caused as much or more misunderstanding than Waldo Frank's! †

However, there was and is, among others, this great difference between Frank and Locke. Frank helped me at a time when I most needed help. I will never forget it. Locke tricked and misused me.

For a short time after the appearance of Locke's book I was furious—

---

* A decade earlier, in 1922, however, Toomer had informed Sherwood Anderson about his desire to found a magazine that would stimulate the consciousness of Negroes.

†Despite these feelings, which Toomer recalled from the perspective of the 1930s, Toomer, after *The New Negro* was published in 1925, gave Locke permission to use the drama ''Balo'' in Locke's *Plays of Negro Life* (1927), even though it is reported that Toomer insisted that the title should not suggest that all the authors were Negro.

because I felt blocked. I could not take my article* and portrait out of it. I could not, without risk of putting myself in a false light, publicly explain the trick that had been played on me. My dear enemies, those who liked to misrepresent me, would have echoed Horace Liveright and said at once, "Toomer wants to deny his race." To have said the thing right I would have had to write something not much less than my auto-biography. Well, I shrugged and let it drop—but not without a pretty sharp sense of the irony of the situation. My writing, namely, the very thing that should have made me understood, was being so presented and interpreted that I was now much more misunderstood in this respect than at any other time of my life.

Yet even this misunderstanding did not strike me as being serious when my emotions cooled. I was living in New York. So far as I knew, I would never live anywhere else permanently. I had my life and work. So far as I could foresee I would have no other life or work. I had my friends and our sufficiently absorbing activities. The racial thing, in so far as it existed, had its proportioned place in the scale of values—and this was all I asked. It made no difference what I was called. The label "Negro" was of no more consequence than any other.

At times, however, I did have a feeling that I was letting the thing slide; and I had a feeling that the slide was gathering momentum. When such feelings came to me, I thought about the situation with some concern. I felt I ought to do something. I felt I should write a book stating who and what I actually was. It was now clear to me that if I didn't, surely no one else would—and why should they?

I can not tell why I did not write that book then. Perhaps it was because I sincerely felt that it didn't matter. Perhaps it was because I did not want to put such emphasis on this one thing, which, in my actual life from day to day, was not emphatic. Perhaps I foresaw that my book might cause even more misunderstanding, though of a different kind. I was, as you can see, in a difficult position; and perhaps the simple truth is that I was not equal to the handling of it. It would be a difficult book to write. It still is.†

---

* "Carma" and "Fern" (from *Cane*) and poems by Toomer are in *The New Negro,* but there is no article or essay.

† After a few additional pages, Toomer apparently abandoned the project, which was leading to another autobiography.

Section II

FICTION

Editor's Note

Some readers will be disappointed that only three stories by Toomer appear in this book. The limited number represents a compromise. Editors at several publishing companies to which I submitted a selection of Toomer's stories feared that the quality and content might damage Toomer's reputation. I have insisted, however, that a representative sample must be included in order that contemporary readers may see for themselves what kinds of stories Toomer wrote in addition to those published in *Cane*. For such illustrative purposes, I wished to include three additional stories that focus on man's problems with ego and emotion. Nevertheless, I believe that the three stories published here represent a sampling of Toomer's best fiction apart from *Cane*.

Composed early in his career, "Withered Skin of Berries" is marked by the style and thought familiar to readers of *Cane*. Lyrically, Toomer explores a woman's gropings for psychological identity, and he considers the problems of racial identity and bigotry. David Teyy is one of the fictionalized characters in whom Toomer pictured himself as the savior/leader of Woman, who must be liberated from society's conventions. Although the story takes place in Washington, Toomer extracted the theme and the bigot Carl from his experiences at the University of Wisconsin in Madison.

Published in *Second American Caravan: A Yearbook of American Literature* (1928), "Winter on Earth" fuses Toomer's lyricism and his Gurdjieffan thought. Assuming society's ignorance to be only one evidence of mankind's need for spiritual reorientation, Toomer suggests the icy desolation that results from man's loss of Eden—his failure to achieve harmony with himself, his fellow man, and his universe.

"Mr. Costyve Duditch," published in *Dial* 85 (December 1928), sketches a man who has "grown out of harmony" with himself. Employing the satirical style characteristic of his post-*Cane* years, Toomer characterizes Duditch as a wanderer whose worldwide travels have failed to sophisticate him to the art of living and interacting with people.

The versions of both "Winter on Earth" and "Mr. Costyve Duditch" in this volume, however, are based on Toomer's manuscripts rather than on the earlier published versions.

The stories which my appeals could not persuade publishers to include are "Drackman," the story of a businessman ravaged by materialistic egomania; "Lump," a story describing a businessman horrified by fear that he has cancer and humiliated by the demeaning experiences at the public clinic to which he has reported for examination; and "Love on a Train," in which a work-jaded physician learns that romance must be accepted as a temporary pleasure rather than a permanent commitment.

Toomer reached the conclusion of this style (I hesitate to term it the apex) in two works not included in this book—"The Gallonwerps" and "Of a Certain November." A heavy-handed satire composed both as a novel and a drama, "The Gallonwerps" castigates a society that applauds those who can deceive it, that hires a nurse (the superego) to control its desires (the id), and that needs a savior who will free the id from the superego. Written after Roosevelt's election and published in the *Dubuque Dial* (November 1935), "Of a Certain November" is an absurdist interior dialogue of the selves of Mr. Doofle Tack, who is helplessly dependent upon the materialistic panaceas, such as "Tropic Glow," which guarantees warmth in the coldest of times. Three longer works of fiction include his novels "Caromb," "Transatlantic" (revised as "Eight Day World") and his novelette *York Beach* (published in *The New American Caravan*, 1929).

In these selections, I have not altered Toomer's punctuation, except to insert commas where appropriate in statements of direct address.

Withered Skin of Berries

I

Men listen to her lispings and murmurs. Black souls steal back to Georgia canefields, soft and misty, underneath a crescent moon. The mystery of their whispered promises seems close to revelation, seems tangibly incarnate in her. Black souls, tropic and fiery, dream of love. Sing joyful codas to forgotten folk-songs. Spin love to the soft weaving of her arms. Men listen to her lispings and murmurs. White souls awake to adolescent fantasies they thought long buried with the dead leaves along the summer streets of mid-western towns. Solvents of melancholy burn through their bitten modes of pioneer aggressiveness to a southern repose. They too spin love to the soft weaving of her arms. White men, black men, only in retrospective kisses, know the looseness of her lips .. pale withered skin of berries...

*　　*　　*

Departmental buildings are grey gastronomic structures, innocuously coated with bile. They pollute the breath of Washington. Washington's breath is sickish and stale because of them. With the slow, retarded process of dyspeptics, they suck the life of mediocrities. They secrete a strange preservative that keeps flesh and bones intact after the blood is dry..Vera is a typist. She is a virgin. A virgin whose notion of purity tape-worms her. Men sense her corporeal virginity. Her slim body, her olive skin, clear as white grapes held to the sun, are pure. Sandalwood odor of her thick brown hair, the supplication of her eyes, her lifeless lips, all pure. Men like to paw pure bodies. They adore them. So Vera came to find out. "They only want to paw me." She blamed the beast in men, black men especially. Pure bodies tease. So the men found out. "Vera is a tease." The thought found its way to her. She set up her creed: Tease the beast.. Vera is a typist. She is neither more nor less palatable than the other morsels that come in from South Carolina, Illinois, or Oregon. But there is a condiment-like irritability in the process of her digestion. Unquestionably, Vera is white. Routine segregates niggers. Black life seems more soluble in lump. White life, pitiably agitated to superiority, is more palatable. Black life is pepper to the salt of white. Pepper in the nose of white. Sneezes are first-rate aids to digestion. Unquestionably, Vera is white. Her fellow workers sneeze about the niggers. Niggers are all right as janitors, as messengers; in fact, anywhere where they keep their place. Niggers, despite their smell and flat feet, aren't so bad. They are good to joke about. Sneezes over colored girls using powder and straightening their kinky hair to look like white. But it is a different thing when niggers try to pass for white. They are slick at it. Youve got to watch out. But there is always a way of telling: finger-nails, and eyes, and odor, and oh, any number of things. Vera listens to them, smiles, jokes, laughs, sometimes with a curious gurgle-like flutter, says goodby to them of evenings outside the office door, and rides uptown to the respite of a Negro home.

Carl. A fellow in the office. From a small town across the lake from Chicago where his father is an independent dealer in oil. Carl got in the government service to earn a little money against the coming of a dream he had. He would be rich some day—when his uncle died. He had plans for the conquest of the Argentine. He had studied agriculture at Wisconsin. He read books, and even took a correspondence course in foreign trade. Spanish he was learning from Cortina. He went out of his way to pick acquaintances with South Americans, Spaniards, and Portuguese. This trait it was that first led him to Vera. She looked Spanish. Casual remarks led to their having lunch together. Carl was sincere. He held roseate and chivalrous notions of womanhood. His enthusiasm bid well to hold out, for a time, against the stale utilitarian atmosphere of governmental Washington. In the office, and during the brief strolls they had after lunch, the inward anemia of Vera fed on it. She liked him. She established a sort of moral equilibrium and dulled a growing sense of deceit by resolving not to tease him. Carl wanted to take her home, to call on her, to take her to the movies, to Penn Gardens, to the dances the office gave. She put him off. Her soft reticence and sly evasions implied purity, evoked an aura of desirability and charm. Carl was buying a car, a Dodge. One afternoon in early spring the departments were given a holiday. It was unexpected. Vera could not possibly have any plans for it, and Carl told her so. He insisted on the falsity of the reasons she gave for refusing to drive with him. Vera was more than usually nervous that day. Carl's stubbornness irritated her. She felt herself getting hot, as if her nerves were heated pins and needles pricking her. That would not do. Carl's friendship made the office tolerable. He took hold her arm. Vera went with him.

Driving down Seventeenth Street, Carl only spoke to call the name of buildings. That was the Corcoran Gallery of Art, that, the Pan-American building. Negroes were working on the basin of an artificial lake that was to spread its smooth glass surface before Lincoln's Memorial. The shadow of their emancipator stirred them neither to bitterness nor awe. The scene was a photograph on Vera's eye-balls. Carl was concentrated on the road. He squirmed skillfully in the traffic that was getting dense. The exotic fragrance of cherry blossoms reached them, slightly rancid as it mingled with the odor of exploded gasoline. As they passed the crescent line of blossomed trees, a group of Japanese, hats off, were seen reverently lost in race memories of reed lutes, jet black eyebrows, and jeweled palanquins. Consciously, the episode meant nothing to Vera. But an unprecedented nostalgia, a promise of awakening, making her feel faint, clutched her throat almost to stricture, and made her swallow hard. Her face was pallid. Carl noticed it and said he guessed it was the heat from the engine and the motion of the car.. A word was struggling with her throat.. They swung into the speedway. Potomac's water was muddy, streaked with sea-weed. A tug, drawing a canal barge from miles in the interior, blew its whistle for the bridge to turn and let it by. Across the river, the green, and white marble splotches of Virginia's hills. Curious for her, lines of a poem came unbidden to her mind:

far-off trees
Whose gloom is rounded like the hives of bees
All humming peace to soldiers who have gone.

She was trying to think where she had heard them. They hadnt impressed her at the time. No poems ever did. She would not let them. A word was struggling with her throat.. Carl called her attention to the superb grace of a Pierce Arrow that glided by. They had reached the point. A hydroplane was humming high above the War College.—That man, what was his name? Who Arthur Bond introduced to me the other night. Who hardly noticed me, he was so stuck up. Whom Art called a genius, and the poet of Washington. The lines, she felt sure, were his. Yes, Art had recited them.—What was his name? He had irritated her. He was closed up in himself. She had felt she could not tease him.—Well, so much the worse for Art Bond. What was his name? Men were fishing, casting their lines from the river wall. Straight ahead, between low banks of trees, the Potomac rolled its muddy course, and, miles away, emptied into the Chesapeake. Smoke from Alexandria was blown up-stream by the river breeze.

"What do you say we run out the Conduit road to Cabin John's and make a day of it?"

Vera answered automatically.

"Sorry I cant to-day. I have an engagement at eight."

"Youve broken what should have been mine enough to break one date with him."

The almost perfect white of his skin was flushed, and rubbed to glowing by the wind. The hair he brushed so smooth was free and rumpled. His grey eyes were eagerly expectant. Vera's seemed to be glowing with prana. The coils of her hair threatened to uncurl and stream out backward like loose waves of silken bunting. Her skirt, rustling and flapping, was pressed close to her thighs.

"What do you say? We'll have dinner there, and afterwards go on to Great Falls. It would be a crime to waste a day like this."

Bud of a word was bursting in her throat.

"Beautiful!"

"Good. I knew youd go. Come on, lets get on our way."

"It is a word I've never said before."

"You bet it is. But youve said it now—no more holding off like you used to do. 'Yes' is a word that once said can be said again. Oh I knew you would someday, Vera, but what made you wait so long? Look at the good times we have already missed. Come on. Lets make up for lost time."

Carl held her hand and was propelling her. A little startled, she looked at him.

"Where are you pulling me, Carl?"

That was a good move on Vera's part. Carl had never seen her playful. Good. He'd play the game.

"To the sand-dunes of Lake Michigan where two loves build a bungalow."

"Really, Carl, I mean it. Where are you pulling me to?"

A fly-like shadow of doubt lit on Carl. He tossed his head, and drove it off.

"Just where I said: to the sand-dunes, where rippling waves make music all the time."

Vera realized that she must have promised something. Well, why not. She let herself be pulled. She'd cover herself with play. Her hair uncurled.

"Beautiful Michigan's azure waves—"

"Fine! Sweet! O poetess of Benton Harbor!"

"How many rooms will the bungalow be?"

Carl was completely red.

"Three."

Shadows of clouds, lazy-like, were gliding over the canopy-trees of the Potomac palisades. Below, the river, eddying in shallows, churning to a cream foam against mud-colored rocks, was carrying the brown burden of a wasted sediment . . . John's Brown's body . . . from Harper's Ferry to the Chesapeake and the sea. Carl and Vera spun along the smooth asphalt of Conduit Road. The country beside the pike was dotted now and then by clustered shanties—poor white homes. Carl was quite happily absorbed in the handling of his car. It was vaguely good to have her there beside him. Vera, since she had come with him, would have been hurt to know her temporary relegation to the position of a pleasant accessory. Silence released her for the uncertain attempt at recapturing a mood which, save as an unreal memory, was new and strange to her. Art Bond. . What was his name? What dreams she had had, always swerved up from the concrete image of a man. The mood that had struggled to a hesitant and spattered ecstasy, that had forced some unused crevice of her soul to a vocalization of beauty, came from—What was his. .? She could not tease him. That hurt her. She had thrust him from her mind. Even his image would not come. The mood lay fallow before the unfound symbol of its evocation.

Carl was chatting over his cigarettes and cheese and coffee.

"You are sympathetic, Vera, and you'll understand. America, now the war is over, dont give a young fellow with push and brains and energy half a chance. Of course you can make money with a million. It makes itself. But what I want is not to loaf around and see it grow, or get tied down to some machine where even if you are a captain of industry youre no more than a petty officer in the army. Thats not what America stands for; but its what it is. And going to be more so in the future. The spirit of the country is one of individual enterprise. But unless it be in the oil-fields—and there the Standard gets you—its dying out, or, rather, its passing on to new lands. Now the Argentine is virginal. Or if not the Argentine, then some of those smaller countries. Theyre now just where this country was when Vanderbilt and Carnegie and Rockefeller first came up. Why a young fellow with go can go down there and clean up. But he's got to be quick about it. Ford and other men are pushing out over the world. . It sounds hard to say it, but I wish the Uncle would hurry up—and do whatever he's going to do. I'm studying hard—and say, Vera, heres where you can help me if you will. Lets talk Spanish when we're together. I dont know so much yet, but you can help me.''

"I'd like to Carl, but I dont know any more Spanish than you do.''

"But I thought—''

"If someone has told you that I am of Spanish descent, its true. My great grandfather was a Spaniard, but I was born in America, just like you. English is the only language that I know. Except for the smattering of others that I've picked up in school.''

"I didnt think that you acted like a foreigner. Theyre all right, you know. I'm not prejudiced against them like I am against the niggers. A couple of them are friends of mine. Foreigners, I mean. But they do act a little different.''

"Why do you hate niggers?''

"Hang if I know. Dont you?''

"Sometimes.''

"Of course I dont hate them like these southern fellows do. And not as much as I hate Jews. The kikes are spreading all over the country; you see their names everywhere. There was one I remember at Wisconsin. He went out for football. We tried to break him up. And then there was Bugger—thats what we called the nigger—he was a good sort of fellow, and we had good fun with him. A good linesman—tackle he was—but he didnt make the team. Ever been to Madison, Vera? Swell place. Ideal location for a college town. A few snobs like there are everywhere, but most of the men came from the middle-west—good fellows, Vera. Youd like them. And there was one colored fellow I remember—say, did you ever see Sang Osmond run? Conference quarter miler from Chicago. I ran against him once. Clean cut fellow, good sport—I liked him. Niggers arent so bad, if only they didnt look so.''

"All colored people arent disagreeable—''

"No, of course not. Theres Osmond. But you cant judge people by their exceptions. Look what we would have come to if we'd tried to believe that all Germans toed the mark of a man, say, like Beethoven.''

"Why judge at all?''

"Good lord, Vera, youve got to have something to go by. Take me, when I go down into South America. I'll feel superior to those greasers—all Americans do. And thats the reason why we're running things.... Come on, lets get out of here and run up to the falls before it gets too dark.''

"Dont forget that I have an engagement at eight.''

"Hang it, Vera, I thought youd broken it.''

"That wouldnt be right, Carl. You wouldnt want me to break one with you. I've been with you all day. And there are other times."

She had meant to make this the first and last.

"All right. Its a go. We'll make it Friday. Dance some place, and then take a drive. Thats closed. Come on, lets hurry up."

Carl paid the waiter.

The Dodge was purring along towards Great Falls.

Parked. They crossed a narrow springy toll-bridge into the clump of wood that vibrates like a G-string to the deep bass of the falls. Dusk, subtly scented violet, sprayed through the scant foliage of clustered trees. Carl's skin was of a greenish pallor. Vera's, almost as purple as the dusk. The agitation of the ground, the fall's thunder, conjured the sense of an impending lightning. Vera shivered. Carl drew her close to him. As they walked, she began to fancy she saw things behind the trunks and rocks, hiding in the bushes. A twig cracked. Vera's jumping upset Carl. But only for a moment. The heavy pounding of the falls was getting nearer. Quarter heaven in the west, the evening star. She pressed his arm. He was holding her waist. Slender, supple waist, trembling at unseen terrors in the forest. Carl would walk in many forests. Across great wastes and plains. The pampa grass, great stationary sea. Villages of untamed Indians. Stealthy marauding savages. This little wood near Washington was tame. Vera, for no reason, vaguely thought of Africa. She shivered. Carl stopped in their now winding path, and kissed her. Her lips were cool. Carl did not think of them as pale withered skin of berries. They reached the high-piled rocks. Footing was insecure. Vera stumbled. Carl lifted her in his arms. Carrying her, he almost fell over lovers hidden in the alcove of a giant boulder. With apologies, he moved on some paces, and set her down. The falls were below them. The foam, the dark suggestion of whirl-pools, were weird, wildly arush. One's shouting voice was barely heard above a whisper. Vera leaned against him. Her mind was blank. It was just good to be held in his arms. A flickering light, a torch perhaps, flared up on the other bank. An intangibly phosphorescent glow gave light. Sandalwood odor of hair. Carl's conscious mind had not planned on love. With a million coming, things could wait. It came. Love was a tender joy, protective-like, that gave soft scents of sandalwood above the din of churning waters, beneath the chaste fire of the evening star.

They too had found a boulder. One's voice could be heard. Vera seated Indian fashion, responding, perhaps, to some folk persuasion of the place, rested Carl's head in her lap. Carl had been talking brokenly, trying to tell himself just how he felt. Her holding him made it easier to think. If it was love, it was curiously without passion. Passion was not love; but it was a part of it. One should pretend not to feel too much until one was married. But hiding it, and not feeling it at all, were two different things. "Once at Madison," he said aloud to Vera, "I felt like this." Her mind wanted Vera to listen. She must not tease or play with him.—Tease Art Bond though. Its almost time, it must be time, for my date with him. What was his name? O wont you come to me. Poet. I will not admit that he ever did or ever could hurt me. Oh yes and just you wait, I'll tease him too. Him whom I cannot tease. Who put beauty, a senseless warm thing like a sucking baby, in my mouth.

"I have never said it before."

"Said what, Vera?"

"Oh, nothing."

"As I was saying, he was an odd sort of chap. Peculiar, and most of the fellows resented it. It wasnt that he was stuck up. We couldnt see any reason why he should be. Enough money, but not too much at that. And I dont guess his folks were anything to brag about. He never mentioned them. In fact he never mentioned anything unless you sort of forced him to it. It looked as though he was acting up to mystery, and all that sort of thing. And then he was dark, and that made some difference. I gave him the duck until it came to summer school and myself and two other fellows from the frat moved over to the Y and on the sleeping porch I found myself in the bed next to him. We got to talking, and walking up the hill together. One day he asked me if I'd like to sail with him, him and two girls. He was strong for girls. That started it. And say, you should have seen him with that boat, as neat as I can handle a six-horse plow. We went to dances, and swam around a bit. One night he took me in his canoe. Just him and I. The moon was shining. When we got out in the middle of the lake, he slid down on the bottom, on the cushions, and began to hum. Yodels and singing were coming from canoes all over the water. I didnt notice him at first. And then, something like a warm finger seemed to touch my heart. I cant just explain it. I looked around and saw him. His eyes, set in that dark face, looked like two stars. 'Put the paddle in,' he said, 'we'll drift.' I did. 'Turn around and slide over the bar, theres a cushion on the bottom for you,' he then said. He saw me try, tip the canoe, and hesitate. 'Come on, dont be afraid, youre with an Indian, pale-face friend.' Saying that, way out in the middle of the lake, surrounded by shores that were once the home of Indians, made me feel strange and queer, you bet. Lights gleaming from the boat-house were far to shore. I made it, and again he started humming. 'Are you an Indian, really?' I asked. He kept on humming. And God if it didnt raise a lump the size of an apple in my throat. 'Whats that?' I asked. 'A negro folk-song,' he stopped long enough to say. 'God, I didnt know niggers could sing like that.' An answer, I guess, wasnt necessary. Abruptly he stopped singing, and I could feel him quiver-like—''

—He does not paw me. His arms embrace the shadow of a dream. I cannot tease him. His dream is a solvent of my resolution. He has taken something from me. It will be harder to face the office. I'd like to hate him for it. Easier to face the office because I share his dream. Will it melt something in me? Why cant I feel? If Art Bond should dream, I could not tease him. Time to go. What was his name? Will no one ever awake a dream in me? Poet. He must be like the fellow Carl is talking about. Him whom I cannot tease. What is his name? Who put beauty, a senseless warm thing like a sucking baby, in my mouth.

"I have never said that before."

"There you go again. Said what, Vera? Youre not listening."

"Oh nothing. Yes I am. Go on, Carl."

"I could feel him quiver-like. 'Carl,' he said, his eyes were gleaming, 'the wonder and mystery of it.' I had a quick foolish notion that he was trying to play up to the role we'd given him. Then I think I began to feel like he did. 'Dead leaves of northern Europe, Carl, have decayed for roots tangled here in America. Roots thrusting up a stark fresh life. Thats you. Multi-colored leaves, tropic, temperate, have decayed for me. We meet here where a race has died for both of us. Only a few years ago, forests and fields, this lake, Mendota, heard the corn and hunting songs of a vanished people. They have resolved their individualism to the common stream. We live on it. We live on them. And we are growing. Life lives on itself and grows.. The mystery and wonder of it.' He paused. And then, 'Deep River spreads over Mendota. Whirl up and dance above them new world soul!' God if he hadnt stirred me. Songs, and young girls' voices yodeling, criss-crossed on the waters. He turned to me and asked, 'Carl, you are a field man, have you ever felt overpowered by the sum of some-thing, of which plowed fields, blue sky, and sunset were a part, over-powered till you sank choking with wonder and reverence?' I had, almost, once. I told him. He closed his hand over mine. Me, a football man, holding hands with a man on the lake. If that had ever got out it would have done for me. But it never did. I could never tell it. Only to you.

You are the first. And thats the point of all I've told you. I feel like that
with you, here by the falls, in the shadow of a boulder where some Indian
made love.''

Carl's words were strange to him.

Vera shivered.

''Chilly?''

''A little.''

Carl shifted positions and took her in his arms. He kissed her lips ..
pale withered skin of berries, puckered a little tight .. and drew her to
him with a tension that was more muscular than passionate...

> John Brown's body, rumbles in the river,
> John Brown's body, thunders down the falls..

''What was that Carl?''

''I didnt hear a thing, sweetheart.''

It would be good to fall in love with Carl, really. With anybody. Tease?
Her mind said that because no man torrential enough—but there had
been men, men with swift brutal passions—they didnt love. They
bruised her with their instincts, bruised and frightened and disgusted
her .. she must keep her body pure.. Carl didnt paw. He loved as she
had long wanted men to. Why couldnt she feel? She recalled that she
had not had a genuine emotion in the presence of a man .. at night,
when she was alone .. since her last affair at home. Ugly. Why were men
so callous? Brutal in insisting on her sacrifice. Then they wouldnt want
her .. she must keep her body pure. Why couldnt she feel? This was pure
love. Why couldnt she feel to return it? Feel for him the emotion that had
spattered in ''beautiful.'' Perhaps—Vera, lead in her heart, faced the
possibility, that, for some unknown reason, maybe she really couldnt love.
Some shameful defect made her incapable of it. She pressed Carl close to
her. Held him to her lips. Tensioned thighs. Her heart beat faster. She
strained. Carl's strength was tender. Why couldnt she feel? Something in
her felt like it was empty. Men poured themselves into her because she
was empty..

''Its time to go, now, Carl.''

''I had forgotten. Of course, sweetheart.''

Deep bass of the falls seemed coming from a throat that had been
turned the other way... John Brown's body... They crossed the toll-
bridge and found their car.

As Carl swung into S Street from Sixteenth, Vera saw Art Bond come
out of her gate, and walk their way. The car passed. He did not see them.

With a hasty goodby she ran up the steps and waited in the vestibule until Carl had gone. Coming down, Vera called to Art who was standing, undecided, on the corner. He seemed impersonalized, a shadow, beneath the great bulk of the Masonic Temple.

"I had a car, and everything," Art was irritably saying.

"I'm sorry Art, I tried to be on time. Is it so very late?"

"How'd you get in anyway? Was that you in that car?"

"I dropped from the stars."

"It was a Dodge. Whose was it? Dave Teyy's?"

"What a simple name!"

Her eyes were sparkling.

"I dont guess its too late yet; that is, if you really want to go."

"And I have been searching, Oh how I have been searching all afternoon."

Vera seemed talking to the apex of the Temple.

"Now whats the use of lying, Vera? You could have found me easy enough if you wanted to."

"David Teyy."

"Oh hang him, Vera. Youre with me now. That is, if you want to go."

Vera looked down into a dark serious face, mobile and expressive, like shifting, sun-shot dusk.

"Of course I want to go, Art. Where's the car?"

"Can I use your phone a minute?"

Vera was hard to talk to, hard to touch to-night. It was to lead her into a mood for loving when they reached the park that Art had hired a car. The Cadillac had hummed up Sixteenth Street, like a shuttle, between the Castle and Meridian Hill, past the portentous embassies. Turning, it had followed the curve of Park Road, across the broad bridge blanketed in a chill vapor. Down the hill, hemmed in by the quickening life of Rock Creek Park. The driver had been dismissed and told to return within an hour. During the whole ride Vera seemed absorbed in herself, and kept to her corner of the car. The wind whistled on the sharp edge of an invisible partition that was between them. Now they sat, Vera hugging her knees, on the slope of a knoll within earshot of the purling of the creek. Great curved massy trees in sharp planes of shadow and moonlight. Mountain clouds, fleecy silver. Massive undulations, barely perceptible—earth's respiration, earth breathing to life. Vera felt dwarfed. She felt that Art could be of no aid to her. Dwarfed by the great heaving blocks of nature. By the shadow of a man. David Teyy. He should be riding the backs of trees, spurring them to swing up and trumpet. Him whom she could not tease. Who put beauty, a senseless warm thing like a sucking baby— Suppose I cannot love him? The thought gave her a sinking feeling, and made her shiver.

"Chilly."

"A little."

Art tucked a robe around her shoulder. He stretched out, lit a cigarette. Women were like that; you had to wait for them. Vera was thankful for the glow of Art's cigarette. It was a small point one could look at. Narrowing her eyes, Art's face looked like a far-off mountain, faintly ruddy, beneath the supernal glowing of a red star. Black man, white man, lips seeking love, souls dreaming.. Man of the multi-colored leaves, dreaming, will your lips seek love? Vera raised her hand, delicate, tapering olive fingers, and pressed it against her lips .. pale withered skin of berries.. The contact was loose and cool. Her heart sank. She shivered. Art reached up and pulled her down beside him.

"Whats the matter, sugar?"

"Nothing, only I dont feel so well to-night."

"Driving all afternoon should have done better for you than that. And with Dave Teyy."

"I wasnt with him, Art."

"Now whats the use of lying, Vera?"

"I tell you I wasnt."

"Oh well, dont lets scrap about it. He's my friend. But I've got to bar him with my girls. He doesnt believe in letting them out."

"What do you mean?"

"You know what I mean."

"Well, he let me out."

"I thought you wasnt with him."

"Art, you are so stupid when you fuss. Why dont you sing, or .. love me?"

"You irritate me. You wont let me."

"There, there. Thats a good sweet boy."

Vera, softly weaving arms. Sandalwood odor of hair. Murmurs. Lispings. Art's arms tightened around her. Vera averted her lips. He kissed her throat. Caught a soft fold in his teeth and bit it.

"You mustnt Art."

"Mustnt love you?"

"Not that way. . . O cant you see I'm empty.. Art, Art I'm empty, fill me with dreams."

"With love."

"No, with dreams. Dreams of how life grows, feeding on itself. Dreams of dead leaves, multi-colored leaves. Dreams of leaves decaying for a vernal stalk, phosphorescent in the dusk, flaming in dawn. O Art, in that South from which you come, under its hates and lynchings, have you no lake, no river, no falls to sit beside and dream .. dream?"

"Red dust roads are our rivers, the swishing of the cane, our falls. I am an inland man."

"Then you have choked with the sum—O tell me, Art, tell me, I know you have."

"Beside the syrup-man?

"Beside the syrup-man."

"He comes to boil the cane when the harvest is through. He pitches camp in a clearing of the wood. You smell only the pines at first, and saw-dust smoke. Then a mule, circling with a beam, begins to grind. The syrup, toted in a barrel, is poured on the copper boiling stove. Then you begin to smell the cane. It goes to your head like wine. Men are seated round. Some chewing cane-stalk, some with snuff. They tell tales, gossip about the white folks, and about moonshine licker. The syrup-man (his clothes look like a crazy-quilt and smell sweetish) with his ladle is the center of them. His face is lit by the glow. He is the ju-ju man. Sometimes he sings, and then they all commence to singing. But after a while you dont notice them. Your soul rises with the smoke and songs above the pine-trees. Once mine rose up, and, instead of travelling about the heavens, looked down. I saw my body there, seated with the other men. As I looked, it seemed to dissolve, and melt with the others that were dissolving too. They were a stream. They flowed up-stream from Africa and way up to a height where the light was so bright I could hardly see, burst into a multi-colored spraying fountain. My throat got tight. I guess it was that that pulled me back into myself—"

—This black man from the South has choked with beauty. He does not paw me. His arms embrace the shadow of a dream. I cannot tease him. Why cant I feel? David Teyy. Can I love him? Vera shivered. Art drew her closer to him. Her arms tightened like strong slender vines across his back. Lips met. Something was tautening her lip-strings to the firmness of a bow. Their thighs were vines. Her heart beat faster. She strained. Art was a wedge .. she tried to push loose .. a black wedge of hot red life, cleaving. Arms strained against his chest. Wedge .. cleaving.. Trees whirl! Stab. Stampede. Spinning planes, shadow, silver. Night thrust back before a burning light. They were rolling, over, over, down the hill. . Trees stand still, glowering, in a stationary sky. Trees continuing to whirl. Art's lips still clung to her. She clawed his face. Pushed at his eye. Her face was wet and grass streaked. Weeds tangled in her uncurled hair. She clawed his face.

"You are a beast. O let me go."

Wedge trying to cleave her.

"Black nigger beast."

Art swung loose, and as if a lash had cut him, groaned. Whip him lash! Art groaned, choked, groaned. Shrinking on a slave-block black man groan! His head swung loose as if his neck had been wrenched... Vera couldnt think what she had done to him. Her eyes were dizzy pendulums of her soul.

"Art.."

"...Go way .. go way .. ohhh."

"Art, what have I—"

"Go way, .. go way .. ohhh.. Go way... O why dont you go way...."

"Art, Art, have I hurt you so? O Art have I hurt you so?"

He sprang to his feet. Vera hoped he would hit her. Swung off across the road, crashed through the bushes, going towards the creek. John Brown's body .. she heard him splashing through the creek .. thunders down the falls.

Vera buried her teeth in the ground to steady the convulsions of her sobbing.

II

Vera was walking down Sixteenth Street to work. Young green leaves looked yellow in the thick flood of sunlight. Morning, clover-sweet and ruddy; melancholy morning. Vera's buoyancy seemed to rest on a nervous and slightly unreal basis. She tried to rid herself of this curious haze by walking. The muscles of her limbs were firm, the skin of her face, flushed and tight. Men passing in sleek expensive cars turned to look at her. Memory of Art was a stinging insect, aflutter, pinned down .. that it was not dead denied by her will. Carl. Carl had proposed to her. She'd put him off. Vera tried to write to her mother. That she could not bring herself to do it gave her a sense of isolation so swift and intolerable that she had rushed from the house, impotently dreading, as in a bad dream. She hid from herself in desperately trivial details of office work. And then, a vicarious peace was vouchsafed her by the innocent loveliness of external Washington. The well-paved streets, the rows of comfortable, inconspicuous houses, the men and women that walked and lived in them, established a perfect sympathy with her in her attempt to defer a settlement with life. If life would only let her alone— save when she beckoned to it. Vera was too aware of her physical loveliness to desire a complete negation. Walking to work helped her to put off. Moving pictures, dances, men whom she could handle. David Teyy. She feared to see him. As a dream, he could be evoked, a final recourse, in dispelling the evil of a too-insistent nightmare. This morning, Vera had no need of David Teyy. The young green leaves looked yellow. The air was sweet with clover. The Masonic Temple, receding over her left shoulder, was a granite chrysalis that had emerged from the mystery of moonlight and shadow into the solid implications of day. A car, full of young girls in brilliant scarfs and sport shoes, drew up to the curb. Vera heard someone call her name. One or two, she slightly recognized. Just a bunch driving to [the] office. Would she go along? They were happy about nothing. Vera caught their spirit. She reached the office tingling and aglow. Anemic thin odor of stale tobacco. She went from sash to sash, throwing up the windows. A digested fellow came in, changed his street-coat for one that had been worn glossy and thread-bare, grumbled at the draft that was coming in, cancelled Vera's efforts for fresh air with quick successive bangs, went to his desk, opened a drawer from which exuded a musty smell, drew out some papers, sharpened his pencils, and, with an habitual show of infinite diligence, virtue, and purpose, started work. Younger voices greeted her upon their arrival. Carl entered, flushed as if just from a shower-bath. He threw up the windows, He and the digested fellow had a fuss. Ingloriously routed, he whispered something into the dark coil that covered Vera's ear. She laughed. The gong rang. Flutter of those almost late. A few stragglers. Tick, tick, tick, tick, pounding of typewriters, metallic slide of files, rustle of starched paper, and the day began. Young girls who worked all month to imitate leisure class flappers. Young girls from South Carolina, Illinois, Oregon, waiting. Widows of improvident men who had been somebody in their day. Boys who had left school. Men dreaming of marriage and bungalows in Chevy Chase. Old digested fellows. Negro messengers. Something was up. The girls were whispering. A group gathered around Vera. The head-clerk looked up uneasily and scowled at them.

"What do you know about it?" one was saying.

"Shows you how slick they are."

"How'd they find out?"

"Oh she left a note-book in her desk. Somebody was looking for papers and came across it."

"What was in it?"

"Nothing, except a date she had to go to the Howard Theatre. Thats a nigger place, you know. It looked suspicious. So somebody followed her home, and saw her go out with a nigger. The chief was told, and he had her up about it. And they say she stood there brazen as anything, and said yes she was a nigger and proud of it. What do you think of that?"

"You could never have told."

"Oh yes you could. Some of them had been suspicious for a long time. And nigger blood will out. Its like Lincoln said, you can fool some of the people some of the time, but you cant fool all of the people all the time."

"But they are slick at it."

"I dont see what they want to be white for anyway. The way they boast about progress and all that youd think theyd be satisfied with their own race. But theyre not, theyre always trying to push into ours."

"Its because these northern politicians—I dont mean the President of course—coddle them. Theyd never even think of having such notions down South. In the South they know where their place is, and they keep it."

"Well, its good we caught her. It'll be a lesson to others."

"Oh, we always do. Sometimes its long, sometimes its short, but we catch up to them. You cant fool all of the people all of the time. I wonder if they know that saying of Lincoln's? Somebody ought to write it on a slip of paper and put it in their desks."

"Lets do."

"Here, Vera, you make some carbon copies."

"Are there as many as that?"

"Well, you cant tell. We've got our eyes on any number."

"Oh I cant see how anyone can be so deceitful."

Carl had drifted up.

"Whats all the row about?"

"Oh just another nigger we caught passing."

"What is it? A game or something?"

"You wouldnt think it was a game if you had been deceived and imposed upon."

"Serious as all that?"

"They'll think so by the time we get through with them."

Carl winked at Vera. The head-clerk came up, smiling behind his scowl.

"And now whats occupying the governments time?"

"Oh, nothing, just something about that Preston person."

"Yes, well, um, well better settle that at lunch. Run along now."

"Yes, Mr. Darby."

"Just as you say, Mr. Darby."

"Aurwewar, Mr. Darby."

Vera, left to herself plunged into work. Carl took her out to lunch. He insisted that she go out with him that night. Vera knew that he wanted an answer. Pressure was becoming intense, almost to suffocation. Not tonight, Carl, she had managed to say only by promising the next evening. He assured her that if she didnt give an answer to him, he would come after her. The afternoon, hugely unreal, ticked away. Reaching home, she plunged into a hot bath and tried to vaporize herself, one with its fumes. The towel but accentuated life. She had a banal observation: now I see why men drink. She tried to sleep. She exhausted herself with the tangled covers. Tossed out of bed and ran down to the phone. Yes, David Teyy would come around to see her; fortunately, he had no date. Vera, dressed, a trifle drawn, but with eyes brilliant in their searching sparkle, compounded of pain and hope and wistfulness, had the sincere impression that for the first time in her life she was really beautiful.

Something from David Teyy ran down the steering-gear, down the brakes and clutches, and gave flesh and blood life to the car. Vera was curled, as if she was in the dark enclosure of a womb. She could drive on forever. Covered by life that flowed up the blue veins of the city. Up Sixteenth Street. David was a red blood center flowing down. She sucked his blood. Go on forever with David flowing down. He had hardly spoken to her. She wished he would never speak. Life flowed away from her to gestate his words.

"What is that, Vera?"

His face, a bronze plate engrossed in sharp lines and curves, emerged from a blood-shot dusk. His words tasted of blood and copper. Why could he not let her be?

"The Masonic Temple, David."

"I mean to you."

"To me?"

"Who live under the shadow of it."

"I have never thought."

"Who live under the shadow of it. Under life."

"How do you know?"

"I have been told that you tease—"

Men who are not strong enough—"

"—yourself."

"I am pure."

"You are a living profanation of the procreative principle of Deity."

Smile, which she could not see in the dusk.

"Because black children are repulsive to me?"

"Because you hold a phallus to the eye, and tease yourself."

"I do not understand."

"That is a rite of profanation."

"Your words cannot make me bad."

"My words were not used in your making."

Smile, she feels.

"You give me sarcasm when what I need is love."

"The necessary complement of giving is the capacity to take."

Smile.

"I cannot understand your words. Let me be."

"You wanted me?"

"After a while. O dont talk now. Please. Let me be."

. . .David flowing down. Vera had wanted to pass the cherry trees. And on out to the point. A word might struggle with her throat.

"Look, the cherry trees. I have seen them bloom. I have seen Japanese in reverence beneath them."

—Would it come?

"Lafcadio Hearn—"

" 'Lafcadio,' that is a soft word, David."

"You are sensitive—"

"Oh to so many things if I would only let myself be."

"Lafcadio Hearn tells of how the Japanese visit regions where the trees are blooming, much as we go to the mountains or the sea, drawn by their fragrance. It is hard to think of them succumbing to gaudy show and blare like our Americans at Atlantic City."

"You do not like Americans, David?"

"Do you feel Americans apart from you?"

"Answer my question first."

"One does not dislike when one is living. Life is inconceivable except in relation to its surrounding forms. I love."

"People?"

"The process and mystery of life. Life feeding on itself. ."

Deep River, Mendota. Vera saw souls drifting to the rhythm of forgotten cadences, whirled up . . . and growing. The inexplicable wonder of it! And our scientists, who can name more strangely minute exceptions than anyone, believing that they have caught it in a formula. Churchmen and scientists contending over formulas, over beliefs! Could anything be more militantly superstitious, more doggedly naive??

. . .David flowing down. David flowing out. David like mass undulations of shadow-silver trees. She wished he would light a cigarette. They were curving into the Potomac Speedway.

—Would it come?

<blockquote>
far-off trees
Whose gloom is rounded like the hives of bees
All humming peace to soldiers who have gone
</blockquote>

"Echoes."

"They are yours?"

"Mine two years ago. Now, more yours than mine? Where did you hear them?"

Potomac swishes and gurgles in the crevices of the river wall. Cars parked beneath the willows are more frequent. Lovers, swift receding oval faces, float in the gloom of back seats.

"Art Bond. He is a friend of yours?"

Vera, restless.

"One of the best. The best, here, perhaps, except for his habit of fastening on the ghosts of my dead selves. Ghosts, the spiritualists tell us, should be allowed to depart, with a bon voyage for the way. That is a serviceable truth that should be brought from the cheap tappings and illogic of the seance room to the practice of broad day."

Smile; serious.

"You believe in ghosts?"

"Your meaning of the word is beside the question. Things die, transmute. Their memory lingers. A preoccupation with them clogs creative life. People who are forever fastening on them give tangibility to the clogs. They can very easily slip from friends to nuisances."

"But do you believe in the ghosts I mean?"

"In the ghosts of hysterical women, their fortune-tellers, ouija-boards, and cards? Perfectly valid as symptoms."

"I do not understand."

"Apis, steer god, cock your ears and listen to the rite of profanation. Vera, you wanted me?"

"I do not understand your words. Let me be. After a while. Lets stop here and run out to the point.—And plunge in the river. Lord, I want to cross over into camp ground."

Mobile river, scintillant beneath the moon.. John Brown's Body..
River flowing from Harper's Ferry to the Chesapeake and the sea. Open
ocean for brown sediment of the river. Tide in, send your tang. Resistant
ripples. Wave in, send your waves. Wash back. John Brown's body rumbles
in the sea. Mobile river, scintillant beneath the moon... Lights twinkle
on the wharves of Seventh Street. Wash red blood. Search-lights play
on Lincoln Memorial and the Monument. Wash red blood. Blue blood
clots in the veins of Washington. Wash red blood. John Brown's body..
Mobile river, carrying brown sediment, scintillant beneath the moon.

They were standing on the point. David's face seemed unreal, and high
above her. The line of his nose was a thin rim of silver. You have teased
me. Your easy phrases when they turned on me, were teasing. Yours is a
sin. Not mine. I cannot help it. You whom I turn to, tease me. Whom I
love. Who carry solution within you. Who could, but by a touch, make
me feel the world not so utterly dreadful, so sinking, without bottom, so
utterly outside, and me alone. You tease me. O you do not know my need.
It is not in you to sin callously. You are here .. why will you not touch
me?.: the dream vanishes, the floor slips, and I dangle, dangle. O you do
not know my need. Tease you? You know I cannot, and you play with
me. O dreamer of Life why do you tease your dream? Do you not see that
I have never wanted to tease? You place my compulsions to your eye, and
play with me. What vision is it that lets you be blinded by the eye? You
sing of rivers. O cant you see? Beneath the scum I am a river. You who
plunge and cause stale drifts to stampede, releasing the river, will you not
even touch me? You cannot sin so. O Christ forgive him if he sins. Virgin
Mother, you will understand if I drown in the river. Forgive him, Christ.
O God, I dangle. Lord God, I want to cross over into the camp ground.

David was humming.

"David, it would be a Godsend for the river to overflow and sweep me
under."

...David flowing down.—Was that his hand that touched me? Are
these his eyes bending over mine? Christ eyes, do not let me cry for loving
you.

"Emptiness desires Nirvana. At best, I thought that that was what you
would want."

—Words, do not take him from his eyes. Glow, Christ eyes.

"Living from herself."

—Christ eyes, do not let me cry for loving you.

Perfect within yourself, incarnate mystery.

"I kneel in reverence before the wonder of it."

David's hand was almost crushing hers. It must have been a tear she felt, so hot it was. Her free hand tingled to the electric of his bent head.

"I am not worthy that you should kneel to me."

Vera shivered. Shook with a strange convulsion.

Roll river!

Something so complete and overpowering came over her that she sank, almost senseless, to her knees on the grass beside him.

*   *   *

"David," she was leaning against him, trembling, "what was it?"

Mobile river, scintillant, flowing to the sea.

"You ask me, who could but kneel before it?"

"I almost sinned, and then God struck me."

They were rolling over the smooth asphalt of Conduit Road, going towards the Falls. Head-lights of approaching cars glared at them. Rushed swiftly by. Across the river, Potomac palisades, great wavy outlined masses, glided leisurely with them. John Brown's body rumbles up the river...

"I have nothing to say to him but 'No'."

"People, Vera, unless you insult them, are insistent for reasons of refusal. Now Art—"

"It is unkind of you to remind me of him—after to-night."

"Ghosts of our dead selves—"

"And yet, if I have gained any strength at all, I should be able to face him. That wont be a ghost until it has been faced. I will sometime. But it will be purely selfish. People cant really forgive. Yet in this case there is nothing to forgive. I dont know how I shall meet him."

"Carl, first. He will want reasons."

"That I love you."

"Will that satisfy your own integrity? It was a half-truth up till to-night."

"It has been a whole truth, always."

"But you see, sweetheart—"

"You do not say that like you would say it if you loved me."

"—your tendency is to make of love a sort of sublimated postponement. Love solves inner complications for a while. It holds little or no solution for the outside world. Perhaps in a better day... Especially is this true of the two worlds you dangle over. Love is inoperative here."

"Then what is?"

"A burning integrity of vision."

"You have it, man of the multi-colored leaves. . O I knew it was you Carl dreamed about. I seemed to love him when the dreams he poured into me were you. I could not feel—"

Vera looked at David, and grew frightened.

"—not with him. I guess I led him on. But it was you who were struggling to birth in a word beneath the cherry trees, you along the river, at the point, above the falls, you. David, David, I love you... You have it, man of the multi-colored leaves, but I?. ."

"When you knelt beside me at the point?"

"I saw only a wonderful glow that I was too afraid to really look at."

"You have never, not once, succeeded in facing yourself?"

"I have run."

"Where?"

"What is it you say? Nirvana. To you."

"Before me?"

"Men's arms, up to a point. And my bed at night."

"Before that?"

"Before my father died, his arms. Before him, mother's."

"And now mine?"

"Now yours, . . if you will let me."

"I seem then, to be in the direct descent of varied and sundry prehensiles—"

"How can you joke?"

"Once learn to laugh at arms and you will find that they will release you. Hasnt your experience taught you that?"

"You are cruel, cruel. Why do you torment me so?"

"Art's spirit working through me, perhaps."

"David."

Tears, by the motion of the car, were shaken from her eyes.

"Seriously, I want you to see this thing through. Answer Carl, and his look will lead you to an answer for the world."

"That I love you."

Clump of wood that vibrates like a G-string to the deep bass of the falls. Night, furtive and shifting where shafts of moonlight stab in quick succession through the veering leaves. Ground trembles to the storm and lightning from clouds of trees. John Brown's body . . John Brown's body thunders up the falls...

"I always feel nervous and unreal in these woods."

"They are under a spell."

"Hold me, David."

David slipped his arm around her, and, bending over, chanted:

> Court-house tower,
> Bell-buoy of the Whites,
> Charting the white-man's channel,
> Bobs on the agitated crests of pines
> And sends its mellow monotone,
> Satirically sweet,
> To guide the drift of barges. .
> Black barges. . .
>
> African Guardian of Souls,
> Drunk with rum,
> Feasting on a strange cassava,
> Yielding to new words and a weak palabra
> Of a white-faced sardonic God—

"Oh dont, David."

"You who would mate with me—"

"Not that way, David."

"—quail at such a simple evocation? What would you do, if a whole troupe of souls who love the earth-sphere too well to go away, were to suddenly materialize before you? You who are still neither in nor out yourself."

"You are only trying to frighten me."

"Well, so I am. Here, see the good fairy beckoning to you from my lips? Do you wish her?"

"David."

Lips that but a few moments ago were the pale withered skin of berries, who tautened you with dew? Brushed you with the sweet scent of cane?

"Now—let us hurry to the falls, David."

John Brown's body was below them. . . Lovers let your dreams fly out the moon. . The golden flare of torches was diluted by the cold white light. Torches flare! It was wonderful to be in his arms.

"Do you know what I say of you, David?"

"I cannot hear you."

"Come, I know a rock."

David smiled at this girl leading him to secret places in his boulders.

"Carl will come to this place."

"How do you know, David? Oh lets not think of him. Tell me, do you know what I say of you? I will tell you. I say that you, man of the multi-colored leaves, put beauty, a senseless warm thing like a sucking baby, in my mouth.''

"How did that come to you?"

"It just came, O man, who knows better yet cant help seeking solutions of mysteries. Wouldnt you love, sometimes, to get rid of your mind?''

"Ask me if I would love to postpone."

"Must you ever refer to it?''

"The western world demands of us that we not escape. The implication of fresh life is its use. Monasteries and sepulchres are the habitats of shades.''

"Not even in love? O David I love you.''

"For yourself; for me?''

"Your questions chill me. Your words. O do not talk to me David. Love.''

Lips that but a few moments ago were the pale withered skin of berries, who tautened you with dew? Brushed you with the sweet scent of cane? Sandalwood odor of hair. Murmurs. Lispings. Love spinning to the tight pressure of tensioned arms. David .. wedge .. cleaving. Bronze sun, hammered to a sharp wedge .. cleaving.. His lips tasted of copper and blood.

"O David, David, not that. Not that, David. How could you—after to-night, your kneeling at the point?''

"Passion?''

"No, David, O no—love.''

"Young girl asking for the moon.''

"What do you mean? O David, you cannot sin so. Love.''

"Young girl asking for the moon.''

"David, you are killing something in me. You cannot sin so. Mother of Christ, forgive him.''

Hands that tautened with dew, brushed with the sweet scent of cane, you are Indian-givers.

*   *   *

Vera lay, a limp, damp thing, like a young bird fallen from its nest, found in the morning, in David's arms. John Brown's body rumbles in the river...

"Cry.''

"I cant, David. I want to go home.''

A shadowy shape was silhouetted above them.

"Beg pardon," it said.

"Carl."

"Is that you, Vera? I cant see. What are you doing here? Oh, beg pardon."

"Its all right, Carl. Sit with us. He is a friend of yours."

"Hello, Carl."

"I cant quite see—well I'll be damned if it isnt David Teyy. Where did you come from? I didnt know that you were in town. Vera, you didnt tell me you knew Dave Teyy. How long you been here? Working? Well I'll be damned. Pardon, Vera. And out here at the falls. What on earth ever brought you out here? This is a surprise. Damn. Pardon, Vera."

"Sit down, Carl. I have something I want to tell you."

Carl crouched down, Indian fashion. The three of them seemed as though gathered round an improbable fire.

"Dave Teyy. Old man, I havent seen you since that summer at Wisconsin. But I've thought of you. Havent I, Vera? Its good to see you. Recalls old days, and everything. Hows the world using you? Piled up a fortune I bet. But no, as I remember it, that wasnt your line. Man of the multi-colored leaves. What was that you used to get off about faces that chiseled dreams? From American marble? Or something like that? Like the fellows used to say, you were a queer duck, but they couldnt help liking you. Damn."

"Carl, this is as good a time as any other. I want to tell you that I cannot marry you."

"But not here, Vera. You cant mean it. Wait till another time. Hell's bells."

"But I do mean it, Carl. And I want to get it over with."

"Cant marry me? Oh this is an h of a time to tell a feller. Pardon, Dave. But it sort of upsets a feller."

"Deep down in your heart you really dont care, Carl. You think you do. But someday you'll find the right girl. Then you'll see."

"You dont love me. Thats it. But thats no reason—what is it Vera, tell me. I thought you did—up till to-night. What is it?"

David was trying to whip her with his will.

"I love David Teyy."

"Oh—well—congratulations, Dave. Hell's bells. Pardon. Guess I'd better be running on."

Something held him.

"Vera, Carl, both of you will sit as you are."

Life was thrashing in David. He would stampede these pale ghost people. He gathered wood, built a fire. Its flare disturbed nearby lovers who grumbled at it and moved away. Carl and Vera could not believe themselves. Fingers pulled down their stomachs. They shivered. Drew nearer the flames. David, holding them with his eyes, was crouching.

"Know you, people, that you sit beside the boulder where Tiacomus made love. Made love, do you understand me? Know you, people, that you are above a river, spattered with blood. John Brown's blood. With blood, do you understand me? White red blood. Black red blood. Know you, people, that you are beneath the stars of wonder, of reverence, of mystery. Know you that you are boulders of love, rivers spattered with blood, stars of wonder and mystery. Roll river. Flow river. Roll river. Flow river. River, river, roll, Roll!

> The river was empty, flowing to the sea,
> From Harper's Ferry to the Chesapeake and the sea—
> ...They hung John Brown..
>
> The river was empty, flowing to the sea,
> From Harper's Ferry to the Chesapeake and the sea—
> ...They hung John Brown.. Roll river..
>
> River was empty, flowing to the sea,
> From Harper's Ferry to the Chesapeake and the sea—
> ...They hung John Brown.. Roll river roll!
>
> John Brown's body, rumbles in the river,
> John Brown's body, thunders down the falls—
> ...Roll river roll!

"Know you, people, that you sit beside the boulder where Tiacomus made love. Made love, you understand me? Know you, people, that you are above a river, spattered with blood. With blood, you understand me? John Brown's blood. Know you, people, that you are beneath the stars of wonder, of reverence, of mystery. Know you that you are boulders of love, rivers spattered with blood, white red blood, black red blood, that you are stars of wonder and mystery. Roll river! Flow river! Roll river! Flow river! River, river, roll, Roll!!

The boulder seemed cleft by a clap of thunder. As if the falls had risen and were thundering its fragments away...

Tick, tick, tick, tick, pounding of typewriters, metallic slide of files, rustle of starched paper. Young girls who work all month to imitate leisure-class flappers. Young girls from South Carolina, Illinois, Oregon, waiting. Widows of improvident men who had been somebody in their day. Boys who have left school. Men dreaming of marriage and bungalows in Chevy Chase. Old digested fellows. Negro messengers. Carl but little changed. The slow process of digestion. Black life pepper to the salt of white. Sneezes. Tick, tick, tick, tick. Vera listless, nervous...

*　　*　　*

Men listen to her lispings and murmurs. Black souls steal back to Georgia canefields, soft and misty, underneath a crescent moon. The mystery of their whispered promises seems close to revelation, seems tangibly incarnate in her. Black souls, tropic and fiery, dream of love. Sing joyful codas to forgotten folk-songs. Spin love to the soft weaving of her arms. Men listen to her lispings and murmurs. White souls awake to adolescent fantasies they thought long buried with the dead leaves along the summer streets of mid-western towns. Solvents of melancholy burn through their bitten modes of pioneer aggressiveness to a southern repose. They too spin love to the soft weaving of her arms. White men, black men, only in retrospective kisses, know the looseness of her lips .. pale withered skin of berries...

Winter on Earth

The physical seasons are still recurring. Winter, spring, summer, autumn—they still recur. The physical seasons recur. The eyes of men who inhabit America have seen these seasons. Ages ago perhaps they started. Ages hence perhaps they will stop. They seemingly start and stop within a period of eighty years for one man. Eighty times a man sees the seasons. But eighty times are not enough for a man to learn that either he has never seen them or else he will see them eternally.

Day and night recur. 29,200 times a man sees day and night. But 29,200 times are not enough for him to learn that either he has never seen them or else he will see them eternally.

Inhalation and exhalation recur. A man breathes 840,960,000 times. But eight hundred forty million, nine hundred sixty thousand times are not enough for a man to learn that either he has never breathed or else he breathes endlessly.

Neither are there enough times or enough man for a multitude of greater or lesser truths to be learned.

What significance does a man derive from his existence?

It was winter.

Intense cold contracted the earth and almost froze the vegetation throughout the entire middle area of America. Nature looked as if she had been turned into a rusty trash-heap and frozen stiff. Fields were colored a dark purplish brown. Foot-paths worn across them were so hard and lumpy that the men who stumbled along them had their spines jolted with each step. A shock rang through anyone who stubbed his toe. Ears and noses knew that the cold was bitter. Blasts of wind swept over the bleak hills and whistled and moaned where anything resisted it. The cold whipped men before it without mercy.

"It is damn cold," said one lean man to another as both stood rocking back and forth and stamping their feet, waiting for the approach of something. Already one foot pained too much to put weight on it. Their threadbare overcoats flapped like gauze and were no protection against zero weather.

"It is cold, hellish cold," said the other as he tried to squeeze into his bones. His jaw was stiff. His head was pulled down into his coat, and he was reluctant to move it. But his long red nose was dripping and freezing; he had to wipe it. It was painful when he tried to remove a wornout woolen mitten from his right hand, the fingers of which were crooked and stiffened. He did so with difficulty, reached into his hip pocket, and could hardly grasp the soiled crusted handkerchief to draw it forth.

"Some poor devil will freeze to death tonight," the first man muttered, as the cold stung his face and nearly took his breath away.

"Yeah. The bastards," the second man cursed against the world.

Their own scrub beards were stiff and brittle.

Their own breaths became watery and froze.

The first man said:

"Old Ormstead always was a cruel bastard, but now he's gone and lost his sense."

"How so?" asked the second lean man. His teeth chattered.

"Leaving them horses out," the first man complained.

Neither of them looked or turned around, but both of them knew that down in the hollow two shaggy old horses were trying to nip grass by an ice-coated pond.

"Ain't they got coats?" the second grumbled.

"Ain't we got coats? What the hell good are coats against this cold?"

"Who the hell fixed this earth?" the second cursed.

"Go south," the first recommended.

"Yeah, and roast to death."

"No you don't. I've been there," the first reassured.

"Why didn't you stay there?" asked the second.

The cold made men everywhere begrudge their energies. Everyone was tight, close-fisted, curt, and surly until he got indoors, where, if it was warm, he thawed out, expanded, and felt jovial and large-hearted.

The newspapers headlined only a fraction of the number who froze to death. But these figures, accompanied by short descriptions of where and in what conditions the bodies had been found, were enough to make sympathetic people wince, and a few of them even went so far as to condemn the civilization that permitted such things to happen. For, to meet death by freezing in a dismal hallway or in some off-street gutter was, they said, a shame and degradation worse than anything that could befall an animal.

Then came the snow.

High above the Earth it formed and flurried in wild adventures down-ward toward the planet's barren surface. The snow-flakes were reckless and courageous. Born in space without protection and without support it was their destiny to ride the winds but always fall toward a nameless planetary form.

The white snow was heedless of the terror men would feel were they crystallized in space far above the Earth and made to whirl and fall upon an unknown surface.

The moon glowed in a black sky like a disk of silver.

Where is the planet Earth?

Where do men think they are?

The Young Man Who Tripped On. The Young Man Who Tripped On.

A young man wearing a tailored suit and smart top-coat which draped with style over his slender somewhat effeminate body—this young man was tripping down the wintry street swinging his cane jauntily and clicking his heels against the sidewalk. His multicolored muffler, showing above his coat, was more of an ornament than a protection against cold. His face, still youthful looking, was the kind that girls go crazy about, though already it had lost the apple look that made it irresistible two years ago. It was not so ruddy pink and full. It was a trifle sallow now, with lips still cupid-like but slightly drooping, and under the eyes were the be-ginnings of bags and dark circles. But his eyes still told the world that there was nothing to do but love the girls. They all fell for him as he tripped down the street swinging his cane jauntily and clicking his heels against the sidewalk.

He had just emerged from an all-night party and breakfast dance. The place, a studio apartment, had been overheated and stuffy, with clouds of smoke and cigarette butts everywhere. Drinks—gin, scotch, and cock-tails galore. There were young married couples, and plenty of single members of both sexes. They were as thick and curling as the smoke. Everyone got drunk enough to cut loose and do just what he or she damned well felt like. Their mouths smelled and tasted of alcohol and tobacco. But they could stand a lot, these young people. The laughter was riotous, somewhat forced. There had been a few scraps and ugly sluggish words, but not enough to cramp things. Petting was going on in all the corners and on all the lounges in the swank apartment. Whoever wished to dance got up, and two others slid into their places on the couches. The music was supplied by a high-priced studio jazz orchestra. And, when this stopped to rest, the radio was turned on.

Our young man had his eye on the pretty girl-wife of a friend of his. The friend from time to time kept his eyes on his wife, because he was still not so dulled and loose as not to care, now and again, what she did, and to see who kissed and petted her. This feeble watchfulness of his friend put a little spice into the affair for our young man. So he watched his chance, his mind made up to put one over on all of them. He did. Unknown to anyone, he cleverly sneaked off with the girl-wife of his dear friend and led her to a back room. He closed the door and locked it. And there, with the noise of the party beating in on them, he had an affair with her. Moreover, he kept her there until almost breakfast time. And when they finally did ease into the party again, and his dear friend, vaguely remembering now that he saw her that he had not seen her for some time, asked his girl-wife where she had been, it gave our young man quite a kick to hear her reply to her husband and his friend: "None of your damned business."

This is why our young man, having had scrambled eggs and coffee and having left his own girl behind, emerged from the party feeling much set up. Striking the cold air outside further braced him. Owing to these causes, he felt like walking—something he hardly ever did. So, just about the time when women who don't know what else to do flock downtown for unnecessary shopping, and long after the people who like machines, run things, had gone to work, our young man sallied forth, snuffed the air, felt a tingle in his cheeks, and began tripping down the street—an attractive youth, swinging his cane jauntily and clicking his heels against the sidewalk. And even now his eyes told the world that there was nothing to do but love the girls. Many whom he passed wished they had him on their lists.

He walked and he walked and he walked—quite unusual, even strange for our young man. And then all of a sudden he forgot who he was. His name, his occupation, his place of residence, the make of his car, what kind of clothes he wore, the number of his bank book, the number of his insurance policy, even his telephone number, in fact all phone numbers and everything just suddenly passed away from him as if they had never been. He was suddenly blank, aware of nothing—but his body kept moving on.

He tripped on and on.

On and on.

He walked on.

His body walked on.

He tripped on and on until finally he stepped clear off the Earth and went on and on swinging his cane with a hollow jauntiness, clicking his heels in cold space.

The moon glowed in a black sky like a disk of silver.

Near what men call the Earth, huge snow clouds massed. Their upper surface was cold and brilliant. Beneath, in the direction of America, all was dark. In this dark space the snow flakes formed and began their journey towards nothing.

Some few men were still upon the streets, a few stragglers, a few night-hawks whose presence made the streets seem particularly silent and deserted. Street lights were large and bright enough to show these people the way home. But their luminosity did not carry far. From the height of a tall building—a skyscraper—if one looked down, feeling dizzy, their feeble glow-like pinpoints could still be seen. But a mile from the Earth, the lights were lost.

Some few men were still upon the streets—people going home from night clubs and all-night cafes, taxi drivers, stray policemen, waiters, bakers, milkmen, two prostitutes—one, an old timer, the other quite new to the game, she having been broken in only the night before after liquor and dope had had effect on her. These people saw the pure snow falling and felt relief from the intense sterile cold.

One man, hilarious, saluted it and cried, "Hail to you, white snow!"

A few people who remained awake late into the night saw it drifting past their windows and before street lights. If they looked up, the snow seemed to come from nowhere.

One such person, alone, high up in the office of a skyscraper, his the only light to be seen in the high rows of ghost windows, this man cursed the snow because if it fell heavy enough it might spoil the scheme he had been working on all night. The next day he hoped to close a deal with a man who was now sleeping in a little cottage far out in the country. This skyscraper man owned a portion of the Earth which, could he show it off to good advantage, could be sold with large profit to himself. No one wished to see or to buy land in a blizzard. So he cursed the snow.

Another man was reading by the window of his room in a modern apartment hotel. When he looked out and saw snow falling, a swift jet of emotion compelled him to put his book down. Forced to feel what he habitually kept hidden, he began dreaming of a girl whom he had first kissed one snowy night several winters ago, and who had ever since consistently refused to marry him.

One old woman who could not sleep, tired of tossing about, finally threw back the covers, feebly felt her way from bed, covered herself with a warm kimono, turned on a light, and, Bible in hand, let herself down into a large chair drawn close to a cold radiator. When the snow came she was looking out, out somewhere, not seeing the rows of houses across the street. Her mind and feelings were roused now and again by memories of quarrels she had had with the families of her married children. These came to mind quickly, and as suddenly passed away. In the intervals between their coming and going, she pictured and felt that she was still a young girl; and she also felt that death was imminent. She had opened the Bible to the page where it tells of the birth of Christ in Bethlehem.

Two others who saw the snow were sitting in a front parlor near the bay-windows with lights out.

"It is tough to be all alone in the world." the boy said.

The girl did not answer. Her cheek was pressed against his heart. She listened to its beats as it thudded regularly against her. There seemed no cause to stir or speak.

"But now I've got you. We've got each other," he continued in a low voice which revealed love mingled with unformed suffering. He pressed her closer to him, kissed her, and as tenderly as he could stroked her hair. His fingers were rather thick and stubby. His face, regularly formed, youthful, but somewhat heavy, gave evidence of having had its share of hard knocks. Against his will, his eyes grew moist.

"It's nothing to get sentimental about. But you're the first one... Gee, it just comes out. When a feller has been alone since he was a kid... I've told you that my old man and mother died on me. Well... This world ain't no joke when it comes right down to it. I've seen the toughest of 'em knuckle under when they thought no one was looking, and blubber like kids. Gee, kid, it'll take time for me to get used to it."

He pulled himself together, and felt reassured by the sense of his muscles and the picture of his trim square build.

"Look, Harry," she said softly, snuggling still closer to him, "look, it's snowing."

"How can you see?" he asked, looking down to see her almost enfolded by him.

"With one eye," she answered. They both laughed.

There was a period of silence while they both looked out and saw snow flakes, like tiny white kittens, alight upon the window-sill.

Then, rousing himself, he said:

"Sorry, sweet—I hate to do it, but it's halfway across town before I get home. Motormen only run cars between crap games at night. Say, look," he exclaimed, pointing to the snow which was now coming down thick and fast, "if it keeps up this way, they'll have to get the snow ploughs out. Now, gorgeous... Up a little bit. Now! There ain't no censor to cut this kiss."

Before daylight, in different places, a number of men-children were born upon the Earth. And there were those who made swift transits, which men call death, into either nothing or into an unimaginable world.

But millions of people did not see the snow until they awoke at various hours the next morning. Already, a white blanket covered everything, and the snow, now in large flakes, was falling faster.

After a few days, Chicago, which is midway America, was almost snow-bound.

Chicago is a depression between New York and San Francisco.

Chicago is the greatest city in the world.

The snow fell upon Chicago irrespective of these phrases.

It brought a pure white beauty to the city parks and streets and boulevards. No skyscraper glistened white like it. There was no drab shanty but what underwent a snow-white transformation.

Shovels had been put to work, and high embankments lined the streets and sidewalks. At first, these piles were almost white, but they soon became soiled and dirty looking. There was too much soot and dirt for pure white snow. During the first phases of the blizzard, the people of Chicago displayed toward each other a good-will and almost joyous friend-liness uncommon in the routine life of city dwellers.

Usually these city folk, and for that matter, most Americans, go down the streets each one shut up behind his own mask as if confined in solitary cells, as if cursed and forbidden to share existence with their fellow-men.

Strange beings! Where do they think they are? Where do they think they are going? What can they possibly tell themselves that they are about? What purpose do they think they serve?

Count all of them. Not only Americans, but human beings everywhere:

they are all more or less the same. Take the measure of the planet Earth. See it somewhere in a vast universe. Why do its inhabitants act the way they do? Who poisoned them?

See this tiny creature wearing high heels, a skirt, and a fur coat. Where has she come from, where is she going—no-one knows. But she is walking down the street rapidly and with some style, going two blocks, and soon to duck into some doorway which will hide her from view. Two blocks is a short distance even when compared to distances which can be known on Earth. It is infinitesimal when compared with transmigration through worlds.

Her face is set, expressionless. She holds herself aloof, body held in and almost rigid. Several people just like her pass by within arm's reach. All are mute. All seem mutually repellent. All are doubtless preserving something from each other. Are they aiming at some great objective? With lips held tight or loose, they look, not at each other, but straight ahead or down—at what?

Where are they going? What are they doing?

Should someone speak to another, the person who spoke would be fearful lest he be rebuffed; and the person spoken to would not like it, and might be offended.

One can be put in prison for speaking to another.

Should one of them be asked the reason, then, if he did not suspect you of being crooked or crazy, he would quickly tell you that his fellow-men are not to be trusted, that they are tricky and treacherous, and that if one of them approaches or speaks to you, it is likely to be for his gain and your loss. This information comes from first hand experience; doubt-less the man who gives it knows what he is talking about. But what would be gained? What would be lost? What is gained? What is lost?

Each one feels that he must preserve something worthwhile in the universe from the attacks of other people who live just where he does and who act just as he does.

Men call such behavior human society in a state of civilization.

Where this lack of ability to be social is most marked—this is indeed a very high state of civilization.

There is much civilization in the great cities of America, including Chicago.

Are human beings born this way? Or do they secretly conspire to make themselves so? Perhaps they are under the illusion that this is the way to become dignified and noble. Perhaps they believe that by acting so they will each gather within eighty years a rich harvest from the Earth experience, and present a radiant face and a great soul when they pass away from their small globe to God.

But while it snowed, some force of Nature thawed men out and allowed them to feel just a little bit that after all they were all in the world together. Doubtless some men took advantage of this good feeling. But there was enough of it to survive these shocks, so that even conductors had a few good words for the crowds that jammed and jostled in street cars. Automobiles got stuck in ruts of snow. Other cars, instead of honking their heads off with irritation and impatience, honked and sounded for the fun of it, gave the stuck cars boosts, and helped them get started. Men gave their arms to women over crossings. And there was occasional camaraderie, gayety, and laughter, as men and women, all bundled up, trudged and crunched back and forth along the snow-packed sidewalks.

*   *   *

An island rose up out of the sea.

From the north it looked formidable and uninhabited. Waves rolled and dashed against a band of rocks, some rounded by the action of the waters, some still jagged and looking as if they had recently broken off and fallen from the towering bleak cliff. Way up, projecting over a wall of solid rock, a hugh boulder-stone appeared to be imperfectly balanced and ready to topple over and hurl down to join the ranks of rocks below it. But this huge stone had been perched in this reckless position as far back as the inhabitants of this island knew of. In their language they called it "Lover's Leap."

Mixed in with their legends was the story of how a beautiful island girl had rescued from shipwreck a great prince of the mainland. They had fallen in love. When the prince departed, this girl, left with a broken heart, had leapt off this rock. And ever since it had been called Lover's Leap. And though few of them ever used it, it did sometimes happen that a young man or young girl dashed away from the town and sought the friendliness of this bleak spot. It was never melancholy which drove them; it was always a deep agony which their stoicism compelled them to face alone with God.

But for the most part, the men and women of this island were too occupied in the struggle and adventure of existence to visit the rock. It was the occasional resting place of screaming white sea birds.

From the south the island stood forth in different aspects. If it were seen against the horizon as the sun-rise illumined and detached it from the sea, it rose up like a legendary castle, and stood isolate and dominant, the sole thing between sky and sea. If it were revealed close at hand as a mist scattered and the sun shone through, it glittered like a gem, its verdant curved hills set in a gold sand beach. But the best time to see it was near noon-time, with the blue sky brilliant and the sea a bottle-green. Then let there be a bracing wind, waves choppy, eager, and a few white clouds moving swiftly overhead. It was then indeed White Island, a miracle of nature, a form so beautiful and wild and free that many on first beholding it doubted that their eyes had seen the real, and suspected it to be the work of instant magic.

On the summit of White Island, high above all else, and where solid rock had once again emerged from under upward sloping green mounds and fields, there was a stone structure. It rested there as if always on the look-out, commanding as it did a full view of the island, the town beneath, and the open sea in all directions. It was nature-worn and ancient. Save for its shape, it might easily have been taken for a sentinel or lighthouse—in the ordinary sense. It was, in fact, a house of God.

It had been built, so the legends told, by the holy men of this island over a thousand, yea, many thousands of years ago. Its construction showed a workmanship of crude simplicity combined with the art and knowledge of a strangely perfect architecture.

For generations this place, save on rare occasions, had been unused. But there were men in each succeeding generation who learned from their fathers how to replace some worn or weakened part with new and strong materials. It received such watchfulness from year to year that it was now practically the same structure and as solid as when first completed. So it stood, high above all else, a symbol to those people of devotion and of the long chain of their ancestors.

Some distance below it, and towards the north, there was a wood, almost a forest. Here and there clearings had been made, and two roads cut at right angles through it. One clearing had been made into a rough farm, but the others were used for cutting wood. And the roads were mostly used for hauling wood from the forest to the town. But they also served of evenings to reach the foot-paths which wound around this wild part of the island. Young lovers from the town liked to stroll along these paths, sing their folk and love songs, sometimes dance about the forest, and now and again pretend to be engaged in some especially dangerous adventure. The smell of wood was mingled with salt air. And often the wind made weird and fascinating whispers, cries, wailings. One foot-path led to Lover's Leap. Another, to a rocky slope from which the sunset could be seen in all its splendour. All paths abruptly terminated at some surprising spot and there disclosed a stark or lovely vista.

Towards the south, there were rolling green hills and fields, places where cattle grazed, and long strips and squares of cultivated farmland. There were springs and brooks, cool and quiet and shaded by green leaves. There were gorgeous flowers, aromatic herbs, and fruit trees. Way down the slope one could see the town, a cluster of red roofs, nestling against a protecting hill. Below and spreading out before the town there was the glittering gold sand beach. And where the beach shelved down, the green sea came. Sometimes it came in gentle laps and ripples. Sometimes it came in great waves and white foam. Then its roar and pounding could be heard and even felt, it seemed, everywhere on White Island.

Behind a high curved arm of land which formed a cove there was a place where sails and spars were made and where ships were built. In the cove the fishing fleet lay at anchor. Bright colored sails were furled. But everywhere in the harbor there was activity. Men in light swift boats passed to and fro. Sometimes their deep voices carried for miles around. A few men worked on riggings. Some were getting their lines in order. Others mended nets. Some few lolled about and smoked and talked, their bronzed sea-faces shining rivals of the sun.

These were a fishing, sea-faring, farming, religious people.

Some men on the island had, in their day, touched almost every spot on the habitable globe. They had gone to the mainland and shipped as mates and captains. They returned invariably to White Isalnd, having seen the main ports of America, Europe, Africa, and Asia.

It was a long and honored tradition among them that no son must die and be buried on any mainland. Either die at sea and be given a sea burial, or else return and die at home.

There was a tale told of how one of them, having been stricken with fever in a foreign port, and near to die, got up in the quiet night when there was no one to restrain him, and, stumbling down to the water's edge, found a skiff, pushed off in it, rowed with the last strength of a dying man until the harbor lights were dim behind him, and there, just as he failed for the last time, slid his body over the side of the skiff and let it sink into the clean cool water, saying with his last breath as he sank down, "Thy son I am, White Island."

Most often those who had a taste for adventuring in far off seas and countries left home quite young. They saw and experienced all in the world they wished to, and then, just at the age of ripe maturity, they returned to the island, told of what they had seen and learned, and with great joy resumed their places among their people.

Now and again one of them would marry a daughter of the mainland. All of them had the world for love and marriage. As a race they were handsome, tall, and strong, possessed of a natural dignity which carried everything before it. Their fearlessness and stoicism were proverbial. Girls and women everywhere were known to love them madly at first sight. To be from White Island was to have a universal passport.

Nonetheless, and though there was no hard and fast tradition against doing so, they seldom married away from home. Now and again, however, one of them did, and brought his wife to live with him on White Island. They never settled permanently on the mainland. And also, now and again, a son of the mainland married a girl of White Island. In both cases, the mainlanders always came to dwell on the island. Indeed, having once seen and lived on it even for a short while, one could not wish to permanently dwell elsewhere, so beautiful and free and noble were it and its people.

In the language of White Islanders, the same word which meant "stranger" also meant "guest." Strangers were received as guests: it was their natural privilege to partake of the best to be had. They were welcomed to the food and drink, shelter, work, song, dance, festivals, and ceremonies of these people. The island life caught them up in its joyous stream. What was their surprise to see the beauty of the island women! What was their strange joy and sense of liberation to hear the whole island burst forth in soft or robust singing! For this was a custom on White Island: they had songs for all their ways of life—craft-songs, songs of the fields and crops and seasons, songs for the sea and fishing, dance, festival, and songs that were sacred. All on the island, from the very youngest to the oldest, knew these songs. There were times for singing: often at dawn and sunset, always during meals, for marriages, harvests, and events of significance to the whole community. But it was no unusual thing for some man in the fields, or some woman in her home, or some child upon the beach, to start singing because they felt like it, and then to have this song taken up and sung by people all over the island. At such times it was as if the whole place was one human organ. Then the song would die away and once again there would be silence save for the sounds of wind and waves.

What was the surprise of visitors to learn how these islanders were governed, and how they shared communal life! All adults on the island worked: it was their joy to be skilled craftsmen, potters, weavers, makers of sails, artists in wood, stone, and with lasting colors which they from ancient times had known how to make. It was said that in one part of the island there was a rich vein of gold; but the islanders kept this knowledge strictly to themselves, and thus it was that nations which had great warships and armies never bothered them. The foreign powers thought the island too small and valueless to be worth even an easy conquest. The islanders themselves never touched the gold. They had no need for it at home; and gold could not buy elsewhere what they had by natural merit on White Island.

The people of White Island governed themselves by a system which seemed very simple, and yet which was in fact quite exacting. When for some reason a new governor was to step forth, the people gathered in and around the house of God upon the summit of their island. Whoever felt compelled by some deep urge within his soul to assume this office, which was at once a privilege and a sacrifice, stepped forth of his own accord and gave his life to guide them. Such a one became at once responsible in his own eyes to God and to his people to be both law-giver and chief instructor in their ancient learning. As he stepped forth, his own conscience had to face the eyes and hearts of those he loved. No one became governor without the ordeal of an inward struggle. No two men had ever been known to step forth at once. Having elected to be governor, and conveyed this fact to the assembled people by fulfilling an ancient ceremony, this man, whoever he was, immediately received the blood and soul allegiance of his people. And so he governed until death or accident or his own inward sense of right and justice caused his removal.

This form of government seemed at first impossible to visitors from the mainland, but they soon became a part of it, and a part of all life on the island. This was their right as guests. They were sternly dealt with if they abused this privilege. Few visitors ever did. The islanders could count on the fingers of one hand the number of people during the past hundreds of years who had violated their kindness. These transgressors became so out of place that they were asked to leave the island; conveyance to the mainland was offered them. When they refused to leave, they were then forced to enter the sea and swim in the direction of the mainland. Two of these were said to have perished in the attempt. A third was supposed to have been picked up by a fishing ship and carried to some distant port.

This severe manner of dealing with whoever violated their hospitality was, of course, well known to people on the mainland. But it was not fear of this eventuality which caused visitors to behave as they should. Indeed, if they knew of it, soon after landing they forgot it because of the joy and warmth with which they were received. It was the islanders themselves, their way of living, the largeness, the simplicity, the wisdom of it—it was this which made it almost impossible for anyone to violate their hospitality. To do so was to violate oneself.

Not all of the men of White Island who went away to foreign places followed the sea. And even those who did carried an unwritten commission to experience all they could, and to understand the lives of all whom they came in contact with. In this way, White Island kept informed by first-hand experience of conditions everywhere the world over.

Certain of the White Islanders deliberately went abroad to study and acquaint themselves with the types and conditions of existence of different peoples: their governments, customs, commerce, arts, religions, sciences, and philosophies.

One such White Islander, having chosen America as his place of residence and study, grew to like this nation, formed deep friendships there, and came to be a figure of great significance in its culture. He lived at different times and for varying durations in New York, Chicago, and San Francisco. And then, having received life and given completely back to life until the age of forty-three, he left America and departed on a long voyage. The people of America never heard of him thereafter. It was assumed that he met with accident. In fact, he returned to White Island, lived long afterwards, and finally, when almost two hundred years of age, peacefully died in the place he loved as he loved no other place on earth.

Another White Islander, in pursuit of the same purpose, went to live and study in the Orient.

And, from among a number, there was a third,—even now his return was expected. The whole island was preparing dance and festival to rejoice and welcome him, by one acclaim, the greatest of White Islanders.

His name was Jend.

He was remembered, twenty years ago, as a youth whose strength and gift of wisdom amazed even them, they themselves a strong wise people. At an early age he had mastered all the crafts on the island. All that could be done with wood and stone he learned, from the felling of trees to the making of simple articles of use, the shaping of spars, the building of ships and houses. He came to understand the soil, the earth: his hand was perfect sowing seed. And to handle a sail and ride the sea were cut for him by nature. He was a striking figure at the helm in a wild high sea: his face, in profile, eagle-like, and, in front view, marvelously cast for man; his body, a muscled symmetry, braced as if it were engaged in victorious contest with wind and waves.

But most extraordinary was the rapidity with which he learned and mastered the knowledge and traditions of his people.

White Island, the legends ran, was so called because the Angels, long ago, had descended and dwelt there. They had been sent down to Earth by God, commissioned to teach and aid the men of Earth to improve their way of living. Everywhere over the broad lands men had departed from universal harmony. And as a result of this their bodies grew sick, and their souls became dis-eased. The Angels chose this spot from which to direct their ministrations because it was isolate from the mainland and the way between was washed with clean waters.

One day as an Angel strolled along the gold sand beach, absorbed in divine contemplation, he was suddenly surprised to see a man-child brought in by the waves and deposited as if by hands before his feet. He took this for a sign that this child's destiny was to be ruled by him. So he gave the child unto the group of Angels who nursed and reared him. When this child had grown to be a marvelous flower of earth-manhood, he and a young Angel were joined in love; and thus arose the race of White Islanders who sometimes called themselves Children of the Sun.

The Angels remained on Earth long enough to see this race well started, to teach them to till the earth, command the sea; to teach them to know themselves and great cosmic mysteries. Here was the source from which sprang the knowledge and the traditions of the White Islanders.

Jend mastered these. From men returned to White Island from far off places he learned diverse languages and customs. In a time of emergency, young as he was, he even became governor of White Island for a short period.

And then came the compelling urge to see and understand the world. So he set off.

Now, after twenty years, he was expected to return.

The whole island expected him. One of their ships had already been sent to convey him home from the nearest mainland port. And on the island itself everyone was preparing for a three day continuous day and night ceremony of rejoicing.

Very gay and active in this preparation was Naril, she whom everyone acknowledged to merit Jend's love. Naril, like most of the women of White Island, was a pagan in the gayety of her body and a priestess in her spirit. Even now she had climbed high to the summit of White Island and stood there, lithe and beautiful in the free winds and bright sun,

near the house of God, alternately praying and dancing with joy for the
first sight of the great Jend, her Jend, as he came sailing home.

*   *   *

The snow drove in blinding sheets across a prairie. Nowhere could
anything be seen save swirls and drives of blinding snow. The glassy road
lay across an endless flat-land, a cold white wilderness in which nothing
grew or could ever grow. Two people drove a car across a prairie in a
blizzard. Four large eyes, straining on the look-out, peered out from
behind a frosted wind-shield. A fog-horn should have shrieked for them,
for they, driving at great speed, peered out and could see not farther in
front of them than where the head-lights shot against the whirling blanket
of white snow and reflected backwards. The car stood still, rushed on, and
set the snow a wild dance all around it. The car was metal. On and on the
man and woman drove. Four large eyes peered out from behind a frosted
windshield. On and on they drove across a flat civilization. They were
in a car. The car was in snow. The snow was in a closed cold world.

Mr. Costyve Duditch

I t was a helter-skelter early-spring day in Chicago. Draughts of wind swept through the huge corridor formed by the tall buildings which flanked Michigan Boulevard; and where the bridge crossed the Chicago River, air currents from the lake blew in, met with opposing gusts, and set up odd swirls which made it difficult for pedestrians to know their footing. One minute, they had to lean forward against the wind; the next, they had to brace themselves back against it. Faces were tense. Skirts and coats waved and beat and flapped. People clutched their hats.

Mr. J. Breastbuck Coleeb was making headway northward up the avenue, approaching the four skyscrapers which stood at each corner of the bridge. On the near side, the London Life Building, and the new skyscraper called 333. And, on the far side, across the river, the Tribune Tower, with its suggestions of Gothic architecture, and the white, unshapely mass of the Wrigley Building.

Coleeb was a man in the early forties, well-trained in the natural sciences and a rather keen observer of human conduct. From the behavior of the human species, more than from the behavior of animals, birds, or insects, he derived much amusement. Squarely built, he gave the impression of being vigorous and rough-and-tumble. The cast of his features was alternately skeptical and humorous. As he drove forward, his jaws were clenched and looked as though he were biting hard on the stem of a pipe. The characteristic squint of his eyes was exaggerated in an effort to keep flying dirt from entering them.

He shot a glance upward at the high vault of grey-blue sky, and, as if from a sky vantage point, he looked down and saw himself, together with several hundred of his fellow creatures, being bullied by the winds. This spectacular concert of biped antics struck him humorously. And then he smiled satirically at the thought that he, a human intelligence, in this trivial circumstance, was giving sufficient evidence of man's helplessness in Nature.

He seemed to be hurrying; but this was more because of his struggle with the wind currents than because of a feeling of urgency to be exactly on time for his appointment in the Wrigley Building at 10:00 a.m.

182

As he neared the bridge, he glanced up and across the river to note the clock on the Wrigley tower. Seeing that he was fifteen minutes early, he returned to scanning with interest the faces he passed by.

And then he chanced to catch a glimpse of something which gave him a shock of unexpected recollection. He noticed, on the farther side of the bridge, coming rapidly towards him, a velour hat of light green color and peculiar shape, a bent head, and a smart morning suit. The sight made Coleeb instantly exclaim to himself:

"As I live! Costyve Duditch!" Then he added: "In his setting."

The figure sped nearer, allowing Coleeb to see its characteristic short-legged gait, its grey spats, its standing collar. He had no doubt of it.

"Here he comes!" exclaimed Coleeb, opening his eyes wide as one does when viewing a racing auto draw near. He exaggerated his expression of amazement.

No sooner had the words been uttered than Mr. Costyve Duditch, he in fact, moving with a velocity which was extraordinary in the face of such uncertain winds, and among so many people—Mr. Costyve Duditch was on and past him. Much as if he had in truth witnessed the approach and passing of a speedy mechanical object, Coleeb jerked himself around and viewed Costyve's departure.

"There he goes!" Coleeb exclaimed, and his face broke into a good-humored grin. "The rascal! Didn't notice me. Wonder when he arrived in town. I must speak to the dear fellow."

His decision to do so was hastened to action by the fact that passers-by along the bridge jostled him and met his stationary figure with unfriendly eyes. Standing there gazing at the rapidly departing figure of Costyve, he was impeding the pedestrian traffic. So, coming to his normal senses, senses which had been somewhat shocked out of balance by Costyve's glancing impact, Coleeb started in hot pursuit of his old friend Duditch.

"Hey there! Costyve!" he called when he had almost overtaken him.

Costyve stopped dead, with hunched shoulders. For a few seconds he neither turned nor budged, but looked as though he were holding himself in blankness prior to some catastrophic onslaught. Then his face brightened and he wheeled around just in time to grasp the hand which otherwise would have clapped him on the back a trifle too vigorously.

"Costyve!" Coleeb exclaimed, as the two men shook hands and looked variously, but both with large smiles, each in the other's face.

"You rascal! You passed me on the bridge and didn't see me."

Costyve smiled with delighted apology, snapped his eyes, and rubbed one of them.

"No wonder," said Coleeb. "We'll need goggles to keep out the dirt, and gas masks to protect our lungs from carbon monoxide before long. When did you get to town?"

"Yesterday," Costyve confessed.

"And leaving to-night?" asked Coleeb, showing his familiarity with the fact that Costyve was continually coming and going from town to town, from country to country.

Costyve nodded in his peculiar way expressive of delighted apology. He seemed to be delighted with the world, apologetic for himself. Delighted with life; apologetic for his own contribution to it.

"Where have you been this time?"

"A short trip," answered Costyve. "To Spain—Toledo and the Balearic Islands."

"Well!" said Coleeb. "How was it?"

"Fantastic! Topping!" Costyve responded, enthusiastically.

"You must tell me about it. When am I going to see you? You leave to-night? Where were you last time?"

"Constantinople," Costyve answered.

"And before that?"

"Persia."

"And before that?"

"Peking," answered Costyve.

"By God!" Coleeb exclaimed, "You do get around, don't you?" And then he told him: "Everybody's been wondering about you."

Costyve brightened and said: "Conceive it!" which was his way of phrasing, "You don't say!" It was evident that it pleased him very much to know that people remembered him and thought of him.

"Yes, indeed," said Coleeb. "We've been wondering where you were, and when you'd come back. Why don't you let people know when you are coming?"

At this question, Costyve immediately showed by a quick batting of his eyelids, and by the protective way in which he drew in his lips and chin, that he was embarrassed. Indeed, with his friends, Costyve wanted to evade the personal factor in his comings and goings. To travel, yes. To see all manner of things, yes, yes! But he was a little touchy on the subject that he, Duditch, personally moved about so much. Hoping to avoid any mention of this, it was a trick of his to arrive in town unannounced; and then, when discovered by someone, he usually tried to give the impression that he had been there all along. But he had not been able to work this technique on Coleeb.

"It is such a bother," he answered, off-hand, but could not hide the fact that he was telling a fib and knew it.

Just then, someone bumped into him. Standing there on the crowded boulevard, the wonder was that it hadn't happened before. So Coleeb suggested that they move out of the way of the pedestrians and find shelter from the wind. They stood in the entrance of a near-by building.

"A bother for whom?" asked Coleeb, feeling that he wanted to have it out with Costyve, "For you or for your friends?"

"For both, I fear," Duditch answered, and fidgeted.

"What is it?" Coleeb asked, rather bluntly, and knowing that he had placed his old friend on uncomfortable ground. "You shy from what you fear may be their criticisms of your wanderings? You feel they think you are a sort of aimless globe-trotter, the proverbial rolling stone which gathers no moss?"

"Something like that," Costyve replied, with simple directness. For a short while he lowered his head.

"Well, what if they do?" asked Coleeb. "Who are they to sit in judgment on how valuable or worthless your comings and goings are? They'd have a difficult case proving that they're better off than you. To have a family; not to have a family. To have a recognized career; not to have one. And so on. Well, what's the real difference? In one case, you do one set of things. In the other, you do another set of things. Either can be worthless. Either can be worthwhile. It all depends on what the given man makes of them. Or so it seems to me."

"That is very true," replied Costyve. "But—" and then, having heard his own position so well defended, he began arguing the case of the settled people against himself, trying to show that they were more productive, more solid; that they had a function in life, that they fulfilled an obligation to society and constituted the backbone of the world; whereas he was like a vagrant, a useless appendage.

Costyve's feeling of inferiority to these settled people of whom he, Coleeb, was one, made Coleeb a bit uncomfortable. Not taking kindly to it, he interrupted Duditch's argument to ask:

"You like to travel, don't you?"

"Oh, yes!" replied Costyve, brightening. One could see that he truly did. And then he added: "It is a way of grooming one's person!" A significant smile lit his face.

"Well then," said Coleeb, "what do you care what people think of you? If the truth be told, half of them are envious of what, from their point of view, is your freedom. From a settled background they envy you as much as you, from a moving one, envy them. And those who don't envy you are always glad to see you and to know that you're in town. So from now on, I won't hear of any explanations or excuses for your not letting us know when you are coming. Do you understand me, my roving gentleman?''

Costyve said that he did, and felt too pleased to look chastened. Something about Coleeb warmed the cockles of his heart.

''By the way,'' asked Coleeb, ''did you by any chance receive an invitation to Constance Hanover's tea this afternoon?''

''Yes, I did,'' replied Costyve. ''I don't know how she knew. Nice of her, wasn't it? It gives one a warm feeling...''

''You don't deserve it,'' said Coleeb, shaking his head at him. ''You just blow in, and blow out, and use cities much as we ordinary mortals use the rooms of our houses. Well, I won't take you to task any more this morning. But this afternoon...'' and he leveled a finger at him. ''I've an appointment at ten. And you seem to be off somewhere.''

He put out his hand, grasped Costyve's, and said:

''About 4:30. Remember where her place is?''

Costyve nodded. ''On Dearborn Street.''

''You do remember your old town, don't you? Well, watch the traffic! I'll see you at 4:30. So long!''

''*Au revoir*!'' said Costyve, and waved his arm as he was accustomed to doing so often at train and ship departures.

And the two men parted to go their separate ways until tea time.

As Coleeb walked against the wind to his appointment, he turned over in his mind what a queer fellow this Costyve was. Reserving serious observations and reflections for another time, he recalled with amusement the various odd stories told on Costyve. In particular, he recalled gossip as to how Duditch liked to be remembered by bell-boys, how he liked to be singled out and hailed in a crowd.

It was told, for instance, that if he were scurrying along anonymous in the throngs of Fifth Avenue, New York, or the Boulevard des Capucines Paris, and someone chanced to notice and recognize him, he was ready to repay this person with his life. The person need not stop and converse with him; he preferred that the person did not. It was enough that he was hailed. ''Good morning,'' or, ''How do you do, Mr. Costyve Duditch!'' He would smile brightly and feel a touch of self-importance. Ships greeting in the night.... And Costyve, God bless him, would mount a crest and sail on.

It was further told that in pursuit of gratification for this strange trait, he had a way of going from city to city carefully selecting hotels with this wish in mind: that after due period of absence, the doormen, the clerks, the porters, and the bell and elevator boys would remember him, salute him by name, complain that they had not seen him for ages, and, in general, treat him as a visiting dignitary of great worth. His calculations were very shrewd. He never returned to a hotel a month after having stayed in it. For, considering the size of the tips he gave everyone, it would have been no mark of remembrance for the entire staff to recall him after so short a lapse of time. No, he never returned to a place so quickly. A year, two years, three years—and if, after an interval of four years they still saluted him, it was one of the high moments of his life. Thus, since he traveled much, he knew almost every hotel in the world, was known by every Hotel Bristol on the Continent, and, unfortunately, sacrificed many pleasant hours by the hearthside in order to gratify this strange weakness.

Coleeb, picturing Duditch in the midst of these antics, did not fail to perceive the distorted wish for recognition which underlay them; and his sense of amusement was replaced by a feeling of pity. He drew a deep breath, shook his head soberly; and then, having reached the Wrigley Building, he entered it.

Costyve, feeling much set-up as a result of his encounter with Coleeb, sped along to fulfill his morning's plan. His day went off like clock-work.

He had a faculty for sleeping well. He slept soundly. Neither dreams nor conscience disturbed him. If he happened to hit the bed flat on his back—that way he slept. If curled on his side, if round on his belly—so he slept till early morning. No day came to find him other than refreshed and full of energy to get up.

Of mornings, his first trick was to thrust his toes from the sheets and twinkle them. Then, with a bright-eyed grin on his face, bouncing up, he would dash in and frisk under a cold shower. Shave. And then into street clothes.

He had many suits. Tweeds, and serges, and fabrics from all quarters of the earth. He also liked tailors to remember him. But whatever else he put on, these two items were indispensable and unchangeable: his spats—his grey spats—and a standing collar. They served to give him an air of distinction wherever he went, and he was strongly inclined to wear them in warm weather and in hot climates. And, also, to discerning eyes, they evoked the pathetic aura of a bachelor—perfectly dressed, but never in his life to possess either mistress, lover, or wife. Ah yes, 'twas said that Mr. Costyve Duditch was a gelding.

However, in other respects, he stood in sufficient answer to those critics of America who say that we are a fatigued and enervated people. For instance, he was indefatigable, with spirits always up. True, now and again he had trouble with his kidneys; but, save for this trifling occasional ailment, he was in sound good health and had an enviable appetite. In fact, he could eat almost any kind of food and cooking with no concern for indigestion. In this, he was an exceptional American. Also, he was free to pick up and leave for remote corners of the earth with never a care about getting fixed up by doctors and dentists before he left. Nor did he require that there be such persons where he went. Central Africa, Tibet, Alaska, the South Seas—it was all the same to him: no place held terror or discomfort. Hence he was free to enjoy the unique strangenesses and delights of each.

What would have happened to him had his spirits flagged? What would have been his outlook had he suddenly contracted gout, or severe rheumatism, or low blood pressure, or Bright's disease?—ah well, he seemed immune from virulent bacteria, organic and psychological—let him be.

Now right after breakfast, he always did something. Sometimes he had definite business to attend to. But whether he had or not, he invariably sallied forth and promptly at 9:00 a.m., hailed a taxi, took a bus or a jin-ricksha, or bounced along the street on foot, according to the place and mood, headed for the business district—no matter what part of the world he was in. For his purposes, Peking was just as good as Moscow, Moscow just as good as Paris, London, New York, or Chicago. All he wanted was to taste some kind of commercial atmosphere first thing in the morning. He had a need to feel in touch with the forms and rhythms of man's tangible necessities. Once in the midst of things, his fertile brain would not wait long before inventing something definite to do.

This morning, after leaving Coleeb, he steered towards the Loop, and paid a round of visits to men with whom he really had business connexions. He visited the offices of his real estate agent and of his stock broker. In both places he tarried just long enough to get a smell of the office atmosphere. His affairs, he found, were going quite well without his personal attention. So, after an exchange of greetings, and after receiving a number of tips which he promptly forgot, he quit his brokers and went to his bank to clip coupons. This done, his urgent business for the morning was finished. But there still remained an hour before lunch. To fill this,

he conceived the notion of inspecting merchandise in various large department stores.

On entering Marshall Field's he should have found himself in a place
of lofty ceilings, large white pillars, and, in general, of rather grand proportions: as they call it, a cathedral of commerce. But neither he nor any
other of the buzzing throng of morning shoppers took notice of the cathedral. They were bent on commerce. Women with eyes close to their noses
pressed along the aisles and crowded about the counters, viewing and
fingering stuffs of silk, genuine and artificial, cotton, leather, jewels...
Costyve himself darted and ducked through the women, giving the impression that he was in urgent search of some special something which was
nowhere to be found. However, as he passed the cut-glass counter, a particularly fine bowl caught his attention and caused him to pause. The
longer he gazed at it, the more it won his admiration. So, at length, he
asked the saleswoman to let him examine it.

He took the bowl in rather nervous fingers and began turning it round,
viewing its designs and rather exquisite workmanship. He came to like it so
well that his mind began searching to find someone to whom he could
send it as a gift. And just then, by God, the bowl slipped from his hands
and crashed on the floor, sending glittering splinters in all directions.
Costyve, in consternation, literally jumped in the air. The saleswoman
made hysterical sounds and gestures. And several people, including the
floor-walker, gathered. Duditch, flushed and flustered, jumpy all over,
fumbled for his bill-case. He stuttered in asking the price of the bowl,
apologized, and, finally, amid much hubbub, the greater part of which he
himself caused, settled the matter by having the bowl placed on his charge
account. This done, and feeling that all the eyes in the world were on
him, all fingers shaking at him reprovingly, he hastened to leave the store.

And then, outside, on Wabash Avenue, with the entire Loop crushing
and crashing about him, he had a sharp feeling that he must also leave
Chicago immediately. The city suddenly seemed to be in the same condition as the bowl. Always when he broke something, which he was continually doing—either literally breaking something, or building up a
scheme or a wish only to have it collapse on him—he felt like this: that
he, the most clumsy person in the world, had shattered the finest things
the world contained. And in this mood, he always headed toward a railroad station or a ship's pier. So now, he jumped into a taxi and was
driven to the Santa Fe station, where he changed the time of his departure
from 10:00 p.m. to 7:00 p.m. Had not Miss Hanover's tea prevented him,
he would have left as soon as he could gather his bags.

For lunch, Costyve avoided his club, fearing he might run into friends who would ask him why he hadn't let them know that he was coming to town. The restaurant selected happened to be a dismal affair, depressing; and save that the food stimulated him, he would have sunk into melancholy worse than he had known in years.

After lunch he bucked himself up and returned to his apartment, there to engage himself till 4:30.

This apartment, a four-room suite in a skyscraper located near the Drake Hotel, he kept on lease year in and year out. Its rent had been raised several times; he had paid the increase cheerfully. It was the one place in the world to which he could turn with a feeling of having a settled habitat. It was the one place which gave him a sense of having anchorage. He did not want to dwell in it constantly. A product of the skyscraper age, Costyve was up-rooted and had to be blown about, restlessly changing place. He had no sentimental regrets about leaving it. But there were comfort and cheer in the knowledge that, furnished with certain of the objects which he cherished, it was there, his own, for him to return to whenever he wished.

One room was his sleeping-room. Another he kept for a possible guest. A third was a sitting-room, containing a baby grand piano, several comfortable chairs, and an odd assortment of objects, such as pottery, weapons, articles of dress and ornament, a tiger skin, a number of ancient-looking manuscripts—things which, from time to time, he had brought home from various quarters of the earth. In addition to these, the room now was littered with Costyve's bags, suitcases, coats, hats, and what not. It had a musty smell owing to its having been occupied so little.

The fourth room, a dark box-like affair which usually had to be lit by electricity, Costyve called his study. Here he kept, in glass-enclosed cases, his books. And here also he hid away in three different covers the notes which for years he had been making and which, some day, he hoped to work over and organize in three separate volumes. Already he had titles for these books of his.

One, dealing with travel as a factor in the shaping of a cultured person, was to be called "The Influence of Travel on the Personality." An alternate title for this book was "How Travel Grooms the Person."

A second book, descriptive of the love-affairs of great men, concerning which, if the book were ever published, Costyve would prove himself a specialist, was to be called "When Love Was Great." He also thought of calling this book "Finesse in Love." He could not quite decide whether he wished to emphasize the bold strength of great men's loves, or the subtlety of management which they displayed.

And the third, treating the creative processes as they are manifest in life and art, was to be titled "There is No Life Without Creation."

Now if, first thing in the morning, Costyve visited the business district, the second thing he did, just after lunch, was to apply himself to his literary work. This also he did irrespective of what part of the world he was in.

So now, having been shot up a high elevator shaft, having returned to his apartment, he cleansed himself of Chicago's dirt, put on a gorgeous silk and gold-embroidered mandarin's cloak which he used as a house robe, went into his study, switched on the lights, and began adding to his given collection the notes he had taken for the past year. There was so much assorting and arranging to be done that, for a while, his activity amounted to no more than librarian's work. In time, however, amid much fussing and fuming, and repeated running to the bath-room for water, he managed to penetrate beneath the surface of his material dealing with the influence of travel on the personality. Opinions and points which had come to his mind during the talk with Coleeb found their way into his notes.

After writing a page which moderately satisfied—and surprised him— he glanced at his watch and was shocked to see that it was already 4:45. He jumped up, put his notes carefully away, hustled into his street clothes, and rushed to Miss Hanover's.

Constance Hanover was a woman of class and refinement—tall, with flowing lines and an easy grace of movement. A charming hostess, she managed all affairs, social and other, exceedingly well, exerting no apparent effort to do so.

To this tea, an informal affair given for no special person, she had invited in addition to Coleeb and Costyve a number of friends and acquaintances whom she wished to see and chat with. Had she known in time that Costyve was going to be in town, she mostly certainly would have given it for him especially. As it was, she planned to manipulate things so that he would become a sort of unannounced lion of the occasion. This she aimed to do, not only because she found Costyve interesting and amusing, but also because his pathetic side appealed very strongly to her and made her want to help and advance him in any way she could.

The room in which she was going to pour tea showed taste in decoration, with an eye for ease and comfort. Its walls were done in soft-toned silver grey; and on its walnut floor there was a modern French rug in grey and rose. On either side of an open hearth, in which a wood fire was crackling, stood a wing-chair and an arm-chair. And across from the hearth, against the opposite wall, a lounge. On a low table everything was in readiness for pouring either tea or coffee. The china and silverware, of old-fashioned design, had been in her family for years. It was recognized by everyone that this room and Miss Hanover belonged together.

Around 4:30 her friends began coming. They drove up in town-cars, taxis—and one or two walked. Two society women, stunningly dressed, and both interested also in the fine arts. A young painter who, in addition to his small canvases, was doing murals for hotels and having quite a success with them. A professor from the university. A critic of literature. A charming young poet who had just finished a long poem in the modern idiom and was undecided whether he ought to be proud or ashamed of it. An actress who was playing the leading part in a rather serious drama which, several weeks before, had come to Chicago from New York. A French diplomat and his wife. A timorous-looking woman, a friend of Miss Hanover's college days. She had been asked to pour tea. And Coleeb.

They were shown in by a manservant, and, after the usual greetings, they were told by Miss Hanover that Mr. Costyve Duditch, just returned from Toledo, Spain, was in town and would be to tea. Without exception, those who already knew him were surprised, delighted, and even eager to see him, while the few others let it be seen how eager they too were. And thus it was that by the time he arrived he found a chatting gathering which was quite willing to lionize him.

Dressed for the afternoon, as if he were in London rather than in Chicago, Costyve made his tardy appearance, delighted and apologetic. His entrance was greeted by a round of murmurs and exclamations such as one would expect to hear on the return of a prodigal; and he had hardly had time to meet the people who were strangers to him before on every side they were asking that he tell them of his latest travels. However, Miss Hanover saved him from breathless confusion by suggesting that he be allowed to have his first cup of tea in comfort, and that thereafter all who wished could ply him with questions to their heart's content.

The wing-chair near the hearth was vacated for him, and Costyve ensconced himself in it, looked very bright and pleased, comfy, sipped his tea, and incidentally took over the office of keeping the fire burning. Ever so often he would lean over, stir the embers with a poker, and, with a quick jerky movement, throw on another piece of wood.

The minute his first cup was put aside, he was asked so many questions that he had difficulty keeping track of them. But, beaming all over—feeling secure and released by the fact that travel, and not he personally, was the subject of discussion—he grew very talkative, now and again threw wood on the fire, and answered, contrived to answer, most of them.

He told them about places, things, and cities in all quarters of the world: in England, Scotland, France, Italy, Germany, Russia, Turkey, Persia, India, and China. The roads, the hotels, the food, the language, the kind of money in each. It is to his credit that he succeeded in adding to the mere information he gave some of his ideas as to the value of travel as an aid, an indispensable aid, in grooming the person. Fortunately, everyone took kindly to these notions; and thus they let him feel that he had a place and function with them and in the world. Indeed they gave him such a sense of wholeness that both the cut-glass bowl and the entire city of Chicago were temporarily mended: he began to regret that he was leaving so soon. Here in this company, in his own town, the purpose and end of his wanderings seemed about to receive not only recognition but fulfillment.

But it was not until he began telling of Toledo and the El Grecos that he really swung into his stride. In describing the city, in pointing out how one never caught the true spirit and meaning of El Greco's genius until one had seen his art in the midst of the very conditions, physical and spiritual, which had given it birth and form, he was able to expand, and, by the use of major examples, to demonstrate that a truly cultured personality could never be formed unless one did travel widely and thus tap the currents of civilization at their sources.

The young painter particularly was interested in what Costyve had to say about El Greco. And so, in a way, was Coleeb. For he, Coleeb, with a good friend of his, had once spent an interesting hour before the El Grecos in the museum in Boston. Mentioning this to Costyve, and asking him if he had ever seen them, Coleeb was not surprised to learn that Duditch was familiar with them and with most things in Boston also.

While Costyve talked on, Coleeb lapsed into silence, slouched in his corner of the lounge, squinted, and began attentively to observe Duditch's behavior.

The first thing he noticed was that Costyve's tone of voice had little or no relation to, no connexion with, the various subjects he talked about. Whatever the subject, whether it were the price of a railroad ticket across Siberia or a Hindu temple; whatever the theme, whether it were gossip about people or serious discussion of art and life, his tone contained an unchanging, odd pathetic pleading, apologetic persuasive quality mingled with a note which suggested that he was delighted with something, perhaps with life, and as pleased with himself as he dared be. This tone of voice appeared to go on by itself, yes, expressing some reality, maybe expressing the fundamental tone of Costyve's temperament; but it rarely if ever changed to suit the various topics of conversation. And so, on first hearing, it seemed to be strangely unrelated not only to the subjects, but to Costyve himself. It gave the impression of being disembodied. A voice, sounding on the face of the earth, pleading and delighted, pleading for no one, delighted with no tangible thing.

Queerly impressed by this observation, Coleeb then turned to note what he could of Costyve's mental behavior. It was not long before he saw that here too, as in his bodily movements, Duditch appeared to be continually coming and going. His face alternated between three distinct expressions. One, a bright-eyed, eager, fertile expression. By this you could know, some seconds before its arrival, that an idea was coming to him. Then, once the idea had come and had been vocalized, sometimes with an odd confusion of words, sometimes with a surprising aptness and clarity, you could tell that it was going by the vacant look which swiftly descended on him. And, third, when it was quite gone, you would know this by the curious silent anticipatory way he would stare at you—an expression suggesting that though his own mind which only a minute before had been full was now blank, that he expected either himself or you to say something of importance immediately.

To these noticed traits, Coleeb added what he knew of Costyve's emotional life: the fact that Duditch was continually building houses of cards only to have them collapse on him, the fact that his growing emotional interests were marked by outbursts of enthusiasm and by an ever increasing fever of activity, and that his waning interest was characterized by a sort of pathetic disillusion and by a semi-frustrated eagerness to find some new attachment to take its place—Coleeb added these known facts to his current perceptions and thus obtained a fairly complete outline of how Costyve acted.

Meanwhile, Costyve himself, still the centre of the company, had left Toledo and El Greco in favor of a seldom visited island off the coast of Greece. And it was at this point that the timorous-looking woman, Miss Hanover's college friend, asked him a question which allowed Costyve to reveal himself in a new light. In fact, in answering it he not only showed forth an aspect of himself unknown even to his close friends, but said something which caused the abrupt termination of the tea.

"But, Mr. Duditch," he was asked by a quivering feminine voice, "suppose you were to die in some far-off outlandish place. Whatever would happen to your body?"

This fearful mention of death threw a vaguely nervous cloud over the gathering and disturbed most of the guests, with the exception of Costyve. He, on the contrary, appeared quite at ease, as if he were fully prepared to face what for others was an alarming aspect of reality. Looking in a matter-of-fact way at his timid questioner, he replied:

"It would be disposed of according to the custom of the place."

"Not even sent home?" she asked, visibly withdrawing from the opposite possibility. All were concerned to hear his answer.

"Home?" he asked. "Do you mean by home, here, Chicago?"

"Yes," she said, trembling. "To your relatives and friends here."

"But my dear lady," Costyve replied. "To a man who has made the world his home—tut, tut—I have not forgotten Chicago—but, beneath the pavement it is all earth, is it not? It is earth here, in New York, in Constantinople, in Mecca, in Bombay, or in some spot without name. What difference does a name make? Would not the same changes occur in my dead organism whatever the place? For sure, they would. So you see, I have no doubt but what some fine morning a strange person using a foreign tongue will enter my room, cast one frightened glance at my body lying there, and say, 'He's dead.' "

Having said this, with more dramatic impressiveness than was his wont, Costyve paused; and the idea of death was about to leave him. But it remained with the others so vividly that each one identified with the picture which Duditch had conjured, and saw himself or herself dead stretched out in a strange room. Even their own usually familiar rooms would be strange if they were dead in them. They felt this with a quick catch of breath.

"Mr. Duditch!" several exclaimed, and looked at him [as if] to say that he had mentioned an impolite and terrifying thing.

It was Costyve's turn to look surprised and dismayed. He could not imagine what he had done to deserve this sudden reversal.

"He's dead" rang ominously in their ears. The longer they heard it, the more aghast they became. The image struck deeper and deeper into them.

"I'm dead," an impossible thing which some invisible force made them grapple with and realize to be true. Shock on their faces, each one tried to view himself and did look at the others. True, every single person there would have it said of him, sooner or later: "He's dead," or "She's dead."

Being not at all like the ancient Egyptians, who used to have mummies brought into their feasts, the present gathering took strenuous exception to such ideas and feelings at an afternoon tea.

Abruptly, one after the other, they arose to tell Miss Hanover how nice her tea had been, gingerly shake Costyve's trembling hand, and leave. In no time at all, Coleeb, Costyve, and of course Miss Hanover were the sole ones remaining. Poor Duditch knew he had broken something, but could not tell what. He was tense, fidgety, and miserable, and made the situation awkward for the other two.

Coleeb regarded him, trying to determine whether his expressed attitude toward death was merely due to lack of imagination or to a well considered unwillingness to place more value on his body than its worth. If this latter, then it was a sign of more intelligence and sense of reality than he was usually credited with. Coleeb could not decide which.

Miss Hanover tried to smooth the thing over; but in doing so she somehow gave Costyve the impression that beneath her kind words she really saw how ridiculous and helpless he was, and pitied him. This made him feel worse than if she had put him out of her house and slammed the door on him. He could not bear to have any one pity him. He made several futile gestures in denial of what he took to be her inner attitude; and then, before either she or Coleeb knew what was happening, Costyve darted toward the hall, left his hat behind, and rushed out the door into the street.

Flying bare-headed down the avenue, his world smashed to bits about him, he was aware of no wish save to see no human being on earth, of no need save to leave Chicago as fast as a train could carry him.

He never could remember how he reached his apartment, got his things together, and arrived at the station.

Once there, he called to his service a staff of porters and had them shoulder more bags, suitcases, and odds and ends than the law allows—himself, like a little general, at the head of them. Several bystanders laughed at the sight of him. But to an observing eye Costyve's departure was a matter of pathos no less than of comicality. For, rushing and active with fuss and to-do, surrounded by things and people though he was, his spirit hugged itself in loneliness and felt goaded by a thousand shattered hopes.

Ah well, it was a matter for this night only. For, on awaking in the morning to find himself speeding over some southwest region of the American wilderness, he would bounce from berth, bowl up the aisle, and out-beam all the men in the shaving-room.

Section III

POETRY

Editor's Note

Of the poems in this volume, most were selected from Toomer's un-published collection of poems, "The Wayward and The Seeking." Only three of these selections, to my knowledge, have been published pre-viously: *The Lost Dancer* and *At Sea* (Darwin T. Turner, *Black American Literature: Poetry* [Columbus: Charles Merrill, 1970]) and *The Blue Meridian* (Langston Hughes and Arna Bontemps, *The Poetry of the Negro, 1746–1970* [New York: Doubleday, 1970]).

The Blue Meridian, the longest of all the selections, is a poetic tribute to the ancestral races of America. Toomer first expressed this tribute in a poem, "The First American," which he subsequently expanded into *The Blue Meridian.* The first 125 lines of an early version of this poem were published as *Brown River Smile.* I published the concluding lines of a draft of the poem in *Black American Literature: Poetry* (Merrill, 1970). A revised and expanded version appeared in *The New Caravan* (Macaulay, 1936). In it Toomer considered more fully than before the spiritual dis-integration of America as a result of war, materialism, crime, and the Depression. The version of *The Blue Meridian* in this volume appeared in *The Poetry of the Negro, 1746–1970,* and is, as far as I can determine, Toomer's final one. In it Toomer, minimizing his allusions to particular places and people emphasizes the importance of universal love as the cure for mankind's ills.

I have made no changes in Toomer's punctuation of his poetry, except in those cases where he used a hyphen but obviously desired a dash.

AND PASS

When the sun leaves dusk
On far horizons,
And night envelops
Empty seas
And fading dream-ships;
When the stars have eyes,
And their light blends
With darkness—
I stand alone,
Salute and pass
Proud shadows.

WHITE ARROW
        Your force is greater than your use of it.
        Existing, yet you dream that breath depends
        On bonds I once contracted for. It is
        A false belief induced by sleep and fear.
        In faith and reason you were swift and free,
        White Arrow, as you were, awake and be.

ANGELIC EVE
>Strong threads have bound your starry life
>Within a silver-silken chrysalis,
>The world's prize,
>>And its first object of envy.
>Strong hands have shaded your clear sight
>Within luxurious slumber,
>Where, safe from the white solar
>And the black sun of night,
>>You have been kept virginal.
>But now, though I am unskilled in magic,
>Too blunt a key to unlock souls,
>You stir, and your waking life
>Makes my eyes luminous to see
>>Angelic Eve,
>The silk as wings upon her feet,
>Emerging from undifferentiated air.

HONEY OF BEING

Always your heart, atomic symbol,
Wherein experience returns
To essence and I know source
And end identical; your love,
Reason and creativeness,
Perfect, our aspirations seek,
And, having found, in ecstasy
Fold their wings upon fulfillment.

SING YES!
There exists in a higher world another being
with whom we may make contact, experiencing
the white-banded light of transformation.

Each being, each life may find his or her perfect correspondence, the other self. Each man may meet the woman who
answers him. To meet without is to meet within. Each woman
may meet the man who answers her. To meet within is to
meet without. The eyes open, the heart trembles and is stilled.
Incredulous recognition! With his whole being each feels the
authentic shock of the other. The spirit is raised and humbled.
We want to weep, we want to sing. What beauty! What unutterable beauty!

No one else has ever seen us, no one else has ever known us,
no one else has ever claimed us. Now we are seen and known
and claimed. This person comes to liberate us, to energize the
deepest unimagined reaches of our soul. And he or she becomes
a sacred presence. When being meets being, a cosmic note is
struck. When man meets woman, a being note is struck. It is
then we love.

Skin knows skin. Touch knows touch. Taste knows taste. The
lines, the curves, the faintest tracings and bold designs of each
are known. Body knows body. Being knows being. Acceptance
is complete and joyous. We are illumined.

Eyes see eyes and sing Yes! Face sees face and sings Yes!
Feelings see feelings and sing Yes! Mind sees mind and sings
Yes! Style sees style and sings Yes! Form sees form and sings
Yes! Rhythm sees rhythm and sings Yes! Breath sees breath
and sings Yes! Man sees woman and sings Yes! Being sees being
and sings Yes!

One never knows his body till he loves. It has been a thing

to feed, clothe, gratify. It has been dumb and inarticulate, a means of shambling through this semi-waking state. Now it is a vibrant organ of contact with the living world.

One never knows sex till he loves. It has been wasted in weak affairs or in purposeless chastity. Now it can conceive or be continent. In either case we feel its potency and force. We sense and realize ourselves as man, as woman, ourselves the products of the cosmic creative force and embodying our portion of it.

One never knows his feelings till he loves. What were ours have passed like sleep from him who wakes. What now are ours have come like waking to him who wakes again.

One never knows his mind. Now he finds his mind. One never knows his style. Now he finds his style.

One never knows his form till he loves. This form, the form of his very essence, lies loose and inactive till it is gathered by the power of love. Each part of him has had its own little form. Each little form has contested with the others, trying to persuade him to fit into it. Then suddenly these petty moulds dissolve and the great form vibrates.

One never knows his sound till he loves. This tone, the sum of all his tones, is not heard till struck by love. His tone of voice has been but the noise of unquickened unrelated self-fragments. It has neither come from himself nor gone to others, sounding them. It has talked but has not sung. Then suddenly his voice sounds with the blended sum of all himself.

One never knows his color till he loves. Each one has a color. Yes, each one has a light. But the color has been hidden beneath the colorless, the light covered by a cloud. Then see the beauty of his color, the radiance of her light!

One never knows his rhythm till he loves. This rhythm, the quintessence of oneself, sleeps till aroused and vivified by love. One never knows the rhythms of his organs. These also sleep, functioning sluggishly, enough for bare sentience but not enough for life. Then suddenly they awake. Each is touched to throb its clear strong rhythm in the whole dynamic equilibrium.

We never know who we are till we love. Then we discover. Then we know man's power and potential. The lost is recovered. The unattainable is attained. We who have been down, we who have been out, rise into our proper place in the great design.

Eyes see eyes and sing Yes! Face sees face and sings Yes! Feelings see feelings and sing Yes! Mind sees mind and sings Yes! Form sees form and sings Yes! Rhythm sees rhythm and sings Yes! Breath sees breath and sings Yes! Man sees woman and sings Yes! Men see men and sing Yes! Beings see beings and sing Yes! Beings see God and sing Yes!

AT SEA

Once I saw large waves
Crested with white-caps;
A driving wind
Transformed the caps
Into scudding spray—
"Swift souls," I addressed them—
They turned towards me
Startled
Sea-descending faces;
But I, not they,
Felt the pang of transience.

THE LOST DANCER

Spatial depths of being survive
The birth to death recurrences
Of feet dancing on earth of sand;
Vibrations of the dance survive
The sand; the sand, elect, survives
The dancer. He can find no source
Of magic adequate to bind
The sand upon his feet, his feet
Upon his dance, his dance upon
The diamond body of his being.

MEN

Different in persons
Diverse in minds
Friends in understanding

Exiles in self
Antagonists in egotism
Brothers in being

Enemies in greed
Dull in routine
Lovers in beauty

Separate in bodies
Many in desires
One in ultimate reality

Strangers on the earth
Prisoners in this world
Natives of deity

PEERS

A rock, you are called,
And hard to touch,
No eyes, no mouth,
No breathing as in men;
Yet we are peers, since
You exist and I exist.
Someday I will see again
Your substance in the sacred flame
And meet you undisguised
In the root of all that lives.

MENDED

> The double I,
> The cleft sky,
> The parted ocean,
> The fissured land,
> Healed over by the passing hand.

ONE WITHIN

Whose life connects
the migratory sea
the sky serene
the restless mind
the quiet being
the light that sees
the black that shines
the voice that speaks
the unutterable mystery

THE BLUE MERIDIAN

It is a new America,
To be spiritualized by each new American.

>*Black Meridian, black light,*
>*Dynamic atom-aggregate,*
>*Lay sleeping on an inland lake.*

Lift, lift, thou waking forces!
Let us feel the energy of animals,
The force of rumps and bull-bent heads
Crashing the barrier to man.
It must spiral on!
A million million men, or twelve men,
Must crash the barrier to the next higher form.

>Beyond plants are animals,
>Beyond animals is man,
>Beyond man is the universe.

>The Big Light,
>Let the Big Light in!

O thou, Radiant Incorporeal,
The I of earth and of mankind, hurl
Down these seaboards, across this continent,
The thousand-rayed discus of thy mind,
And above our walking limbs unfurl
Spirit-torsos of exquisite strength!

The Mississippi, sister of the Ganges,
Main artery of earth in the western world,
Is waiting to become
In the spirit of America, a sacred river.
Whoever lifts the Mississippi
Lifts himself and all America;
Whoever lifts himself
Makes that great brown river smile.

The blood of earth and the blood of man
Course swifter and rejoice when we spiritualize.

We—priest, clown, scientist, technician,
Artist, rascal, worker, lazybones,
This is the whole—
Individuals and people,
This is the whole that stood with Adam
And has come down to us,
Never to be less,
Whatever side is up, however viewed,
Whatever the vicissitudes,
The needs of evolution that bring
Emphasis upon a part—
Man himself, his total body and soul,
This is the moving whole.

Men of the East, men of the West,
Men in life, men in death,
Americans and all countrymen—
Growth is by admixture from less to more,
Preserving the great granary intact,
Through cycles of death and life,
Each stage a pod,
Perpetuating and perfecting
An essence identical in all,
Obeying the same laws, unto the same goal,
That far-distant objective,
By ways both down and up,
Down years ago, now struggling up.

So lift, lift, thou waking forces!

The old gods, led by an inverted Christ,
A shaved Moses, a blanched Lemur,
And a moulting Thunderbird,
Withdrew into the distance and died,
Their dust and seed drifting down
To fertilize the seven regions of America.

We are waiting for a new God,
For revelation in our day,
For growth towards faceless Deity.

The old peoples—
The great European races sent wave after wave
That washed the forests, the earth's rich loam,

Grew towns with the seeds of giant cities,
Made roads, laid silver rails,
Sang of their swift achievement
And perished, displaced by machines,
Smothered by a world too huge for little men,
Too empty for life to breathe in.
They say that near the end
It was a chaos of crying men and hard women,
A city of goddamn and Jehovah
Baptized in finance
Without benefit of saints,
Of dear defectives
Winnowing their likenesses from synthetic rock
Sold by national organizations of undertakers.

Someone said:
    Blood cannot mix with the stuff upon our boards
    As water with flour to make bread,
    Nor have we yeast, nor have we fire.
    Not iron, not chemicals or money
    Are animate to suffer and rejoice,
    Not what we have become, this angel-dough,
    But slowly die, never attaining birth
    Above the body, above its pain and hungers,
    To beat pavements, stand in lines,
    Fill space and drive motor-cars.

Another cried:
    It is because of thee, O Life,
    That the first prayer ends in the last curse.

Another sang:
    Late minstrels of the restless earth,
    No muteness can be granted thee,
    Lift thy laughing energies
    To that white point which is a star.

The great African races sent a single wave
And singing riplets to sorrow in red fields,
Sing a swan song, to break rocks
And immortalize a hiding water boy.

    I'm leaving the shining ground, brothers,
    I sing because I ache,
    I go because I must,
    I'm leaving the shining ground;

Don't ask me where,
I'll meet you there,
Brothers, I am leaving the shining ground.

But we must keep keep keep
    the watermelon—
He moaned, O Lord, Lord,
This bale will break me—
But we must keep keep keep
    the watermelon.

The great red race was here.
In a land of flaming earth and torrent-rains,
Of red sea-plains and majestic mesas,
At sunset from a purple hill
The Gods came down;
They serpentined into pueblo,
And a white-robed priest
Danced with them five days and nights;
But pueblo, priest, and Shalakos
Sank into the sacred earth
To fertilize the seven regions of America.

Hé-ya, hé-yo, hé-yo,
Hé-ya, hé-yo, hé-yo,
The ghosts of buffaloes,
A lone eagle feather,
An untamed Navajo,
Hé-ya, hé-yo, hé-yo
Hé-ya, hé-yo, hé-yo.

We are waiting for a new people,
For the joining of men to men
And man to God.

When the spirit of mankind conceived
A New World in America, and dreamed
The human structure rising from this base,
The land was as a vacant house to new inhabitants,
A vacuum compelled by Nature to be filled.
Spirit could not wait to time-select,
Weighing in wisdom each piece,
Fitting each right thing into each right place,
But had to act, trusting the vision of the possible,
Had to bring vast life to this vast plot,
Drawing, in waves of inhabitation,

All the peoples of the earth,
Later to weed out, organize, assimilate.
And thus we are—
Gathered by the snatch of accident,
Selected with the speed of fate,
The alien and the belonging,
All belonging now,
Not yet made one and aged.

O thou, Radiant Incorporeal,
The I of earth and of mankind, hurl
Down these seaboards, across this continent,
The thousand-rayed discus of thy mind,
And blend our bodies to one flesh,
And blend this body to mankind.

The east coast is masculine,
The west coast is feminine,
The middle region is the child—
Reconciling force
And generator of symbols.

    Thou, great fields, waving thy growths
       across the world,
    Couldst thou find the seed which started thee?
    Can you remember the first great hand to sow?
    Have you memory of His intention?
    Great plains, and thou, mountains,
    And thou, stately trees, and thou,
    America, sleeping and producing with the
       seasons,
    No clever dealer can divide,
    No machine or scheme can undermine thee.

The prairie's sweep is flat infinity,
The city's rise is perpendicular to farthest star,
I stand where the two directions intersect,
At Michigan Avenue and Walton Place,
Level with my countrymen,
Right-angled to the universe.

It is a new America,
To be spiritualized by each new American,
To be taken as a golden grain
And lifted, as the wheat of our bodies,
To matter uniquely man.

I would give my life to see inscribed
Upon the arch of our consciousness
These aims: Growth, Transformation, Love,
That we might become heart-centered towards
    one another,
Love-centered towards God, dedicated to the creation
    of a higher type of man, growing up to Him.
Let new eyes see this statue in the bay,
Let this be quarantine to unbend dreams,
Let old eyes see it in Wall Street and the Loop,
And through this clearing house
Let all pass checks who may.

But out of our past comes hell,
Rushing us, sweeping us,
Winding us, blinding us,
Mistakes and hates,
Habits, blights, and greeds,
Out of our past they come
And they are hell.

The eagle, you should know, American,
Is a sublime and bloody bird,
A living dynamo
Capable of spiritualizing and sensualizing,
One or the other predominantly;
Its spread from tip to tip denotes extremes
Of affirming and denying,
Creating, destroying—
And the majestic flight may disappear;
Now we have become air-minded, it seems,
The eagle is a flying-machine,
One wing is broken,
The plunge to earth is panic before death.
There is force gone wrong.
Somewhere in our land, in cellars or banks,
In our souls there is a forgotten trust—
What is it we stamp upon our money?
May we stamp it upon ourselves
    In God We Trust.

        In one of the depression years,
        Or was it a prosperity year?
        I forget. I forget, too, whether the

Republicans were in, the Democrats out,
Or vice versa. At any rate, it was during
The time of man, and some said everything was
All right, and some said just the reverse,
That I met a girl upon the streets—
"So you are, eh, ready for anything,
A fly little bum? It's OK with me.
Let's go to a night club
Where we men who disembowel the day
Drink and coax reluctant lust,
Come jazz. Make the place as swank as you like,
I've got millions, they all know me,
And, kid, who knows, it may be
Our luck to see the dancing Wow,
The rage of this old town, the one
That everybody's crazy about,
I said the Wow,
The Bold Bitch of Babylon.''
I got a surprise, believe me I did,
She replied—
"Yes, I too have let friends suffer for a day,
But never always. I see yesterday and tomorrow,
From me are drawn the powers that heal,
Sweeten, give new faith and make us remember
That to live is to grow, to grow is to love,
And this is what we are here to do.
You, then, must convince me that you know
The undying seed and its destiny,
The yesterday before birth, the after-death
   tomorrow,
The now of man and woman—
So will I believe you worthy to let me.''

(The nature that man should have, and woman,
The trust and faith in one another,
The depth and beauty of relationship—
That after chaos they may manifest again
And build their worlds.)

An airplane, with broken wing,
In a tail-spin,
Descends with terrifying speed—
"Don't put me on the spot!''—
From beings to nothings,

From human beings to grotesques,
From men and women to manikins,
From forms to chaoses—

Crash!

Of what avail that with neon lights
We make gas-tanks look like Christmas trees?
Of what avail the battle
Of the school-books and the guns?
What use bombs and anti-bombs,
Sovereign powers, brutal lives, ugly deaths?
Are men born to go down like this?
Violence is violence.
Our holidays leave us as we were,
Our schools do not regenerate,
Precisely the educated are the brains of war,
Our churches do not transform—
So here we are. In war, in peace

> Blood does not mix with the stuff upon our boards,
> As water with flour to make bread,
> Nor have we yeast, nor have we fire.
> Not steel, not chemicals or money
> Are spirited to suffer and rejoice,
> Not what we have become, this angel-dough,
> But slowly die, never having birth
> Above the body, above its ego and hungers,
> To sit at desks, stand in lines, ask for jobs,
> Fill space and pass time
> Within a prison system all of wardens.

Nor does it help to know that thus
The pioneers and puritans have legacied us,
They, indentured to all men before them.

> Nor can we eat, though food is here,
> Nor can we breathe, though the world is air,
> Nor can we move, though the planet speeds,
> Nor can we circulate, though Nature flows,
> Nor can we love and bear love's fruit
> Though we are living and life is everywhere.

> It is because of thee, O Man,
> That the first prayer ends in the last curse.

In truth, in no ordinary way
Can anyone quit any racket.

Men and women—
It begins with us,
So we must end it.

On what vermilion peak will squad-cars cluster
When the universe sounds judgment-day,
Vigilant for what gong-alarm
To get what anti-cosmic outlaws?
Down what rosy-golden streets will the black cars
     cruise,
Watchful for what syndicate
Of racketeers and hijackers,
And where the bull-pen, what the bars,
And who the men who will thus help God?

Men,
Men and women—
Liberate!

Yet, in this crashing world
Terrorized by bullet-athletes,
I unbolt windows and ten-cents greet
A happy simple thing—
An organ grinder with jaunty hat,
With wayward roaming feet,
And his monkey,
Sauntering along a spring street,
Diddle-lidle-le, diddle-lidle-le.

Late minstrels of the restless earth,
No muteness can be granted thee,
Lift thy laughing energies
To that white point which is a star.

There is land—I have worked it with my hands,
There are materials for every known and unknown
     need of man,
There are houses built and more to build,
Calling to the creator in each person,
There are men, there are women,
There are all the coming generations,
There is Life—but,
On land are shadows not of trees or clouds,
On materials marks not made by Nature,
On men and women ravages no animal could make,
On children brands,

On life a blight not put by God—
Gargoyle shadows,
Finger marks,
Ghosts like us,
A blight in an image recognized,
I having seen myself—
O Man, that thy mask
Streaks the space between the sun and earth,
Streaks the air between thyself and thyself.

Driven by what the cosmos has put in me
Let me then affirm to those, the mazed,
Who like myself have seen self-streaks,
Who too have felt the sear
And would rather suffer it than pass it on—
We are made to grow, and by growing attain,
Rising in new birth to live in love.
The brotherhood of man cannot be realized
By stunted men, nor by those dismembered,
Closed in themselves, cut off from the mainstream
And therefore frustrated and bent to live in hate;
Exiles can but gang against themselves and earth,
Suffering the wrong turn as it works out
With ever stronger compulsion towards catastrophe.
We who would transform ex-I to I
And move from outlaw to I AM,
May know by sacred testimony—
There is a right turn,
A struggle through purgatories of many names,
A rising to one's real being
Wherein one finds oneself linked with
The real beings of other men, and in God;
The kingdom *exists,* and is to be *entered.*
This seeming detour meanwhile leads
To a near highway just beyond where all roads end,
And along this, despite the prowlers of this planet,
Men and women can love one another,
Find their plot, build their world,
Live this life with unstreaked dignity
And lift a rainbow to the heavens.

> *White meridian, white light,*
> *Dynamic atom-aggregate,*
> *Lay waking on an inland lake.*

To depression
The stock of debris descends,
Down go its greed-events,
Control by fear, prejudice, and murder.
Let go!
What value this, paper of the past,
Engraved, ingrained, but meaningless?
What life, that for words and figures,
For power to spend and rear vain monuments,
Two hold guns and the rest are destitute?
Let go—and we'll carry all America in our hearts.
This is no ship we want to sink with,
But wreckage;
This is no ark through deluge into the future,
But wreckage manned by homesick ghosts.
Let go!
Let it go that we may live.
A pin, a watch-fob, a card of identification,
A name, pain, and emptiness,
A will to perpetuate what has been, blind
To distinctions between the useful and the useless,
And, of course, an ego.
Let go!
That which you have held now holds you.
And as it sinks would drag you down.
A chair of pessimism, a desk of disillusion,
Doors and windows of despair,
Denials run wild, violence,
Rampant negatives—
A fine suite, it is said—
A modern office
Machined and ventilated
For everything but man.
Walk from it,
Wake from it,
From the terrible mistake
That we who have power are less than we should be.
Join that staff whose left hand is
Demolishing defectives,
Whose right is setting up a mill
And a wheel therein, its rim of power,
Its spokes of knowledge, its hub of conscience—
And in that same heart we will hold all life.

It is the world we live in,
Then let us live in it.

Islanders, newly come upon the continents,
If to live against annihilation,
Must outgrow themselves and their old places,
Disintegrate tribal integrators,
And fix, as their center of gravity,
As their compelling ideal
The symbol of Universal Man—
Must outgrow clan and class, color,
Nationalism, creed, all the fetishes
Of the arrested and dismembered,
And find a larger truth in larger hearts,
Lest the continents shrink to islands,
Lest human destiny abort
And man, bristling against himself, explode.

So I, once an islander, proclaim,
Not as if I were the first,
But remembering one who went before me.

Our crocks are adequate and breathed upon,
Shaped first by hand, now machined,
But not whole. Cracks are in them,
Lids shut out the radiant air,
Shut in unholy rust,
And we, incontinent
Or small by shrinkage,
As if souls were denim,
Are tight after the wash of experience.
Yet we are not, nor are we made
Of cheap materials;
Throughout we are perpetuating stuff,
Existing in every world conceived by man,
Enduring in the real world itself,
Made to flow and expand
Through feasts and fasts,
Through sufferings and ecstacies
To balance, and the sacred reconciliation.

Mend and stretch, and then—

Unlock the races,
Open this pod by outgrowing it,
Free men from this prison and this shrinkage,

Not from the reality itself
But from our prejudices and preferences
And the enslaving behavior caused by them,
Eliminate these—
I am, we are, simply of the human race.

Uncase the nations,
Open this pod by outgrowing it,
Keep the real but destroy the false;
We are of the human nation.

Uncase the regions—
Occidental, Oriental, North, South—
We are of Earth.

Free the sexes
From the penalties and proscriptions
That allegedly are laid on us
Because we are male or female.

Unlock the classes,
Emerge from these pockets;
I am, we are, simply of the human class.

Expand the fields, the specializations,
The limitations of occupation,
The definitions of what we are
That gain fractions and lose wholes—
I am of the field of being,
We are beings.

Open the religions, the exclusive creeds,
Those tight parodies of God's intention;
There is a Root Religion
And we are of it, whose force transforms,
Whose way progressively reveals
The shining terraces of one reality.

Uncase, unpod whatever blocks, until,
Having realized pure consciousness of being,
Knowing that we are beings
Co-existing with others in an inhabited universe,
We will be free to use rightly with reason
Our own and other human functions—
Free men, whole men, men connected
With one another and with Deity.

In another Wall Street of the world
The stock of value ascends.

What then am I bid,
By what free arm and yielding hand,
Offering what currency,
For this.—

Matrons of shrinkage,
Feed not on these children,
But rather break your arms
Than impede their growth;
Lift those shadows,
Cut the binds of apron-strings,
That young gods may dance.

The skins have dried, so let them pass,
So let those who once lived and garnered
Release all seeds to us,
That we in turn may plant and gather
And pass on to those to come
Sound grain, right soil, air, rain and sun.

The cold white eye is in cold storage,
Down is the ad that reads,
"A dime to heaven in an elevator,"
And in this sacred factory
Of minerals, plants, animals and man,
Right direction is in his hands—
Man, master of himself and husbandman
Of earth and growth and every breathing creature,
Thus to live, thus to work, thus to love.

It is a new America...
In brand new cities,
Slanting up incredible buildings,
Bright pilasters are pathways to the sun.

I held a fair position as men rate things,
Even enviable—
I could taste flavors in a grain of sand,
My eyes saw loveliness,
And I had learned to peal the wind,
In short, I was a lucky fellow.
People shook my hand, said nice things,
And sometimes slapped me on the back;
Curious, then, that I, of all people,
In the month of the nasty mouth,
Should have found myself caught
In a backbay leased by public and private
    scavengers;

Such was the case—but I found
A river flowing flowing backward to its source.

I met a woman—
Much that I am I owe to her,
For she was going where I was going,
We together,
And a buried being was called to life,
A beauty and a power, a revelation
Of what life is for, and why we are;
Except that on the way we parted.
Why? Who knows what breaks the whole?
Ego? Separation occurred and each re-tasted
The illusion of split dominance.
I and she pushed we apart,
We divided us—
There was no use staying,
The essential thing had been lost
And we would have helped each other lose it more,
So off we went, and singly buried it.
She entered a world, all hers only;
It is for her to say if it is hers or not.
You can have the world I wound around me,
Though I would not wish it on an enemy.
Now and then I see her from a distance,
Sharply remember our way together,
And feel, deep beneath the layers,
Gratitude—and the task of man.

Upon my phonograph are many records
Played on sides in sacred and profane extremes;
Sometimes I hear Gregorian chants
Or Bach's "It Is Consummated";
Sometimes I hear Duke Ellington
Or Eddy Duchin sing popular contemporary;
And some rare times
I hear myself, the unrecorded,
Sing the flow of I,
The notes and language not of this experience,
Sing I am,
As the flow of I pauses,
Then passes through my water-wheel—
And those radiant others, the living real,
The people identical in being.

Water-wheel, as the unending stream flows
To turn thee to thy function,
Send thy power to the stones
That they may grind, that we may live,
And do it excellently,
But may thy motions sometimes pause,
May you be still within the flow
That always was and always is.

Sun upon clean water is the radiance of creation—
And once, far out in the vast spread,
Our eyes beheld a sacrament;
Her face was marvelously bright,
My brain was fiery with internal stars,
I felt certain I had brought
The gods to earth and men to heaven;
I blessed her, drawing with the fingers
Of my spirit the figure of the cross;
I said to her—
"All my senses will remember you as sweet,
Your essence is my wonder."

    Sweetheart of the lake!
    Marvel of the prairies with starry eyes!
    Angel child! Princess of earth!
    Girl of the mesas and the great red plains!
    Star of the sky! Joy of the sun!
    Pride of the eagle! Beloved of the thunderbird!

It is a new world,
A new America

Fifty times walk up the Palmolive Building,
Or the Empire State, following the pilasters,
And, if it is the Empire State, you will find
On top at last a curious mooring-mast,
If the Palmolive, a curious revolving light;
Above you will arch a strange universe,
Below you will spread a strange earth,
Beside you will stand a strange man.

To be spiritualized by each new American

Curious engine, compact of gleaming steel,
Trees, bone, blood, and compressed steam,

Your cabin is the captain's house,
Your whistle is the eagle's scream,
Accelerate your driving-rods—
Irresistible the whirling drive of great wheels.
Thundering black fire-being, down straight-a-ways
You roar with demonic speed, leaving
In your wake evident world-rails;
The double accents of your rods proclaim,
"My captain has new fuel and direction,
He will thunder me past semaphores,
Through blocks of all dimensions,
Past waiting stations and waiting beings,
Past all determined symmetries,
Beyond my head-light's searching reach..."
Irresistible the whirling drive of great wheels.

Each new American—
To be taken as a golden grain
And lifted, as the wheat of our bodies,
To matter superbly human.

The old gods, led by an inverted Christ,
A shaved Moses, a blanched Lemur,
And a moulting dollar,
Withdrew into the distance and died,
Their dust and seed sifting down
To fertilize the seven regions of America.
This new God we have—
Man at last triumphant over not-man,
Being born above anti-being,
And in this being, and everywhere,
The god who is, the God we seek.

The old peoples—
The great European races sent wave after wave
That washed the forests, the earth's rich loam,
Grew towns with the seeds of giant cities,
Made roads, laid silver rails,
Factoried superb machines,
Died, and came alive again
To demonstrate the worth of individuals,
The purpose of the commonwealth.

    Blood does mix with the stuff upon our boards
    As water with flour to make bread,
    And we have yeast, and we have fire;

To implement ourselves by things,
To use as means, what we are, what we have
    become,
Americans, to suffer and rejoice, create,
To live in body and all births;
And we can eat, and we can breathe,
And we can move, and we can circulate,
And we can love and bear love's fruit
For we are men and women living.

The great African races sent a single wave
And singing riplets to sorrow in red fields,
Sing a swan song, to break rocks
And immortalize a hiding water boy.

Earth is earth, ground is ground,
All shining if loved.
Love does not brand as slave or peon
Any man, but feels his hands,
His touch upon his work,
And welcomes death that liberates
The poet, American among Americans,
Man at large among men.

The great red race was here.
In a land of flaming earth and torrent-rains,
Of red sea-plains and majestic mesas,
At sunset from a purple hill
The Gods came down;
They serpentined into pueblo,
And a white-robed priest
Danced with them five days and nights;
And pueblo, priest, and Shalakos
Sank into the sacred earth
To resurrect—
To project into this conscious world
An example of the organic;
To enact a mystery among facts—
The mime-priest in the market-place,
Daubed with mud to grace the fecund,
Clown, satirist, and invocator,
Free dancer—
In the Corn Dance, the Kosharé.

A strong yes, a strong no,
With these we move and make drama,

Yet may say nothing of the goal.
Black is black, white is white,
East is east, west is west,
Is truth for the mind of contrasts;
But here the high way of the third,
The man of blue or purple,
Beyond the little tags and small marks,
Foretold by ancient seers who knew,
Not the place, not the name, not the time,
But the aim of life in men,
The resultant of yes and no
Struggling for birth through ages.

We are the new people,
Born of elevated rock and lifted branches,
Called Americans,
Not to mouth the label but to live the reality,
Not to stop anywhere, to respond to man,
To outgrow each wider limitation,
Growing towards the universal Human Being;
And we are the old people, witnesses
That behind us there extends
An unbroken chain of ancestors,
Ourselves linked with all who ever lived,
Joined with all future generations;
Of millions of fathers through as many years
We are the breathing receptacles.

There is greatness in the truth,
A dignity to satisfy our wish,
A solemn tone to make us still,
A sorrow to fill our hearts,
A beauty and a vision in the truth.

Mankind is a cross,
Joined as a cross irrevocably—
The solid stream sourcing in the remote past,
Ending in far off distant years,
Is the perpendicular;
The planetary wash of those now living
Forms the transverse bar—
This, our figure on this globe.
And upon our God we are a cross,
And upon ourselves we are a cross,
And through life and death
And all the currents, we are held to it.

O thou, Relentless Stream...

The Mississippi, sister of the Ganges,
Main artery of earth in the western world,
Is a sacred river
In the spirit of our people;
Whoever lifts the Mississippi
Lifts himself and all mankind,
Whoever lifts himself
Makes that great brown river smile;
The blood of earth and the blood of man
Course swifter and rejoice when we spiritualize.

The west coast is masculine,
The east coast is feminine,
The middle region is the child—
Reconciling force
And generator of symbols,
Source of a new force—

My life is given to have
Realized in our consciousness,
Actualized in life without celebrity,
This real: wisdom empowered: men growing
From womb to birth, from birth to rebirth,
Up arcs of brightness to the resplendent source.

    No split spirit can divide,
    No dead soul can undermine thee,
    Thou, great coasts and harbors,
    Mountains, lakes, and plains,
    Thou art the majestic base
    Of cathedral people;
    America,
    The seed which started thee has grown.

The prairie's sweep is flat infinity,
The city's rise is perpendicular to farthest star,
I stand where the two directions intersect,
In any town or county in the land,
Level with my fellow men,
Right-angled to the universe;
Where God's dimensions touch our lives
And work their nameless magic.

    Blue Meridian, banded-light,
    Dynamic atom-aggregate,

Awakes upon the earth;
In his left hand he holds elevated rock,
In his right hand he holds lifted branches,
He dances the dance of the Blue Meridian
And dervishes with the seven regions
          of America, and all the world.

Lift, lift, thou waking forces!
Let us have the power of man,
The tender power of the loving hand,
The irresistible urge
Of brain and heart and limbs
Moving on and on
Through the terms of life on earth
And then beyond
To aid the operations of the cosmos.

Beyond plants are animals,
Beyond animals is man,
Beyond man is God.

The Big Light,
Let the Big Light in!

O thou, Radiant Incorporeal,
The soul of our universe, hurl
Down these seaboards, across these continents,
The thousand-rayed discus of thy mind,
And above our waking limbs unfurl
Spirit-torsos of exquisite strength!

Section IV

DRAMA

Editor's Note

Little has been written about Toomer as a dramatist although the dramatic form of "Kabnis" (*Cane*) has suggested his interest in that genre. Throughout his writing career, however, Toomer flirted with theater—generally with little response. Toomer was innovative as a dramatist. In *Natalie Mann* he experimented boldly with Symbolist settings and Expressionistic dance while most American dramatists were clinging to Realistic and Naturalistic styles. In *The Sacred Factory* he created an Expressionistic drama as good as some Expressionistic plays produced in New York during the 1920s. Bad luck and bad timing may have interfered with Toomer's efforts to find producers (only *Balo* was produced—by the drama society of Howard University). Kenneth Macgowan, a director who was not reluctant to produce experimental theater, may have offered the most accurate assessment of Toomer's failure to achieve commercial success as a dramatist. Rejecting *Natalie Mann*, Macgowan asserted that it lacked the prime requisite of good drama—a strong plot line. Toomer's plots, in drama as well as in long fiction, are thin; for his interests lay in thesis, characterization, and language. But Toomer's dramas enunciate his ideas more clearly than his fiction or poetry do.

Completed in 1922, *Natalie Mann* depicts a young, middle-class, Afro-American woman who achieves self-liberation with the assistance of Nathan Merilh, a partly autobiographical, partly idealized representative of Jean Toomer as savior. Natalie Mann is contrasted with Merilh's fictional creation, Karintha, a Southern black awakened to sexual freedom at an early age, who ignores society's dictates. Natalie and Karintha are contrasted also with other Afro-American women: lower-class Etty Beal, misdirected and abused by the middle-class, who has freed herself defiantly; and middle-class Mertis Newbolt, who, intimidated by her group, rebels too late.

It is interesting to study the descriptions of Nathan Merilh's relationship with Afro-American society in Washington and with white artistic groups in New York. Consciously autobiographical in his presentation, Toomer uses the allegation that Nathan Merilh has passed for white in New York;

but Toomer's own position about his racial identity when he wrote this drama is probably best revealed in the description of Merilh's room, which emphasizes European and African influences almost equally.

The dialogue and the dance are also of interest in the drama. Through imitative dialogue, Toomer satirized the banality, hypocrisy, and conformity of the Negro middle-class. Through dance, used to express a theme rather than merely to provide visual diversion, Toomer suggested that liberation of the self is not achieved through suppression of the physical self but through heightened awareness and use of the physical self.

For contemporary readers, however, the most exciting aspect of *Natalie Mann* may be Toomer's focus on black culture and the black condition in America. When Toomer wrote *Natalie Mann*, no Afro-American writer had succeeded in having a serious play about blacks produced on Broadway. Broadway audiences knew black playwrights only as authors of musicals— those which had been popular at the turn of the century; and, later, *Shuffle Along* (1921), a sensational musical that inspired a number of imitations. Most of Toomer's white contemporaries who wrote serious dramas about black protagonists evaded criticizing America's treatment of its black citizens. For example, in *The Nigger* (later called *The Governor* [1909]), Edward Sheldon described the dilemma of a fair-skinned governor-elect who learns that he has an Afro-American ancestor. In *The Emperor Jones* (1920), Eugene O'Neill centered his plot on Brutus Jones' tyranny as emperor of an island in the Caribbean. Even Ridgely Torrence, who wrote for black audiences (*Three Plays for a Negro Theater* [1917]), softened his presentation by showing how the influences of Christianity persuade a black grandmother to abandon her plan for vengeance against whites.

Through the works of both black and white playwrights, America's theatergoers of that period might have pictured Afro-Americans primarily as comic or pathetic primitives, restricted and oppressed only by their personal or racial weaknesses. In contrast, even while he assailed the hypocrisy and ignorance of middle-class Afro-Americans, Toomer attacked white America for judging blacks according to spurious standards of morality and art, repressing black artists, and exploiting black women.

Moreover, Toomer praised the black heritage. He revealed the cultural richness of black folksong and folktale. Rather than evade identification with Africa, Toomer utilized a portrait in Merilh's study to symbolize Merilh's African heritage, just as a second portrait suggests his European heritage.

In *The Sacred Factory*, an Expressionistic drama, Toomer climaxed his spectacle of humanity's disintegration. It is a presentation of both the monotonous, profitless, mechanical birth-to-death cycle of a working-class family and the intellectual-spiritual confrontations that frustrate and defeat middle-class American men and women. Toomer severely castigated the spiritual disintegration of America—a factory that creates robots and adopts the materialistically oriented drugstore as its church. Although Toomer may justifiably be questioned for his beliefs about the effective ways for women to fulfill themselves, he is contemporaneous in his concern about the misdirection of women and about their suppression in marriage. Like some psychologists whose views antagonize many women today, Toomer envisioned Woman as the embodiment of emotion and Man as the embodiment of thought and reason. Rather than accepting the tradition that evaluates reason as superior to emotion, however, Toomer insisted that a generation of liberated, self-knowing beings must fuse the two forces. If one force must dominate, Toomer suggested repeatedly, emotion is preferable. The emotion-oriented individual may realize himself or herself. The thought-oriented individual may attain materialistic goals but will not become liberated through self-realization.

In the typescript of both dramas, Toomer was inconsistent in his punctuation, capitalization, and spelling. I have sometimes made changes to achieve consistency in these areas.

Toomer also ignored or used inconsistently other stylistic and structural conventions. For example, in *Natalie Mann* stage directions are sometimes underscored to indicate italics, but sometimes they are not. In *The Sacred Factory,* however, Toomer did not underscore them at all. To conform to common practices in printed dramas, I have italicized all descriptions of character and all stage directions except for the statements of time (and sometimes, place) at the beginnings of scenes.

I could not resolve as easily, however, my own questions about some of Toomer's practices that may reflect stylistic choices (if these typescripts were intended for a publisher) or may reveal mere carelessness and indifference (if Toomer desired only to have working scripts to present to producers and directors of dramas). For example, in *Natalie Mann,* Toomer regularly typed "Mr." and "Mrs." without the periods customarily used to indicate that these are abbreviations. Because I question whether Toomer saw stylistic significance in these omissions, I have supplied the periods after these titles. On the other hand, even though I suspect that Toomer was considering typing ease rather than style when he omitted apostrophes from such contractions as "don't," "it's," "th'," and "t'," I have reproduced contractions exactly as they appear in the typescript of *Natalie Mann.* In this instance, I feared that, if I made any changes—even to improve the clarity for new readers of Toomer, I would mislead readers of *Cane* into believing that, in *Natalie Mann*, Toomer had altered his practice of omitting apostrophes from certain contractions. In the typescript of *The Sacred Factory*, however, Toomer inserted apostrophes in contractions, as this text reveals.

I have duplicated Toomer's use of two, three, or four periods to indicate a pause for thought, but I would not care to affirm that the length of the pause should be equated with the number of periods. I have preserved, and call attention to, one spelling practice that I consider deliberate. When he desired a mild exclamation or interjection, Toomer wrote, ''Oh''; but ''O'' indicates a stronger, more passionate, lyric cry from the soul.

Perhaps the most interesting editorial question of this sort relates to the names or designations Toomer used to identify speakers in the dramas. For example, when he indicated the middle-class females of an older generation, Toomer generally used either the title and last name or the full name (Mrs. Mann, Nora Hart). On the other hand, when he identified talented young women with whom the audience is to sympathize, he regularly used the first name only (Etty, Natalie, Greta). Considering these practices, one is tempted to wonder about the significance when ''Newbolt'' is consistently used to identify a young woman who has repressed emotion in order to satisfy middle-class morality: Is the use of ''Newbolt'' a careless practice by a writer who knows that an actress in the role would need no clearer cue, or is it a careful writer's attempt to distinguish the woman's character from that of other women in the drama? Similar questions might be asked about Toomer's designating males by last name and title (Mr. Mann, Mr. Hart), by last name only (Merilh, Kemp, Law), or by first name only (Tome). I am very hesitant to propose that these designations must be the result of conscious craftsmanship; they may reflect merely the author's subconscious response or relationship to his diverse creations. Nevertheless, some of the patterns of naming speakers suggest the possibility at least that Toomer consciously used these identifiers to indicate the character's prominence, social relationship to other characters, or role in a given scene. For example, the woman who is identified as ''Nora Hart'' when she is at a meeting becomes ''Mrs. Hart'' when she is involved in a more intimate discussion interrupted by her jealous husband. Even more strikingly, the characters who have been identified as ''Father'' and ''Mother'' in *The Sacred Factory* become ''Husband'' and ''Wife'' after the man dismisses their child. Later, they become ''John'' and ''Mary'' as soon as Mary decides that she cannot continue as his wife. To permit readers to consider these issues, I have copied whatever name or designation Toomer used to designate a speaker; therefore, what may be misconstrued as evidence of careless proofreading is the result of a reasoned decision.

Beyond the minor alternations already discussed, I have made as few changes as practical. I have corrected obvious typographical or spelling errors, and I have modified punctuation or interpolated words in order to improve the clarity. Toomer hyphenated many compound words that authors of today would write as single words. In addition, he sometimes wrote as independent entities two words that present-day authors would yoke into a single compound. I have retained his hyphenated words; but, in those occasional instances in which context indicated that two words are to be read as a single unit, I have linked these with hyphens.

NATALIE MANN
A Play in Three Acts

CHARACTERS

Mary Carson ⎤
Mr. Carson ⎥
Nora Hart ⎥
Mr. Hart ⎬ [black] citizens of Washington
John Kemp ⎥
Mrs. Kemp ⎦

Mertis Newbolt, who tries to evade one of the prime urges of life by fatiguing herself with less fundamental issues
Mr. Newbolt, her father
Mrs. Newbolt, her mother
John Newbolt, her brother

Natalie Mann, a personality who achieves herself
Mrs. Mann, her mother
Mr. Mann, her father

Nathan Merilh, an instrument of achievement
Therman Law, his friend

Etty Beal, a dancer
Tome Mangrow, her partner

Waitress in cabaret

Galt ⎤
Kaufmann ⎥
Brown ⎥
Greta ⎬ [white] citizens of New York
Carnoux ⎥
Maria ⎦

Incidental characters

ACT I   The action takes place in Washington.

1

Mary Carson's parlor. It is scrupulously neat and clean, almost to [a] fault.
Yet one feels rather at home in it. The walls are papered with no special
reference to taste. Old fashioned, nondescript pictures hang here and
there. An open hearth, with log fire, is in the center wall. A large bay-
window is to the right. An upright piano to the left. A Venus, in bronze,
is forward to the left. A group of three people, as if backed away from too
hot a fire, are over by the window. Mary Carson is middle-aged, very sharp-
featured, brown hair, and has an aggressive, high-strung poise. John Kemp
is around fifty. The expression of his face is tolerant. Nora Hart likewise is
middle-aged, futile, yet anxious, it would seem, to lessen the degree of her
futility.

MARY CARSON

I think it is such a pity that no one has helped her to find herself.

JOHN KEMP

Can an outsider really help, do you think?

MARY CARSON

No, of course not. The major promptings must always come from the soul.
But what I mean to say is, just a few touches and suggestions, the environment of a decent home. She's never had it, you know.

NORA HART

Dear, dear. Your opinions are so unconventional, Mrs. Carson. If I could
give my children what she has always been used to I could rest content.

MARY CARSON

Oh youre just like most superficial, social-grabbing mothers. In fact, you are almost the perfect type, Mrs. Hart. (*They laugh.*)

NORA HART

Never had a home. Dear, dear. Why the Manns have one of the finest houses that I know of. Besides, Mrs. Mann is certainly a very well-read woman. And a college graduate.

MARY CARSON

Thats just your trouble, Mrs. Hart. You think that a house makes a home, that being well-read is a synonym for intelligence, and that a college diploma carries with it the certification of a perfect life. But I can tell you that a home is nothing without a woman that loves it, loves her husband, and is willing to sacrifice herself for him.

NORA HART

I guess youre right. But it is such a pleasure just to step inside their door. It is so well-appointed and artistically done, you know.

MARY CARSON

That is the shell. Polished and smooth, isnt it? Looks better than this place. But I can tell you that the egg is rotten. At least so far as Natalie Mann is concerned.

KEMP

What you said a moment ago about sacrifice interests me, Mrs. Carson. You are an artist, you know.

MARY CARSON

Yes, but I thank God not one like Mr. Merilh is trying to be. You cannot approach the beautiful over the dead or maimed carcasses of others. Selfishness that masquerades as art is a work of the devil. And you cannot meet obligations by ignoring them.

KEMP

You acknowledge, then, obligations superior to art?

MARY CARSON

Yes I do. Art, art. What do you or Mrs. Hart, or Nathan Merilh know about it? Just so much talk and pretence. Aping, imitation, plagiarism and pretext for slurring the duties of life.

NORA HART

Dear, dear, what an iconoclast you are, Mrs. Carson.

MARY CARSON

Dont use words that you dont know the meaning of, Mrs. Hart. (*They laugh*.)

NORA HART

But isnt Miss Mann engaged to Nathan Merilh?

KEMP

That's what I've heard. Theres opportunity enough in that, it seems to me. Perhaps then she'll find herself.

MARY CARSON

Dont talk nonsense, Mr. Kemp. Nathan Merilh is a mere boy. She is already a woman. I saw her from the window today. There is really something quite majestic in the way she walks, and the carriage of her shoulders. He is not man enough for her. He looks more like a freak than a human being. Flies down the street (*mimics him*) with his head bent down, and wont even speak half of the time.

NORA HART

Dont take him too serious, Mrs. Carson. I'm sure that he's just acting. At least thats what everybody says.

KEMP

I dont think so. Its real all right, and you must make allowances for genius, you know.

NORA HART

Genius? Do you really think so?

MARY CARSON

He has the freakish look of genius, but I can tell you that thats all. He is wholly undeveloped. I have tested him. His mind cannot get above his body—and it never will. He ridicules the spiritual. And thinks he must indulge his passions as they come to him. Absolutely no restraint or elevation whatsoever. (*to Kemp*) You must be very careful how you handle such a word, Mr. Kemp. (*Kemp and Nora laugh*.) Remember, it is applied to Socrates and Plato.

NORA HART

But he must have a fine mind. He knows so many of the successful writers
in New York. And such a boy, too.

MARY CARSON

Its all from books. He reads, and gets someone else's ideas, thats all.
Look out, or he'll be picking you. (*laugh*)

KEMP

But you will have to admit that even that is above the average.

MARY CARSON

Oh he's a good thief all right.

NORA HART

Now dont say that, Mrs. Carson. You are so hard on people.

MARY CARSON

The truth is often hard.

(*Pause. The bell rings. Mrs. Carson goes to the door.*)

MARY CARSON

Oh, good evening Mr. Law. Its awfully good of you to come. I didnt
know whether to expect you or not. You are such a hermit. That is, unless
Mr. Merilh is along.

[THERMAN] LAW

(*as they come in*) Its not that. (*bows to the others but does not shake
hands*) I simply cant conceive of people wanting to see me. (*They laugh.*)

MARY CARSON

Well, I can assure you that I do. We were just talking about Mr. Merilh.
I know that he is a very dear friend of yours, but you know that I am
very outspoken.

LAW

That is a gift that few can share with you, Mrs. Carson.

MARY CARSON

Oh thank you. But Mr. Law, you are flattering.

LAW
Didnt intend to be.

MARY CARSON
No, I'm sure you didnt. And that is what I admire in you. Men are so deceitful.

KEMP
Not all men surely.

MARY CARSON
Yes, all men. I will except Mr. Law.

NORA HART
And wont except Mr. Kemp?

MARY CARSON
No, because I know too many bad things about him. (*They laugh.*)

LAW
Mr. Merilh said that he would be here shortly.

MARY CARSON
You have seen him then?

LAW
Yes, certainly.

MARY CARSON
And is he coming with Miss Mann?

LAW
I dont think so.

(*The evident surprise is not able to form itself in a sequence of gossipy questions, for the bell again rings.*)

MARY CARSON
Oh, good evening Miss Newbolt. Its awfully good to see you. Come right in, wont you.

[MERTIS] NEWBOLT
(*shaking hands*) I am frightfully busy—teaching all day, and then trying

to learn something myself at night, but I just had to come. Anything that moves for race betterment should be supported—even at personal sacrifice. Who did you say was to talk?

MARY CARSON
Oh it isnt to be a one-man affair. All of us are to contribute.

NEWBOLT
Splendid idea. Are any more to come?

MARY CARSON
Why yes, we are expecting Miss Mann and Mr. Merilh.

NEWBOLT
Natalie Mann? I didnt know that she was interested in such things.

KEMP
Perhaps she can become so? A meeting of this nature is so unusual around Washington that one doesnt get a chance to find out if one is interested or not.

NEWBOLT
I dont think so. Goodness knows there are activities aplenty. Besides, I've known her since high-school. She never would apply herself.

LAW
That is, wouldnt apply herself to what?

NEWBOLT
Oh, anything.

LAW
For instance.

NEWBOLT
Well, she'd never study.

LAW
Maybe the subjects didnt suit her nature. Or perhaps they were presented in a very uninteresting sort of way.

NEWBOLT
Why Mr. Law, I'm surprised. Washington schools are every bit as good as

you can find anywhere in this country. And as for the subjects not suiting her nature—it is the purpose of school and education to bring discipline and order into unruly, scattered natures. Man is a social animal, Mr. Law, and must be made, if he wont accept his condition gracefully, to conform to the existing order of things.

NORA HART

You are right. He certainly must. Just suppose that some of those rowdy colored people from the south-west were allowed to come up in this section and do just as they pleased.

LAW

I wont object to your platitude (*Newbolt bristles.*) about man being a social animal, Miss Newbolt, but I think I find you inconsistent. You say conform.

NEWBOLT

Yes, I do.

LAW

Do you?

NEWBOLT

Why certainly, Mr. Law. I said I did. Do you doubt my word?

NORA HART

No, I'm sure he doesnt Miss Newbolt.

LAW

To take a minor example, would you call it conforming to the established order of things when you told the manager of that theatre that you had just as much right to any seat in the house as the purest white person God ever made?

NEWBOLT

No indeed I wouldn't. But thats a different thing.

LAW

Quite different, I agree with you. But cant you conceive of it being possible that Miss Mann might revolt against the established schooling just as you object to the existing system of segregation?

NEWBOLT

Indeed no. I have reasons, based on a democratic justice, for my protest.

She was too young then, and is too indolent now, to even gesture at a reason. And besides, the way she runs around with men is simply scandalous. White people are always condemning us for immorality, and it is just such examples as hers that give their scurrilous remarks a slight basis in truth.

NORA HART
Dear, dear. You certainly are right.

MARY CARSON
But our women are not immoral, and I can tell you that. Our girls are more decent and modest than the whites. Look at the styles of F Street if you dont believe me.

LAW
I wish Merilh were here to tell you what he thinks about that.

MARY CARSON
Some superficial and unfair criticism, I dare say.

LAW
You are not quite fair to him, Mrs. Carson.

MARY CARSON
Yes I am fair. I know him better than you do. He works on the fairness and the fineness of your own disposition; he imposes on your friendship to make you think as he does. But you have a mind of your own. Better than his, I can tell you. Why dont you use it? What do you let him bluff you for?

LAW
Perhaps you havent heard his thoughts in this case.

MARY CARSON
Oh yes I have. He has spouted them until I gave out; that is, I got tired of listening to his freakish notions. I can tell you that they are all wrong.

LAW
Well, I dont care to argue the point, but kindly observe this, Mrs. Carson: truth is never fostered by a wholesale condemnation.

MARY CARSON
Words, words, words. It sounds just like Nathan Merilh. Why dont you use your own mind sometimes?

LAW
That is what I had hoped to do to-night.

KEMP
Suppose we drop the personalities. How about the meeting. May it not begin?

NEWBOLT
Why I thought it had already begun.

NORA HART
And so did I.

MARY CARSON
I was waiting for the others. Miss Mann especially. I really want to do something for her.

NEWBOLT
Why waste your time?

LAW
Do you think the application of true intelligence is ever actually wasted on anyone?

KEMP
Let's not drop into the old line again. Perhaps—

(*The bell rings. Mary Carson opens the door for Natalie Mann.*)

MARY CARSON
Oh, good evening Miss Mann. I'm so glad you've come. We were waiting for you.

Natalie enters. Her living personality is reflected in the sparkle and anima-tion of the men's faces. She is about twenty-four. Easily more of a woman than any of the others present. Searched for a surface beauty, her face does not reveal it. Indeed, in repose, it inclines to heaviness. Mertis Newbolt, as her stiffness takes on an added vitality, is decidedly the more attractive of the two. Yet a preference for Mertis, even in Washington, would be laughed out of court.

NATALIE [MANN]
Hello everybody.

KEMP

Good evening, Miss Mann.

LAW

How's Natalie.

NORA HART

How do you do, Miss Mann.

NEWBOLT

Pleased to see you I am sure.

NATALIE

I hope you didnt wait for me. I could easily have been around sooner, but folks never gather on time.

NEWBOLT

Some people do not.

MARY CARSON

We are waiting for Mr. Merilh. (*A quick and pained shadow passes over Natalie at the mention of this name. The others notice it, and mentally check its significance.*) Wont you play something for us, and perhaps by that time he will have come.

NEWBOLT

(*as if to herself*) I dont see what we have to wait for him for.

(*Natalie, with none of the silly modesty of so-called parlor-artists, complies. She runs her fingers over the keys, musing. Recalls the presence of the others, and plays a light inconsequential piece, which is obviously quite foreign to her mood. Then, unconcerned as to consequences or possible inferences, pours her very soul into the Presto agitato of Beethoven's* Moonlight Sonata. *During this, the bell rings. She, of course, does not hear it. Mrs. Carson comes in with Nathan Merilh. He is twenty-six. Looks like a boy when he laughs, like an old man when he is concentrating. When he walks, his head leads the rest of his body. He is dressed in tweed, and wears a brown flannel shirt. He stands rooted to the door-sill, his mind and emotions being wholly unprepared for such abandoned expression. Having spent her riotous mood, and much subdued, but deeper, Natalie swings into the* Love Death *from* Tristan and Isolde. *Merilh glances swiftly at the group, crosses them from his mind, and approaches Natalie. His face is tense with emotion, his whole being concentrated on her, on*

*her playing. Pain flashes his face. Then a stern joy. Natalie stops, turns
and sees Merilh, rises, and with a beautiful restraint in freedom is about
to return the pressure of his arms when Nora Hart gives a society cough.
Nathan, rudely pulled from his emotional absorption, in a reflex action
turns to the reality of the room.)*

[NATHAN] MERILH
God-damn you! (*With face blazing, he strides out of the room and the
outside door bangs behind him.*)

NORA HART
How uncultured.

MARY CARSON
He is crude. And he included you in his curse, Mr. Law.

NEWBOLT
He is a beast.

MARY CARSON
No, not as bad as that, Miss Newbolt. Just freakish.

NORA HART
But to curse in the presence of ladies. I think its awful. And the ingrati-
tude. I only wanted to remind him—O I have never had such a thing
to happen to me before. Everyone I've known has been such a gentleman.

LAW
It wasnt meant especially for you, Mrs. Hart, I can assure you.

MARY CARSON
Oh dont attempt to apologize for him. You simply make it worse. Of
course he meant all of us. There is a common streak in him. Very common.
It takes unusual occasions to bring it out. (*to Law*) I'll never forgive him
for including such a friend as you have been to him.

(*With the exception of Newbolt, they all avoid looking at Natalie. This
delicacy, together with the time taken in coversation, allows her to
somewhat compose herself.*)

LAW
You dont understand. It was—

MARY CARSON

I understand sufficiently well to forgo you your apology, Mr Law.

LAW

(*somewhat tartly*) If you will kindly let me say one word I think you will see that my statement is an apology only for those whose unreason persists in calling it so. I believe I know Nathan Merilh well enough to say for him that it was not you or Mrs. Hart or anyone present as persons that he cursed; he cursed us as immediate symbols of an environment which almost seems malicious in obtruding itself between the spontaneous union of souls, between even a creative concourse of one with one's own soul. So far as the cursing goes, it was absolutely unpremeditated. You belittle him, and violated your own discernment in imputing petty motives to his action.

NATALIE

(*flashing a glance of thanks to Law*) I hope I will not inconvenience you, but I think I had better go.

MARY CARSON

(*rising, the perfect hostess*) Oh not at all, Miss Mann. I'm really awfully glad you came. And I hope that next time we will be able to progress without such rudeness. Do come again. Say next Thursday evening. I want to talk to you.

NATALIE

(*slightly ironical*) Thank you so much. Good night everybody. Good night, Therm.

ALL

Good night, Miss Mann. (*She leaves.*)

MARY CARSON

(*returning from the door*) There, what did I tell you. How superb she is, and what a woman. Marriage to a man like that would ruin her. How childish of him. Not an ounce of modesty or control.

NEWBOLT

But she was simply brazen, Mrs. Carson. Only a loose woman could give herself like that. And such a good family. They must be ashamed of her.

LAW

If you would say "jealous," Miss Newbolt, I could agree with you.

NEWBOLT
Do you mean to impute that I am jealous.

LAW
Oh no, certainly not you, Miss Newbolt—just folks in general.

NORA HART
Dear, dear, I cant for the life of me see what there is to be jealous of, unless its her money and her home.

MARY CARSON
My dear Mrs. Hart, wont you ever rise above material things and a life furnished with tinsel and bric-a-brac?

NORA HART
Dear me, I'm afraid I'll never suit you, Mrs. Carson.

MARY CARSON
Dont, for God's sake, act to suit me; I'm not your husband. But I do wish that youd become less superficial.

KEMP
Well, we havent left the old mark yet. (*yawns*) What time's it getting to be?

MARY CARSON
Oh dont speak of time, Mr. Kemp. You show your plebian blood.

KEMP
Thats all well enough for those who can sleep as long as they want to in the morning. But bread-winners, and those who do the world's work, have to guard against the time.

MARY CARSON
The conceit of the male.

LAW
A very matter-of-fact and unenviable one, I can assure you.

NORA HART
Dear, dear.

MARY CARSON
I do wish you would get something else to say. "Dear, dear." If you cant

think, then borrow or steal. Anything to break the monotony and silli-
ness of it. Crazy people repeat words like that.

NORA HART
Do they really? Mr. Law, you can tell us about that.

KEMP
She's hinting that youre a little off, Law.

NORA HART
Mr. Law knows that I meant no such a thing.

NEWBOLT
Well, arent we going to have the meeting?

NORA HART
Oh, but my dear, we have been here so long already.

NEWBOLT
But I cant waste a night like this. (*Law and Kemp exchange glances.*)

MARY CARSON
Why I guess we might at least begin.

NEWBOLT
Yes, lets do.

KEMP
I second the motion.

MARY CARSON
(*beginning, but not so sure of herself as when she was talking about
personalities*) You are aware, I suppose, that the world is drifting into an
almost complete materialization of thought, and chaos. This newest fad,
psychoanalysis, says that everything is sex, physical sex. They wash love in
the dirty water of their own hypotheses. The old scientists, saying that the
soul was nothing but a property of matter, fooled themselves and degraded
the mind's conception of immorality. But they did leave the loop-hole
open for a noble love. A love nursed in the sanctity of home. Now these
young up-starts and pretenders presume to take all of the beauty out of
that. And then there are the socialists. Who are they? Materialists, materialists bent on a crude material conquest of the world. They would
disrupt the home. But they are strong. Physically strong, and the idols
they hold up to the masses are calculated to capture their credulity. Who

wouldnt be a socialist if he was offered, gratis, an equal share of the world's wealth? But anyhow, all these forces are tending towards materialism. Now the colored people are by nature spiritual. They actually see ghosts. Let the scientific ignoramuses who will, call that superstition. They know how to cast spells and control unseen forces. They are the coming people. We are a section of them. We are an intelligent section. Therefore it is our duty to combat materialism with our own God-given spiritual weapons. We must consecrate ourselves to that cause. (*pause*)

NEWBOLT

Thats all very nice, Mrs. Carson, but dont you think there are more immediate problems which we ought to clear up first, before going so far afield? Lynching and Jim-crowism, for example?

MARY CARSON

They are the outgrowth of materialism, my dear, and will die out of their own accord when it does.

NEWBOLT

But in the meantime, hundreds are being brutally butchered, and millions made to suffer the injustices of segregation.

LAW

Besides, how are you going to combat this materialism that you speak of unless you go for its concrete manifestations?

MARY CARSON

Thought, Mr. Law, is the ruling power of the world. Beautiful thoughts will supplant evil ones. They will reshape the whole contour of the world.

KEMP

Thats Christian Science. My wife's in it, and she wont give me a minutes peace.

MARY CARSON

Call it what you will. I call it Truth.

LAW

But it cant be Truth, Mrs. Carson, for you are way off on the question of socialism, and I'm afraid that the purpose of psychoanalysis is not quite clear to you.

MARY CARSON

Of course you'd say so. Mr. Merilh is a socialist and a bolshevist and an analysist and a freakist and I dont know what all. You get it all from him. He hands it to you on a tin spoon, and you swallow it whole. Why dont you use your own mind, Mr. Law?

LAW
As I said, thats what I had hoped to do tonight.

KEMP
I quite agree with Mrs. Carson about that socialist business. But what I'd like to know (*to Mrs. Carson*) is just what role your art plays in all this.

MARY CARSON
Art is the inevitable result of spiritual sight and inspiration. It serves its purpose in forwarding the greater end.

NORA HART
Dear, dear, all of this is too much for me.

(*A voice from the dining room calls to Mrs. Carson.*)

MARY CARSON
Do come out and have a cup of tea.

(*They all rise as if glad of any pretext for motion. They chatter as they pass out. The curtain descends.*)

2   The same evening

The Mann home. Parlor. To the rear is the hall. A mahogany cabinet, which may be a victrola, is seen through a central door. The wood-work is white. The paper is a thick buff. The floor is of hard wood, polished. A small, expensive rug only partially covers it. The bay-window is to the left. A dark mahogany table sits in it. That it may be seen from the street, a floor lamp. To the left, front, Mrs. Mann is reading a finely bound book. Beside her, a small portable table with a reading lamp. On the other side of this, an extra chair. A grand piano is to the right. A wide door in the right wall. To the left of this is a comfortable sofa. Natalie enters, dispirited. She crosses idly to the piano. Her natural carriage conceals her inward state from all but a discerning eye. Mrs. Mann glances up as Natalie enters. She adjusts her tortoise-rimmed glasses. Her gestures are brief and determined. She does not stop reading as she off-handedly questions Natalie.

MRS. MANN

You are home early, my dear. Did you enjoy the meeting?

NATALIE

Yes, very much—what there was of it.

MRS. MANN

I'm glad you did, my dear. Young folks are so frivolous and irresponsible these days. Who was there?

NATALIE

Oh, Mr. Law and Mr. Kemp, Mrs. Hart, Miss Newbolt, and—Nathan came in.

MRS. MANN

(*looking sharply*) How is it he didnt come home with you, my dear?

NATALIE

I dont know, mother—that is, he must have had another engagement, as he only stayed a short while.

MRS. MANN

That is strange. You do not know where he has gone? I understood that Nathan was to be one of the principle contributors.

NATALIE

Well, he was, mother.

MRS. MANN

You look tired, my child. Well, never mind, tell me all that was said. I am sure it must have been very interesting.

NATALIE

How can I remember all that, mother.

MRS. MANN

Goodness knows you couldnt have circled the encyclopedia in such a short time. And your memory is certainly long enough to stretch a few short blocks. What is the matter, Natalie?

NATALIE

Oh nothing.

MRS. MANN
But there is something, Natalie. I insist that you tell me.

NATALIE
Well, if you must know, Nathan cursed at them and left.

MRS. MANN
Nathan cursed at them and left? Why what a strange thing for Nathan
to do. Surely there must have been a very grave provocation.

NATALIE
I dont think so. He's just freakish at times.

MRS. MANN
And that is a very unusual thing for you to say. One would expect such
thoughts from a person who has never seen or read of people other than
common and business and professional men. If my memory does not fail
me, it was you yourself who used to take up for him when I, I am ashamed
to say, idly repeated what idle gossips said about him. What could possibly
have changed you so. You are not yourself tonight. (*Feeling that something
is wrong, she does not even so much as gesture towards her daughter in
open affection or love.*)

NATALIE
Oh, its nothing. That is what they said about him tonight after he had
gone.

MRS. MANN
Not Mr. Law surely.

NATALIE
Therman Law is true blue.

MRS. MANN
I am sure he is. But I am not so sure of you.

NATALIE
Why mother.

MRS. MANN
No, dont "why mother" me. Something has changed your attitude. You
must tell me.

NATALIE

Well, I do not want to be engaged to a man whom people are always making fun of.

MRS. MANN

That is not worthy of you, Natalie.

NATALIE

Well.

MRS. MANN

Nor will indignation serve the purpose. What I want is the simple truth. (*She suddenly realizes that Natalie has willfully been with-holding something from her. Intuitively she feels that she is to blame. A shadow of pain crosses her face. Starting to go to Natalie, she checks herself.*)

NATALIE

Well, the truth is, mother, that I cannot tell you.

MRS. MANN

Daughter!

NATALIE

(*letting herself go*) Oh, bother "daughter." "Daughter," "daughter." "My child," "my child." That is all I've ever heard. For years you have sat there under that lamp and read, and read. Read of mothers and children, of wives and husbands, of their problems and disappointments, of their need for guidance and love, while all the while my own life has whirled and eddied past like a river which you glance at now and then from the remote security of a steel-span bridge. Whenever the river has risen higher than its accustomed mark, people on the shore have shouted, and you, using you hands for a megaphone have called down, "Dont flow so fast, dont rise so high, dont whirl and eddy so." You are not a mother; you never have been. You are a powdered and scented and proper bundle of donts and prohibitions. I have never expected that you understand me; all the reading in the world cant change your temperament. But a daughter's starvation rations should include at least a bare crust of love. All the old hens in this city—and the young ones too, have tried to peck at me and pull me down. I dont complain that you have often believed them—you are more like them than you are like me, but it has nearly crushed my soul to feel not even a spark of blind faith and sympathy...

MRS. MANN

Daughter! Have you been holding all this malice in your heart towards me?

NATALIE

It is not malice, and I will not have you call it so. You can upbraid me for some petty misdemeanor against the lying, respectable social code, and I must thank you for a parental benevolence calculated to secure for me a sweet and harmless good. The minute I recall your duties and failure as a mother, I am accused of malice. You wanted the truth; now I've given it to you.

MRS. MANN

Your good breeding should never permit you to forget the respect due your elders—

NATALIE

Another one of your failures.

MRS. MANN

I shall speak to your father about this the minute that he comes home.

NATALIE

Oh mother, cant you see even this once that stiff codes and the accustomed threats can do no good? (*She goes over and kneels beside her mother's chair.*) Cant you, you, your real self meet me this once? Mother I need to love you. More now than at any time before. I need to feel your love. O it would be wonderful to touch you, and feel something large and dark and warm—

(*Men's voices are heard, and a key rattles in the lock.*)

MRS. MANN

Your father, Natalie. Heaven knows what he'd think if he saw us like this. (*Natalie, taking up a book, sinks into a chair on the other side of the reading lamp. Mr. Mann enters. He is followed by Mr. Hart.*)

MR. MANN

Come right in, Hart. Mother, daughter, Mr. Hart.

MRS. MANN

Oh how do you do, Mr. Hart. I'm so glad to see you.

NATALIE
Good evening, Mr. Hart.

MR. HART
Quite well, I thank you. How are you both?

MR. MANN
Rest your things here, Hart. (*indicates the sofa*)

MR. HART
Havent long to stay. Just a minute then.

MR. MANN
Come this way a second, Hart. I want to show you a pet rooster of mine.
(*They pass out the door to the right, pour drinks from a bottle of boot-
leg* [whiskey], *and return.*)

MR. HART
Quite a game-cock you have back there, Mrs. Mann.

MRS. MANN
Yes, isnt it, Mr. Hart. (*Hart and Mann find room on the sofa.*)

MR. MANN
Tell them that tale you got off, over at the club, Hart.

MR. HART
Would Miss Natalie care to hear it?

MRS. MANN
Oh I'm sure she would.

MR. MANN
Go ahead, Hart.

(*The curtain begins to drop* [*during Hart's speech*]. *It is timed so as to
cut off the stage in the midst of the laughter that is to follow* [*his speech*].)

MR. HART
(*getting comfortable*) Well, it seems as though a revival was sweeping over
a certain backwoods section of Georgia. Only a shallow stream ran through
the place. This wasnt deep enough for anybody to walk across and thereby

establish the certainty of his holiness. So when a local preacher wanted
to demonstrate that he was really full of the Spirit, he climbed up a
tree (having picked one where the ground underneath was soft). He
walked out on a sturdy branch, spread his arms, and cried, "Lord God
Almightly if I'm full of You, now let me fly." Flapping his arms bird-
wise, he jumped into the air—and flew like a rock straight down to
mother earth. (*All but Natalie laugh.*) The incident proved, of course,
only that preacher Harbut was not wholly pure. The next Sunday, Rev.
Jamese, who occupied the pulpit of the rival church, not to be outdone
in subjecting himself to test, stopped off abruptly in the middle of his
sermon. Dropping down on his knees he cried, "If the Spirit like a dove
has settled on my head, O Lord, then let me hear Your voice. If the Spirit
like a dove has settled like a dove on this poor humble sinner, O Lord,
Great God Almighty, let me hear Your voice." Sure enough, just at that
moment a low rumbling voice came from the yard. The congregation
scrambled to their knees, and were too frightened to even look around.
The preacher himself shut his eyes tight and repeated his request. Again
the voice answered. This time, however, old Rev. Jamese slyly opened
one eye. He saw a little boy peeping in the window and grinning. Hitched
to a buggy was an old grey mule. It didnt take him long to see where
God's voice had come from, so he motioned the boy to move along. The
young fellow, misinterpreting the preacher's gestures, pulled back the
lines and said, "Come on mule, aint no ole preacher round here gwine t
hurt you." The congregation looked out the window and saw the hoax.
And there would have been some tall goings on if the Right Rev. Jamese
hadnt succeeded in convincing them that the Holy Spirit often spoke
from a mule. (*Natalie has not taken her eyes from her book. The others
laugh heartily.*)

(*Curtain*)

3   The same evening

*Mrs. Hart's. The parlor. Very much on the same order as Mary Carson's.
The furniture is more up-to-date, the fire-place has been bricked-up, and
a table, suggesting the Manns', is in the bay-window. Mrs. Hart and
Kemp enter.*

MRS. [NORA] HART
Come in for a short while wont you, Mr. Kemp. I do hate so to break
off right in the midst of an interesting conversation. Mr. Hart is out—

(*She calls.*) Mr. Hart! Yes, I guess he's at the club with Mr. Mann. They're such good friends, you know. He goes there or somewhere every night, and then objects if I have too much company here at home. Dear me, even marriage cannot teach men what it is a woman wants—I mean they never seem to consider her at all.

KEMP

I dont know what it is—I've tried hard enough, but I'm a failure like the rest. (*They are seated.*)

MRS. HART

Oh I didnt mean you, Mr. Kemp.

KEMP

Of course not. You are too gracious to include present company. Nevertheless the fact is that I'm one of them. Any man's wife, who, with no physical ailment, dives into Christian Science, has been mistreated. The whole suffrage movement is a summation of domestic dissatisfaction and protest. Women dont want to vote, and all that sort of thing. They are innately too refined and artistic to want to mix up with the dirt and graft of politics. I am curious as to just the real reason why you joined.

MRS. HART

Why I'm not a suffragette, Mr. Kemp. Neither is Mrs. Carson. We believe that the place of woman is in the home.

KEMP

Pardon me. I understood that you were.

MRS. HART

I have no sympathy at all with these modern women. Feminine virtues mean absolutely nothing to them. I think it is simply disgusting to see a woman smoke. And some of the other things they do..! Besides, as I said, the home should be the very center of a woman's life. These modern women are bent on its destruction. No woman who sits in an office all day can come back at night and make the real atmosphere of home.

KEMP

I quite agree with you on that last point, but there are two thoughts one must hold in mind. One is, that it is only a degraded politics that becomes synonomous with office holding. Pure politics is a very powerful agent for the adjustment of just such grievances as you hold. Another is that the home, as distinguished from our ideas of what it should and should not be, is subject to change and modification. In a large sense, the woman's movement is an instrument—

MRS. HART

Dear, dear, Mr. Kemp, you are so involved. If Mrs. Carson were here, she would accuse you of imitating Mr. Merilh.

KEMP

Nathan Merilh has ideas, Mrs. Hart, and vital ones. He nearly knocked me off my feet the first time I heard him. I knew him as a boy, you know. But he's far from being the only mind in Washington. Mrs. Carson has her own grievances, and I dont begrudge her them. But she shouldnt put the whole town against the boy by such silly rot.

MRS. HART

I am sure that you are quite right, Mr. Kemp, quite right. Dear, dear.

KEMP

All I want to say is this, and then I'll stop. You cant blame individual men and women for the failure of the home. I've tried, and you've tried. It is a larger thing, more general forces that thwart and defeat us.

MRS. HART

That is true. That is true. But you were speaking about Mrs. Carson having grievances. Do you really think so? What do you imagine they could be?

KEMP

You should know better than I. You are closer to her. One cant help wondering. And in lieu of facts, supplying one's own conjectures. I shouldnt care to express myself.

MRS. HART

But you have your opinions?

KEMP

Naturally.

(*Pause. Conversation lags. Mrs. Hart revives it.*)

MRS. HART

I thought the expression on their faces was so beautiful tonight—until he turned and cursed me. Oh, I have never had such a thing happen to me before. It was so unlike the gentleman. And such a good family.

KEMP

You were saying that you thought the engagement broken off. Do you know it for a fact?

MRS. HART

Well, not beyond all dispute. But you see, the girl that does day work for me is a friend of the Merilhs' cook. You know how things get around. The Merilh cook has heard Mr. Merilh and Mr. Law talking. Some of the things they say are quite awful. I would never have believed them if he hadnt proved himself so unlike the gentleman tonight.

KEMP

What did he say about her?

MRS. HART

Oh, that she was too much a chameleon of her environment, that she'd have to blaze her own way before he'd admire her enough to marry her, that so far as love went he saw a hundred women every day whom he could love. I dont in the least pretend to understand it all—I dont like to talk about it. But one can see from that, that its just as Mrs. Carson says— she is way too good for him.

KEMP

I wonder what he means by love.

MRS. HART

Mrs. Carson says that he is like all the other socialists, and wants to com- munize women—whatever that means.

KEMP

And have you yourself any thoughts on love?

MRS. HART

I believe love to grow from admiration between two people of the same social class.

KEMP

Has that been your experience?

MRS. HART

Well—that is—you see, I have only had one love, and so my own experi- ence would not count for much. Dear, dear.

(*Pause. Conversation lags.*)

KEMP

Someone was telling me that Merilh is writing plays using the Negro folk-songs. Curious thing that a chap like him should dig down into that. There's lots of meat in them sure enough, but he's always seemed to me more intellectual and critical than anything else.

MRS. HART

Oh he is. He has no heart at all. Cold, cold all over.

KEMP

Do you think its sincere?

MRS. HART

Well, I wouldnt like to say, Mr. Kemp, for much harm can be done by unguarded words, but he has always kept himself so aloof, and when he goes away he never mixes with colored people. I believe he is frightfully prejudiced, and so does Mrs. Carson.

KEMP

You mean against color?

MRS. HART

Oh against everything.

KEMP

So I've heard. But one mustnt place too much assurance on what one hears.

MRS. HART

No, of course not. But I cant see how he can possibly be sincere about the spirituals. I dont like them myself.

KEMP

Dont you?

MRS. HART

No I dont. We havent been working these many years to get away from those low conditions simply to have them served up on a silver or any other kind of platter by the name of art.

KEMP

Each one to his own way of thinking, I suppose. Well, I really must be going.

MRS. HART
It has been so good of you to stay this long.

(*Just as Kemp is about to leave, Hart enters.*)

[MR.] HART
Hello, Kemp, glad to see you. What are you leaving for so soon?

KEMP
Must. The wife wont use Christian Science when I'm away from home.

HART
Well, drop around anytime. Glad to see you.

KEMP
Thanks. Good night.

BOTH
Goodnight, Mr. Kemp. (*Kemp leaves.*)

MRS. HART
He just brought me home from Mrs. Carson's, Harry, and I asked him to stay until you came home.

HART
Guess if I hadnt come home until one o'clock you'd have kept him all the same. I've told you often enough that I dont like these men hanging around when I'm not here.

MRS. HART
He wasnt hanging around, Harry. We had quite an intellectual evening.

HART
Now whats the use of saying that, Nora? Nobody else'd believe it, if you do. You cant bluff the world with that sort of stuff.

MRS. HART
Its not my fault if the world chooses to interpret everything in its own evil way.

HART
But it is your fault if you give it a chance to question you with its evil, and thats all there is to it. So just dont do it.

MRS. HART
Well, I will do it if I choose. (*She leaves.*)

HART
Yes, and you'll be choosing your own life thereafter.

(*Curtain*)

4   The same evening

Mertis Newbolt's bed-room. It is small and cramped. An oak bed is against the left rear wall. To the right of this, a door opens into the hall. It is now closed and locked. To the right, by a gas-jet, is a dresser. On it, together with some toilet articles and books, are two pictures, presumably her father and mother. Two chairs. Mertis leans back in one, reading. She is tense. Yet, as if someone were looking at her, she assumes nonchalance. It is the Bible she reads.

MERTIS NEWBOLT
(*reading from the* Song of Solomon [King James Version])

Let him kiss me with the kisses of his mouth: for thy love *is* better than wine. [. . .]
A bundle of myrrh *is* my wellbeloved unto me; he shall lie all night betwixt my breasts.
My beloved *is* unto me *as* a cluster of camphire in the vineyards of Engedi. [. . .]
Behold, thou *art* fair, my beloved, yea, pleasant: also our bed *is* green.
The beams of our house *are* cedar, *and* our rafters of fir. [. . .]

Stay me with flagons, comfort me with apples: for I *am* sick of love.
His left hand *is* under my head, and his right hand doth embrace me. [. . .]
O my dove, *that art* in the clefts of the rock, in the secret *places* of the stairs, let me see thy countenance, let me hear thy voice; for sweet *is* thy voice, and thy countenance *is* comely. [. . .]
My beloved *is* mine, and I *am* his: he feedeth among the lilies. [. . .]

Thy lips *are* like a thread of scarlet, and thy speech *is* comely:
thy temples *are* like a piece of a pomegranate within thy locks. [...]
    Thy two breasts *are* like two young roes that are twins, which feed
among the lilies. [...]
    How fair is thy love, my sister, *my* spouse! how much better is thy
love than wine! and the smell of thine ointments than all spices! [...]

    O that thou *wert* as my brother, that sucked the breasts of my
mother! *when* I should find thee without, I would kiss thee; yea, I
should not be despised.

(Rising to her feet, she nervously turns the pages back to Leviticus.)

    (reading) Speak unto the children of Israel, saying, If a woman
have conceived seed, and born a man child, then she shall be unclean
seven days; according to the days of the separation for her infirmity
shall she be unclean.
    And in the eighth day the flesh of his foreskin shall be circumcised.
    And she shall then continue in the blood of her purifying three
and thirty days; she shall touch no hallowed thing, nor come into
the sanctuary, until the days of her purifying be fulfilled.

(With an abrupt change of mood, she turns to Christ's Sermon on the
Mount.*)*

    (reading) And seeing the multitudes, he went up into a mountain:
and when he was set, his disciples came unto him:
    And he opened his mouth, and taught them, saying,
    Blessed *are* the poor in spirit: for theirs is the kingdom of heaven.
    Blessed *are* they that mourn: for they shall be comforted.
    Blessed *are* the meek: for they shall inherit the earth.
    Blessed *are* they which do hunger and thirst after righteousness:
for they shall be filled.
    Blessed *are* the merciful: for they shall obtain mercy.
    Blessed *are* the pure in heart: for they shall see God.
    Blessed *are* the peacemakers: for they shall be called the children
of God.
    Blessed *are* they which are persecuted for righteousness' sake: for
theirs is the kingdom of heaven.
    Blessed are ye, when *men* shall revile you, and persecute *you*, and
shall say all manner of evil against you falsely, for my sake.
    Rejoice, and be exceeding glad: for great *is* your reward in heaven:
for so persecuted they the prophets which were before you.

(Someone raps on her door. Quickly putting the Bible aside, she grabs up one of her school books. Opening the door, a hand pushes in a letter, and a voice says:)

LANDLADY

Pardon me for not giving you this at dinner time. But I saw your light, and thought it might be important.

MERTIS

Thank you, Mrs. Banks. You didnt disturb me. Thank you. Goodnight.

LANDLADY

Goodnight.

(Mertis, without looking at the letter, throws it on the dresser.)

MERTIS

(returning to her preoccupation) Nathan Merilh—that is a strong name. Nathan Merilh... O God why did I go to Mrs. Carson's. O I'll never go there again. Never. *(She throws herself, sobbing, across the bed, and the curtain descends.)*

5   The same evening

The Black Bear Cabaret. Quite a commonplace affair. The floor-boards run several feet up the walls. The walls themselves are painted a cheap (now dirty) yellow. No windows are visible. An orchestra, of piano, saxophone, banjo, and drums, is over the right, rear. This side of the orchestra, a door, used by performers. Another door (front, right) opens on the street. In the left wall an opening shows an additional room—a sort of overflow and annex. The dance-floor, in the center, is surrounded by tables and chairs with metal backs. These are all occupied, mostly by young fellows and girls. Nathan Merilh has a table to himself (front, and slightly to the left). To his right, two couples drink near-beer. Just behind him is a handsome, but somewhat brutalized man, obviously of the place. The orchestra is resting. Merilh is interested in a large-eyed, full-breasted young woman who is one of the group of four. Law comes in.

MERILH

Dont tell me what they said, Therm. I've got it all in here. *(taps his pocket)* There's a study for you. *(nods towards the large-eyed girl)* What do you make of her?

LAW
Trying to amuse herself, forget herself maybe.

MERILH
Trying hell. Trying not to amuse herself, trying not to forget herself. She's from the South—some little burg I guess where her father's the big nigger of the town. Her voice is a little thin, but beautiful. I'd like to hear it when she's off her guard. She's got a singing laugh—but it flutters. And her walk is conscious and stiff. God, its criminal—and there you have it, Therm, a perfect symbol of what happens to the physical charm, the emotional possibilities of that type of girl after she has been respectably familied, pressed, rolled, straightened, powdered by the goody-goody sheep-dust of the Negro's benefactors. It would be a pain even if there were a compensating rational increase—which there is not in her case; for the triumph of reason, on the part of most of those who trumpet it, is forced into the hypocrisy of explaining a palpable mis-use of emotion. Well, never mind about that. That girl—I dont know what she's fit for—might be the bed, or the stage, or nursing—damn if I know—but whatever it is she is fundamentally capable of doing it creatively. Look at her now—'fraid even to give herself up to bubbles of near-beer and a soda-straw.

(*The party at the table, having become aware that Merilh's remarks are directed at them, show signs of resenting it. A rather pretty waitress comes indolently forward.*)

WAITRESS
What are you fellows goin t have?

LAW
What'll it be, Han?

MERILH
Ginger-ale.

LAW
All right. Make it two. (*Waitress, after smiling at Merilh, goes.*)

(*The handsome fellow slips up to their table.*)

TOME [MANGROW]
Corn?

LAW
How much?

TOME
Two bucks.

MERILH
All right. (*Law slips him the money, and receives a bottle [of corn whis-key]*.)

(*Tome goes back to his table. The waitress returns with the drinks.*)

MERILH
When's the dancing, sugar?

WAITRESS
Solo's next.

MERILH
Who is she?

WAITRESS
Some broad from up the way who calls herself "Jypsy Queen."

LAW
Oughtnt it be "Shimmy Queen?"

WAITRESS
Na, she aint so much on that. Some though. But not as much as I could do. (*gives a shrug by way of illustration and takes Merilh's tip*) Thanks.

(*She goes. The orchestra begins to shift and get ready. The lights dim. Spot-light on the floor. Jypsy appears. Every inch of her is living. But despite her smiles, her face shows bitterness.*)

MERILH
Know her, Therm?

LAW
Seems as though I remember the face.

MERILH
God, you ought to. Thats Etty Beal.

LAW
Jesus Christ!

(*The music and the dance commence. A sublimated shimmy. Or rather, the higher interpretive impulses of the girl attain a sort of grotesque compromise with the frankly sensual demands of the place and time. She dances in an intense vindictive abandon. Coming close to Merilh's table, she recognizes him, and from sheer impulsive mockery, beckons him to partnership in her dance. Merilh accepts the challenge. He swings into the obvious implications of the rhythm. Then, gradually, they establish a rhythm of their own. The orchestra instinctively stops. The dance becomes a spontaneous embodiment of the struggle of two souls, against external barriers, for freedom and integrity. It reaches a high point, a flourish, a triumph—and a close. The orchestra is the first to clap. Then the whole house. Lights. The manager comes forward and congratulates them. As Etty and Merilh are returning to his table. Tome steps up.*)

TOME
Look a here you dictie nigga, I dont like your dancin' with my gal. (*Merilh tries to push by. Tome grabs him by the sleeve.*)

TOME
You listen to what I'm sayin' to you, hear.

ETTY [BEAL]
Tome, this is an old friend of mine.

TOME
I dont give a god damn who he is, he aint goin t handle you. It was his kind who threw you down, an I aint fought for you t see them come an pick you when a blind man could see that youre pure gold.

ETTY
He is right, Han. You will excuse me, wont you? (*She is about to leave.*)

MERILH
(*detaining her*) Just a moment Etty, and Mr. Tome. I cant say a thing without sounding like a Y.M.C.A. secretary apologizing for the prudery of a young-folks home, but since Mr. Tome doesnt seem to hold a personal grudge, there is no harm in your sitting at the table with us until the next dance, surely? (*Etty looks at Tome.*)

ETTY
All right. (*recognizing Therm*) Why hello, Therm.

LAW

Hello Etty. Nothing better than to see you.

ETTY

Oh, let me introduce Mr. Mangrow. Han, this is Mr. Mangrow. Therm (*Tome and the men shake hands.*) Mr. Mangrow has been my silent partner ever since—well, you know when. (*They are seated at the table. Those who have been curious at other tables become occupied with their own concerns.*)

MERILH

How long do you stay here?

ETTY

Leaving tonight.

MERILH

Whats the trouble?

ETTY

I dont like it. I quit dancing for churches and community centers because I couldnt stand the people. I quit the stage; there youve got to be vulgar, but you cant be sincere. Cabareting is killing all the finer stuff in me, but in most of them theyre honest, and I get response. This damn place is filled half of the time with college boys and school-marms. I dont like it. What are you smoking?

LAW

Pardon me. One gets out of the habit.

(*The orchestra starts a dance tune. Couples fill the floor. After they get going, the music should be muffled, stopped altogether if necessary, so that the conversation at the table may be heard.*)

MERILH

Would it be intruding to ask how it will be before the real flame dies? Usually, I mean.

TOME

Hell, this aint no coroner's inquest sho'.

ETTY

Cant tell, Han. I am a fool to fight, and it might go any time. I've seen two pass. The girls have turned to common whoring... Ah Jesus but

I'm bitter underneath. And what for? No one that you can lay your hands
on is directly to blame. I cussed the old man till I was black in the face.
I've spit on church altars. Tome here has beat a hundred white-men. But
what for? The old man got his ideas of right and wrong from his old
man. The preachers have got to earn a living just the same as me. And
white-men when all they want from a nigger woman is her body want
that because their own women folks havent been taught how to satisfy
them. Do they know more about the needs and beauty of art than these
pickle-heads around this town? Tell me that. The hell they do.

> TOME

What's the use of going over all that, Birdy? (*turns to Merilh*) What do
you want to know for, anyway?

> MERILH

Come, old man, I may not have faced all of the experience that you have
on your plane, but I've bucked it in my way. Hell, thats not what I
want to say to you—its this, a river, blocked, spreads out over the plain,
and if it does no other damage, it wastes and dissipates itself. The thing to
do, is to dredge the bottom, get it full of melting snows and April rains,
and then by the cumulative velocity of its own current there is no such
thing as blocking it. Thats unnecessarily involved, I admit—I've been
beached on some old jargon I thought I was rid of—but anyway, you get
what I mean. To be concrete: I've got a girl who's at the cross-roads.
Either she breaks her environment, or it'll break her. I cant help her,
because she'd only cling to me. Besides, I'm just piecing myself together.
What I want is not a house-wife; its nothing personal like that. Just two
things have meaning for me: creation, and the power to achieve it. What
I see in her is talent, maybe a sort of genius, I dont know; what she sees
in me is man. And why? Simply because she isnt free to look at the world
from her own angle. Do I want to free her? I do not. Do I want you to
free her? You cant. I want you to take her, and like a rubber ball, bounce
her against an altogether new set of realities until, learning direction, she
ceases to rebound into your hand, or anyone else's.

> ETTY

Nathan Merilh—

> TOME

(*swinging around*) Look a here, are you one of those Merilhs?

> MERILH

One of what Merilhs, Mr. Mangrow?

TOME

You know who I mean: the ones who got their dirty money beating ignorant colored folks out of insurance, and swindling them when they were slaving to buy a home.

ETTY

Let that drop, Tome. Cracking old nuts doesnt give you the kernel.

(*Tome strikes at Merilh, catching him on the shoulder and knocking him backwards. Nathan's agility saves him from a fall. Etty, with a decisive strength, shoves Tome into his chair, and places her knee on him.*)

ETTY

This aint th time for rough stuff, Tome. Now cut it, thats all.

(*A few of the couples on the floor stop dancing to look on, but as they see that no fight is coming off, mix again with the dancers. Tome, demonstrating physical protest, transfers his real action to words.*)

TOME

You know what I said I'd do to the first one of them I caught. Now leave me alone.

LAW

You certainly cant hold against him, Mr. Mangrow, something that his parents might have done.

TOME

Aint he wearin the clothes his old man gave him? Where'd the money come from? Aint he got dictie airs? Where'd they come from? Aint he had easy times and nose-bags always full? Aint he got education? Aint he been sitting here like a god-damn duded doctor probing words in wounds the likes of him have caused? Aint he got clean sheets and a soft bed to tuck into tonight? Where'd they all come from? Where'd they all come from? And what is he going to do with them? Steal an rob, an pay the police to protect his stealing. Aint I got cause to fight?

MERILH

(*to himself*) Apologizing, defense, and supplication seem to sum it up tonight. I've got to shake out of this. (*to Tome*) I'd let you beat me up—

TOME

Let, hell. It aint for you to let.

MERILH

—if any good could come of it. But it cant. I'm for you now—

TOME

A lot of good thats doing me.

MERILH

—but I might not be by the time you finished swinging that hammer at my jaw.

ETTY

(*smiling*) I'm afraid you wouldnt be for anyone in particular then, Han. (*They laugh*.)

MERILH

Guess youre right, Etty.

TOME

She sho is, Mr. Merilh. (*Nathan puts out his hand to Tome. They shake*.)

MERILH

You struck a point tonight, Mr. Mangrow, a challenge. "What am I going to do with them?" Broaden it, and you have the problem that confronts the world today. What are we, all of us, going to do with our accumulations of knowledge, wealth, and institutions? Are we going to forswear our obvious duty to survive them, to direct them towards the welfare of a universal mankind, or are we going to let them bury us, all of us, by the uncontrolled destructive agencies that are inherent in them all? I have been fortunate in wealth, Mr. Mangrow, but still more fortunate in disposition, energy, and point of view. You think that money has made them possible, but you are mistaken. My family's money, my family's position, have been almost maliciously hostile to them. I have had to fight through. Money would have made me like my father. Education would have made me believe as all the upper classes do. My sole obligation would have been to preserve, to increase, what an all-wise God in His unfailing charity and beneficence had given me. Those who didnt have, werent supposed to have. Else He'd have given it to them. Duty to others? Duty to myself and to my God who never failed to look after all His children. And you? You would have been one of those divinely destined to achieve your recompense in another world. As it is, some years ago I accepted the challenge, "What am I going to do with them?" I said to Etty a little while ago, "Just two things have meaning for me: creation, and the power to achieve it." I do not mean that selfishly; I mean creation for each one according to his gifts, power to every man so that he may develop what is potentially within him. It is but an insuring wisdom on the part of the more fortunate to see to it that the most humble receives justice in the form of concrete opportunity. (*The dance ends. The tables are reoccupied.*) "What am I going to do with them?" You may not have intellectually understood a single word I've said. It does not matter. A conviction has found a lodging in your heart that will not hereafter allow a single questioning as to my motives. Actual achievement? God, who knows. . . .

(There is a silence, filled by the chattering at the surrounding tables. Etty comes out of her reverie.)

ETTY
About that girl, Han. I'd like to, but it cant be done. I understand you. Its swell of you to want to do it. I wonder how the hand would have played with such a trump for me. But you cant see into this game. Tome and I play it. One more? And from that life? Nope, Han, it cant be done. *(Realizing that her time to dance is near at hand, she makes a nervous motion, and rises. She shakes hands with Merilh and Law.)* Thanks for the dance, Han. By-by. *(Slipping across the floor, she disappears, and the men are left to a moody abstraction.)*

(*Curtain*)

ACT II

1   Evening, three or four days later

A sewing circle at Mrs. Hart's.

MARY CARSON

It is just as I tell you—there is a common, unbalanced streak in him.
A god, I mean, a gargoyle, with club-feet of clay. How else can you
explain it?

NORA HART

Can there be no possible doubt about it, dont you think?

MARY CARSON

Of course not.

[MERTIS] NEWBOLT

But the accounts of it do differ, Mrs. Carson.

MARY CARSON

What of that? Strip away the points of difference, and you still have the
fact. You cant possibly get away from that.

NEWBOLT

Yes, but I insist that they are so different that there must be error
somewhere.

MARY CARSON

You heard that he went to a cabaret immediately after leaving my home?

NEWBOLT

Yes.

MARY CARSON

That he had been drinking, that he danced a vulgar dance with a loose woman of the place, that he got into a disgraceful fight with one of its low denizens? Well, what difference does it make who the fight was over? If it was about Natalie Mann, as you say, then his degradation is the more complete. What was simply ignominious becomes infamous. To drag a respectable name into such a place. If you care for him, as I half suspect you do, it would be best not to insist upon your version.

NEWBOLT

Mrs. Carson!

MARY CARSON

Oh, that's all right about Mrs. Carson. You take my advice and steer clear of the whole affair.

NORA HART

Dear, dear, what will the up-shot be?

MARY CARSON

Mrs. Mann has emphatically answered that. Natalie has formally broken the engagement. Nothing better could have happened. Absolutely nothing. She is far too good for him.

NEWBOLT

So I've heard you say, Mrs. Carson. But breaking engagements really settles nothing. Does it? Any more than becoming engaged?

MARY CARSON

(*looking sharply at her*) So you are being led by Mr. Merilh into ideas of free love. I am surprised at you, Miss Newbolt. I gave you credit for having more firmness than that. And ideas of your own.

NEWBOLT

Mrs. Carson, you are obsessed by a very wrong notion of Mr. Merilh, and such a repetition of it becomes irritating and tiresome.

NORA HART

Dear, dear, you mustnt quarrel. You know Mrs. Carson doesnt mean anything by what she says.

MARY CARSON
When did you get to know so much?

NORA HART
I mean you mean nothing wrong, nothing to hurt.

MARY CARSON
That is very different.

(*The bell rings. Nora Hart opens the door for Mrs. Mann.*)

MRS. MANN
Good evening, ladies. You must pardon me for being late, but very important business unavoidably detained me, I can assure you.

THE LADIES
Good evening, Mrs. Mann.

MARY CARSON
Yes, I understand. Natalie—

MRS. MANN
Oh it did not concern her, Mrs. Carson.

NORA HART
But she must be very broken up over the affair.

MRS. MANN
Not at all I assure you, Mrs. Hart. Natalie is a very sensible girl, if I do say it. And very obedient, as a daughter should be. I simply put my foot down, and that ended it.

MARY CARSON
How firm and sensible of you, Mrs. Mann. I have often wondered why you did not do as much before. Anyone can see that Natalie is much too much the woman for him.

MRS. MANN
Do you really think so? Of course she is. But up to this scandal, nothing that he had done had jeopardized his name or his position.

MARY CARSON
His position?

MRS. MANN

Why yes. You surely have heard. His father has disinherited him.

MARY CARSON

No!

NORA HART

Dear, dear, what is the world coming to.

NEWBOLT

Really?

MRS. MANN

True. It now appears that the person whom he fought was one of those desperado bootleggers, or whatever they are called. Nathan Merilh had been financing a league of them. It seems as though the fight started over a division of the illegal spoils. There was nothing for Mr. Merilh senior to do but to withdraw the financial support that he has so innocently been giving such a nefarious business. He has washed his hands clear of it all. Nathan, I understand, is to leave for New York.

MARY CARSON

Who would ever have thought that he could stoop so low.

NEWBOLT

You could have predicted it, I am sure, Mrs. Carson.

MARY CARSON

That is because no silly love has blinded the purity of my vision as to just what he is. I would advise you to follow suit.

NEWBOLT

I am not so sure of it.

MARY CARSON

Sure of what, Miss Newbolt? You do not mean to insinuate that I too am in love with him? How childish. How absurd.

NEWBOLT

I dont see why not. If I am, and Natalie Mann is—

MRS. MANN

I want to assure you, Miss Newbolt, that my daughter's connection with Mr. Merilh is a thing of the past. Absolutely of the past.

NORA HART
And Mrs. Carson is married.

NEWBOLT
(*completely giving way to a revolt towards honesty*) Oh rot. Rot, I tell
you. I'm sick and tired of all this childish make believe, this lying. Yes,
I love him. And there is not a woman in this city who can boast of two
grains of vitality who wouldnt if she dared to. I listen to you women with
your chatter and your vain pretense at a moral superiority. What are you?
Nothing in God's world but camp followers to a pack of lies. Natalie
Mann ceases to love him because her mother forces her to break an engagement. Mrs. Carson cant love him because she has a husband tucked
away in her clothes-closet. What stupid, lying rot! I love him. I dont
care who knows it. (*preparing to leave*) Tell it to the Board of Education,
if you dare. Ask them to remove me on the grounds of my avowal. Tell
them I am unfit to teach your children. Then face me that I might brand
you all as hypocrites. Hypocrites! (*She leaves.*)

MRS. MANN
What an unspeakable fury.

NORA HART
I never would have believed it of her. And to think that only the other
night she said that Natalie was brazen—Oh, I—

MRS. MANN
Did she? She did? The hussy. I'll teach her to cast aspersions on a child
of mine.

NORA HART
But I am sure she could have meant no harm, Mrs. Mann.

MRS. MANN
Meant no harm? Now dont you get silly, my dear. It is high time we
found her out. You have become a public benefactor, Mrs. Hart.

NORA HART
Dear, dear, I dont know what the world is coming to.

MARY CARSON
(*trying to bite her own way to a generalized sincerity*) Well I'll tell you,
Nora Hart: it is approaching an honest recognition of certain fundamental
facts—

MRS. MANN

(*interrupting*) Yes, I quite agree with you, my dear Mrs. Carson. But you certainly cannot call the scene that we have just witnessed an example of that honesty. It was sheer vulgarity. Nothing else. And so unbecoming.. She has been casting aspersions at my girl. I'll teach her. Why what would the coming generation amount to if we entrusted them to such hands. Think of it. Your duty as a mother and as a citizen of this glorious Republic demands that you keep the educational system uncontaminated. Action must be taken at once. But you can leave this entirely in my hands. I have dealt with such cases before.

MARY CARSON

I wouldnt go too far if I was you, Mrs. Mann.

MRS. MANN

My dear, I can well dispense with your guidance. I have handled such cases before. Washington is becoming corrupt fast enough without our passing over such a flagrant violation of right conduct. And on the part of a teacher. Think of it.

MARY CARSON

(*with a too facile resignation*) Well, shall we sew?

NORA HART

You are right. Let us. (*They pick up their work, and revert to the usual.*)

NORA HART

Did you see that new creation in the Boston House today?

MRS. MANN

Yes. Oh I'm so glad you saw it. Wasnt it perfectly lovely?

NORA HART

Charming. The dresses seem to be getting longer.

MRS. MANN

I have noticed that. Well, its high time. Quite enough girls have shown the men their limbs. (*They laugh.*)

NORA HART

I bought some new material to-day.......

Etc. etc. etc...

(*Curtain*)

2   The next evening

Parlor of Mertis Newbolt's rooming house. Indistinguishable from Mary Carson's with the single obvious exception that there is an old-fashioned stove in the place of an open hearth.

MERTIS [NEWBOLT]

I asked you to come over, Mr. Law, because I feel that I can be frank with you. I know that Nathan Merilh has [been], and your friendship—it is a fine and beautiful thing, Mr. Law—has never once failed him. You've heard of course, exaggerated as such things always are, what happened last night. I dont care to go into the details of that except to say that I was honest. I have not often been. At times I have been petty and lying, and most unfair. You know that, and you have not begrudged your hostility. But I feel that it was not me you were hostile to, but my trivial hypocrisy. I have a great burning need for honesty, and I believe that you are large enough not to hold old grievances as obstacles. Am I right?

LAW

I am hardly prepared for this, Miss Newbolt. People have hurt me, and I have formed a shell. I never come out—except to Nathan Merilh. He hurts sometimes, cuts deeper than all the others put together. But its the difference of his motives. And at such times I think of myself stretched on an immaculately clean enameled table with a firm but kindly surgeon bending over me, probing for a bullet in an ugly wound. Something strong and resolute wells up inside of me to meet him. I become disdainful of anesthetic, and my spirit seems to float outside of me into life unconditioned by questions of mere pleasure or pain.... Well, thats me. Its you who should be talking. (*half musing*) Curious.. I've never told that to anyone ... to him..

MERTIS

(*conscious of an established rapport*) We all have shells, but they do not always contain us. Sometimes we burst through. Society hammers us back, and wagging tongues stitch ugly seams. They say that set bones are stronger than unbroken ones. Souls grow like that. They are broken and set, broken and set until they become so knotted that a force equal to death—but its my own case I want to talk about. I broke some years ago in Philadelphia. I had a child. The family hushed it up, and I went away. Ever since then I've tried to choke the force of life. Finding that I was not strong enough, I tried to fray it in any and all sorts of odds and ends. Teaching would not absorb it all. I took on extra studies. Studies would not absorb it all; I plunged into social service. Going amongst the

Negroes in the alleys I came upon scenes that burnt my imagination and memory like a forest fire. I had to give that up. I tried to throw myself into the cause against the wrongs suffered by my people. I still am at it. I believe in it. But how can the question of where you sit in a car compare with the vital problem of living? I mean with sex, Mr. Law, with sex relations, with the question of the home. With motherhood, with father-hood, and the conditions under which public opinion says that they must be performed. Something is wrong. There is no natural justice in the way I have had to suffer, to deny myself. I was blind, quite blind, in my need and revolt some years ago. Last night, a veil seemed to fall from my eyes. Almost without cause. Oh I cannot tell you how mean and contemptible I felt for all my past lying, for my two-faced servitude. I could have cursed them, and cursed myself with more bitterness than ever Nathan Merilh dreamed of. Since then I've thought, and thought— my brain is tight like an oak-knot. I have envied Natalie Mann her freedom. I have envied her her love. I still do perhaps, but I'll be honest if it kills me...

(*Pause.....*)

LAW
Have you decided as to just what is wrong?

MERTIS
Well, yes, but only generally. We must be sincere.

LAW
So much for attitude. Any details?

MERTIS
They are swirling in my head but refuse to be caught in words. I dont know.

LAW
I feel that I may be impertinent in saying so, but the psychology of the average colored person is so subject to a color interpretation of every-thing, that I must give the suggestion that the problem and its solution rest on facts and considerations that for the most part take no account of race. The general literature of the day is full of it. If anything, the whites are more concerned than we, for the simple reason that greater numbers of them are at the social level prerequisite for its recognition. There is one point, however, at which race enters. It is this: for three hundred years at least, an unsympathetic and unscientific white posture has gestured with scorn and condemnation at what it calls the benighted

moral looseness of the Negro. It has used its own moral pretensions as a
foot-rule of universal measurement. It has scoffed and played superior
to the French. But the French are too intelligent to do more than satirize
and laugh at it. The Negro, cursed by his ignorance of moral evolution,
of moral relativity, and lack of any sense of autonomous development, has
not been so fortunate. He has knuckled to. He has cupped his whole
nature in an imitation of bigotry just to prove to the white man that what
he says is not true. The result is obvious: what should be the most colorful
and robust of our racial segments is approaching a sterile and denuded
hypocrisy as its goal. What has become of the almost obligatory heritage
of folk-songs? Jazz on the one hand, and on the other, a respectability
which is never so vigorous as when it denounces and rejects the true art
of the race's past. They are ashamed of the past made permanent by the
spirituals. My God, imagine the look on the face of Dvořák. But I am
digressing. In spite of this peculiarity, the problem is a general one, and
it may be called not so much one of moral tolerance as one of moral
determination. Determination to find an individual truth, determination
to allow the same privilege to others, determination to interfere with no
one except [when] such a one obviously intends a social harm, and then
restraint must be exercised not on the grounds of moral dogma, but on
the basis of practical expediency. . .

MERTIS

What you say is very true. But it seems to me that is more of an ideal
than anything else. What we need is a technique of attainment. I am
going to lose my job for merely being honest. Everybody cant afford to
lose their jobs.

LAW

If everybody lost them, no one would lose them.

MERTIS

Thats right. But even if everyone thought alike, not everyone would
have the nerve to say so—that is, unless there was a spontaneous utterance
like there was the day that the armistice was signed—which is impossible.
Can you picture Mrs. Hart or Mrs. Mann admitting a flaw in the accepted
fabric?

LAW

Hardly. It falls the burden, therefore, the sorrow and the joy of those
who are driven to it. You will pay for your honesty. Many others have.
But honesty, like love or art, germinates the seed of its own recompense.

MERTIS

(*in a lighter vein*) I am sure that if Mrs. Carson were here she would long ago have accused you of repeating Nathan Merilh. (*They laugh.*)

LAW

She is a curious case, I'll swear. To hear her talk you'd think she was bent on sarcasm and a wholesale destruction, that she disliked everybody, inpartially, including herself. But thats not her. Get her alone, and you will see a side of her (if she likes you) that, like the blue sky, is evenly beautiful. I dont know what it is, but people excite her.

MERTIS

I heard Mr. Kemp mention art the other night. She is an artist?

LAW

Dont you know?

MERTIS

Indeed I do not. And I've lived in Washington, on and off, nearly all my life.

LAW

That is what she says. Might as well wash dishes so far as the people around here know or care about it.

MERTIS

But it is surely not my fault. I didnt know. No one has ever mentioned it. What does she do?

LAW

She paints.

(*The bell rings, and the landlady shows in Natalie Mann.*)

LAW

Hello, Natalie.

MERTIS

Good evening, Miss Mann. (*She is puzzled at the visit, as Natalie does not look at all hostile.*)

NATALIE

How are you both? No, I wont be seated, thank you. I just came around to tell you that whatever mother does, I absolutely have no hand in it. I never disliked you, Miss Newbolt, and when mother told me what you said—exaggerated of course,—why the queer thing was that, instead of resenting your remarks about me, I began to like you immensely. I hope we will be friends.

MERTIS

I am sure that we will, Miss Mann. (*They shake hands.*) Wont you stay awhile?

NATALIE

I would like to, but I promised Mrs. Carson that I would come around tonight.

MERTIS

(*as Natalie leaves*) Come to see me again, wont you?

NATALIE

You bet I will. Goodnight.

BOTH

Goodnight.

(*As they prepare to resume their conversation, their gestures are such as foreshadow a personal intimacy. Then Law's mind reverts to Natalie.*)

MERTIS

You were saying that Mrs. Carson paints. She and Mr. Merilh should be good friends, it seems to me. But it is evident that they are not. At least that is the impression that she gives—

LAW

(*not having heard her*) Say, did you ever see anybody like that girl Natalie. God, but she is a corker.

MERTIS

Miss Mann is quite remarkable.

LAW

Just that one act in coming here to you.

MERTIS

Yes, Miss Mann and Mr. Merilh will make a splendid couple.

LAW
So they will. Old Han. Well . . . What was that you said? Something about
Mrs. Carson?

MERTIS
I was saying . . . . . .

(*Curtain*)

3   The same evening

Mary Carson's.

NATALIE
I believe it, Mrs. Carson. I feel that way. But I dont know. Mother's
objection doesnt count a feather in a barnyard. Its Nathan: he's so set
against it.

MARY CARSON
I wasnt thinking particularly of Mr. Merilh. I think it would be good in
many respects if you did break from him. I have said it to others, and
now I'll say it to you: he is not near the man for you. He is cold. He
reasons. He doesnt know what love means. If he put his arm around you
it would be because his mind told him to. You would starve in a week
under such treatment.

NATALIE
I have felt that at times. His mind gets so absorbed. But then .. when
he is with me.. O Mrs. Carson you really cant known.

MARY CARSON
I can imagine it. That, however, does not meet the requirements of a
home. Love, to be lasting, must be spiritual. It takes that type of love to
withstand the strains of marriage. A permanent contract between two
people is a duty. What duty, tell me, does Nathan Merilh recognize that
is not a selfish one? He would leave you after the first month. Or if he
didnt, he would make your life so miserable that you would wish he
would. I know him better than you do. Now you take my advice. He
talks about creating. Why what is more creative than a real home? How
many women have them? How many men are married to women who

know how to make them? Point out to me one decent home. Our children might just as well be searching for warm air in an ice-box as to look for love in these stables decorated with beds. Oh dont tell me about them. I know.

NATALIE

You bring up so many points that it is difficult to answer you.

MARY CARSON

I dont need answering. Answer them for yourself.

NATALIE

At bottom I am certain that I feel as you do. But my mind seems to want to—

MARY CARSON

Thats Nathan Merilh, not you.

NATALIE

But as I have told you, Nathan would agree perfectly with you about the poverty of the home. He believes that it could be made creative; he knows that today it isnt. He thinks it could be a wonderfully effective center for all the people whose demands it fulfills. His point to me is, that in my present unawakened condition, as he calls it (there is a surprise in store for him), I could neither make a home that would satisfy him, nor bring to it a "technique" that would allow the development of those gifts which he sees in me other than instinctive motherhood. He has more confidence in my talent than I have myself. Or at least, he emphasizes it more.

MARY CARSON

Talent. Talent. What talent is to be compared with the talent of creating a home? Like all men, he is selfish.

NATALIE

He claims that in a more happy society you yourself wouldnt be spending your energies—

MARY CARSON

What does he know about me. He is impertinent. He thinks he can take his mind and lay down a rule of conduct for a sex whose needs he does not understand, and with which he wouldnt sympathize if he did. It is the ego and selfishness of the male. Why dont you show a little gumption? Take him.

NATALIE
But I thought—

MARY CARSON
Oh I dont want you to marry him. He is not man enough for you. But you should be married.

NATALIE
To whom?

MARY CARSON
I dont know. Anybody.

NATALIE
(*wryly laughing*) That is so difficult, Mrs. Carson.

MARY CARSON
(*less didactic and superior*) You should be married. It is the only thing. You are too fine to become a prostitute. You are too fine to become a white man's concubine. What else is there open? You couldnt be an old maid if you tried. All this talk about talent is aimed in the air. Dont you suppose that other girls of this group have had talent? Where is it? Tell me that. The white people of this country wont let you develop it. Art is as prejudiced as politics or industry. What becomes of colored students in the art schools? What happens to them in the conservatories? They wont admit you half the time, and when they do they are so mean that instead of beauty you are filled with bitterness. Talent is sacred. Defilement of it is worse than religious agony. Oh yes, you have talent. Dont you suppose that I can see it? I have known it all along. I have wanted to spare you the suffering. Nathan Merilh seems senseless to pain, and he is strong. But it would kill you. Of course, there is Europe. But you know that your father would not stint himself for what he considers a harmless pastime. O these men! And what can Nathan Merilh do for you? He hasnt got a red cent to his name. His father is putting him out. If he wasnt selfish before, he'll have to be so now. There is a fineness about you. You dont want to have to touch the ugly sordid things of life. You were cut out for polish and courtesy. Let him go if he wants to. Let him drink and eat the dirt of life. He may be able to stand it. He is a man. But you would break your heart in disappointment and bitterness. Get married. Any man will do. Surround yourself with a home. Make your own home. And live there...

NATALIE

It hurts me to say it.. I have seen a different side of you tonight ..
something in me that is deep and protective goes out to it ... but I would
rather die outright, be burnt or lynched, than to build myself such a
sepulchre, to cheat death by calling it home.

(*Curtain*)

4   The same evening ... an hour later

*Nathan Merilh's study. The walls are lined with dull black stained book-
cases. Above them is a rich grey wall-paper. There is but a single picture
[on] each wall. The frames are of simple, narrow black wood. A Henri Lefort
lithograph portrait of Tolstoy hangs on the left. On the right, an etching
of the breast and face of a powerful black man. His forehead is massive
like Tolstoy's. His lips fuller. He has no beard. An elemental, yet subtle
daring fills his eyes. The central portrait is a remarkable idealization
which might easily be a composite of the other two. Beneath each picture,
supported by the tops of the book-cases and the central mantel, is a yellow
candle in a brass holder. The ceiling is impressionistically reminiscent
of Africa. An open hearth is in the central wall. A low fire of pine logs
burns. Before this is a screen such as Hunt Diederich might do in Negro
figures. A leather sofa obliquely faces the audience. To the right, a grand
piano. Above this, in the right wall, a curious triangular stained-glass
window. The shade of the piano lamp is done in African figures. To the
left, Nathan Merilh sits before his desk. Behind him, on a slim pedestal,
rests a reproduction of the African Guardian of the Souls. A guitar is in
the corner. Merilh, bent over, is playing on a mandolin and humming
Negro spirituals. "Deep River." "Roll Jordan Roll." "Steal Away." And
one or two near folk-songs which he and Natalie have written. During
this [playing of music], Natalie slips in. She intently searches [the face of]
Nathan for a few moments, then goes to the piano, and plays the songs.
Merilh glances in her direction. He continues to play. She likewise sings.
Before the music has spent itself, Nathan crosses to Natalie, and with a
force that the conventions would call rude, takes her in his arms. She
responds, equal in vigor. They move to the sofa. Finally, Merilh stiffens
and pushes her away.*

MERILH

Moments like this, and I completely understand the force that drives you.
Moments like this, and I am almost willing to sum creation in a passionate

love. But the illusion that it will last forever is not strong enough to grip me. Could I admit it, with even an attempted admission, there arises something in me more insistently fundamental than passion itself. It simply will not tolerate passion as an end. Not a thing in God's world can challenge the fact that it, and it alone, includes the end. Insatiable, tender-cruel, sensitive-callous, evil-good, but always strong, it uses the whole of life to nourish it. You? Why, it would devour you and forget that you ever lived, unless you prove sufficiently independent and vital to force its lasting recognition. (*looking, with a burning intensity, straight at her*) The question as to whether you can do it or not is answered, for I see no fear fighting with courage for possession of your eyes.

NATALIE
But you may see your own strength and convictions mirrored there.

MERILH
The eye's reflection of surfaces is deceiving, but if there were nothing more sustaining them than my image, its pressure would have forced them to collapse in a spurt of blood. You would be blind. Instead, your eyes are like brilliant sheens bearing the burden of an unleashed soul. O you are beautiful. Such beauty was never destined for one man. You would make me feel like a miser whose lofty ambition has led him to contemplate hoarding the sun... (*more to himself*) Hum, old images .. guess the poetry of love for me lies in action...

NATALIE
I wasnt listening, Han.

MERILH
I said that I guess I'd rather love you than talk about it.

NATALIE
Why dont you then? (*He does. Again he frees himself.*)

MERILH
This wont do. I leave tomorrow. There are things to talk about, things to decide.

NATALIE
You say that you would rather love than talk. Yet you always pull away. And even when you dont, I feel as if you are about to. Tell me why.

MERILH
I thought that I had told you.

NATALIE

You have. Tell me again. (*Instead, he embraces her. Again he breaks away.*)

NATALIE

Well then, convince me that I am wrong, and that you are not selfish. Convince me that I am more artist than woman. Tell me how I may love you five minutes and feel secure.

MERILH

That must come from you.

NATALIE

Then give me the thoughts. I think that I can listen now.

MERILH

You mean that you havent before?

NATALIE

Not that, Han. But they were all distorted by my one desire. You dont know me as well as you think you do. Why must I spread myself around the globe when everything I am converges to you?

MERILH

I dont want you to spread yourself. Thats one of your faults now. You havent learned to use your energies. You think they all focus on me. Youre wrong. One that is swollen and more insistent than the others does. And youre not detached enough to see it in relation to the rest. What you need is experience, and the vision and perspective that springs from it. You need the bruising contact of reality to rub your other faculties to glow. When you have achieved that, you will look back with an indulgent smile upon the child-woman that you are to-day.

NATALIE

Suppose that I dont care two figs about smiling indulgently, and vision, and all the rest?

MERILH

(*ignoring her remark*) With me, Mrs. Nathan Merilh would read my stuff, maybe act my plays. I dont want that. I want to see Natalie Mann— no shadow or reflection, however perfect—Natalie Mann creating and recreating life and beauty. On the domestic plane, I dont want to meet an imperfect double, eat with one, sleep with one, talk to one. I get tired of myself. What would happen to you?

NATALIE

(*somehow giving the impression that she is indulging him*) Arent you a little selfish, Han? If I want to melt myself in you, ought not my own desire be considered?

MERILH

Hell no . . . if it really were your desire. But it isnt.

NATALIE

You judge too much for other people.

MERILH

Because I know the mechanism which determines what others say. And I know that it violates the principle of integrity, the principle that is the foundation of every individual life, that has been coaxed and clubbed to sleep in most of us.

NATALIE

But the Hindu desires Nirvana.

MERILH

That is understandable from the condition of his life. Self-effacement is but the spiritual counterpart of suicide. No one who has truly tasted of the joys and sorrows of creative life willfully desires nothingness. A child who has fashioned a whistle wants to live to hear it blow. And then he wants to keep on making whistles—and blowing them. With a show-maker, carpenter, an artist, a scientist, its all the same. If there is such a thing as a universal principle, the understanding of it lies in its thirst for creation. The cruelty of destruction is comprehensible as the complementing side of the desire to create. A one-sided destruction, annihilation, or absorption proceeds from a thwarted, stunted, denied creativity. You have not found yourself. You cannot function. You can conceive of no joy transcending the bliss of a surrender to a partial love. You think that your love for me is the sum of all your capabilities. But even a char-woman gets more from life than bed and home and babies. If only once in a life-time, she is conscious of her own being. At that time she knows that a man does not include the universe. Your possibilities are greater. You would curse me if you awoke too late to realize them. That beauty and vitality which is so rich and nascent in you now would become a sterile bitter thing. Look at the faces of the women you know; look at the men. They are cracked masks, too fragile to withstand the mutual hatred and resentment. The call to love, the call to create, is castrated by the servile toleration of custom, of ingrained modes of thought, by man's frantic desire to fit

his nature to them at whatever cost. You would become a spiritual eunuch.
I will not let you. Life lies outside of me.

NATALIE

When you become earnest and eloquent, I think that you are almost
divine.

MERILH

God damn me. Its you I'm talking about. I know what I am, and what
I'm going to do. You dont, and I want to set you straight.

NATALIE

You are very certain of yourself, Han.

MERILH

Yes, sure. I am conscious of my power. I know my purpose. And you
should know yours by now.

NATALIE

I do, Han.

MERILH

(*slightly nettled*) What do you mean?

NATALIE

Just what do you mean, Han.

MERILH

Then you agree with me? You understand what I say?

NATALIE

I think that you have just stated the case of the creative soul with more pre-
cision and strength than I have ever before heard it. Bernard Shaw (*Merilh
gives her a sharp glance*) puts it graphically, "This is the true joy in life: the
being used for a purpose recognized by yourself as a mighty one; the being
thoroughly worn out before you are thrown on the scrap-heap; the being
a force of nature, instead of a feverish, selfish little cold of ailments and
grievances, complaining that the world will not devote itself to making you
happy." You see, I know what you mean. I want that, almost as much as you
do. But as you say, I am not quite free yet.. You are going to free me..
Look at me, Han.. You have not heard my side of the equation.. Look
at me intently; I want to tell you something.. Now ... Han, I love you.
It is you who do not know what that means. You have never given me a

chance to act it, or explain.. Tonight I shall do both.. I want to tell
you a folk-tale. There was an African princess, and her name was Coomba.
Her father, king of many towns, enslaved the man she loved and sent
him to the west-coast, to a pirate slave-ship. Coomba followed through
the forests. She sold herself that she might accompany her lover to the
other shore. Reaching America, they worked side by side in the fields by
day. They planted rice and cotton. They harvested cotton and rice. They
cut the trees and cleared the ground. They were the real pioneers. And
when night came, their wretched cabin was a love abode. Coomba was
well-formed and beautiful. Ali, as straight as a phallic pole. One day, in
her sight, Ali was killed. Before night-fall, Coomba had been cruelly
violated. The story tells of how, that night, America heard the first folk-
song.. I love with the passion of that woman. My love is the need of
working with you day by day. Of planting and harvesting. Of clearing
ground. Of seeing the sunset in your eyes at night. Like Coomba, when
passion cools, or dies, then, it will be that I will sing my first song. You
would deny me a transient sacrifice to love. But you cannot do it; my need
is stronger than your desire to evade it. You said a little while ago that
something in me was swollen. You implied that it should be reduced to
the relative and normal. Follow that thought and you will see that the
straight line to creation runs directly through you. I am a woman, as
conscious of her immediate needs as you are of her far-off ones. I will
not be denied. (*She takes him in an embrace that will admit of no quali-
fications.*)

(*Curtain*)

ACT III

1   A year has passed. Nàthan [Merilh] and Natalie in New
     York

*It is a large front-room, on the second floor. Two windows in the central
wall. The light coming through them is anemic. Solid, old-fashioned
houses are seen across the street. A double iron bed is to the left. A dresser,
running water, two trunks, and a table on which rests a small gas-stove
are over against the right. Impossible pictures scattered on the walls. There
are some books in uninviting piles about the floor. Nothing, practically,
to suggest Merilh's study in Washington, except the mandolin and the
guitar. The effect would be indescribably commonplace and dreary but
for the energy of Merilh, bent over a typewriter, near the right window.
He wears white flannel trousers which an even dirt and steady wear have
turned nearly grey. His brown flannel shirt is open at the neck. Less
aesthetic surely, but more vital. Natalie, in a plain coat-suit, comes in
from work. Interrupting Nathan only by a smile in response to his nod,
she immediately sets about the preparation of supper. Dusk replaces the
anemic twilight. Natalie lights the gas. Merilh puts his work aside. Noticing
this, Natalie asks:*

NATALIE
Whats it going to be tonight?

MERILH
(*lighting a cigarette and pleasurably stretching*) Sort of an—

NATALIE
(*seeing his cigarette, interrupts*) I thought you had given them up?

MERILH

So I had. But I'm fatalistic about such things, I guess. At bottom I feel
that one's heart pumps on to a destined end, and what one does neither
shortens nor lengthens the time. A reincarnationist would derive me from
the Orient, I'm sure.

NATALIE

Well, it is your own life that you are living. (*Merilh arches his eyebrows.*)
What about tonight?

MERILH

Sort of an International or Cosmopolitan Club I guess you could call it.
They had something like that at the university; but as I was never invited, I dont exactly know. I was too much like the real thing for them I
suppose. Ooooo my! (*stretching*) Yep, young America shall gather under
this roof tonight. Jews and Germans and Irish and Russian and Latin, God
Almighty's Anglo-Saxon, and Niggers! Wheeee! (*Laughing, he goes over
to banter and rough-house Natalie.*) Need a little exercise, and cant see
any reason why you shouldnt be the butt of it. Youre elastic, strong,
and vigorous. And you cant hit back. Thats the very essence of good exercise.

NATALIE

Stop, Han, I'm getting supper.

MERILH

My dear, never scramble my eggs with the obvious. Hast thou lived with
me this long—pardon me, my dear—this short year to no purpose? Hast
thou not learned, O most priceless and indispensable of women, that my
mind is a singularly high-powered one? And that it disdains references
to the apparent and commonplace? Dost thou think I sit all day scouring
my wits for unique thoughts and images only to have my efforts crowned
by such a bit of culinary platitude?

NATALIE

I'll see to it that you are crowned, if that is what youre looking for. (*Nathan
still pesters her.*) The municipal authorities should provide struggling
playwrights and poets with a sand-pit and a playground.

MERILH

Not at all necessary, I assure you, when one's sweetheart fills his room
with P's!

NATALIE

(*laughing*) You are really too clever even for a crown. But you'll get it if you dont leave me alone.

MERILH

Come. I dare you. I am stronger than thou. By the time I get through bruising thy parts, the bed alone could comfort thee.

NATALIE

Yes, and while the bed was in the process of comforting me, thou, most worthy of Lords, would starve.

MERILH

Ah, but you swing that economic bludgeon with a heavy hand.

NATALIE

See, youre already getting the worst of it. So you'd better stop. Tell me, how is the play coming on?

MERILH

Fine. But I had temporarily forgotten that it was primarily for you. I was having the man say great things just as you came in. I'll have to change that part of it. (*They laugh*.) Seriously, I think I have succeeded in putting more of myself and of you, and of the people we know, in it than in anything I've done.

NATALIE

Are you merciful?

MERILH

If mercy is an attribute of honesty, I am.

NATALIE

Take them easy, Han. Use me if you will. I've used you, and its only fair that you should. But those people—Oh theres lots of good there, Han. I couldnt see much then,—I do now.

MERILH

Is it true perspective, I wonder, Natalie? Or the old habit of magnifying the virtues of the dead?

NATALIE

But they are not dead, Han. They are very much alive, and you would think so if you knew—

MERILH
Knew what?

NATALIE
How do you think we got along those first months? You didnt think that
it was money I had brought from home?

MERILH
Sure, what else?

NATALIE
That held out only a few weeks. The folks completely cut me off.

MERILH
And then?

NATALIE
Mertis Newbolt.

MERILH
You mean she sent—

NATALIE
Precisely, and even after mother had had her put out. Even with the ex-
pense of her own doctor's bills. She had been quite sick you know . . .
she and Therm—

MERILH
Damn . . . But I can match you. Where do you think that typewriter came
from?

NATALIE
I'm sure I've wondered and asked enough. It mysteriously made its appearance one day when all we'd had to eat was bread and peanuts.

MERILH
(*laughing*) Therm Law.

NATALIE
His generosity, and your impractibility. No wonder you sneaked it in.

MERILH
Shhhh! Division of labor and faculty provides that you be the practical

one. I sometimes have to out-wit your sense, just as its often necessary that you circumvent my lack of it. But to return to those goodnesses you were speaking about. Therm and Mertis are exceptions, you'll have to admit.

NATALIE

Exceptions in what, Han? I mean fundamentally.

MERILH

Opportunity and circumstance is an easy answer, and in accord with the democratic dogma. But that doesnt satisfy me. As an honest statesman I could use it. As a sociologist. But for art it is irrelevant—when it is not actually weakening. It makes one sympathetic to the point where he is inhibited from touching the vital elements that inhere in social evil and oppression. It is one of the contributing causes to the anemia of American Negro art. The Negro, judged by a superficial white standard, is some degrees below equal. To portray the Negro realistically is to give evidence of that fact. Few can ignore the public for their art. It is like placing the gelding as an arbitrary of horse. Silly owners hasten to castrate their males. And pseudo-artists, happening along before complete emasculation, ignore the art appeal of the remaining stallions to pay obsequience to a horse-fancier's ideal gelding. Hell!

NATALIE

Well, if things break right, stallions' broods may yet trumpet to the wind.

MERILH

You damn bet they may.

NATALIE

Do you know what really struck me about the case at Washington? Curious thing, it wasnt the fuss and the racket or the episode of the detectives. It hasnt a thing to do with feeling. And its a strange thought for me: its the tale that grew up around your going to the cabaret that night. Not the gossip or its consequences, but the fact that underlies the gossip. This: suppose that they should take some simple and beautiful fact of life, and apply the same processes. What would you have? An epic tale, a folk-tale, or a folk-song. In the twinkling of an eye, and all from nothing, you became the bold leader of a desperate band of outlaws. You might just as easily have become an heroic center, they might just as well have invested you with legendary powers. So you see it is not that their minds are inactive, but that they use them in a futile way.

MERILH

Hum.. And its just that futility that I'm going to turn over. There is but a thin line dividing your "futile" from the down-right malicious. The two are synonomous in Therm's and Mertis' case, if not in ours. They'll kill her, and hound him most to death.

NATALIE

I wonder if we hadnt better run down?

MERILH

Therm's got sense enough to write if he really needs us.

(*As they sit down to supper, the curtain descends to mark the passing of three hours. When it rises, the "club" has assembled. At least fifteen people are in the room. They are on the bed, on the trunks, on the floor, backs propped against the walls. For the most part, they chat in groups.*)

KAUFMANN

(*to Merilh*) But Merilh, you try to boil everything down to your own formula. It cant be done.

MERILH

I havent any formula, Ben. Unless you call my method of work a formula. But I have a philosophy, and I believe it to be inclusive. And I'll continue to believe so until some experience in life convinces me to the contrary. It seems to me that when you say "formula" you state your own case perfectly. Your part-philosophy excludes from it all but aesthetic values. You are in the same boat with Galt here, who cant see any but economic, or Brown, who cant see any but racial, or Greta, who cant see any but sex.

KAUFMANN

You say that because I will not include the Negro's features in my Classification.

MERILH

What in hell do I care about your "classification"?

GALT

And because I wont include your revolted bourgeois and intellectuals in the proletariat.

BROWN

And because I see you as inimical to the race.

GRETA

And because I cant admit of fundamental art impulses that dont originate in sex.

MERILH

You twist my motive. Exclude or include, its all the same to me. You are still interesting. And each one doubtless will create in his own way. Ben started the argument by accusing me of narrowing life to a formula. I deny the validity of his charge. I repeat, I have a philosophy, and I believe it to be inclusive. That is all.

CARNOUX

Listen here, Han; you believe in moral freedom—I do not confuse that with moral license. I want you to follow me closely, and then hold your peace if you dare. For convenience sake, let us say that man has three bodies. We will call them the soul-body, the mind-body, and the physical-body. Now we will take any imaginary woman with whom you are in love. I could read poetry to her, and you would not object. She could read poetry to me, and you would not object. That is, you would not be jealous of my sharing the body of her soul. All right. I discuss science with her; she discusses science with me. You do not object. In other words, I share her mind-body without arousing your jealousy. Mind now, this is still theory. Suppose I shared her physical-body; logically you could not object, could you?

MERILH

I could not.

CARNOUX

Having established that point, let us take an actual and concrete case. Suppose I shared all of the bodies of Natalie?

MERILH

I might knock your jaw loose. (*laughter and joking*)

CARNOUX

Precisely. Which proves what? Why, simply, that there are times when man acts on sheer unprincipled impulse, impulse pre-determined by centuries of feeling and thought which for the most part we are wholly unaware of. Is that not so?

MERILH

It is.

CARNOUX
Q.E.D. No philosophy of conduct can be inclusive.

MARIA
Oh bother argument and philosophy and all that bosh. We came here
for a good time, for art.

KAUFMANN
But all great art is philosophical.

MARIA
What nonsense. It is not. You might just as well say that all great art
is scientific—that art is science; that science is art.

KAUFMANN
But you cannot deny Danté and Goethe.

MARIA
Does Goethe live because of his philosophy? And you must know that
so far as thought goes, Danté is hopelessly out of date. A first-rate college graduate can shoot him full of holes.

KAUFMANN
What, then, do you call great art?

MARIA
Great art is a fresh, spiritualized record of one's world.

KAUFMANN
But how is one going to see one's world without a point of view?

GRETA
Oh for God's sake dont go into all that. I thought you were tired of argument. Kaufmann is inconsistent, anyway. He should be pumping aesthetics
instead of philosophy.

KAUFMANN
But what is aesthetics if not a philosophy of the beautiful?

GALT
Cut it out, you bears. Will somebody read something to us? If not, I'll
have to begin.

CARNOUX

Spare us!

GRETA

Come on Merilh, you've been writing all day. Fetch out.

OTHERS

Thats right, Merilh, give us something. (*Etc.*)

(*Merilh fumbles around with some papers. The rest comfortably re-settle themselves. Nathan selects a MS, shows it to Natalie who picks up the two instruments, giving the mandolin to Brown. These latter begin to play and hum an adaptation of a Negro spiritual. Merilh reads. As he progresses, one by one the others in the room join Natalie and Brown in humming. When Nathan finishes, the curtain begins to descend. The humming continues till it is down.*)

MERILH

(*reading*)

Karintha

> Her skin is like dusk on the eastern horizon,
> O cant you see it, O cant you see it,
> Her skin is like dusk on the eastern horizon
> . . . When the sun goes down.

Men had always wanted her, this Karintha, even as a child, Karintha carrying beauty, perfect as dusk when the sun goes down. Old men rode her hobby-horse upon their knees. Young men danced with her at frolics when they should have been dancing with their grown-up girls. The old men secretly prayed for youth. The younger fellows counted the time to pass before she would be old enough to mate with them. This interest of the male, that wishes to ripen a growing thing too soon, could mean no good to her.

Karintha, at twelve, was a wild flash that told the other folks just what it was to live. At sunset, when there was no wind, and the pine-smoke from over the saw-mill hugged the earth, and you couldnt see more than a few feet in front, her sudden darting past you was a bit of vivid color, like a black bird that flashes in the light. With the other children one could hear, some distance away, their feet flopping in the two-inch dust. Karintha's running was a whir. It had the sound of the red dust that sometimes made a spiral in the road. At dusk, during the hush just after the mill had closed down, and before any of the women had started their supper-getting-ready songs, her voice, high-pitched, shrill, would put one's ears to itching. But no one ever thought to make her stop because of it. She stoned the cows, and beat her dog, and fought the other children.. Even the preacher, who caught her at mischief, told himself that she was as innocently lovely as a November cotton-flower. Already, rumors were out about her. Homes in Georgia are most often built on the two-room plan. In one, you cook and eat; in the other is where you sit and sleep, and where love goes on. Karintha had seen or heard, perhaps she had felt her parents loving. One could but imitate one's parents, for to follow them was the way of God. She played "home" with a small boy who was not afraid to do her bidding. That started the whole thing. Old men could no longer ride her hobby-horse upon their knees. But young men counted faster.

> Her skin is like dusk,
> O cant you see it,
> Her skin is like dusk
> When the sun goes down.

Karintha is a woman. She who carries beauty, perfect as dusk when the sun goes down. She has been married many times. Old men remind her that a few years back they rode her hobby-horse upon their knees. Karintha smiles, and indulges them when she is in the mood for it. She has contempt for them. Karintha is a woman. Young men run stills to make her money. Young men gamble to make her money. Young men go to the large cities and run on the road. Young men go away to college. They all want to bring her money. These are the young men who thought that all they had to do was to count time. But Karintha is a woman, and she has had a child. A child fell out of her womb onto a bed of pine-needles in the forest. Pine-needles are smooth and sweet. They are elastic to the feet of rabbits... A saw-mill was nearby. Its pyramidal saw-dust pile smouldered. It is a year before one completely burns. Meanwhile, the smoke curls up and hangs in odd wraiths about the forest, curls up, and spreads itself out over the valley. Weeks after Karintha returned home, the smoke was so heavy you tasted it in water. Someone made a song:

> Smoke is on the hills. Rise up.
> Smoke is on the hills, O rise
> And take my soul away.

Karintha is a woman. Men do not know that the soul of her was a growing thing ripened too soon. They will bring their money; they will die not having found it out.. Karintha at twenty, carrying beauty, perfect as dusk when the sun goes down. Karintha...

> Her skin is like dusk on the eastern horizon,
> O cant you see it, O cant you see it,
> Her skin is like dusk on the eastern horizon
> ...When the sun goes down.
> Goes down...

> (*Curtain*)

(*The curtain rises on the same scene; it is morning [and the guests have left]. Natalie has just finished her breakfast. Merilh is still in bed. Natalie goes out, and presently returns with some letters. She hastily reads them.*)

NATALIE

There is a letter here from Mertis, Han. And one from Therm.

MERILH

(*He has caught the word "letter." His mind is wide-awake, his body still relaxed from sleep.*) Rejections or checks?

NATALIE

I said that they were from Mertis and Therm, Han.

MERILH

Well, what in hell did you wake me up for them for? The ink, I suppose, will have faded by the time you come home to-night.

NATALIE

(*repressing a desire to reply in like terms*) Not the ink, Han, but whats behind the ink. I read Mertis' and it made me open Therm's.

MERILH

Whats up?

NATALIE

Mertis is very sick. She wants us there. Therm also says to come.

MERILH

If its as serious as all that, what on earth can we do? You know I dont like this bed-side sobbing stuff.

(*Natalie crosses to the bed, and takes hold of his shoulders with deter-*
mination.)

NATALIE

Listen to me. Youre not awake. I said that both Mertis and Therm want
us to come. Neither one of them cares any more for tears than we do.
Mertis is sick. How sick I can only—

MERILH

Whats the actual trouble with her?

NATALIE

You are so damned meticulous where other folks are concerned. You
know as well as I do that she and Therm have been going together.

MERILH

And I also know that they have as much sense in that respect as we have.

NATALIE

Sense, yes. But Mertis is different. She cares not at all; then she cares a
whole lot. She doesnt apply her sense. She starves, and then takes enough
to kill a glutton. Thats her trouble now. She doesnt say so in so many
words—neither does Therm—but I know thats it.

MERILH

Hasnt she definitely mentioned it before?

NATALIE

Only vaguely. And Therm?

MERILH

We share ideas, but Therm has always kept his emotional life to himself.
I used to admire him for it. I thought of it as delicacy and discretion as
contrasted to the common bragging of most men. Now I'm not so sure.
Perhaps underneath he's really ashamed of his own ideas. Not sure of
them from the logic of his emotions. It takes the actual maturity and
conviction of experience to break away from ingrained notions. He has
known only child-women. I half suspect that his ideal is still that of innocence. And that he conceives the tragedy of woman as residing in its
so-called betrayal.

NATALIE

And so, his, their, need of us. Her family is there.

MERILH

So? A sort of broad-side of all that is prudish, respectable, and proper, eh? Guess youre right. When shall we go?

NATALIE

The one o'clock train if you can make it.

MERILH

All right for me. But how about you?

NATALIE

The job doesnt count. I'm expecting a letter from Watkins.

MERILH

Really? The first I've heard of it. What will you get?

NATALIE

Some minor role. I wanted to surprise you.

MERILH

Well you have that, right enough. Look out. Get off me. Produce or starve it is from now on.

NATALIE

Not quite that, Han. You know that I shall always be grateful.

MERILH

The hell you say. Look out. Get off.

(*Curtain*)

2   Washington. Evening of the same day

The parlor of Mertis Newbolt's rooming house. Merilh and Law. Law, in a rocker, is not quite able to control his restlessness. He is visibly depressed.

LAW

Etty Beal's in town tonight, Han. Over at the same place. Giving a benefit dance. Dont know how they roped her for it. All the old fossils will be there.

MERILH

Shall we go?

LAW
If you say so—that is—

MERILH
Yep, we'll go over when Natalie comes down. I want her to see Etty. .
How has the family used you?

LAW
Rotten. . . We were married yesterday.

MERILH
You mean—

LAW
They insisted. But it wasnt that—I wanted to . . Have you seen your family?
Your father?

MERILH
Havent had time, and dont know that I shall.

LAW
I saw him on the street the other day. He said that you could stop with
him. I told him I thought you would be down.

MERILH
Kind of him.

LAW
You still have feeling?

MERILH
None whatsoever. In fact I never had any. Its been years since what he did
or didnt do affected me. Around the house he was no more than a sort
of animated shadow. I only noticed him when he got in the light. "Father"
implies attachment. Of what sort? Really, that in exchange for bread
and butter he demands obedience. What a farce. Most men, denied suitable expression in the world, come home at night and try to bully their
families. He wasnt like that. He bulldozed the world, developed that
attitude towards everything, and seemed to have no desire to consider his
family as anything more than a convenient segment of it. He killed my
mother, and then became sentimental over it. I lost respect for him. I
tried to grow close to him on that proposition of financing a little theatre.
He thought only of money and profits; I, only of art. I saw we couldnt
make it. After that, he might just as well have died for all he meant to

me. How far we drifted apart, how little he understood me, or I him, for that matter, is measured by his silly acceptance of the truth of that rumor. He said I'd have to go. That was all. We had no words; I was too disinterested, or disgusted, to even question him. To give him chance to forgive me. Conscience will smite him in the approved way when he is about to die. He'll make provision for me in his will. He neednt—that is, so far as I am concerned. I have no more claim on him than I have on Rockefeller.

LAW

Christ but youre getting hard, Han. Thats what Mrs. Carson says about you.

MERILH

(*laughing*) So she's added that to the other demerits has she? How is the dear soul?

LAW

All right, I guess.

MERILH

Done anything?

LAW

Not that I know of.

MERILH

Still talking about the glory of the perfect home?

LAW

Still talking. In fact she advised me to get one as soon as I could.

MERILH

You and Mertis?

LAW

Yes.

MERILH

(*quite seriously*) Well, she was right, there. It would have been the best thing.

LAW

But you and—

MERILH

A difference in fundamentals and temperament, I guess, Therm. I saw you like myself because you were close, like a reflection in a mirror. But youre not that—at least not yet, and I doubt if you ever will be.

LAW

But my God, Han, Mertis is dying . . .

(*Natalie comes in. Her face is flushed. She looks belligerent.*)

MERILH

What is it, Natalie?

NATALIE

Those people, her mother, especially her mother. The old wench. After tirading me as the example and cause of her daughter's fall, she actually burst into tears and hung on my neck. It must have been harrowing for Mertis. She cant talk now. (*Law starts. Natalie restrains him.*) It would do no good, Therm. They'd only start on you. Their grief is real—but so is their sense of moral outrage. I think we'd better go, unless you want a scene.

LAW

(*standing, uncertain*) I think we'd better—but cant I see—

(*Mertis' brother bursts into the room, followed by the mother who is weeping and being supported by the father. He is much smaller than she. He braces his short banty legs as they all confront Law. Law is too in-wardly shrunk to boldly face them. He does not bluff.*)

MRS. NEWBOLT

(*between her sobs*) O she is dead. She is dead. My little flower is dead. She is dead.

JOHN NEWBOLT

(*the brother, to Law*) And you killed her. I could take my fists and beat your brains out. Youre not fit to talk to. You should be taken to the first lamp-post and strung up. Thats what should happen to you. You take a respectable girl and ruin her. You killer. Youuuuu! Why couldnt you have taken a rat? Why did you have to take a respectable girl? My sister? I could beat your brains out.

MR. NEWBOLT

Young man, as the father of the girl whom you have wronged I call upon you in the name of a just God to make amends. Our Heavenly Father will punish you. "Vengeance is mine saith the Lord." O did I not fear to take His whip into my hands, you could see . . . Where is your conscience? Where is your sense of duty? Where is your respect for the purity of womanhood? Where is your manhood?

MRS. NEWBOLT

O he is no man. He is no man. No man could have done such a thing. He is a brute, a coward. Thats what he is, a sneaking coward.

(*Merilh, who has been seated, a sort of curious spectator, rises to go.*)

MERILH

Well, what are we waiting for?

NATALIE

(*restraining him*) Just a minute, Han. I have a debt to pay, and I may just as well cancel Therm's at the same time. (*to the Newbolts*) Are you through? Have you said all that you dare to say? If not, be quick about it, for I want to take the sum, once for all, and be done with it.

MR. NEWBOLT

(*properly indignant*) Young lady—

NATALIE

"We have finished." I'll say it for you. All right then. I begin. And dont you even so much as interrupt me with a word. You accuse me. You accuse Mr. Law. You accuse us in the name of all that is proper and established in the moralities. You are fearful, august, secure on the pedestal of vindictive Right. Or at least you think you are. And we, like guilty penitents, are supposed to bow and cringe, at least apologize, before your God-championed Righteousness. You would willingly enough construe reason as apology. I shall deny you even that. Now listen to me. You, Mrs. Newbolt, are the worst offender. You know as well as I do that Woman, in the truth of her own soul, does not gauge a man's strength by his ability to resist her desires, but by his power to fulfill them. Love, respect, the values of manhood, of womanhood, of life itself, do not rest on the basis of denial; they are only thinkable in terms of actual accomplishment. You call Mr. Law a sneaking coward; the God whom your husband talks about, if he has the sight men give him credit for, knows that you are a sneaking hypocrite. Hypocrisy, which is the worse form of cowardice, fits all that you have said. Mr. Newbolt there speaking as if "rat" and "respectable" could divide the essential fact of Woman. As if a violation of one would not also violate the other. As if "whore" and "sister" bifurcated the insistency of sex. The one, sterile and pure; the other, fruitful, but impure. What wild-oats nonsense. And you, Mr. Newbolt senior, talking of duty. What sort of duty do you call it that so restricts a daughter's needs that she must become a mother under conditions that convince her of its sin? O how futile it all is.. But I feel better... (*to Merilh and Law*) Shall we go?

MERILH

Yes, lets. (*They go out, leaving the family more confused than indignant.*)

(*Curtain*)

3   The cabaret. Same evening, an hour later

The place has been made as respectable as possible. The orchestra is behind a rather well got-up electric decoration. Growing palms, rented especially for the occasion, are here and there. A row of national flags with a large Stars and Stripes is swung from the ceiling. Directly over the dance floor, a large gilt sign reads: "Charity Benefit." All the tables are filled. Tome Mangrow sits at a small table to the left. At his [left], two chairs are vacant. Mr. and Mrs. Hart, Mr. and Mrs. Carson, Mr. and Mrs. Mann, and Mr. and Mrs. Kemp form a group towards the center. The women chatter incessantly. The men are ill-at-ease, or downright bored. From the talk it is evident that Mertis Newbolt's death has already reached them.

KEMP

No offense, I guess, to light a cigar.

MRS. KEMP

Oh, John.

MARY CARSON

Thats all right, Mrs. Kemp. Let him smoke. They usually do in these sorts of places.

MRS. KEMP

I am glad to see that my husband is not acquainted with their practices. But he shant smoke if it annoys the others. Besides, it would teach him a little self-control. Denial, you know, even in petty matters, is a decided strengthener of the Will.

MRS. HART

I'm sure I dont mind.

MRS. MANN

Of course I shall not object.

MR. MANN

He wont get flabby, Mrs. Kemp, for this one neglected opportunity, I'm sure. (*Each one tries to press upon the other his own brand of cigar, as is the custom. They smoke.*)

MRS. KEMP

Neglecting opportunities, even trivial ones, breeds the habit of neglect. If you wish a tragic example of what that leads to, I can do no better than recall to you the sad instance of that Miss Newbolt. Why only a year ago, who would have thought it possible. She seemed so perfectly under control. Just one slip, and I dare say it was a petty one, and look what she has come to.

MRS. MANN

It was not a petty one. I can assure you, my dear Mrs. Kemp. It was very grave indeed. It would have been a perfect disgrace for this to have happened had she still been in the schools. Providence has been more than usually kind to us.

MR. HART

Providence chose a lovely form to work through this time.

MRS. MANN

You flatter me, Mr. Hart.

MR. HART

Not at all, I assure you.

MRS. HART

They say that her family came down. I wonder what class of people they are. Of course you havent met them. They are not exactly our sort, I dont think. I knew them on sight before they left the city that first time. That is, I mean, before Miss Newbolt had that first affair.

MRS. MANN
What first affair, my dear? I never heard of it.

MRS. KEMP
Oh it happened in Philadelphia one summer, and was soon hushed up.
But somehow, bits leaked out. You know how such things are.

MRS. MANN
Indeed? Someone must have been slack in looking into her record. I shall
have to investigate this immediately.

MR. MANN
Let is drop, mother. The girl is dead. No earthly good can come of it.

MRS. MANN
But whoever it was who let her slip into the schools is not dead. He must
be reprimanded for so gross a neglect of his duty, lest other undesirables
be put in charge of the sacred office of instructing our children. You are
too lenient, Mr. Mann.

MARY CARSON
Leniency becomes a virtue where an over-strictness is a fact.

MRS. HART
What an original proverb.

MARY CARSON
As usual, you can be depended upon to talk nonsense.

MRS. HART
Dear, dear. Does nothing I say ever make sense?

MARY CARSON
It would seem not.

MRS. HART
You are so hard on people.

MARY CARSON
So I've heard you say. It wouldnt at all harm you to imitate me in that.

MR. HART
Speaking of imitation, this dance tonight is to be a sort of imitation of
something isnt it?

MRS. MANN

I really couldnt say. (*to Mrs. Kemp*) My dear, you arranged for it. Tell us what it is going to be.

MRS. KEMP

Why, I had Mr. Parson arrange—that is, look after the details of it for me. I really can't deal directly with that type of woman.

MRS. MANN

Is she not respectable?

MRS. KEMP

Oh yes, perfectly. But the life they lead breeds certain what you might call irregularities, even vulgarities, that try the patience—

MRS. MANN

For the good name of our Society, I hope and trust that she will have the discretion and good sense to leave her vulgarities at home—if she has one. Artists and dancers and actors don't usually have them do they?

MRS. HART

You mean, homes?

MRS. MANN

That is what I had reference to.

MRS. HART

Why theres Mrs. Carson, I'm sure.

MARY CARSON

You will kindly leave me entirely out of the discussion.

MRS. MANN

But my dear, you are such a perfect example to refute the spurious contentions of libertines and homewreckers that art is incompatible with modern conditions in the home. I think that the balanced and exemplary achievements of your life should be taught in all art schools. This very day I shall recommend that my advice be followed in the art departments of our local schools. I have noticed a tendency to looseness on the part of some of those engaged in drawing, dancing, and athletic games. It must be stopped. It is not given to everyone to serve her community by the simple fact of example. You should consider it an honor, Mrs. Carson.

MARY CARSON
Thank you. When does the dance begin?

(*Natalie and Merilh enter. They cross, instinctively, to the table occupied by Tome. Nathan smiles blandly at the group as they pass. Natalie perceptibly stiffens. The men all speak. Likewise Mary Carson. The others pretend to ignore them. Mrs. Mann pulls her husband to his seat, thus spoiling his attempt at a public reconciliation. Tome and Merilh greet like old friends.*)

MERILH
Hello old man, hows it?

TOME
Fine, fine, just as fine as silk.

MERILH
(*presenting Natalie*) Mr. Mangrow, Miss Natalie Mann.

TOME
Sho glad to meet you, Miss Mann. Youall sit down, wont you? I reckon it was you I was keeping these seats for, and didnt know it. (*They laugh, and are seated.*)

MERILH
How'd she happen to come again?

TOME
You mean Etty? (*Merilh nods.*)

TOME
(*with candor*) You. She has never quit talking about that dance youall had together, and that talk. Is this the young lady?

MERILH
Which one, Tome?

TOME
The one you spoke about that night. Etty often wondered if she did right in refusing you.

MERILH
(*with a sly laugh*) Yep, this is the one.

TOME

Where is the other gentleman who was with you?

MERILH

A little under the weather tonight. When does she come on?

(*The orchestra begins to tune.*)

TOME

Right away, I reckon. She started to blow at the last minute. She'll come on now though.

(*Lights go out. Spot-light on the dance floor. Etty appears in a brilliant costume of black and gold. The same Etty—only, this time, her lips are malicious rather than bitter. The dance begins. At first, it is such as would prove delectable to the most respectable taste. Gradually, however, and as if by a purpose formed before-hand, it approaches the vulgar. Gasps of disapproval come from the tables. At its lowest phase, Etty whirls to a stop, and stands, inviting, daring, imploring, demanding Merilh.*)

NATALIE

She wants you, Han. Go on.

(*Merilh steps upon the floor. As before, they at first dance to the music, then establish a music and rhythm of their own. The orchestra stops. As if from some indefinite region, a music is evoked, an interpretive music, symbolic of the dance and triumph of souls. Beginning as a medley of national, racial folk-tunes, it spirals into a music that is individual and triumphant. At the very crest of creation, something inside of Merilh gives away, and his limp form is saved from sinking to the floor by the firmness with which Etty holds him. Women shriek. There is a general commotion. The lights are snapped on. Tome rushes to the floor. He and Etty assist him to the chair. His faint breathing comes in gasps. Natalie is curiously aloof and composed.*)

NATALIE

Will someone kindly call the ambulance? (*A man goes out.*)

(*Etty sinks to her knees and presses her lips against Merilh's limp hand. The men are ineffectually solicitous. Mrs. Hart begins to cry. Mrs. Kemp is hysterical. Mary Carson passes her arm across her eyes as if to convince herself of the reality of the whole thing. Her husband fans vigorously to keep her from fainting. Several other women get tearful. Suddenly, Mrs. Mann, who has remained stiff as a board up till now, gives way to most*)

violent tears and sobbing. Natalie seems to growing by inches. A truth,
of which she is at this moment fully conscious, leaps up in her eyes. With
a magnificent gesture she cries:)

NATALIE
What are you weeping over, you silly women, who see him only a man!

(*Etty springs to her feet before Natalie. They face each other, not in*
jealousy, but in the glow of an instant and mutual recognition.)

(*Curtain*)

THE SACRED FACTORY
A Religious Drama of Today

CHARACTERS

A Workman
His Wife   } The Worker Group
Their Children

Eight People   The Mass Group

The Father, John
The Mother, Mary   } The Family Group
Their Child, Helen

A Being

Additional People

The scene is a dwelling place, a description of which will soon be given. But this dwelling place is Life in the modern western world. There are assembled in it three groups of people. One, a workman and his family. The second, a family group of cultured people. The third, a mass group of diverse human types. These groups are used symbolically. But they also live and act and interact concretely: Each exists realistically in its own right. Each has its own concrete sequence of experiences. And the characters of the cultured family group are similarly individualized. The drama as a whole results from the coordination of these three group lives, from the coordination of the lives of the people composing them, and from their actions converging to a mutual climax.

There is one stage setting for the entire drama. . . .

There are three parts or chambers, separated from each other by pillars (a) and (b). These pillars, or dividers, placed to the front of the stage, mark and define the separation of the three chambers to anyone sitting in the audience. But the space behind them is quite open, so that, though the chambers appear separated if seen from a view squarely in front, an oblique or side view would show them all of the one structure, there being no walls between them, passage between them being in reality unobstructed. The audience must be able to see that passage between the chambers, so far as actual construction is concerned, is in fact free. This must be quite evident, so as to stand in sharp contrast to the fact that the actions of the drama take place, for the most part, within the chambers, within each separately—a set of actions for each, not only as if there were a structural partition between them, but also as if what takes place, say, in the right-hand chamber did not exist for what takes place in the left-hand chamber. Only at the end of the drama is there a mass communication and movement between the chambers, when all converge and concentrate in the central one.

The central chamber, domed or vaulted, should give the effect of being lofty and spacious. One must be able to know and feel at first sight that it is of the order of religious structures. It is, of course, seen from the inside. It is quite plain and simple, yet at the same time deep and rich. It conveys the impression of being an inner chamber in an Eastern temple. But it must not be Oriental. It conveys the impression of being, on a small scale, the choir of a cathedral; but it is simpler in design, and not so open, so easy of access.

Its walls are concave.

A triangular opening (not too large) cut in the rear wall about one-third of the distance down, admits the rays of one brilliant white star. On either side of this, but lower down, there are two slit-like windows containing stained glass.

Other than these, there are no apparent outside openings in this chamber. There are no openings at all in the other chambers, so that the entire form is closed in. That is, it should give this appearance, whatever may be the technical demands for moving on and off stage, which will be few.

The dominant color of the stage should be a pale blue. This color is vivid and electric in the central chamber. It is dull and heavy in the other two. But at all times and everywhere it should, of course, be sufficiently bright for the clear perceptions of the actors and their actions. It may prove to be desirable to use lighting effects of various hues to supplement and symbolize from time to time what takes place in the left-hand chamber.

Additional light and mellowness should be obtained for the central chamber by having two lamps of appropriate design suspended or supported on either side of a slightly elevated platform placed in the middle and against the rear wall. This platform is to be occupied by that Being who enters this chamber only at the end. Save for this, the platform remains vacant during the course of the drama. The central chamber remains vacant during the course of the drama, save at times when people stray into it from the other chambers, as will be indicated, and save of course at the end, when there is a mass movement from both other chambers into this central one, and a concentration of people about Him who will then occupy the platform.

In contrast to the spacious, lofty aspect of the central chamber, the other two are low, and give the impression of being compressing and constricting. If the central chamber suggests the choir of a cathedral, these two suggest the underground cells, almost the dungeons of the same cathedral.

In these two the main actions of the drama take place.

In the right-hand chamber (looking from the audience), there takes place, in pantomime, the life history of a worker-family—that is, the life history of the family of an ordinary day laborer. The history begins from the time of the marriage and concludes with the death of the man.

The action of the pantomime is stark and simple. After a somewhat stiff and awkward and none too joyous dance expressive of their marriage, the movements of the pantomime quickly resolve themselves to this: The man goes out to work. The woman moves about in various circles, but always in circles, all day. The man returns in the evening. They eat. They get sleepy. They go to bed. They get up. The man goes out to work. The woman moves in circles all day. The man returns. They eat. Get sleepy. Go to bed. Get up. Etc. Etc. At intervals children are born to them. The children soon begin following their mother in her round of circles. One by one, in time, they go out, never to return. The man and woman continue the same rounds—only, gradually but noticeably, their movements begin to show the effects of drudgery and age. Gradually they both decline. The man dies. This death wrings gestures of dumb anguish from the woman, who, in her movements of active despair, accidentally moves from her own into the central chamber and is drawn towards the platform. This movement of the woman into the central chamber and towards the platform should coincide with the similar movement which will be taking place in the left-hand chamber at this time, and the sequence of the worker-family pantomime should be directed and timed with this coincidence in mind.

The pantomime should convey the feeling of human existence, stripped of all interest, stripped of wish, of hope, of possibility, reduced to a dull maintaining of itself, mechanically performing under unfavorable conditions no more than is necessary for such maintenance. It should be apparent that the few simple things they do are repetitive, as if what they do in one day is no more than the counting off of a series of numbers, like 1, 2, 3, 4; and what they do the next day is a repetition of this series. They are, obviously, manikins, marionettes; yet it must be felt that they are in fact human beings, not marionettes.

There is, for this chamber, no special lighting other than the dull blue light already mentioned. There are no windows, no openings, other than that (which, for the worker-family is as if it did not exist) which leads into the central chamber. But one of the lamps in the central chamber should be so placed that its reflection is barely perceptible in this chamber.

What furnishings, if any, are in this chamber are only those necessary to the actions of the pantomime. Something for a bed, for a table, for chairs, etc. These, if present, should be quite realistic.

The left-hand chamber is similar to the right. Actually, it will have to be larger, since it will contain eleven people and will have to provide room for their actions. But it should give the impression of being especially cramped and down-pressing. It has no openings save that unnoticed one into the central chamber. Through this opening a reflection from one of the lights comes.

In this chamber there are two or perhaps three benches, similar to those seen in schools and churches, with upright backs. These are placed one behind the other, facing the audience. They are capable of holding eight people. Of these eight, four are men and four are women. These people are a mixture of human types: crude, cultured, sanguine, cynic, etc. Only one of them is especially marked in appearance. This is a woman, dressed in flowing white, and pure and lovely to look upon. She sits just a bit apart from the others, on the rear bench, last seat to the left. She does not take part in most of the mass actions of the others. And, unlike the others, her eyes are never shut, nor is her body held in a rigid posture.

The seven people are seated on the benches, their bodies rigid and their eyes closed—except at those times as will be indicated.

Behind the benches there are three seats, raised above the benches, so that those who are to occupy them can be seen by the audience as being elevated above those who occupy the benches. When the curtain goes up, these three seats are empty.

Before the benches—that is, between them and the footlights, and on the same level with them—there are three seats. Two of these are of the size for adults. These, placed just about the width of the benches apart, face each other. Between them there is a child's chair, back against the benches, facing the audience. This seat will later on be occupied by the child of the man and woman who are already occupying theirs.

Father and mother—or, simply John and Mary—face each other.

John, Mary, and their child Helen compose the family group.

The eight seated on the benches compose the mass group.

The relationship between these two groups is not a constant. For instance, sometimes it appears that the mass group is the great world impinging on the family group, in different ways and with different consequences for John, Mary, and Helen. Sometimes it appears tht the mass group may represent the fragmentary workings of Mary's subconsciousness. At other times, one or both of the groups appear to exist and manifest quite separately.

The details of the actions and interactions of these groups will be indicated as the drama proceeds.

Neither John nor Mary is meant to be a fully drawn and rounded character in the realistic sense, and neither are they meant to be just the opposite of this; namely, they are not meant to be just abstract types or symbols. They are meant to be both of these, in a sense, combined—or better, both of these alternately. At one time they are realistic characters. At another, they tend to become vehicles for introducing some idea, feeling, or action necessary at that phase of the drama. Their individualization is maintained.

A psychological summary of John and Mary:

By nature, Mary is emotional and intelligent. Prior to her marriage to John, which took place upwards of ten years ago, she had become some-what intellectualized, and therefore less emotional and less intelligent. John is intellectual and intelligent. After her marriage to him, her super-

ficial and alien intellectualization diminished, owing to the fact that she
became occupied with being a wife and mother. But John's mind, though
feeding her own, also tended to dwarf hers and turn it in his own direction, while his mental way of living made it difficult for her to live
emotionally. Dissatisfaction with John, and hence, from this angle, with
life in general, accumulated in her to produce an emotional restlessness
and a vague searching for "something else." This dissatisfaction is approaching a breaking point at the time the drama begins.

Side by side with this restlessness, there exists in Mary a genuine sense of
possibilities in life greater and more worthwhile than any she has thus
far experienced. But she is not, at the beginning of the drama, fully aware
of this sense, and she does not distinguish it from the dissatisfactions
caused by her domestic life. Neither does John see this distinction. He
treats both feelings as if they were identical. He tries to rid her of them,
on the grounds that unless they are cleared up and out, she, Mary, will
increasingly disturb both of them, to their misfortune, and there is a
chance that she may become pathological. She feels that John is somehow right, and somehow wrong. She feels that she is likewise. But she is
unable to make head or tail of it until later. Hence, her attitude towards
herself, her own wishes, and towards John and his wishes, swings from
positive to negative. As long as it does so, she sits in her seat. John is certain that he is right. But he also sits in his seat because he has nowhere
else to go.

Mary has the instincts of a wife and mother.

She has a capacity to be religious.

John is quite certain of himself, and has, within limits, cause to be. He
has succeeded in directing himself (so to speak), and in controlling external conditions (provided that the demands made on him are moderate—
he tries to keep them so) to his own satisfaction. He has set for himself a
strange aim in life, which will be disclosed later. Mary is necessary to it,
so he tries to make her fit in with this aim. He is, more than he can admit,
already apprehensive of the result.

In his service he has a realistic intellect, over-weighted in its own direction,
but very keen to penetrate and understand the half it does see. Buried
in him there is the remnant of a rather splendid idealism.

John is not—decidedly not—religious. But he is intelligent enough to know
that another epoch might have produced in him a different point of view,
different actions. He will not readily admit this.

He is courageous, as will be seen.

Both John and Mary are, at root, good human stuff.

*The sense of human possibilities, actual human constriction and degrada-
tion, pathology, clear sight, understanding, aspiration, struggle, gaiety,
loveliness, wonder, satire, the grotesque, machine routine, human stuff,
force unformed, blindness, groping, vacancy, human action, unhuman
ones, dialogue, stark utterances, songs, chants, pantomime, lights, color,
settings—these should be skillfully coordinated on the stage to produce
the effect of one dramatic whole.*

ACT I

When the curtain goes up, the stage presents this scene: The eight people are in their bench seats. Seven of them sit rigidly, eyes closed, giving the impression that they are straining to be something or to get somewhere in their sleep. One, the woman figure in white, sits in firm repose, eyes open, contemplatively straight to the front.

The three seats behind them are vacant.

In front, the child's chair is vacant. But the father and mother are in their seats (facing each other), also rigid, with eyes closed, and also giving the impression that they are sleeping people who are straining to be something or to get somewhere. The man is less tense and rigid than the others.

From this left-hand chamber, there is, at first, no sound, no movement.

The central chamber is vacant and still.

The right-hand chamber is vacant and still.

The stage is static. And yet it is charged with the potential energy of the left-hand group. It is held so for some minutes.

Then from behind scenes, from the rear of the central chamber, there comes an incantation, followed by a choral hymn. This hymn is necessarily religious in character, but it has a dynamic, almost a martial undertone.

The Incantation.

I am that I am
I am that I am
I am that I am
The Father.

I am that I am
I am that I am
I am that I am
The Mother.

I am that I am
The Son
That I am
I am that I am
The Son.

Blessed that I am
The Father
Holy is the Mother
That I am
I am that I am
The Son, In Glory.

(*This in no way affects the stage. It soon concludes.*

There is a pause, an interval.

The stage is static.

Then from off stage—to the right—there enter the laborer and his just-now-married wife. They enter their chamber. The marriage dance begins. And from this time on throughout the course of the drama there continues to take place the pantomime of the worker-family.

After the pantomime has expressed three or more rounds of repetitive existence—sufficient for the audience to become familiar with it, so that it will no longer need to attend to the pantomime but can transfer its attention to the left-hand chamber; each time the audience glances at the pantomime it will quickly see and recognize the same thing—then in the left-hand chamber John and Mary, husband and wife, show signs of life. He opens his eyes, and releases his body into a posture of ease and certainty, and smiles somewhat cynically but nevertheless in a way to convey that he is decidedly pleased with himself. His glance rests upon his wife and remains there. He understands what he sees, and he is also puzzled by it. He does not move from his chair.

She opens her eyes, relaxes the rigidity of her body, and has difficulty in holding her balance. Her glance rests upon her husband. It alternates between the type of certainty which comes with familiarity and "I don't know what to make of it all." She is evidently more puzzled and disturbed than he is.

They regard each other. From him: affection, analysis, humor, cynicism. From her: affection, dissatisfaction, criticism, an upward lift, and something verging on revolt.

Neither of them notices or appears to sense the presence of the Eight behind them. These, one excepted, still sit rigid.

While mother and father still regard each other, from off stage—to his left—a child, their child, a girl of about 10, enters, and, unnoticed by them, wanders about everywhere looking at and sensing everything. She wanders about the left-hand chamber, regards her parents and the people sitting on the benches. She crosses through the central chamber and, in the right-hand one, regards the pantomime of the worker-family. She returns to the central chamber, and soon her attention is attracted to the triangular opening through which shines the brilliant white star. Just as she leaves the worker-family and enters the central chamber, a strain of religious music comes from off stage, quite faint. When she sees the triangle, the singing grows slightly stronger. These are the words that are sung:)

> To that glory
> Which is above,
> Below,
> Everywhere, in everything
> We sing
> To Him who is that glory.

(She gazes at the triangle in wonderment.

The song shortly ends, and the child, after intently regarding the star some moments longer, eagerly moves from this chamber in the direction of her mother.

Bright, wide awake, with eyes sparkling she enters the left-hand chamber, approaches her mother, and with a sense of mystery and wonder, asks:)

          CHILD

Mother—

(The mother, as if used to it, turns her regard towards the child. The father keeps his attention upon his wife.)

          CHILD

Mother, where am I?

(This question falls into silence. At first, it is as if the mother did not hear it. And then, she seems to hear the echo of it. She is perplexed by it, does not know exactly how to take it. Hence she cannot even attempt to answer it, but remains silent for a time. The father takes no part in this, and appears not to have even heard the child's questions, not to have noticed her, save as she draws attention and responses from the mother. Trying to rouse herself, the mother asks flatly:)

          MOTHER

What did you ask, Helen?

(The child repeats her question, but her tone of voice indicates that already a bit of its pure quality has been lost.)

          CHILD

Where am I, Mother?

(Something in the mother won't permit her to understand the nature of the child's question—though she does sense it, and doesn't just now want to; so she is forced to meet it in a matter of fact way.)

          MOTHER

Why Helen, what a question. You are ...... why you are in this room, Helen. Where else would you be?

(The child is slightly confused and baffled by the inadequacy of the mother's reply.)

          CHILD

I know....... But I mean, *where am I?*

(This time the child's question strikes nearer to the corresponding questions in the mother: Where am I? What is it all about? It disturbs her, but as she does not want this disturbance to be apparent to Helen, she covers it again. Though she knows it is not literally so, she asks herself if perhaps Helen has been sleeping, has just awakened from a dream, and has not yet quite come to herself. Perhaps so. Hence she, the mother, tries to calm and reassure Helen.)

MOTHER

Helen child, there now. (*laughingly*) Where are you? Where are you? Of course, can't you see? You are in your mother's room. See your pictures hanging on the wall? And your new dress laid out? See them?

CHILD

Yes, Mother.

MOTHER

Well, then, now go and do something for your mother. Go find your mother's glasses and bring them to her. There's a good girl.

(But before Helen can move off, the mother asks:)

MOTHER

Have you been sleeping, Helen?

CHILD

No, Mother.

MOTHER

(*slightly reprehensive*) What have you been doing?

CHILD

Oh, lots of things.

MOTHER

What, for instance?

CHILD

Thinking.

MOTHER

What?

CHILD
Just thinking.

MOTHER
Gracious, Helen! Thinking!

CHILD
Is it naughty to think, Mother?

(*The mother is aware of how thinking has frequently induced in her unpleasant feelings, and hence, often, the wish to suppress it. She does not
want to suppress it in her child, but she does wish to turn Helen's attention
to something else.*)

MOTHER
No, not exactly, but thinking is . . . for . . . . grownups.

CHILD
Do you and Father think?

MOTHER
(*caught*) Why, yes, certainly, Helen.

(*The father smiles curiously and with a trace of removed amusement.*)

CHILD
About wonderful things? Are Mr. and Mrs. Brooks wonderful things to
think about? And automobiles and bridge, and golf, and money, and art
and science and sermons? Are all these thrilling to think about? I wish I
could think about them, Mummy.

(*And then, already half feeling that she has been doing something not
quite right, but urged to tell it anyhow, she approaches nearer to her
mother and with a trace of guilt confides to her:*)

CHILD
I have, a little, Mummy.

MOTHER
Have what? Helen.

CHILD
Well, why does Mrs. Brooks look like a duck, and why does Mr. Brooks
look like a fox terrier? And why do you look like—

MOTHER
Helen, you mustn't say such things.

(*Helen giggles.*)

MOTHER
(*severely*) Helen.

(*Helen tries to suppress her giggling. Then feels she wants to cry. Alternating between these states she moves away from her mother, walks slowly, and then soon both moods of giggling and crying give way to a bright-eyed pensiveness. She remembers her original question, again senses a wonder and mystery. So, just as she first entered the room, so now she again turns to her mother and asks expectantly:*)

CHILD
Mother, *where am I?*

MOTHER
(*more open and more serious*) Again and again that question. (*as if to herself*) Where *are* you?

(*She looks about her, as if expecting to see the answer. Then quickly she wishes to evade this mood, so she almost snaps out:*)

MOTHER
You are with your mother, Helen.

(*But this time Helen is somehow encouraged to pursue.*)

CHILD
And where are you, Mummy?

MOTHER
I, I? Why I am here. Can't you see?

CHILD
Yes, Mummy, but where is here?

MOTHER
Now Helen, don't be ridiculous. You know as well as I do that we both are in your father's house.

CHILD
And where is Father's house?

(*Without movement, someone of the Eight repeats this question as if it were asked in sleep.*)

ONE
Where is my Father's house?

(*This is not noticed by the family group. When it is finished, the mother answers Helen.*)

MOTHER
We live in Chicago, Helen. But this is absurd. Have you forgotten, Helen? You haven't brought me my glasses yet. Now run along dear, and bring them to me.

CHILD
Yes, Mummy.

(*She starts off, and then recognizes that she, as a matter of fact, does not know where they are. So she asks in point of fact:*)

CHILD
Where are they, Mummy?

MOTHER
(*mistaking nature of question*) What a persistent child you are! (*half teasing*) Where are the glasses? Where is the house? Where are you? Where am I? (*and then with sudden and serious intensity*) Where am I? What wouldn't I give to know that. To understand what it is all about. To be able to prove or disprove the faith I have.

FATHER
It is far simpler to prove doubt. And one answer is as good as another. It is a matter of economy. But I suppose you will find God before you find that.

MOTHER
If I had choice, I'd rather.

CHILD
Rather what, Mother?

MOTHER

(*really addressing husband*) Rather waste much to find something worthwhile than economize and become a dried-up mummy.

CHILD

What is a dried-up mummy?

MOTHER

Your father economizes.

(*One of the Eight, his eyes remaining closed, abruptly stands up where he is, leans forward and says decisively:*)

ONE

Our Father economizes.

(*He sits down, as before. The family group is unaffected by this.*

There is a pause, a silence.

Then—)

CHILD

Mother, do you know where I am? And where you are? And where anything is? Do you, Mother?

MOTHER

I only know where men say things are.

CHILD

Where?

MOTHER

We are on Earth.

CHILD

Where is Earth?

MOTHER

The Earth is a little speck of dust in the universe.

CHILD

What is the universe?

MOTHER
It is a great vast elephant full of stars.

(*The child is impressed by this picture. Then she asks:*)

CHILD
Was the great elephant born?

MOTHER
Yes, Helen.

CHILD
Who was its mother?

MOTHER
Space.

CHILD
Who was its father?

MOTHER
God.

(*There is a slight pause. Then the child moves towards her mother, kneels beside her. The child's posture indicates that now there can be a real contact and exchange between them.*

At this point, there is a crude laughter from one of the Eight. From now on, those on the benches, sometimes singly, sometimes en masse, will take, from time to time, an active part in the drama. Unless especially indicated, what they do appears not to affect the family group, and vice versa. Unless affected, the members of the family group hold the positions they had just before the action of the Eight commences—they hold these positions until the Eight action is over for that time.

Or, if the Eight action is too long for the positions to be held during it, or if it does not seem advisable that they be held, then the members of the family group relax into natural but unexpressive postures, and remain so until the Eight finish. Whereon, if the family action is a continuation of something cut into by the Eight, then the family members retake the expressive gestures, etc., they had just before the Eight action began. If the action is new, then of course their movements are made to express this new phase.

Now, when any one of the Eight speaks or moves or manifests in anyway, he or she opens his eyes during that manifestation, and, when the action is finished, closes them. When in action, their bodies become less rigid, though a certain stiffness is always retained.

It will be indicated when necessary whether the voice is male or female.

In the following, the Eight remain seated).

SOME ONE OF THE EIGHT (*male*)

Haw, haw, haw.
Haw, haw, haw.

(*Pause.*)

A SECOND (*female*)
What a mother!

A THIRD (*male*)
O, what a mother!

A FOURTH (*female*)
How incompetent.

A FIFTH (*male*)
No wonder we go hungry to our graves.

(*The mother, though not outwardly hearing this, is moved from her chair, leaving Helen alone beside it. The mother moves towards the front of the stage and shows by gestures, etc., that she experiences some vague but deep distress. The distress is not articulate, nor is it dynamic. She remains away from her chair during this manifestation of the Eight.*)

A SIXTH (*female*)
Have you ever been a mother?

SECOND
No.

SIXTH
Well then, shut up.

(*Pause. Silence.*)

> ONE (*male*)
What a father!

> A SECOND (*female*)
O, what a father!

> A THIRD (*male*)
No wonder we go hungry to our graves.

(*The father does not budge.*)

> A FOURTH (*male*)
Have you ever been a father?

> FIRST
No.

> FOURTH
Well, then shut up.

(*Pause. Silence.*)

> ONE (*female*)
What a wife!

> A SECOND (*female*)
Have you ever been one?

> FIRST
No.

> SECOND
Well then, shut up.

(*Pause. Silence.*)

> ONE (*male*)
What a husband!

> A SECOND (*male*)
What? No? Shut up.

(*Pause, longer. Silence.*

Then—)

>ONE (*female*)
It is painful to be born, not knowing why or where.

>A SECOND (*male*)
What?

>FIRST
It is painful to be born, not knowing why or where.

>SECOND
Who ever heard of being pained by that.

>A THIRD (*male*)
I've got to have a kidney removed.

>A FOURTH (*male*)
What?

>THIRD
A kidney must be taken out.

>FOURTH
Well, what of it? It won't hurt.
Take gas.

(*Pause. Silence.*)

>ONE (*female*)
Somewhere there is God,
When in deep I know
That God is somewhere,
When in deep pain I know.

(*Snatches of this are repeated by several. Soon this is chanted in unison. The chant becomes musical, semi-religious. This breaks off abruptly.*

Pause: Then someone stands up and says:)

>ONE (*male*)
I am hungry for food.

A SECOND (*male*)
What?

FIRST
Food.

SECOND
Let's eat. (*stands up*)

A THIRD
(*standing up*) Let's eat.

(*One after another, with the exception of the figure in white, they stand up, and as each one does so, he says, "Let's eat."*)

ALL
Let's eat. Let's eat. Let's eat. Let's eat.

(*With one accord they sit down, and are silent.*

This group returns to its rigidity.

The mother then returns to her chair, looks with perplexed and disturbed affection at Helen, and strokes her hair. They remain so for a few moments, and then, still kneeling by her mother Helen asks:)

CHILD
Is there something beyond this room, mother?

MOTHER
I think there is.

CHILD
Is it more wonderful than this room?

MOTHER
I think it is. (*to herself with feeling*) I have faith that it must be.

CHILD
Who lives in it?

MOTHER
I don't know, Helen.

CHILD
People like us?

MOTHER
I don't know, perhaps so, Helen.

CHILD
Are they funny like you and Father?

MOTHER
Helen! What a thing to say.

CHILD
I didn't mean it, Mummy, but you know—

MOTHER
Yes, I think I do know.

CHILD
Well, anyway ...... people like us live in it?

MOTHER
I suppose so.

CHILD
And what is beyond that, Mummy?

MOTHER
I don't know, Helen.

CHILD
Another room?

MOTHER
Yes, another room.

CHILD
Who lives in it?

MOTHER
How can I know, Helen?

CHILD
Does God?

MOTHER
Yes, God lives in it.

CHILD
And does He live like we do?

MOTHER
Yes Helen, just like us.

(*Helen suddenly giggles, owing to some funny pictures that have occurred to her. The mother is a bit surprised and provoked by Helen's giggles at this point.*)

MOTHER
What is the matter, Helen?

CHILD
(*trying to stop giggling*) Oh, nothing.

MOTHER
Why are you laughing?

CHILD
Oh, nothing. Because.

MOTHER
Because of what?

CHILD
Only because.

MOTHER
You must tell me truly, Helen.

CHILD
(*frankly*) Well then because I wondered if people like ducks and dogs and rabbits came to see Him—

MOTHER
To see who?

CHILD
Came to see God. And if He played cards, and went to the movies, and wanted to buy a Rolls-Royce car, and live in the best part of the universe, and—(*laughs*)

MOTHER

Helen! You mustn't talk this way about God.

CHILD

Well, Mummy—

MOTHER

Yes, I know, Helen. It is really my fault. I have been talking nonsense.

FATHER

You certainly have.

MOTHER

Just a moment, John. Helen has asked me something seriously; she has received a ridiculous answer. But I must try to answer her. Helen, we *are* like God, only . . . . . only God is not like what we see and know of ourselves—

FATHER

Goodness! If not metaphysical or mystical, you certainly are obscure. Why not page the Bible? Or at least you might call in Mr. Plato. But don't you think we have had enough of this? Besides, there is a matter between you and myself that I think we might profitably consider now.

MOTHER

I would like to, John. But Helen?

FATHER

There are much better things for a child of her age to do, much better than for her to form the habit of questioning the unanswerable. Of all futilities, this is the most futile. We might at least not encourage it.

MOTHER

Have I—?

FATHER

Certainly you have. Both in yourself and Helen. If she must come to this new pastime—

MOTHER

John—

FATHER

That is just what it is. Have I told you my new name for it? I call it
"chasing God." You will soon be expert at it. Another year or two. But if
Helen must come to it—as indeed she must—God in one hand, and in
the other, women's clubs—as she must unless extreme good fortune and
my efforts aid her to avoid it—if she must "play God," then time enough
when she gets to be your age. But I should think, Mary, that you
particularly would want to keep her from it.

MOTHER

Why I particularly? And besides John, what right have you—John, you
cannot know what you are doing.

FATHER

As I have many times told you, it is not a question of right. Who is there
to decide that? It is a question of fact. But we will come to that. It is not
good for children to overhear the conversation of their parents. Suppose
we let Helen go and do—well, what children of her age usually do.
(*without waiting for the mother's agreement, but addressing Helen*) So
now, Helen, my dear child, suppose you—well, suppose you just run
along and go about your business. There's a good girl.

(*Having said this, he immediately turns his attention upon the mother,
the question of Helen having been thus settled. The mother would like to
do something, at least soften Helen's dismissal. Her gestures indicate this.
But she does not know what to do. Besides, she also wishes to settle
certain matters between herself and John. During the conversation
between her parents, Helen has increasingly felt cut off from them and
outside of what was taking place. She has felt ill at ease and out of place.
She has withdrawn into herself, and drawn away from them. The phrase
"just run along and go about your business" comes at a time and is said
in a way to rather stun the child, and also to negatively electrify her. She
rises to her feet, backs away from her parents a pace or so, and then in
turn regards each of them semi-helplessly. The father is certain that he has
done, if not the right thing, then the best possible. The child receives no
further response from him. The mother would do something, but feels
powerless to. So she soon lowers her eyes, and composes herself upon her
chair. The child receives no further response from her. So she, Helen,
draws still further away from them. Suddenly she gives a cry as if stricken.
She crumbles in a heap upon the floor, crying. Then slowly she pulls
herself together, stops crying, and rises to her feet—a different child.
Freshness, wonder, etc., have not gone from her, but they are passive.
Then, looking to neither right nor left, but with a set glance straight*)

ahead of her, she begins to slowly walk, circle about this left-hand chamber. Her pace gradually accelerates as she walks. After about three or four rounds, she walks, in a matter of fact way, up to her chair between her parents, unnoticed by them, and sits down. Here she will sit (not stiffly), unnoticed by everyone for the rest of the drama until towards the end. From time to time her head will move in the direction of one or the other of her parents, in a way to indicate that she is aware of, and being influenced by, what they say. As the drama moves on, the child will gradually fall asleep in her chair. She will remain so until awakened towards the end.

The father and mother do not hear the child's cry. From the moment they cease responding to her, they become unaware of her. But they remain silent, and do not begin their own conversation until after Helen has taken her seat between them.

Just after Helen makes her first round of this left-hand chamber, the first child of the worker-family should commence its rounds behind its mother. But the attention of the audience should not fail to notice Helen taking her seat between her parents.)

(*Curtain*)

ACT II

The curtain rises upon the same scene. The people are just as they were before the curtain fell. The second act is a continuation of the first; it begins as if there had been no curtain break.

The husband and wife begin their conversation.

The husband speaks with a sort of incisive intellectuality. He knows what he says, but he does not feel it. The wife, on the other hand, tends to feel but not know.

During John's monologues, Mary expresses from time to time by means of gestures, etc., the emotional equivalent of what is only intellectually said by John.

HUSBAND
I think it is time, my dear, that we talked things over.

WIFE
It is almost time for something else.

(*The husband is a bit alarmed in spite of himself.*)

HUSBAND
What do you mean by that?

WIFE
I mean—

(She hesitates, since she is not quite certain or prepared to say just what she does mean. This gives the husband the opportunity of continuing as he had intended.)

HUSBAND

Well, we will come to that later. The fact is, that recently—I say recently because during the past few months I've noticed it more—I have noticed signs in you of a, well, call it unrest, which, from my point of view, is both unfortunate and unnecessary. And, though not wishing to be an alarmist, I should say that it is dangerous, or can be so. For this reason: Our nerves are such fragile things these days, so easily snapped or injured, and particularly so in women of your age, that it is difficult for them to withstand the strain of interior conflict. They have all that they can do to keep their own against outside pressure. And when to this there are added the quite arbitrary—arbitrary and artificial because a person causes them in himself, but could avoid them—the quite arbitrary strains of one's own psyche—well, it is no wonder that our poor nerves snap.

WIFE

So you think I am heading for a nervous breakdown?

HUSBAND

I shouldn't say exactly that. But I do think that you are causing an avoidable uneasiness and perhaps unhappiness for both of us. And all the while, the remedy, if I may call it that, is so simple.

WIFE

And it is?

HUSBAND

I am coming to that. I was simply pointing out that unrest, that all forms of psychic disturbance can and do place an undue strain upon the nerves which may snap under it. It is but a short step from neural disorganization to a general psychological pathology, the main symptom of which is this: that whoever is the victim of it persists in believing the visionary to be real. The taste for fantasies of all sorts becomes a vice. But no one who is a victim of this taste calls it a vice. Oh, no. On the contrary, they give great high-sounding names to it. They call it "the divine urge," "the thirst for perfection," and what not. In fact, they become what someone has called "rainbow chasers," but rainbow chasers of the worst sort. For instance, all of the numerous cults, new and old, are mainly recruited from such people. Witness Theosophy, Christian Science, and I might even add, Suffragism.

WIFE

John, what are you driving at?

HUSBAND

Just this—

WIFE

Please remember that I have heard most of your facts and theories many times before. Well, what?

HUSBAND

Just this—you are more restless and disturbed than ever before. This is so, isn't it?

WIFE

Yes, it is so. Of course, John. My only wonder is that you haven't noticed it before. Do you think I choose to be so?

HUSBAND

I have, my dear.

WIFE

Well, why did you permit me to go on. Why did you not do, or at least try to do, something. You might at least have opened the way to our talking it over before. Not that talking will do much good, but then— But instead, you have gone along your own way—With all your knowledge and ability there seem to be so many things you cannot do. I have often questioned lately whether it is because you won't or can't. I used to feel that it was because you didn't wish to; now I begin to think that it is because you can't.

HUSBAND

In a sense, you are right. My ability, Mary, is restricted to a relatively small number of all those things my understanding knows there are to do. But, as I have said before, I neither wish nor feel compelled to undertake more than this small number. It is, as you know, my principle in life only to attempt what I am reasonably certain I can do, and, not to evade or anything of the sort, but simply not to undertake what I cannot do. Quite frankly, I have been, and still am, apprehensive that I shall be able to do too little for you in this condition you've gotten into. That is why I haven't wanted to talk about it. But your case is growing critical—

WIFE

John, will you please not speak of me as if I were your patient in a clinic.

(*Pause, slight.*

One of the Eight, male, stands up abruptly and says with force:)

ONE
We are all in a clinic.

(*Pause.*)

There are no doctors.

(*Sits down.*

Slight pause. The family group does not hear this. John continues.)

HUSBAND
Well, then—you are reaching a point where you will do something if I do not.

WIFE
(*half to herself, ironically*) *This* is to be critical.

HUSBAND
And I don't want that.

WIFE
Man never does.

HUSBAND
I don't know about man, Mary, I only know about myself (*pointing*), this one person here. And I repeat that I do not wish you to be forced to take, as they say, the reins in your own hands.

WIFE
And pray why not?

HUSBAND
Because you could neither hold nor guide them.

WIFE
(*sarcastically*) And you?

HUSBAND
If you don't mind, dear, I really feel the situation to be too serious for us to descend to merely taking cracks at each other. Yes?

WIFE
Yes, John. I did not mean to.

(*There is genuine feeling in these two passages. They are both slightly embarrassed by it, John particularly.*

Pause.

One of the Eight, male, stands up abruptly, and says with force:)

ONE
Everything is serious
Everything is critical.

(*Slight pause.*)

Everybody takes cracks, and nothing else but.

(*He sits down.*

Slight pause. Family group does not hear.

John finds it a bit difficult to re-begin.)

HUSBAND
The fact is, Mary, that without seeing any signs of it, I know that already you must be—if I say "playing with," you will understand that I do not mean just that—you must already be playing with two possibilities, while you continue to live the third—

WIFE
And they are?

HUSBAND
(*continuing to generalize*) For a married woman of your type in the state you've gotten in, there are three, and three only.

WIFE
Which are?

HUSBAND
(*continuing to generalize*) They arise in women's minds the world over, but each woman assumes that she only, uniquely, is concerned with them. Women the world over have tried to live according to one or the other of them, or to all of them, and the results of such attempts have been every-

where and in all cases similar. But each individual woman assumes that her attempt will somehow lead to unique results.

WIFE

John! Will you please be concrete!

HUSBAND

Well then—while you continue to live with me, you are considering, first, having a lover, or any number of them.

WIFE

That is not true. Never in my life have I even thought of having lovers. God, how men destroy what they would build up.

HUSBAND

(*with real feeling*) Forgive me. You are right.

(*Pause. John, with difficulty, regains his intellectual level, but he does not speak until in himself he has done so.*)

HUSBAND

It was my mistake. I should have confined it to a single lover, just one. One. That is so? Mary.

WIFE

(*after hesitation and conflict*) Yes, it is so.

(*Pause.*

Several of the Eight speak now, but without standing up.)

ONE (*female*)

That would be adultery.

A SECOND (*female*)

Well, what of it?

A THIRD (*female*)

There is no such thing as adultery.

A FOURTH (*female*)

Well, what of that?

THIRD
Everybody wants a lover.

A FIFTH (*male*)
Everybody everywhere wants love.

(*Pause. Silence. The husband continues.*)

HUSBAND
Also, you have been considering getting a divorce. In which case, after a divorce, you contemplate either earning your own living and existing, as they say, independently, or getting married again, and this not primarily for yourself but to have a father for your child. And this is so, or not? Mary.

WIFE
It is.

(*Pause.*

Several of the Eight speak, without standing up.)

ONE (*female*)
There is no divorce.

A SECOND (*male*)
Divorce is not practical.

A THIRD (*female*)
Divorce is difficult.

A FOURTH (*male*)
There can be no divorce.

A FIFTH (*female*)
Divorce is selfish.

A SIXTH (*male*)
Divorce is sinful.

(*Slight pause. Same voices.*)

ONE (*female*)
There is divorce.

SECOND (*male*)
Divorce is practical and necessary.

THIRD (*female*)
Divorce is not difficult.

FOURTH (*male*)
Divorce should be had for the asking.

FIFTH (*female*)
Divorce is unselfish.

SIXTH (*male*)
Everybody is divorced.

(*Pause. Silence. The husband continues.*)

HUSBAND
And then, my dear, there is the possibility of your continuing to live with me more or less as you have been.

WIFE
John, before you go further, I wish you—and I think it only fair to ask it and be answered—I wish you, now that you have told me about myself, to tell me also about yourself. Am I alone in wishing something other than I have?

HUSBAND
No, you are not. I too have wished and do wish for something other than I have. But the terms of our wishes are very different.

WIFE
You mean that you have never thought of having a lover or of getting a divorce?

HUSBAND
I do not mean that. On the contrary, I have. Given what we are in, this, our present situation, then thoughts and wishes for a lover or a divorce must have been induced in both of us. I have. You have. No, it is about something else that our wishes differ. It is mainly with this something else that I am concerned. But I can only approach it, I can only expect to cope with it on the condition that I prepare certain very necessary things before hand. One of these, and the most important, has to do with you

and, if you will, my concern with the three possibilities already mentioned. I say it frankly, that I am going to talk and put all my force in favor of our continuing to live together as man and wife. Not only do I wish you to choose this possibility, but I also wish that you and I may live it just a bit differently from the ordinary run of people. I don't, for instance, look forward to a life with you in which your desires for a lover or for a divorce, though they come to nothing outside, continue to wrangle and swell and grow inside of you, and spoil all that is fine. Nor do I expect you to look forward to such a life with me. This is what generally happens. So, rather than have these desires spoil things now and surely later, I am going to deliberately uproot and kill them.

WIFE

John, what *are* you saying? What *are* you trying to do?

HUSBAND

Just that, Mary. It may be painful, but the pain will only be temporary. You can trust my judgment that afterwards you will be thankful. And I, dear, will be thankful to you.

(*Mary cannot quite believe what she has heard, yet she does believe that she has heard accurately and understands what John is about. She experiences a mixture of fear, indignation, acceptance, and rebellion. She continues to sit there for a moment, and then, when the following is said by the Eight, she leaves her chair, moves towards the front of the stage, and expresses by gestures, etc., what feelings are at work in her. John retains his mental composure.*

Pause.

The Eight now speak, without standing.)

ONE (*female*)

What kind of pain is this?

A SECOND (*male*)

All pain is futile. The only thing worthwhile is to be dead to pain.

A THIRD (*female*)

Whoever heard of constructive pain.

A FOURTH (*male*)

Constructive pain!

A FIFTH (*male*)
Can surgeons give it?

ALL
Surgeons can only hope they can.

FIFTH
Can judges and governments give it?

ALL
They don't even hope.

FIFTH
Can God give it?

ALL
I have never seen him do it.

FIRST
Who is this man who is going to give constructive pain.

SECOND
Who does he think he is?

THIRD
Where does he get off?

(*Pause.*

Mary returns to her seat and again faces John.

Neither of them has heard the above. John is still composed. He continues.)

HUSBAND
Your trouble, my dear, began some years ago. To begin with, a big mistake was made by someone or something. You should have been married when you were eighteen.

WIFE
To whom?

HUSBAND

To a man who corresponded to you, and who could have provided the means of your fulfilling, quite instinctively, without philosophy, the needs and wishes which you, as a young woman and potential mother, then had.

WIFE

Well, John. This from you. You are right. You speak platitudes. But you are so impractical and beside the point that I don't quite understand you. (*then, more rapidly and with more feeling, as if summing up for herself as well as for John much thought and personal experience in just this field*) You know as well as I do that there was no man of this type whom I could have married then. But why rehearse this? You know better than I do that this is a condition met with everywhere: Young men who might in other ways be possible, too often haven't and may never have the means. Young men who may have the means are too often in other ways impossible. The usual assortment of young men, and their seniors also, lack both.

HUSBAND

True—for a woman of your type.

WIFE

All women are of my type, though some of them forget or try to forget it. Women do want marriage. Real marriage. Few get it. A woman can no more truly marry a talent than she can a bank account. Neither can she marry a profession, nor qualities like industry, good humor, kindness, or the reverse of these. But she has, I had, nothing else to choose from. This person who should be a man is simply a talent in a male body, which is often none too good. That person who should be a man is merely a bank account; this one, merely a profession; that one, merely the quality of industry, or kindness, or what not. Well, if it just happens so, a girl when still young marries something, call it a man if you will. I cannot. When I was eighteen, as you say, this blessing just did not happen to me.

(*Pause.*

At this point, the Eight, with the exception of the figure in white, all engage in play. The play is genuine. One by one they rapidly open their eyes, release the rigidity of their features and bodies, and become good to look upon. They become graceful, happy, joyous. They leave their benches, chatting, playing, and having delight in one another. They walk about, flirting playfully, exchanging greetings, never loud or boisterous. They give the impression of being on a well-tempered and really enjoyable excursion or party. The family group takes no part in this, nor is it affected. Snatches of songs begin to be sung. Soon they converge to the front of the stage in a graceful gay assemblage, and sing in unison. They should sing some of the simple, humorous, gay, clean lilts and melodies to be found in the folk, or almost folk, music of all countries. It would be good if the songs were selected from several countries: England, France, Germany, Russia, America—a humorous gay Negro song. But this variety is not necessary. Nor is it at all necessary that the singing be good technically. But it must be felt. It must be genuine.

The singing ends, and the people, now happily fatigued return to their benches. They quiet down, but they are still happy.

Then—)

> ONE (*female*)
Oh it is good to just be living.

> A SECOND (*female*)
It is wonderful just to be here.

> A THIRD (*male*)
Goodnight, my friend, and sweet dreams to you.

> A FOURTH (*male*)
Ladies, good night, good night.

(They fall asleep gradually, and then gradually resume their rigid postures.

Pause—a bit longer than usual.

Then—husband and wife resume their conversation.)

> HUSBAND
What you say, my dear, only confirms my point. Certainly there were causes why you did not marry. And certainly there were effects following from your not doing so. These effects are just that misfortune I referred to. To put the matter simply, because you did not marry then, and have a home and children, you were forced to do something else. This something else was as contrary to your nature as being a wife and mother is in accord with it. You began to look for something else to do—mere compensations for the hunger of your basic needs. First you tried this, then that,

and finally you somehow stumbled on the career of so-called intelligent discussion, which demanded a great deal of reading and practice to keep up with. And so you became a cultured person, one, indeed, of the intellectuals. To your misfortune. It is damaging enough to become a so-called intellectual at any period of one's life; it is almost fatal to become one before you have become a man, or before you have become a woman.

(Pause.

Several of the Eight speak, without standing up.)

> ONE *(male)*
>
> What is a man?

> A SECOND *(female)*
>
> What is a woman?

> A THIRD *(male)*
>
> Who knows?

> A FOURTH *(female)*
>
> Who cares?

(In the following, whenever a male speaks, his voice is made effeminate; and, whenever a female speaks, her voice is made masculine.)

> ONE *(male, effeminate voice)*
>
> I only care about philosophy.

> A SECOND *(female, masculine voice)*
>
> I only care about big business.

> A THIRD *(male, effem. voice)*
>
> I only care about science.

> A FOURTH *(female, mas. voice)*
>
> I only care about art.

> A FIFTH *(male, effem. voice)*
>
> I only care about religion.

> A SIXTH *(female, mas. voice)*
>
> I only care about suffragism.

(*Pause.*

Then—)

        ONE (*male*)
I want to sleep.

        A SECOND (*male*)
What?

        FIRST
I want to sleep.

        SECOND
Let's sleep.

        A THIRD (*female*)
Let's sleep.

        ALL
Let's sleep. Let's sleep. Let's sleep.

(*They do.*

Pause. The husband continues.)

        HUSBAND
It is particularly unfortunate to become a so-called cultured person in this
age we live in. And for this reason: Never have there been so many notions
and theories about life, and about how one ought or ought not live. Never
have so many notions and theories been so easy of access. Indeed they
are thrust upon you in such quantities from all sides that the moment
your nose touches the so-called educated or cultured world, you cannot,
even with effort, possibly avoid them. Most of the notions and theories
are wrong, and many of them are vicious. Now you can't hold wrong
notions about life without gradually killing your native, instinctive real
intelligence for living. Each wrong idea kills one right instinct. Enough
wrong notions kill all right instincts.

        WIFE
But John, why do you restrict your observations to the cultured classes?
Is the "man on the street," the "average man," somehow magically
exempt from contagion?

HUSBAND

Because this is particularly true of your cultured classes, though the man
on the street is certainly not exempt. Wherever you may look, conditions
are similar. There is hardly one of our instincts, there is hardly one of our
functions but what has or finds just that wrong notion most appropriate
for killing it. For every grain of that sound native intelligence which is
our birthright, and which we all are born with, for every grain of this
intelligence there is, floating in the atmosphere, eager to be absorbed,
just that wrong notion which will destroy it. Our atmosphere is so foul,
the race of mankind has breathed it so long, each succeeding generation
breathing in the dirt of all its ancestors (*At this point, the child, still sitting
between its parents, should act as if she were trying to push or shove her
parents away from her. Of course, she can do no more than gesture. Then
she acts as if she were inhaling, say, coal-gas fumes. Gradually she wilts
and becomes torpid, but does not yet fall completely asleep.*), that the
problem of sane intelligence for mankind as a whole seems hopeless. For
instance, those systematized wrong notions which we call education—our
great and glorious system of education soon destroys whatever there is in
us to be educated. So-called philosophy kills the mind. So-called morality
kills conscience. So-called religion kills the function of feeling religiously.
For such a concrete thing as our body and its processes there are a host of
wrong notions which are gradually damaging and destroying it. For the
ordinary processes of eating and eliminating, there are so many wrong
notions and practices that we have lost instinctive knowledge of how to
eat and excrete, and no single person can really tell us how. How should
you eat? Your mind does not know and the process does not take place
rightly of itself.

(*Pause. The family group is not affected by what follows.*

One of the Eight abruptly stands up, leans forward, and speaks.)

ONE (*female*)

Let me, dear friends, glorify the Drug Stores. When man prays to God, it
is always because he wants something. But only children can pray to God
for gifts which add joy and beauty to that which is already joyous and
beautiful. The rest of us pray to be rid of pain, or to have granted some
modifications of our ugliness. Let us therefore face the facts.

98% of us suffer from constipation, noticed or unnoticed.

98% of us suffer from bad stomachs, noticed or unnoticed.

98% of us suffer lack of vitality.

49% of us suffer in our manhood.

49% of us suffer in our womanhood.

>   A SECOND (*male, shouts*)
> Give me castor oii.

>   OTHERS
> Shhh. Let the sermon continue.

>   FIRST (*continuing*)
> Glory belongs to our Drug Stores, not to God, for He helps us not in our
> ailments.

But simply for walking in them and plunking your money down, our
Drug Stores give relief to our every ailment.

See how the blessings repose row upon row, shelf upon shelf, in *this* store,
the perfection of cleanliness, purity, and sanitation.

Only modesty about their mission prevents our druggists from calling their
store what it should be called. It is, my friends, a church, a temple.

For proof, you have only to recall that we are a religious people, accustomed from long ages to daily devotions and pilgrimages. But where
now do you find us most? In our so-called churches? Or in our Drug
Stores?

Then glorify our sacred residences.

Glory to the Drug Stores.

See each bottle on the shelf. See the shelves row on row.

Remember all you are familiar with. Anticipate the taste of all new marvels.

Thousands of bottles. Thousands of stores.

Each year new bottles. Each year new stores.

Let us no longer be ashamed of them. Let us fearlessly acknowledge them.

Let us acclaim them. We are disciples.

But let us first of all be practical.

Speak out any one of you. Confess your ailment.

Let here and now the miracle take place.

> SECOND (*male, shouts*)
> Give me castor oil.

> FIRST
> It is not for neophytes. But, choose and pay for any one or more of these, less good, but also blessings of our chemists: Nujol!

> ALL (*exclaiming*)
> Ahhhh!

> FIRST
> Cascara!

> ALL
> Ohhhh!

> FIRST
> Magnesia!

> ALL
> Aaaaa!

> FIRST
> Eno!

> ALL
> Wheeeee!

> FIRST
> Epsom Salts!

> ALL
> Yeaaaa!

FIRST
You have but to choose and swallow. The rest will be done to you.

ALL
We have but to choose and swallow. The rest will be done to us.

(*All, with the exception of the figure in white, now stand up, file from their benches, and begin walking about the chamber in lock step, with the first person in the lead. As they walk, they repeat, "You have but to choose," etc.*

Shortly, the procession forms ranks towards the front of the stage, the leader in front of them. She then says:)

FIRST
Give us drugs, give us medicine,
Give us science, art, religion.

ALL (*as if said at a football game*)
Give us drugs, give us medicine.
Give us science, art, religion.

(*Repeat.*

Then—more matter of factly—)

ALL
Give us whatever you will.
Whatever you may call it,
On this sole condition:
That without effort on our part
It does things for us.

(*Slight pause.*)

ALL
All drugs are blessings,
We have but to buy and swallow,
The rest will be done to us.

(*Then, with one accord they drop to their knees, and, pointing towards their leader, who remains standing, say:*)

ALL
She is our saint
She is our saint.

(They now become solemn. They rise to their feet, and, in silence, lift their saint upon their shoulders. In grave procession they carry her and deposit her on the middle of the three seats to the rear of, and elevated above, the benches. Here she remains, as if propped up, with eyes closed, until near the end of the drama. Of course, she no longer takes part in the doings of the Eight. These—that is, the six figures—having deposited her, make half ludicrous, half grotesque genuflections before this, their saint, and then in silence straggle to their bench seats. They sit down, close their eyes, and soon become rigid.)

(Curtain)

ACT III

People and scene the same as when the curtain fell. This is a direct continuation.

The husband continues.

HUSBAND

Education kills what is to be educated. Philosophy kills the mind. Morality kills the conscience. Religion kills religion. Drugs of one sort or another gradually kill all of us. Life kills us. That most ideas and notions (and most living) are wrong is evident from the fact that whoever is influenced by them grows steadily worse. Outside, people are putting up a front and show of well-being more and more, which means that inside and in reality they are getting worse and worse. You meet Mr. Brown on the street, and you say to him: Hello, Mr. Brown, how are you? And he says: I never felt better in my life. Fine, just fine! He is a liar. Inside he feels like a dump heap. Well, he goes along as he must. Each person collects his allotment of the Earth's garbage, and calls that a life.

WIFE

John, I have never heard you talk like this. What you are saying is terrible.

(Pause.

During the following, one of the Eight, male, gets up from bench, leaves it, and, half stealthily, half like a trapped rat, begins moving silently about the chamber, feeling its walls, not seeing well, but giving the unmistakable impression that he is trying to find a way out. He does not succeed, but returns to his bench.

The Eight now speak, without standing.)

ONE (*male*)
This is a raw deal, this business.

A SECOND (*female*)
It is a raw deal.

A THIRD (*male*)
It is a dirty business.

A FOURTH (*female*)
What is?

FIRST
Life is.

A FIFTH (*male*)
Are you just finding that out? Where have you been all these years?

FIRST
It is a tough job, a raw deal, I tell you.

(*Slight pause.*)

ONE (*male, effeminate voice*)
Oh let's talk about philosophy!

A SECOND (*female, masculine voice*)
Oh no, let's talk big business!

A THIRD (*male, effem. voice*)
No! let's discuss science!

A FOURTH (*female, mas. voice*)
No! let's discuss literature!

A FIFTH (*male, effem. voice*)
Oh, let's talk about art!

A SIXTH (*female, mas. voice*)
Oh no, let's talk about suffragism!

A SEVENTH (*male, effem. voice*)
No! let's discuss theosophy!

AN EIGHTH (*female, mas. voice*)
No! let's discuss Christian Science!

(*Pause. Then—*

Each one in turn and all stand up.)

ONE (*male*)
I want to eat.

A SECOND (*male*)
What?

FIRST
I want to eat.

A THIRD (*female*)
Yes, let's eat.

ALL
Let's eat, Let's eat. Let's eat.

(*All sit down and become rigid.*

Pause. Silence. Husband continues.)

HUSBAND
It is so, my dear. I may say things more terrible. But if you will realize
that it is now an open fight between myself and, well, something—that I
am backed against the wall, opposed by odds—I have never admitted how
great they are—you will understand why I am forced to say just what I do
say.

WIFE
John, tell me what you are fighting for. What for? Always I have felt you
against. Always negative. Cutting at this thing. Destroying that—

HUSBAND
Never cutting intelligence, but always trying to cut into it.

WIFE
But why? For what purpose? You have intelligence. You have knowledge,
but your use of them is negative. They are positive. But your use of
them—John, is there any positive thing to you worthwhile?

HUSBAND

I have just answered, Mary. Intelligence.

WIFE

But why? For what?

HUSBAND

Intelligence for living.

WIFE

But how can you live intelligently when you exclude so much of life? You do John—you do. You live like a needle.

HUSBAND

Perhaps I do. Thank you, Mary. A needle. That had never occurred to me, the image I mean. A very good one. More accurately descriptive than all of my characterizations of myself. Thank you. However, you must remember that a needle, narrow though it may be—well, the image has served its purpose and we should not overwork it. Besides, I should like to return to what I was saying about you.

WIFE

Before you do, John, will you answer me just this one question? You must believe what you are aiming at now to be worthwhile, else you would not spend so much time and force on it. What is it then? Can't you just tell me now? Can't you just answer me, plain and simple? Perhaps I am all ready to agree with you. Then why waste and strain us both unnecessarily? Can't you? John.

HUSBAND

Yes, I could answer. But my answer could not do what I must do. In some strange way I am dealing with much more than just you, you, this one person, Mary. I could answer, but the plain simple answer would not do. Enough of this. Even I begin to talk obscurely. If I keep on in this way even I shall begin to feel urges towards the Universal Something. (*half to himself*) It would be ironic if I fell a victim of the disease I set myself to cure. (*openly*) No, enough of this. Enough of myself for the moment. We will return to you.

Where were we? Oh, yes, I remember now.

You, my dear Mary, back there at the age of eighteen, you escaped, as you called them, the usual assortment of wrong young men. But in a very short time you absorbed and began to be influenced by a more than usual assortment of wrong notions and ideas. And from that time on, all that was really fine and sound and true in you began gradually to be destroyed. In particular, your capacity to be a woman, a wife, a mother.

WIFE

I do not care to dispute you.

HUSBAND

You cannot.

WIFE

Perhaps not. But I should like to ask you: Suppose John, that instead of taking up with all those, from your point of view, wrong notions, I had, instead, picked one of the wrong young men? Then what?

HUSBAND

The results would have been similar, only the terms would have been slightly different.

WIFE

You see that?

HUSBAND

Certainly I do.

WIFE

(*intensely*) How can you see so clearly and feel nothing?

(*Pause.*

The Eight speak. John is unaffected. Mary is forced from her seat, and moves about the front stage expressing by gestures, etc., what takes place in the Eight group.

One rises to his feet and says:)

ONE (*male*)

Only through pain will you cry out to God. Only through suffering will you seek to find Him.

A SECOND (*male*)

Someone speaks.

FIRST

Repeats.

A THIRD (*male*)

As if we haven't already had pain enough to have many times over sought and found Him.

FIRST

Still not enough.

THIRD

Well, we have had enough of your gloomy doctrines.

SEVERAL

Yes, Yes. Enough of gloomy doctrines.

(*Slight pause.*)

A FOURTH (*female—stands up*)
If I ever find Him it will be through joy.
I will stream towards Him, and burst upon Him.
I will drift towards Him on little joys,
I will stream to Him in great joys,
I will come before Him in ecstacy.

SEVERAL

I must be so. It must be so.

A FIFTH (*female—does not stand*)

Yes, Yes, Why must we be whipped and cuffed and beaten. Why must we find all tastes nasty, smells offensive, sights ugly and revolting. Why must we hate, be poisoned, and despair. Only if God is the Great Sadist can it be so. Should He be supreme in cruelty, then I want to be ever and ever farther from Him. But He is not so. God is Good. He must be all-loving, supremely joyous.

FOURTH
I will stream towards Him, burst upon Him.
I will drift towards Him on little joys,
I will stream to Him in great joys.
I will come before Him in ecstacy.

ALL (*except the first*)
I will stream towards Him, and burst upon Him.
I will drift towards Him on little joys, etc.

(*Slight pause.*)

FIRST (*male*)
Still not enough of pain and suffering
Only through pain will you cry out to God.
Only through suffering will you seek to find Him.

ALL (*except the fourth*)
Still not enough of pain and suffering.
Only through pain will we cry out to God.
Only through suffering will we seek to find Him.

(*The lines on pain and joy are repeated alternately by all. The alternations and stanzas come more rapidly. Then they stop abruptly. The wife returns to her seat. Silence. Pause. Then everyone, with the single exception of the husband and she who has become a saint—everyone on the stage, the wife, the child, the Eight, including the figure in white, yes, even the worker-family, bows, inclines his head. Then the Eight sing, very faintly, the choral hymn. Not too long. It ends shortly. Everyone becomes as before.*

Pause. Silence. Then—)

ONE OF THE EIGHT (*male*)
I am tired. I want to rest.

ANOTHER
I am weary.

ANOTHER
I want to rest.

ALL
Let us rest.

(*Pause. Silence. Then—*)

THE CHILD
Now I lay me down to sleep,
I pray the Lord my soul to keep.

> If I should die before I wake,
> I pray the Lord my soul to take.

(She then falls asleep, and remains so until towards the end of the drama.

The Eight grow rigid.

The family of the worker pantomime, never interrupted, goes on as before and always.

Pause. Then—

The husband resumes his talk.)

HUSBAND
You were asking if you would have done better by picking one from among the usual assortment of wrong young men, and, I will add for you, wrong old men. No matter. No worse. The results would have been similar, with slightly different terms. In this day and age, the position of a young girl ready to be married is damnable, from whatever angle you look at it. Here again, as in every real life condition, the number of possibilities are quite definitely limited. And none of them seems to promise much of anything. Well yes, they promise. But they contain very few real prospects. If a young girl marries, as for instance our Helen may do—

WIFE
Please do not mention Helen.

HUSBAND
But my dear—

WIFE
No, please don't. If it must be so, then let this be just between you and myself.

HUSBAND
There was no special point in my mentioning Helen. None whatever. I simply happened to think of her as an example.

(To the surprise of her husband, Mary suddenly rises to her full height, and glares at him with a mixture of despair and fury. This glare shocks him, and her feelings, somewhat felt by him, cause him also to rise. For

the time being, she is the force, while he is a bit unsteady and uncertain. They stand facing each other, she, still furious, he by posture, etc., asking: What on earth is the matter?

While they stand so, one of the Eight speaks—not heard by Mary and John.)

ONE (*male*)
Tonight I kill him.

A SECOND (*male*)
What?

FIRST
I kill him. I murder him tonight.

SECOND
Aw shut up. Tomorrow I'll read about it better than you can tell me.

(*Silence. Pause.*

While she is standing, something unusual happens to Mary. The force which is at work in her—it is neither suppressed nor controlled—suddenly is transformed from despair and fury into an energy which almost seems to form in her a new character. She grows calm and firm. She has achieved a larger stature. This, she retains. When she speaks to her husband it is with more certainty of herself, more understanding of, and even compassion for, him. But she somewhat restrains from manifesting these qualities, so that, though he senses a change in her, he interprets it as being favorable to him—at least she is more comfortable to be with than when she glared at him in fury.)

WIFE
Sit down, John.

(*He does. She also.*)

HUSBAND
What *was* the matter?

WIFE
(*calmly and directly*) You made me furious, and then something happened rather wonderful within myself, and I thought better of it.

HUSBAND

Well, well, I am sorry—

WIFE

That is over now. Continue, John, what you were saying. It was about a young girl. If she marries.

(*Having been placed upon his feet and helped a bit, John can now continue.*)

HUSBAND

Yes, so it was. I was saying—what? Oh, yes. The prospects of a marriage-able girl. If she marries, the chances are great that she will get some man not suited to her and not able to wisely regulate their life in the midst of contemporary conditions. If she gets the wrong, or an incapable man— first experiences of anything so primary and intimate as marriage indelibly stamp our temper towards all its factors. No woman can ever afterwards escape the consequences of, or grow out of, what happens to her during her first years of married life. If, for instance, when she first marries, she does not really become a wife, but merely enacts the role of one for a sufficient length of time, then she will be almost spoiled for ever being truly a wife, and to become one thereafter under any circumstances will be difficult, if not impossible. Thousands of young married women, now, at this time, are being spoiled in this way. And the men are being spoiled for ever really being men and husbands.

WIFE

What you see when you do look, never ceases to amaze me. (*half musing to herself*) What freak of nature, I wonder, could have cut anyone so completely in half.

HUSBAND

Why a freak, my dear, unless saneness, straight clear thinking about facts, can be classed as such? And as for my being a half, by which you mean, I suppose, that I lack just that which would make me wholly acceptable to you—for what other standard of a whole person could you have than the standard of your own subjective wishes?—well, you also, from my point of view, when measured by my wishes, you also are a half. And so far as I have observed, any person is no more than a half to any other; that is, no person is wholly acceptable to any other. No person can ever be. There must always be discrepancies, gaps, lack of perfect contact. Even a perfect man, if there were such, would lack imperfections. No other single person could feel him to be wholly acceptable. So what then? It is all a question of adjustment. One can ask no more than to be able to meet a given maladjustment rapidly, so as to be ready for the next. The wise man is he who has reduced maladjustments to a minimum and who has gained the skill of an expert in meeting all of them. My wish for you is that you will become a wise man. Doubtless you would like me to become a saint. (*then smiling strangely to himself*) Who knows? Perhaps I am.

WIFE
Now that you say it, I know that is my wish.

HUSBAND
It is not possible. Not as you understand it.

WIFE
Neither is it possible for me to become your wise man.

HUSBAND
It is, Mary.

WIFE
It is not, John.

HUSBAND
But let's not close the issues as tight as this just yet. If you don't mind. There are a number of things I would like you to consider first, and in the light of these you will certainly see things more as I do. Shall we continue what I was saying a short while ago?

WIFE
If you will, John.

HUSBAND
I was speaking of what happens to a young girl if, when first married, she fails to become a wife. There is a similar consequence if a woman becomes a mother, but does not at the same time experience motherhood. She bears children certainly, but if conditions, including her husband, are not what they should be, then she cannot become, in a real sense, a mother, and it will be difficult after this first experience for her ever to become one. There are many children; there are few mothers.

WIFE
You mean that I failed in this because of you?

HUSBAND

Certainly not. I was not thinking of you and myself at all in this case. Though it must be admitted that neither one of us has been what we could have been. But you might profitably think of these facts in connection with our Helen. It will not be long now before she will have to face and meet just the conditions of which I am speaking. Suppose, for instance, to move on a bit, suppose our Helen marries and takes a place of her own, but does not make a home of it. Suppose she, like thousands of young married people everywhere, takes an apartment or rooms at a hotel, places which can never be homes; or even has a well-appointed residence, but without, say, children, or she continues to live with us—then it will be difficult thereafter for her ever to make a home. But the instinct to make one will continue for some time to have a sort of distorted life, and it will find an outlet in any one or more of the vices which young people, married or unmarried, are engaging in more and more.

In general, if a young woman marries, she usually marries wrong—

WIFE

You are a strange man, John.

HUSBAND

Why strange?

WIFE

Because on the one hand you talk as if there were nothing to live for but adjustments, the fewer the better; and on the other hand one might believe you felt man to be capable of a really human dignity.

HUSBAND

(*hurriedly*) There is no contradiction there. Or if there is, it will be removed now very shortly. To continue—if a young woman marries, she usually marries wrong. There are more maladjustments than either she or her husband can take care of. What happens? Let us say that she lives along with her husband. If she has children, her second and third are likely to be either accidents or attempts to fill a vacuum. Soon she may also seek a lover either to fill this emptiness or in resentment against it. Failing to find this satisfactory, as she must, she will then turn to any one or more of a number of less exacting but far more dangerous compensations, notable among them being newosophy, old thought, and Christian Discovery. She will turn to something which, without demanding any effort on her part, will let her feel that she feels in contact with the great scheme of things, with God himself as her personal supervisor. Having a vacuum

which should never have been there in the first place—but having a
vacuum and failing to fill it with her family or anything else on Earth,
she somehow gets the universe in it. In brief, she gets God to fill her
cavity. But of course she cannot, not completely, unless she becomes out
and out pathological. The result is: the birth of "divine urges" of all
types and characters. She is now a full-fledged "rainbow chaser." This is
the ultimate, the almost irreducible maladjustment.

WIFE
Like myself, you mean.

HUSBAND
Not exactly. There is this difference: That you have been married not to
just Tom or Dick or Harry, but to a man who, whatever his other alleged
shortcomings, has, up till now, been able to handle, to manage you. Not
perfectly, to be sure, but enough to prevent your committing the usual
follies, including that of falling head over heels in love with God.

(This statement, made with the cold assurance of a surgeon who has made
a skillful operation and removal of an abnormal growth, with a sort of
cold impersonal egotism—this statement appalls and angers Mary. She
now has the distinct feeling of having been the subject of an operation
which, to be sure, she has felt in progress, but never so sharply, and
never with the clear recognition that each act of John's was a part of a
deliberately worked-out plan. Even now, on first hearing it explicitly
stated by John himself, she is half incredulous. But as the following takes
place she quickly obtains a realization of it and of its meaning. She acts
upon this realization. Through the following conversation there is a rapid
and forceful integration of Mary's character to the point of action. Mary
rises from her chair.)

WIFE
Can you mean—

HUSBAND
Precisely what I have said, Mary.

WIFE
How could you have dared to—

HUSBAND
It was not a question of daring—

WIFE

You did not know what you were doing. How were you justified, even to yourself? You cannot create one single living thing, not even the tiniest, and yet you dare to kill, to kill deliberately. You used your mind—

HUSBAND

Not to kill. But to remove an abnormal growth, much as a surgeon would —to cure.

WIFE

Upon me ... an operation ... by a blind hand ... deliberately .....
these years ..... my life ..... my faith ..... my possibilities .....
under anesthesia ....., deadened to be cured. It is appalling. Terrible!

(At this climax, Mary's feelings are suddenly transformed into a clairvoyance which will result in action. Her force is contained and it expands and deepens her. She experiences a concentration of herself in one inevitable decision. And at the same time she understands John and what he has unwittingly meant to her.)

HUSBAND

No, Mary. Never under an anesthesic. On the contrary, from fantasies about life and about yourself, I have helped you to wake up.

WIFE
(with firm decision) John.

HUSBAND
(standing up and rising somewhat to meet a situation which he is not and never will be aware of) Mary.

WIFE

Yes, you have helped me to wake up. More than you know, and in another way, John.

HUSBAND
Yes, Mary.

WIFE
How can I tell you?

(The fact is that Mary cannot. This is indicated on the stage in the following manner: Up to this time, John and Mary have been facing each other

*as living people having a mutual experience. Now, however, John becomes
suddenly cut off from the real Mary, and from this point on he ceases to
respond to her or be aware of her in any way. He sits down in his chair,
crosses his legs, lights a cigarette, and, instead of attending to the Mary
who is still standing, he appears to be contemplating, with some self-
satisfaction, a Mary seated in the chair opposite him. Later on, he will
even begin talking to this Mary. The actual Mary continues addressing and
acting with John, but, of course, gets no response from him.)*

WIFE

How can I tell you? How can I make clear to you, who know neither of
them? Yes, one you do know from seeing it in other people—how can I
tell you who have felt neither, how can I make clear to you the difference
between two feelings, a difference I myself have just come to realize?
John, there is an unrest caused by conflicts and dissatisfaction of all sorts
which have their cause in what you call maladjustments. I am not sure but
what you are right; in fact, I am sure you are right in attempting to rid me
of such feelings. I have no doubt they do give rise to—rainbow chasing, to
play or love or whatever you wish to call it, to play with mere fantasies of
God. But there is another feeling, a sense, of altogether different origin.
It does not come from maladjustment. It has nothing to do with any of
the ordinary emotional dissatisfactions. It is quite different. So very
different. It is a sense, yes a sense of possibilities, of one's own innate
power to grow. It is the most real thing I know. Where it springs from
must be clear and sound. What it moves towards must be true and marvelous. But to you John, both these feelings are the same to you. You
treat them as if they were. This is your great—it was almost your terrible
mistake. To cure one, you almost killed the other. In me. In yourself
you have suceeded in curing and killing both. For myself, I thank you.
For you—the deepest compassion that I have ever known.

(Slight pause.)

John, you and I, united by a custom as man and wife, we, the two of us,
should have been born in one single being. This being would have had
your perception and knowledge of the actual world, a world in which
facts must be seen and events understood. This being would have also
had my sense and faith in the world of possibilities, a world intangible to
senses and even perhaps to intellect, but to faith, real. In one Being, your
knowledge and my faith would have been each other's complement; this
blending would have given rise to a vision of oneself and of the world
oneself exists in, a vision more complete and accurate than either faith or
knowledge, separate, can have. We were not born in this one Being. You

have wanted me to have your knowledge. I have wanted you to have my faith. We have succeeded only in opposing them. It has been knowledge opposed to faith; faith opposed to knowledge. You and I opposed—until now; the struggle is ended. I have gained in understanding, and for this I thank you. John, I bless you because you have helped me to be as I am. But you are still faithless. I cannot help you. So I, separately, must act according to my faith, and now according to my need. So you, separately, must act according to your lack of it. Good-by John.

(She moves swiftly towards him, kneels before him, and repeats:)

MARY

Bless you. Good-by John, and bless you.

(She rises to her feet, turns away, and moves off. Then suddenly she remembers Helen. A short intense sound, almost a cry comes from her. She stops, turns around, sees Helen sleeping there in her chair, rushes to her to take her in her arms, and carry her with her. She makes the attempt, without waking Helen. But Helen is heavy. She has to put her down, replace her. Realizing this to be inevitable, she again turns away and moves off. She moves about the chamber, looking in intent search here and there, but at first without seeing the Eight. Soon she begins to make movements as if feeling the walls for a possible opening through which to find her way and get out. She feels along the opening into the central chamber, as if it were also a wall. At one place, she does find an opening. Through this, she gains entrance to the central chamber. But, once in it, she seems not to be able to see anything, and she feels a great fear. She quickly steps from it back into the left-hand chamber. Here she again begins moving about. Suddenly she sees, elevated in her seat, the first saint. She looks at this figure intently, questioning it. She is not satisfied with what she sees and feels. She moves away. After a short while, she begins to sense and then see the presence of the Eight, the figure in white excepted. She is not surprised by what she sees. She sees the vacant bench seat. After looking about and deciding that there is nothing else for her to do, she moves to this seat, and sits down. Here she will remain until, as indicated later, a member of the Eight, but with her eyes open, intense, seeking, and though she may take part in some of their actions, she does not completely identify herself with them.

After Mary takes her seat among the Eight, there is a pause, a silence. Then one of the Eight speaks in a firm deep voice, not exclaiming, but with the conviction of its necessity:)

ONE (*male*)
Which way! Which way!
Which way out of this!

(*Pause.*)

(*Curtain*)

ACT IV

People and scene the same as when the curtain fell.

The husband, John, remains looking at the vacant seat across from him as if Mary were in it. His posture is self-satisfied but a bit of affection and kindliness has come into it.

One of the Eight rises to his feet abruptly and says:

ONE (*male*)
I've been to War.

A SECOND (*male*)
What?

FIRST
I've been to War.
I fought for my country.
I fought for all that's best in life.
I killed men and I saved men.
I've been to War.

SECOND
Oh, you don't say.
Well, how'd you like it?

FIRST
Fine! Great!
For the first time in my life I felt I was being fully used.
I say, I was fully, wholly, gloriously used for the first time in my life!

A THIRD (*female*)
Oh, War is Fine!

A FOURTH (*male*)
Oh, War is Great!

A FIFTH (*female*)
Oh, War is Fine and Great and Glorious!

ALL
Oh, War is Fine and Great and Glorious!

(*Saying this, they—with the exception of the figure in white, but including
Mary—get up, leave their benches, join hands, and dance around the
chamber after the fashion of that dance called Ring Around the Roses.*

Then they sit down, cease all movements, and tend to become rigid.

Pause. Silence. Then one stands up and says:)

ONE (*male*)
I've been to War.

A SECOND
What?

FIRST
I've been to War.
I fought for my country.
I fought for all that's vile in life.
I killed men and I saved men.
I've been to War.

SECOND
Oh, you don't say.
Well, how'd you like it?

ONE
Awful! Terrible!
For the first time in my life I felt I was being fully misused.
I say, I was fully, horribly misused for the first time in my life.

A THIRD (*female*)
Oh, War is Awful!

A FOURTH (*male*)
Oh, War is Terrible!

A FIFTH (*female*)
Oh, War is Awful, Monstrous, Terrible!

ALL
Oh, War is Awful, Monstrous, Terrible!

(*Saying this, they—with the one exception—get up, leave their benches, join hands, and dance around the chamber after the fashion of that dance called* Ring Around the Roses.

Then they sit down, cease all movements, and tend to become rigid.

Pause. Silence.

Then one of them slowly rises to his feet, and addressing his remarks to no one in particular, says, with seriousness and gravity:)

ONE (*male*)
There is something wrong here.
I tell you, there is something wrong.

A SECOND (*female*)
There is something wrong.

(*Slight pause.*)

A THIRD (*male*)
Which way! Which way!
Which way out!

FIRST (*repeating*)
There is something wrong here.
There is something wrong.

A FOURTH (*female*)
To think that we have come to this.
Ages of human effort have brought us to this.

A Fifth (*male*)
This is no time for thinking. This is a time for doing.

(*He stands up.*)

Who wants to do?

All (*with the one exception, rise successively to their feet and say:*)

I do. I do. I do.

(*Then there is confusion. They look here, there, wring their hands, sway, etc., and say at random:*)

Something has happened
Something was promised.
Something must happen.
I say with my heart: something must happen.
It is a nightmare.
It is horrible.
Nothing means anything.
Life is nothing.
Who is responsible?
What must we do?
There is much to do.
God give me strength.
God cannot.
Who is responsible?
Who? Who? Who?

(*While the above is happening, two people, a man and a woman, detach themselves from the mass; and both, though separately, move about the chamber, feeling about, searching the walls as if they felt themselves to be trapped rats who wanted to get out. The woman feels about to no result and is shortly caught up in the following mass action. The man, however, just like Mary before him, does find his way into the central chamber. He has difficultly in seeing about in it. Also it evokes fear in him. But he moves about it, here, there, now boldly, now in fear. He remains in it until just after the mass action of the Eight, at which time he returns to the left-hand chamber, takes a casual glance at the new saint, and sits down. Just after the random sayings reach: "Who is responsible?*

*Who? Who?," the fifth person, male, dominates the scene by saying
loudly:)*

FIFTH
Who caused this?

*(He is echoed by several. Then they all begin pointing accusing fingers at
one another. They hiss as they do so. The fifth person, however, hisses
louder than the others, and they therefore are drawn to point at this one
whom the Fifth has singled out. In this way, all are brought to agreement
in accusing and pointing and hissing at this one, male.*

*The Fifth leaves his bench, goes towards the front of the stage, turns,
addresses the accused, and says:)*

FIFTH
Come out here, you.

*(The accused is shoved out by the others. He moves towards and stands
helpless and passive before the Fifth.)*

FIFTH
(addressing him) Now don't you speak, because we know you did it.

(He addresses the others.) Come friends and brothers. Here he is.

(They come forward, semi-menacing, and gather around the accused.)

MARY
What has he done?

FIFTH
We are not here to ask and answer questions.
We are here to do.
Now grab him and choke him.

(They do.

*They kill, him, not with great passion or violence, but with a common-
place rustle and bustle. Once they have killed him, a mood of tenderness
grows in them. They gently lower him, and lay him out before them.
Then as they gaze on him, they begin to feel "awe," and then "reverence."
One by one they kneel before him. One by one they say:)*

He once was with us,
Now he is no more.
He once was with us,
Now he is no more.

(This is repeated.

Pause. Then—)

ONE (*male*)
He has passed over the great fear into blessedness.

ALL
He has passed over the great fear into blessedness.

FIRST
Henceforth he is a saint.

ALL
Henceforth he is a saint.

ALL
He has passed over the great fear into blessedness.
Henceforth he is a saint.
He is a saint henceforth.

(Then they chant these lines. A mumbled lament alternates with the chant. While thus engaged, they lift the saint's body tenderly, carry it in procession to the rear of their benches, deposit and prop it up in one of the two remaining vacant seats. Here he, the second saint, also remains until near the end of the drama. Of course, he takes no part in the doings of the Eight. These, having propped him up, make half-ludicrous, half-grotesque genuflections before this, their second saint. Then a silence falls on them.

Then they get up and slowly circle round their benches, alternately repeating the chant and the lament, but now, at random, no longer in unison.

They return to their benches, sit down, and grow rigid.

Pause. Silence.

The husband, John, now speaks as if to Mary, but as if Mary were still sitting opposite him. Mary, among the Eight, of course does not hear him.)

HUSBAND

(*reminiscently, with an easy pleasure and self-satisfaction*) You will remember, my dear Mary, that when we, you and I, were first married, I was able then as now to provide you with all the so-called material things you wanted. I was able to provide all that was necessary for the type of life we planned to live together. And though I was younger, knew less, and was less a man than I am now, I—and you also my dear—we seemed able to give each other what each wanted.

(*The Eight should now faintly hum a love lyric. Very short. The husband stops while this goes on, and when it is finished, continues.*)

HUSBAND

We cared for each other very deeply, Mary. And life went well. That is, as well as any two people could reasonably expect it to go. Of course there were discrepancies. Even then I was too singly and too often mental —that is, intellectual—for you. I see that now. But then, back there over ten years ago, I just assumed without thinking much about it—I just assumed that our types were similar. It was not till later that I began to see differently.

(*Pause.*

The Eight now speak, and as each one does so, he stands up.)

ONE (*male*)
I want to eat.

ANOTHER (*male*)
What?

FIRST
I want to eat.

A SECOND
I want to eat.

A THIRD (*female*)
Let's eat.

ALL
Let's eat. Let's eat. Let's eat.

(*They sit down, and grow rigid.*

Slight pause. Then the husband continues.)

HUSBAND
It was when I began to see that you were not really intellectual, but
merely intellectualized, owing to your forced association with the so-called
cultured world—it was when I began to be able to distinguish between
what you were by nature, and what was quite foreign to you—that I
began to suspect our differences. At first, they seemed no more than the
differences between two types, one intellectual, the other emotional. And
I saw no reason why we should not and could not complement each
other. I began indeed to work towards this end. You on your part might
have done more—But never mind now. It was still later that I saw beginning to grow in you—just that which has caused our real difficulties.
But it is premature to mention this just now. To get back—At about
the same time, you, from your side, must have begun to note what were
differences if not discrepancies in me. Of course you did. But in spite of
all this and despite the ups and downs of life when even at its best, things
went well with us.

(*Pause.*

As he speaks he stands up.)

ONE OF THE EIGHT (*male*)
I want sex.

A SECOND (*female*)
What?

FIRST
I want sex.

SECOND
I want sex.

A THIRD (*male*)
I want sex.

ALL
Let's sex. Let's sex. Let's sex.

(*They sit down. Grow rigid.*

Silence. Pause. The husband continues.)

HUSBAND
Helen was born, and your motherhood remains one of the bright parts
of my memory. I remember looking about me at that time, and the odds
seemed favorable that we would avoid both the snags and the dead levels
of inertia that most marriages go to pieces or rot on. I have never been
what you could call a hopeful temperament. I have never hoped to get a
great deal from this life, and, as you know, I have no illusions as to any
life hereafter. So when I say that the odds seemed favorable, you will
recognize that to be a conservative estimate.

(*Pause.*

As each speaks, he stands up.)

ONE OF THE EIGHT (*male*)
I want to sleep.

A SECOND (*female*)
What?

FIRST
I want to sleep.

SECOND
I want to sleep.

A THIRD
Let's sleep.

ALL
Let's sleep. Let's sleep. Let's sleep.

(*They sit down. Grow rigid.*

Pause. Silence. The husband continues.)

HUSBAND

There seemed little likelihood of your ever seriously wanting another man. And of course, I considered myself capable of holding you, which I still do, when it is a question of another man. It is not this, it is not any apprehension of your picking up and leaving me for anything so tangible as a lover or a divorce, it is nothing so tangible that disturbs me. It is something else. And it is this that I am coming to.

(*Pause.*

Here the Eight make a distant deep rumbling sound. It is faint. It is audible. It is like the sound of a great wind or of a great human crowd coming from far off. This sound, or complex of sounds, lasts a while, and then ends abruptly. John, suddenly and for the first time, is visibly disturbed. He acts as if he had been swiftly brushed by some great outside force, with which he is not in harmony, and which he can do nothing with. By the use of force he controls himself and continues.)

HUSBAND

I noticed it, that which made me apprehensive—about five years ago. And I never mentioned it. But now that I must—(*with feeling to himself*) But why must I? For what seems too long a lifetime I have held it. So, (*he indicates by gesture how it has been locked up in himself*) why now? (*easier*) But why not now? (*quite at ease*) My dear Mary, I will recall to you those periods when I was convalescing—a strange thing, that accident—when I was convalescing from that accident which almost killed me— well, I was then much absorbed in my own thinking. You often used to ask me what I was thinking about, as if you sensed that it was not abstract, but might concern you. It did. However, not you only, but me also. (*growing momentarily intense*) You hear? Myself! Me! *I was affected then.* (*He gives a strange laugh, and becomes more at ease.*) That was the most important period of my life, and I came out of it, outwardly perhaps the same, because I planned to look the same; but inwardly I was a changed man. How changed, you will see.

(*At this point, the rumbling complex of sounds again begins coming from the mass group. It is louder than at first, and more of a babel. At intervals, longer at first, shorter as the action continues, and with volume and confusion increasing, it will continue to come from the mass group during John's speech until, as will be indicated, it reaches a semi-climax and abruptly ends. This sound coming from the mass group forces John to speak louder so as to be heard above it. His own story, his own thoughts now also begin to evoke feeling in him. External and internal pressure combine to make of him a tragic character. He holds to his discourse to the end.*)

JOHN

(*continuing*) To begin with, that accident and the narrow escape I had, made me realize how basically precarious life really is. (*He rises to his feet. The eyes of everyone open suddenly and they all look at him. He says with intensity:*) In an instant—can you realize that?—*in an instant it can all be over.* A swift disease, an accident, the wrong bottle, a stray bullet, and *one life* is finished. One life. My life. Your life. Snapped out like that. Nothing here. Not one scrap. Nothing there. Gone. Finished. Done with. In an instant. (*calmer*) Well, so. It is nothing to get excited about, but it does make ideas about living for something grand and important sound very hollow, doesn't it? In fact, the phenomena of uncertainty and accident entirely rules out the thing called *my* life. My life? How mine? I haven't got any. What have I got? Just this one thing: Pleasure. Pleasure only. For fools there is much else: pain, suffering, strife, urges. Well, God cares for them. I care for my own pleasure.

But pleasure is not a constant. Therefore one's only aim should be to make it so—as long as it lasts. When it is done, it is not life that has finished (I have ruled life out), but it is simply pleasure gone. But why tell reasonings? Better that I tell results. The result was this: that what I had always more or less done, but unconsciously, I, at the time, formed into a principle. I decided to live for pleasure only. But pleasure derived from what? Many things which delight people did not delight me. Pleasure, then, from what? After a searching and sincere questioning of myself, I soon discovered that I invariably derived pleasure from one special thing—namely, from myself. I was always pleased with myself provided that I handled myself in a way which was creditable in my own eyes. So, simply, I then resolved always to so conduct myself that I should have the pleasure of being pleased with myself. (*His voice is now high. There is a lull in the sounds from the mass; all eyes are on John.*)

To be pleased with himself. Each man wants it. He wants nothing else. The whole world seeks the perfection of this pleasure. This, the perfect life. This is perfection. This is God. But there are fools, idiots, hypocrites, cowards amongst us. Some people won't admit it. They are fools. Some people do admit it. They are naive sentimental pups. A toothache downs them. They don't know how. They would not try to if they did. They are cowards to their own convictions. But I—for me life and pleasure are one. But a pleasure very subtly distilled in perfect Egoism.

(Pause.

John's face has become somewhat diabolical. But there is in it a certain fearlessness. A ruthless frankness, but frankness nonetheless. The courage of a man who is willing to declare himself, fight it out alone if need be, and pay in any terms the price of his convictions.

The Eight draw back and away from him, appalled by his declarations. Also they are forced to admiration. John does not see them, nor does he hear when someone shouts:)

ONE OF THE EIGHT *(male)*
Anti-Christ!

(This is the sign for babel, rumblings, etc., to break forth from the mass group. It rises to a violent swift climax, and stops abruptly.

Pause. Long silence. John holds his last posture and is unaffected by what now takes place.

Slowly the figure in white rises to her feet. The child, Helen, now opens her eyes, and from now on they will remain open and she will witness all that takes place. But she is not part of the happenings, nor does she feel or understand them. She takes them in; she does not respond to them. She remains seated. The first movements of the figure in white attract the eyes of the Eight. They are hungry to look at her. They are incredulous. Then their incredulity is replaced by wonder. Their eyes follow her as she moves with stately grace to the front of the stage. They want to follow her, but are hesitant, withheld from doing so at once by a feeling of respect, near reverence, which she calls forth in them. Mary is the first to arise and approach this figure. Mary kneels to the right side of her. One by one the others follow, kneeling and forming behind her in a semi-circle. With bowed heads they remain in silence. Each one in turn then feels compelled to give expression to the birth of feeling within himself, feelings for which he has no words, no vehicle, no language. They, the feelings, then begin to come forth from each one by means of pure sound vocables, now hummed, now sung in the form of unfinished hymns. These rise and fall, alternately. Then there come in succession three crests at which the singing is suspended to allow three of those kneeling to become articulate in words.

These are the words expressed at the first suspended crest:)

ONE (*male, looking up while he speaks towards the face of the figure in white*)

Madonna,
Yours is the force of grace
To bend and supplement
Bold strides,
Like arches are to spans
From Earth to Endlessness.

(*The low singing begins immediately after he has finished. It swings down and rises to the second crest, where it is suspended.*)

MARY (*looking upward toward the face of the figure in white*)

Bright lines have traced
Your body on my body,
Your soul upon my soul,
Indelibly.
No thought, no wish, no action
Can make this not so.
What was traced is blended.

(*Singing as before.*

Third crest.)

ONE (*male, looking upwards*)
This marriage is a sacrament,
It is a magic
Which time alone must now
Condense and crystallize
In matter
And produce on Earth
A ritual.
Towards this we go.

(*The low singing begins again immediately after this. It swings down, rises again, diminishes, grows faint, barely audible, and ceases.*

Pause. Silence.

Then the figure in white turns round and begins moving towards the rear of the chamber. She is followed by the Eight in reverential silence. Of herself, she mounts and occupies the one vacant chair beside the saints. The Eight kneel before her. But this time their devotions are simple and genuine. When finished, they return to their benches and resume their seats. They do not close their eyes, nor do they become rigid. Mary, however, does not return with them. She remains kneeling near the figure in white. The Eight have no sooner composed themselves in their benches than the figure in white dismounts from her pedestal, and goes directly through the opening into the central chamber. Once in this chamber, she moves directly towards the platform and kneels before it, her face towards the wall in which, higher up, there are the triangle and star. Mary, from her kneeling posture, sees the figure in white descend. When she goes into the central chamber, Mary follows her. Mary experiences no difficulty in going in; but, once in, she again goes swiftly here and there, as if half blinded and unable to bear the fear and wonder which the chamber evokes in her. But before long, and before being forced out again, she notices and instantly recognizes the figure in white kneeling before the platform. With movements expressive of a new-found joy and radiant assurance, she moves towards this figure and kneels behind her.

There is a pause. A silence.

Then one of the Eight speaks in a quiet, even, matter-of-fact voice:)

       ONE (*male*)
I once knew two people, man and wife.
They were good people.
The man was one thing; the wife, another.
There was nothing and no one to
reconcile them.

       A SECOND (*male*)
There never is.

       FIRST
There can be.

(*Pause. Silence.*

Then John resumes his talk, and in this passage concludes it. His mood and features are those which he had just before the figure in white arose. Only, both mood and features are somewhat reduced, and he in general is more contained. He is now entirely concerned with himself, his own views, thoughts, and problems. His words are no longer addressed to Mary, or to anyone in particular outside himself. In fact, what he now says is straight soliloquy. As he speaks, the Eight, with eyes open, regard him. As he continues to speak they begin to gesture in his direction and then at him. Their faces should express no personal feeling either for or against him. So far as he personally is concerned, their faces are impersonal. But the features of each face should reveal a tragic intensity as if set in a mask. By the movements of their arms, the Eight should express the slow and general motions of great forces, forces contained in human beings but now soon to be released from them. At first the motion of the forces is slow and general. It becomes more rapid and concentrated. By the end of John's speech it should be known that the forces, though not directed at him in particular, are nevertheless circling him, and will soon have him amongst them. The child, Helen, is a witness of all this, but keeps to her seat and does not take part.)

JOHN

Just I, alone, in a vacant world. No. Not alone. Mary is necessary. Just I and Mary, the two of us in a vacant world. With her to reflect me, and, in a sense complement me, with her to reflect me and supply the parts which Nature—ass that she is—should have built in just one machine, with Mary to reflect me I would be content to be the God of a desert universe. Upon thinking it over, however, it seems to me that something more would also be necessary. I need a world of fools against which I can stand in contrast. Seemingly, the world as it is, is quite good for my purposes. If only one could be in it and yet remain perfectly isolate if he wills to. But this world in which I live—pardon me—in which I am pleased with myself, I am but a minute part—and, reason compels me to admit: a relatively helpless part. I am but a minute part of a world of huge elemental forces and of some two thousand million human beings, the whole of which impinges upon any and every single particle. Those who know my attitude might well call me insane. Well, no matter. I exist, have pleasure, in an age of this world which is particularly disturbed and chaotic.

This age was not made for any great permanence. Save, perhaps, mine. This age was not made for, say families, such as I, had I lived in another epoch, might well have wanted and have had. Much less was it made for one great Family. (*A buried idealism comes to birth here for a moment, and for this brief time it burns splendidly.*) It was not made for one great State. For one great Art. One Science. One Philosophy. One Religion. Yes, even I would have been religious had there been One. (*slight pause*) What a thing for me to say—the echo of a past dream passing by just at

this time to criticize the aim for which I have spent my life. Oh, nonsense.
To continue, then, John.

This age was not made for any great permanence whatever, save mine. In
fields more varied, and in some respects richer, than ever before, it makes
men overnight, and breaks them as quickly. Are they not idiots who plan
and pin their pleasures on hoped-for achievements outside themselves?
Would they plan to build on quicksand? They do plan. And they are
idiots. Moreover, the man who builds today, may himself not live to see
his building smash tomorrow. *In an instant,* it can be all over. Man has
about as much chance to do something in an idealistic sense as an ant has
to cross a boulevard. No wonder that even sound realists sometimes draw
back and either kill themselves or become rainbow chasers. What then can
a wise man, gifted with a bit of force and courage, equipped with stuff to
play the game—what can a wise man guarantee himself? Just this: to be
able to have the pleasure of being pleased with himself. This is the quintessence of it all, the ultimate good sense.

(*Slight pause.*

[*Speaks*] *with sudden intensity.*)

So then, I have declared myself.
See me, you fools and idiots!
See me, you pleasure pups!
See me, you great men: Artists, Scientists, Philosophers, Saints!
I am a saint for you!
I! I! by God, so sane as to be mad!

(*At this point the Eight, in silence, leave their benches and begin weaving
all about the chamber, about John, lines of accelerating force. Twisting,
turning, darting, shooting, growing even more and more intense, more
converging, more concentrated.*

*John now notices them. At first he tries to draw back and protect himself,
isolate himself. Then he is forced to try to shove them away from him. He
uses every device not to be caught in their movements. But shortly he is
caught up in and with them. He becomes one of them. All together they
weave, twist, turn, dart, shoot. Then in a concentrated, solid mass they
all rush to the front of the stage, and suddenly arrest all motion.*

Pause. Silence.

Then one of the Eight says with intense revulsion:)

       ONE (*male*)
This is a nightmare.

(*Slight pause.*)

       A SECOND (*male*)
It is a nightmare.

(*Slight pause.*)

       A THIRD (*female*)
Nightmare.

(*This is repeated by several more; and, as the conviction grows in them,
they begin drawing away from each other, as if each one were some horrid
figure to be hated and feared.*

Then—)

       FIRST
It is a nightmare. (*He points to one after the other.*) You. You. You. You.
You are horrid shapes I hate and fear. You I hate. You I fear. You I want
to run from. You I want to kill. Look! Look! You half-goat, half-bear. (*He
points at, and either withdraws from or goes towards the one named.*)
You crocodile! You hyena! You toad-jackal!

(*He begins moving amongst them, half running, half dragging himself,
grabbing and pulling this one to him, repelling that one, naming each
one as he passes.*)

       FIRST
Wolf-gazzle! Rabbit-vulture! Goat-bear!
Hyenna! Toad-jackal! Snake!

(*The last named, the Snake, hisses back at him.*)

       THE SNAKE
Mule-bat!

(*The Mule-bat gasps as if struck, almost stricken.*

But before anything further can come of this, the others now begin to call each other the names he has called them. They also begin moving amongst themselves, half running, half dragging, grabbing, pulling, pushing. This grows in intensity as it goes on, until soon they are contorting about like a mass of envenomed worms, stinging and choking each other.

Before they begin contorting, they cease naming each other. Names are replaced by the sounds of painful struggle; cries of pain, of fear, hatred, curses. These also gradually diminish and cease. They have gotten down to business, and silently go about the process of choking each other.

Then, one of them, in the midst of the contorting, suddenly recognizes a need, and begins looking around to find a suitable object. He says:)

        ONE (*male*)
Here. Here. Who?
We need another Saint.
Which one?
Here. Here. Quickly.
We need another Saint.
Anyone will do.
Only Quickly, Quickly. No time to lose.
Who?
Who for a Saint?

(They all now temporarily cease contorting, and, while looking around amongst themselves, repeat:)

        ALL (*at random*)
        Who for a Saint?
        Who for a Saint?

(Then, shortly, the first person selects one. He goes up to him and says:)

        FIRST
Here, this one.

        THE SELECTED (*male)*
Me?

        FIRST
Yes, you.

FIRST (*to the others*)
Here now. Grab him and fix him.

(*They do. They choke and finish him quickly.*

Then they hastily and without ceremony carry and hoist him into the third seat in saints' row. Without more ado they quickly return to contorting, to choking each other.

Then, first from one and then another, and so on, these now sincere cries, groans, and supplications are forced out:)

> Oooh
> Christ
> Have mercy.
> Enough, enough
> Pity
> O, God
> No longer
> Deliver me.
> O, God. O, God.

(*These cries are wrung from the very depths of them.*

All cries become supplications.

This is now crescendo.)

SOMEONE (*cries*)
Which way! Which way!
Which way out!

This a sign; and, having heard it, they all in one moment cease contorting and fall apart. One falls, almost prostrate. Another on knees, body bent, arm supporting. Another drags himself on his belly around the chamber. Another stands as if stricken rigid. One tries to support himself on him, etc.

Broken sobs and supplications continue to come from them. But the sounds are faint, because they, the people, are spent, almost done for.

Sobs and supplications cease.

Silence. Pause.

The worker-wife is beating herself in dumb anguish and despair while moving about the right-hand chamber.

Then, an extraordinary force begins to work in them, all with the exception of John, who will remain huddled on the floor. According to their diverse states it animates them. Then, as they rise upward and forward, one after the other, each turns his eyes for the first time directly towards the central chamber. It is seen that each one senses and feels that the central chamber contains that which each one wants and seeks with his whole heart. The central chamber draws them. They are drawn to it, as if energized by some power which transcends them. While still in their various postures they become irradiated. And then with one accord they begin limping, dragging, crawling, helping each other, somehow moving towards and into the central chamber.

The worker-wife finds her way into this chamber at the same time.

From offstage, additional people now also run, hobble, crawl, somehow come in, all into the central chamber.

There should be enough in number to convey the sense of momentum and to give a sense of fullness to the central chamber. But it should not be crowded.

Coincident with the movement of people into the central chamber, a door—the size of a man, cut into the wall behind the platform and leading directly to it—opens, and the Being, male, of this chamber enters. He is dressed in a rich but simple white garment, on the breast of which, embroidered in gold, there is a triangle surrounded by a circle. He stands in firm repose upon the platform.

The people who come in all face him. They kneel and form a semi-circle around the platform.

The central chamber is now in silence. All have entered and are in their places.

Just as the last person kneels before the Being upon the platform—just then, the three figures who up till this time have been sitting immobile in saints' row, open their eyes and dismount from their chairs much as men quit seats at a lunch counter. They dismount and just walk off the stage, using the left-front exit.

When they have gone out, John pulls himself together, rises to his feet; and, while trying to adjust his clothes, rub dirt off, and, in general, set himself right, he walks, somewhat bent but not broken, towards the place occupied by his former seat. Once there, but now standing up, he makes one last and considerable effort to compose himself. To be what he is. To shake off all trace of what he has just been through. He succeeds in drawing himself up to his full height, squaring and bracing himself. He succeeds in composing himself, but his composition gradually settles into and is transformed into that of stone statuary. Just before his eyes close, he says in a firm but compressed voice:)

JOHN
I shall not die, because I have never lived. But this is the end of pleasure.

(His eyes close. His face sets. He becomes transfixed as stone. It is as if he had died, no funeral or burial being necessary.

So he stands.

When he is transfixed, the child, Helen, who has been sitting there, following all movements with her eyes, including those of John, but not moving from her chair—now Helen leaves her chair, and no longer noticing John, moves about the left-hand chamber as if she is lost and is looking everywhere for something or someone. She fails to find what she is looking for. When the choral hymn begins to be sung in the central chamber, the child then enters into this chamber, still searching.

In the central chamber there has been silence.

Now the Being on the platform repeats the incantation. This incantation should begin the moment after John is transfixed.)

The Incantation

I am that I am
I am that I am
I am that I am
The Father.

I am that I am
I am that I am
I am that I am
The Mother.

I am that I am
The Son
That I am
I am that I am
The Son.

(*Curtain*)

Section V

APHORISMS AND MAXIMS

Editor's Note

In 1931, while he was deeply involved with his mission as spiritual reformer, Jean Toomer published *Essentials*, a collection of maxims and aphorisms commenting on human life. Prior to this private printing of a limited edition, Toomer had tried to sell the book to commercial publishing houses; but they had rejected it, perhaps agreeing with Ogden Nash that it was interesting but that the Depression was not a time in which to expect financial profit from it. During the seven years following *Essentials*, Toomer continued to write down lines and statements that he arranged into "Remember and Return," a longer book including many maxims and aphorisms from the earlier one. Despite his efforts, he failed to persuade a publisher to accept this second collection.

In a preface to the manuscript of "Remember and Return," Toomer explained the intention of the book, his reason for choosing the form and the structure:

> The reality of man's life, as I perceive and understand it, is complex beyond the possibility of formulation. How represent in sequence that which exists simultaneously? Where begin, where end? Yet a book about man must be written in sequence, and it must begin and end. Thus a book about human life, in its very structure, is a first-class misrepresentation, no matter what facts and truths it may contain.

> If it is to approach true representation it must be *made* to do so by a dynamic, creative and critical relationship established between the words and he who writes them and he who reads them. As such relationships are as rare in literature as they are in life, it follows that even the excellent books, due both to their defects and to man's negligence, tend to become agents of error and arrestation.

> My realization of this "inadequacy" has not deterred me from writing, but it has kept me from attempting to construct a mental "system" under the illusion that such a system would be an accurate and complete representation of man's reality.

> On the positive side, this same realization gives me some assurance that this present collection of views and ideas, though incomplete as

mental description of my world-view, though full of gaps as regards my psychology of man and the creative functions, has an intrinsic honesty, if not truth, in that it simply presents, for whatever meaning they have to others, the perceptions and understandings that came to me over a period of years, not while I was trying to write a book about man but while I myself was experiencing the realities and the illusions of man's life.

In relating the lines to each other, in grouping the lines and statements into sections and the sections into the whole book, I was guided by the principle of psychological association, and also by the aim to produce a certain inner revolving of ideas, meanings, and effects.

My intention was to arrange the statements in such a way that the mind of the reader would be able to catch hold of the central themes and follow them through. These themes, I need hardly say, are expressions of my root-experiences. If I have been successful in this, the lines do build up, and continuous reading is not only possible, it will prove worthwhile.

Though the ordering of the book is not the order in which I wrote the lines, it is, I hope, an order which will enable other people to grasp and experience my *meanings*—and, after all, it is precisely these meanings and their development, not the facts or realities as such, that I primarily aim to convey.

Books, I think, are much more faithful as presentations of meanings than as representations of complex reality. In this they are similar to music and other forms of art which, in expressing the *essentials* of human experience, thereby inevitably express some portion of underlying reality, since man himself is an integral part of the universal realness—even though his body-personality often causes him to be a disinterred part, even though he sleeps through it all.

Their function, as I see it, is to feed, to communicate, evoke, point out, open the eyes, make clear, guide, and, more rarely, to reveal. . . .

In this volume, I have included only a small sample from Toomer's four-hundred-page manuscript, arranged on pages according to his original intention. I have included the beginning of Section I (Nature Is Not Unnatural . . .), most of Section III (Split-Men . . .), the beginning of Section V (Two Forces Behind Human Values . . .), and all of Section VII (Indications . . .). These sections focus on human nature and human values. In other sections, Toomer wrote about such topics as his life, literacy, evil, reading and writing, education, human relations, the prison system, morality, death, human relationships, materialism, and progress.

I

NATURE IS NOT UNNATURAL ...

The records of the wise and most human men show that
they had in common this one essential aim—to
restore the people of the earth to their right
habitation in the universe.

We have reason to ask no more, and certainly no less
than this: that we return in full consciousness
to be and to function as befits us in the Natural
Scheme.

By Nature I mean not only the Nature described by
naturalists, but also the Nature described by
those who perceive spiritual reality.

I refer to the vast and marvelous Order of Life throughout
the worlds, from which man has plainly deviated.

Are we in parts that we need be made whole?
    I think we are.

I think moreover that there are in us some parts
    that never will be, never can be, never should be,
    joined.

Can hate be joined with love? Should it be?
    I think not. Can false beliefs be joined
    with knowledge, prejudice with impartiality,
    egotism with a love of all that breathes?

If, then, we would become unified we must also work
    to eliminate these disintegral parts.

Catharsis must accompany development, and development
    must be supervised by the unifying principle.

To develop without catharsis is fatal. Witness
        our world today.

To develop without balance, without unification,
        without harmonization is also fatal. Again
        witness our world today.

To develop *and* cleanse *and* unify—this is the
        creative way, the way of man.

Nature is natural. Human nature, by nature, is all
        right. It is the acquired or false "nature" of
        men that is all wrong.

Therefore our aim must be, not merely to change but
        utterly to eliminate these false growths—in
        fine, to *remove* whatever is obstructing our nor-
        mal development.

Change human nature? Not at all. Get rid of ob-
        structions and *cultivate* human nature.

Life is mystery in motion.

It would be very distasteful but very fruitful if each
        one realized that the main trouble with the world
        is himself.

All men have faults.

Small men are blind to their own, and therefore
        remain small.

Great men are those who overcome their own faults.

III

SPLIT MEN . . .

We are split men, disconnected from our own resources,
        almost severed from our *Selves*, and therefore out
        of contact with reality.

Not altogether so, else we would not live, or, if we
        did, there would be no questions about our plight,
        no contradictions between our actual behavior and
        the ideal state of being.

These threads of union existing between the conscious
        and the subconscious, between the mask and the
        man, are responsible for our sensing the tragic
        discrepancy between what we are in behavior and
        what we might be in being.

And they are our hope of salvation. For as long as
        they obtain, threads though they are, we can use
        them to bridge the gap and re-member ourselves.

It is because of this split, and because what-we-feel-
to-be-ourselves *locates* in the lesser divorced
part, that we are *out of life*.

Do we not know we are out of life? Each one knows
as the chief fact of his earthly existence that
he is an exile, an orphan, out of touch with "something" he ought to be in touch with.

The deep drives of men, however contaminated by egotism, greed, and lust, are essentially drives to get
in touch, to enter into life—and here we commit
the second tragic mistake.

The first mistake was that which caused the split.
We in our own existences perpetuate this mistake
and commit the second by believing that we can
enter *into* life by driving *outward*.

Ah, people, how "logical" but how fatal. How logical
that we who already are *out*, should be persuaded
that what we desire is to be gained by going *out*
after it, still further out.

Thus, for one thing, we promulgate the cult of "living"
which is devastating the Western World, which has
devasted every historical people who succumbed
to it.

Indeed this persuasion to go out is so powerfully upon
us that to us there seems no other possible direction; and we drive ahead to create a huge worldly
world, only to find ourselves the more entangled;
and we scoff at those "mystics" who suggest that
the way to become free is to disentangle ourselves
from this world, who teach that the way to enter
into life is precisely to enter *into* it.

A "mystic" too was he, the Christ, who taught the way
which most modern Christians go directly counter
to, even inventing machines so as to go counter
more efficiently.

I am not saying that this is a deliberate infidelity.
On the contrary, I am saying that, though anti-
Christ, it is logical to those who themselves are
out of life.

Is this mysticism? There is no fact more "brutal"
than this: that we men of this modern Christian
era, implemented by machines, have pushed out with
such force that we have created a world so utterly
out of life that it is bent upon the wholesale
destruction of itself.

What else? Is it not inevitable that a world so out
          of life must also be out of hand; that neither gov-
          ernments nor people, using variations of the means
          which brought this world into existence, can check
          its mad course?

Will you, then, the individual, persist in going out
          and contributing to a world that is not only anti-
          Christ, anti-all-religions, but counter even to
          bare creature survival?

Or will you stop to consider this perfectly simple
          proposition: that we are out of life because we
          are split men, and therefore if we would enter into
          life we must do nothing to increase this split,
          everything to mend it.

Rather let us overcome our out-of-life "logic" before
          it overcomes us. The way to do this is to become
          *psycho*logical, learning and using the means for
          re-turning our drives so that instead of seeking
          out we seek *in* for contact with that Greater Part,
          which now is and always has been *within* life, await-
          ing our union with it, even while conscious—we exist
          in exile.

Thus and thus only will we re-member ourselves and
          become *whole* men aiming to become *complete* whole
          men, existing not in what we call life but in
          that which is Life.

There is no end to "out." *Out* is an endless direction
to nothingness, crossed by pains of the flesh and
flared by ghastly competitions for prizes which
vanish as we grab them.

Behind each man there is a Self. That he is not aware
             of it does not mean it is nonexistent, that he is
             unconscious of it does not mean that it is unconscious.

Behind each Self there are lesser and greater Selves
             ranging up to that Great Self called Deity.

There may be terrors as well as marvels in this, the
             real universe, but a man will not be related even
             to the least of these until he contacts Himself,
             and through this contact comes in touch with all
             real existences.

For human beings who desire to surrender themselves to
Something Greater Than Themselves, there are directions as to how to do it formulated by those
who have done it.

People who believe that the scriptures are out of date
testify in this way the extent to which profane
desires have driven them out of life.

The return to human nature is not to be confused with
        the "return to Nature."

True, as a *means* of returning to human nature it is
        necessary to detach ourselves from the harmful
        properties of civilization and attach ourselves
        more closely to Nature and her processes.

But the development of man is an *emergence from* Nature,
        a development beyond the lower orders of life, a
        liberation from *dependency* upon Nature, a freeing
        from the trap of animal survival, a birth *above*
        the body, and hence a birth *above* Nature, into
        spheres which are characteristically *human* and
        at the same time *universal.*

The return to human nature is a psycho-spiritual movement
        through which we detach ourselves from the harmful
        properties of our false natures, attach ourselves to
        the creative functions of our true natures, and enter
        purely into those cosmic processes which are particularized
        in human beings.

The developed man precisely is not a superior monkey;
        he precisely is master of all earth-creations,
        son and servant of his Creator.

V

TWO FORCES BEHIND HUMAN VALUES ...

Human values are empowered in two ways: by force of
      beauty and by moral force.

He, using the force of beauty, is an artist who makes
      record of beauty, intending that this record speak
      for itself, that this beauty work its own miracle.

He, using moral force, is a teacher who himself speaks
      and directly works effects.

Artist and teacher have common values and aims. That
      they use different powers and different means should
      make them complement each other.

How stupid, then, are those artists and teachers who
      battle each other on acount of their different
      ways to the same goal.

If I do not often mention the Beautiful it is because, during these latter years, beauty seems to have forsaken me and this world (remaining only for the few who keep us reminded), so that the majority be driven to those labors which purify and make ready for beauty to exist enduringly within the lives of all men.

And how, in those years ago, I prized the Pure—little knowing the complicated procedures that are the necessary means to this simple state of being.

I was logical then. My mind worked on the direct line between simple desire and simple achievement. Yes, logical—and innocent of the labyrinth that existed in those regions of myself and in other people which my mind did not see, but which we must face and negotiate—either working through and developing out of the maze, or else becoming lost and trapped in it.

Since then I have become psychological, to include ever more of that labyrinth—and this is the simplest explanation I can give to those who expect poetry from me, get psychology, morality, and something of religion, and are puzzled.

I am not less poet; I am more conscious of all that I am, am not, and might become.

And with this increased consciousness of my totality has come an increased consciousness of the human world totality. To become aware of these real complexities is to know that in order to realize even the simplest ideal of daily living, such as having harmony among the members of one's own household, one must learn and employ those Great Means worked out by the great teachers of men for the Great End.

Seek ye that, and all these other things will be added unto you. In no other way are they sure to be added—and, unless they are related to the central meaning of man's existence, what meaning have they, even if we get them?

I count it good that any poet stops writing his own small verse, that any man stops doing his own small work, and becomes a student of the Great Work.

I would count it good if all men of the earth stopped in their tracks and went on strike against all usual activities, until they had learned the Meaning and the Means of essential human living.

VII
INDICATIONS ...

Science is a system of exact mysteries.

We desire to see the right thing done by human will and intention, not by chance.

There is a hope among people that human beings can work out their
salvation by some means less drastic than a radical transformation of the human psyche. Of our many false hopes, this is the
chief futility.

A teacher is one who brings tools and enables us to use them.

A symbol is as useful to the spirit as a tool is to the hand.

Men are inclined either to work without hope, or to
        hope without work.

Talk about it only enough to do it.

Dream about it only enough to feel it.

Think about it only enough to understand it.

Contemplate it only enough to be it.

Bibliographical Note

Bibliographical Note

The complete listing of holdings in the Toomer Collection, which is housed in the Special Collection Section of the Fisk University Library, Nashville, Tennessee, deserves a volume of its own. It is possible, however, to summarize within this volume of largely unpublished works other unpublished materials in the Toomer Collection that are of major interest.

Acquired by the Fisk University Library in 1963, the collection includes a variety of materials: letters, telegrams, announcements, documents (library cards, a marriage license, a passport, etc.), photographs, manuscripts of published and unpublished works, and a collection of letters by Margery Latimer, which Toomer attempted to publish as a book. The extensive correspondence includes originals or copies of letters to and from such individuals as Sherwood Anderson, Kenneth Burke, Marjorie Content (Toomer), Hart Crane, Waldo Frank, Georges Gurdjieff, Margery Latimer, John McClure, Gorham Munson, Margaret Naumburg, Georgia O'Keefe, and A. R. Orage. Among the photographs in the collection are those of Toomer, his first wife and his daughter, the Pinchback family, and Sparta, Georgia.

Among the unpublished manuscripts in the Toomer Collection are four novels: "Caromb," "The Gallonwerps" (two different versions), and "Transatlantic," which Toomer revised and expanded to "Eight Day World" (which he also revised). The novelette "Istil" was later revised and published as *York Beach*. There are more than a dozen short stories, some of them without titles. Among the manuscripts of unpublished short stories are "Clinic," "Mr. Limph Krok's Famous 'L' Ride," "Love on a Train," "Lump," and "Drackman." Toomer hoped to publish some of the stories in a collection to be called "Winter on Earth." Although his plans for the collection were thwarted, he was able to publish individually such pieces as *Winter on Earth* and *Mr. Costyve Duditch*.

In addition to several untitled dramas, the collection includes such dramas as *The Colombo–Madras Mail*, *Drama of the Southwest* (incomplete), *The Gallonwerps or Diked*, and *Man's Home Companion*.

There are more than eighty poems, which Toomer hoped to publish in collections entitled "The Blue Meridian and Other Poems," "Bride of Air," and "The Wayward and the Seeking."

443

There are several autobiographical manuscripts. The distinctions among these have been discussed earlier in the note introducing the section on autobiography. Other nonfiction materials include more than fifty lectures on religious, philosophical, and psychological subjects and more than fifty essays on such topics as individualism, religion, literature, race and race problems, and "diking." (According to Toomer, diking is the art of manipulating people in such a way that they not only fail to perceive that they are being controlled but even enjoy the process.) There are also several longer manuscripts on philosophical, psychological, social, and spiritual subjects. These include "Angel Begori," "The Crock of Problems," "Talks With Peter," and "Values and Fictions."

The most complete record of critical comment about Toomer is John M. Reilly's "Jean Toomer: An Annotated Checklist of Criticism," *Resources for American Literary Study* IV, i (1974), pp. 27–56. The most extensive published biography of Toomer is Darwin T. Turner's "Jean Toomer: Exile," *In A Minor Chord* (Carbondale, Ill.: Southern Illinois University Press, 1971), which includes a selected bibliography of Toomer's published and unpublished fiction, poetry, dramas, and nonfiction.

Index